OP 15⁴

Laura Meredith Wilson
October 30, 1939.
Grosse Pointe

THE BOOK OF TALBOT

* * *

TALBOT CLIFTON

IN SIBERIA, 1901

THE
BOOK OF TALBOT

BY
VIOLET CLIFTON

MORTEM·AUT·TRIUMPHUM

HARCOURT, BRACE AND COMPANY

NEW YORK

PRINTED IN THE UNITED STATES OF AMERICA
BY THE POLYGRAPHIC COMPANY OF AMERICA, NEW YORK

TO
GOD
FOR TALBOT

★   ★   ★

CONTENTS

* * *

ILLUSTRATIONS AND MAPS

✳   ✳   ✳

✳   ✳   ✳

I
THE LITTLE BOOK OF ALASKA
★ ★ ★

CHAPTER I

* * *

BEGIN AT THE BEGINNING.

But indeed when is the beginning?

Is it when soul and unborn body mysteriously meet in a womb?

Then the soul is launched into time: 'Such and such a treasure from out of matter, and from out of time this venture shall bring Me.' That may be the expectation of God.

The beauty of God to be increased, somehow, by the adventures of this being, of this thing welded of soul and of body. The body fashioned by time, and by race, and by generation following generation; the soul emerging after its age-long enfoldment in the Thought, in the Beauty.

Begin at the beginning.

Talbot Clifton was born in 1868, and he suckled his mother so fiercely that she had a wound in her breast. 'That', said Nurse Patch from Devonshire, 'that was the start of the discord between them.'

He went to Eton and to Cambridge and then, for eighty days he was on the sea, sailing to Australia. The schooner was nearly overcome by gales.

Talbot learned the signs that are in the clouds: promise of fair, and threat of foul weather.

Before he was twenty years old he had been twice round the world, choosing adventure rather than the enjoyment of the ancient vast estates in the Fylde, which wealth had come to him when his grandfather died. Talbot was then but sixteen years of age; his father had died when he was a child.

After that there was a time in Wyoming when he learned to throw the lasso, and learned the signs that are in the eyes and in the ears of a horse. Bucking horses, and men whose hands went quickly to their hip pockets, these were his teachers. He nearly

3

forfeited his life because, serving his turn as cook, he forgot to clean the roasted birds and set them down upon the table, stinking under the pie-crust.

Then came the year 1894.

With a revel begins the diary of that year, with a revel the diary ends.

After leaving Liverpool, he had written that he was pleased to go, but that it was a curious feeling to leave England for five or six years.

At Los Angeles, for three months he played polo, rode steeplechases and drove a coach; the first man there to do so for pleasure.

Then with a boy, Santiago, with ten mules, one horse, and with provisions for four months, he started for Durango in Mexico.

The journey was rough; there was lack of water; there was vermin; the mules bolted and were caught. "These mountains have never been shot." Bear and deer were the quarry, but soon, because he had an abscess on his chest, the hunter was bound to lie in a ranch and to send the boy Santiago to hunt for food. "Did nothing all day. Lay on my back. Learnt Spanish, sketched, and Shakespeare."

That went on for days, till, maddened by pain, he wrote: "I can do nothing to relieve my chest. I can't move, damn it, and chest is worse than ever. Wish it would get right into my heart and kill me."

Mario, owner of the ranch, went in and out. Sometimes he was beneficent, procuring milk and ointment; at another time he took all Talbot's whisky and vomited in his room.

Then Talbot, suffering still, rode on, and he met a man who had been bitten by a snake; he had been bitten in the head and it had swelled up; Talbot could pity him. So he lent him a mule and the three men rode together. "I cannot sleep at night so I learn Spanish and the speech of Antony." By perilous paths in the mountains by moonlight, and by lovelier dawn, so the men gained Durango.

"Very ill, wrote thirty pages of my novel." And again: "Chest aching. Sat up all night writing poems like a demon a-blood-curdling; these relieve my mind."

4

Later on, Talbot stayed in Mexico City; was inebriated by the life, and painted picture after picture as though the sun and the colour so demanded. At the end of July he was back in San Francisco. "*July 29.* Rode Guadaloupe three days ago. Guadaloupe broke another man's collar-bone. One death, two collar-bones and several more casualties, but will ride him at the races in Monterey. Drove to the park to the Heads in my drag. It went beautifully and everyone seems pleased with it. Had a charming day." He went to Monterey. "Magnificent trees but gloomy. Wandered about, then went to bed." And next day: "Dismal outline of trees blacker than ivory-black, yet not black."

Some days later August had come, and he wrote: "Went in the evening to see a water-party supposed to be like Venice, but in this quarter of the globe like hell. Female got us drunk. Don't know what I am coming to."

★   ★   ★

These words were the last to be written in that year's broken diary. But it is known that in the autumn Talbot joined the Church for which his forefathers had suffered. It may be that the low aims and the self-seeking of the men about him drove him sheer and sudden to the God self-sacrificed. "It was like finding an orchid on a dung heap." That is what he said of a Mass heard in a low part of the city. He was at variance with himself; he was cast down by hollow-hearted women. So he turned to where was enshrined that Lady who is clean
as the scent of apple-blossom, as the scent of the
bean-flower. Virgin and Mother, she, Mary,
could make good to him the
lack of mothering, which
lack had frozen (1)
his boyhood.

CHAPTER II

*   *   *

THE FOLLOWING YEAR TALBOT SAILED FROM ENGLAND TO return to California; and it was in the summer that he reached Montreal.

The day after his arrival: 'Come and hunt with us in Quebec,' some Canadians said. Talbot was ready to start, but he fell ill. After delaying for a day or two, the hunters went off whilst miserably he remained behind. In the same hotel with himself was staying a company of actors and actresses whose looks and performances were equally pitiable. One evening, feeling less ill, Talbot went downstairs to talk to them. He took with him Bob, his dog—then remembered that upstairs he had left his handkerchief. "Go and get handkerchief," he ordered, and Bob scampered off, for that was a service sometimes asked of him. From the half-open drawer he took one in his mouth and re-appeared with it in the hall below. The leading actress thought this delightful; and without sense, pushing past Talbot, she swept down upon the dog which bit her twice in the leg.

"There was the deuce to pay, and the doctor," who feared hydrophobia. The poor lady left the next morning, "after having cried all night at the cruel marks the bite would leave on her little leg. Pity, that she was not bitten in the face instead, as that might have taken off an inch of rouge."

But Talbot fell ill again and the doctor visited him twice a day: "Although his visits are expensive it is a great relief to see anyone." Loneliness in a hotel was more bitter than in wild places, where would be at least a brook or a tree for company, or, failing these, the wind to hear and the clouds to watch. From this room no sky was visible and man had tampered with the very air. What wonder was it that such a place should be— to Talbot—terrible. He suffered a double distress, for added to his own dislike of towns there was in his nature the long-inherited usage of the country. For some eight hundred years,

6

from their home windows, the Cliftons had looked out upon their lands, as far as eye could reach. The houses in which they were reared, century after century, were set about with lawns and woods, so that trees had served those Cliftons for neighbours—trees always, never human beings.

The Montreal newspapers were so puritanical that Talbot flung them away, owning the while that those of San Francisco were not puritanical enough. On Sunday Talbot went to Mass and Benediction, then, thankful to leave Montreal, he travelled on to San Francisco.

In 1894, Talbot had been the summer hero of San Francisco, and that partly because he had been the owner and the rider of the horse 'Guadaloupe'. Before he bought the splendid chestnut it had been gelded that it might become tamer, but it was still untamed. What price Talbot paid for the creature is not known. 'It's the grandest bargain ever made,' was all his friend 'White-Hat' McCarty would say, reflectively boring more holes in his white hat.

At the Country Club at Del Monte Talbot would take his seat for dinner at the table of Dick Tobin who rode better than he: Tobin who, with Hobart and Baron, was a most expert gentleman rider. A newspaper of the day recorded that as Clifton sat down there would be a great hush and people would nudge each other whispering: 'That's the man who's going to ride Guadaloupe.'

'Every morning at eleven o'clock Clifton held a reception at the stables where young ladies had thrills as they watched Guadaloupe endeavouring to bite the tips of his owner's fingers, whilst Clifton would quote McCarty's opinion that 'he's a cannibal but he's a winner'.'

On the Bay District Track that year was held the first race ridden by gentlemen, and the newspapers were filled with news of 'gentlemen riders climbing into pigskin, riding for glory only'; 'aristocrats who ride in the first gentleman's steeplechase held in California'. 'One rider represented San Francisco's noble Four Hundred, another Canada's untallied élite. Talbot Clifton on Guadaloupe upheld the chivalry of England.'

Riding so for England.

'Twenty to one against you,' shouted a bookmaker, as Talbot

entered the betting ring, clothed in 'all the glory of the Clifton yellow-and-brown racing colours'.

'Twenty to one against you!' again yelled the man, leaning out of his box.

Talbot parted with one of his twenty-dollar pieces and put the ticket in his pocket.

'Bet you ten to one you don't show,' cried the man in the next box.

The English gentleman yielded up another gold piece. Then the crowd lifted him overhead and carried him from box to box, at each of which he left a twenty-dollar piece, receiving a ticket in return. The laughing crowd carried him to the Club House balcony and cheered him three times.

Guadaloupe came in third, but, always treacherous, veered round in front of the judge's stand and threw Talbot over his head. Talbot, though bruised, held on to the reins and re-mounted, and again the great crowd, pleased at his nerve, cheered him.

'Training down amid the aristocratic seclusions afforded by the track of the Burlingame Club in San Mateo County, Talbot Clifton, the day before he negotiated for Guadaloupe, bought a filly out of a selling race which he sought to pay for with a draft on Coutts' of London. Norman Brough, clerk of the scales, begged for more negotiable local currency, and then learned that Clifton was a blood of the first water. With a well-bred sigh of regret, Clifton called a coloured boy who was loafing around the scales.

' "Boy," he said, "will you please go down to my room at the Palace Hotel? Here's the key. When you enter my room you will find two silver boxes. The one on the right has cigarettes in it. Leave it alone. The other contains about nine hundred pounds in English notes and American gold. Bring me about—how much did you say I'd bid for that filly, Mr. Brough? Seven hundred dollars, eh? Well, my boy, bring me about seven hundred dollars."

'Then Brough interrupted. 'My dear sir,' he said, 'don't you know that coloured boys are only human? Better arrange with the owner and bring him down to that silver box.' '

Talbot nearly won a great race for which he entered Guada-

8

Guadaloupe and the son of Stamboul

loupe. He was leading, but the animal threw him at the water jump, and, though no part of him was broken, Talbot was stunned and had to go back. Later, in Monterey at the hurdle race, Guadaloupe did break Talbot.

'He's a vicious brute. Don't ride him,' said his friends.

'He jumps out of control,' added Tobin.

All the same Talbot rode.

So that day at Monterey they cleared a stone wall, but Guadaloupe, headstrong, crossed another horse at the water jump and fell, throwing Talbot. Weeks of pain followed, because the doctor who first attended him was an estate agent whose spare time was given to doctoring and surgery. This man set his shoulder blade and dressed his lacerated tongue, but failed to notice that his collar-bone was broken. Another doctor was called in by Talbot's friends and, with agony, the first operation was completed. Next day in the sick man's room was furious contention, the first doctor storming at the second one, and Talbot and his friends in chorus cursing the fool. The villain attached Talbot's buggy and horses, which attachment was released on a bond. A big law suit followed.

When that year Talbot was leaving San Francisco a man came to him wishing to buy Guadaloupe: "I'd prefer not to sell him," said Talbot, "I'd rather shoot him. He's not fit for anyone to ride." The man pressed him; Talbot put the price high to stave him off.

"A horse that takes the bit in his teeth and bolts deliberately through temper (and not through fear) is useless to a man. Nothing will stop Guadaloupe when he gets frenzied, and he will kill himself some day." Still the man insisted and Talbot, getting angry at his obstinacy, let him have the horse. Within a week Guadaloupe had killed his new owner.

On the day before leaving, Talbot had a wild drive which a local newspaper reported in this manner:

'White-Hat McCarty and Talbot Clifton, in a buggy behind a runaway horse going at one-minute gait, was what people on Golden Gate Avenue saw Thursday afternoon. The horse was a son of Stamboul, and it was the first time he had ever been on any thoroughfare more lively than a stock farm. The car bells frightened him and he bolted.

9

'For several weeks Lord Clifton had been anxious to possess a son of Stamboul, and during a recent trip to Southern California he found what he was seeking—a genuine son of the great horse. After purchasing the horse Clifton was anxious to try him out on the Park speed track. He knew that his animal was a wild, strong horse, but Clifton boasts that he has never yet seen the horse he would not drive. The son of Stamboul was therefore put aboard a car and sent to this city.

'HEARD THE CAR BELL RING

'Thursday afternoon Clifton and McCarty were preparing to drive out to the race track. Nothing would suit the Lord but to have his new horse put in harness. McCarty protested, but in vain. Lord Clifton would drive, and McCarty could take the cars if he preferred; but McCarty would not allow it to be said that he was less plucky than Lord Clifton, and both men were seated in the buggy when it left the stable.

'McCarty handled the reins and managed to keep the fiery horse in check till a car crossed the Avenue with its bell ringing loudly. That was something too metropolitan for the son of Stamboul from the country, and it frightened him. He ran off at a gait never before seen on Golden Gate Avenue, and McCarty, by heroic exertions, kept him straight till Baker Street was reached. On one side of Baker Street is a board fence, and McCarty managed to head the animal straight for it.

'On flew the buggy, and it did not stop until several feet of the fence was torn away and the buggy badly scraped. The horse was trembling in every limb and McCarty concluded he had had enough of Stamboul's son for one afternoon.

'But not so Lord Clifton. He insisted upon driving his new horse to the track. The buggy was squared up and the two men made the remainder of the trip in safety.

'THE WILDEST RIDE OF HIS LIFE

' 'It was the wildest trip of my wild life', said McCarty that night. 'That horse has not had a strap on him for five months. He has never been in the city in his life and is a strong animal with a 2.23 record. I thought 'Lord' was joking when he proposed to take him out, but Clifton is dead game and is afraid of nothing. I never saw a horse in all my life go at the speed we made along the avenue. One of my arms has been paralysed since, and I do not expect to be able to use it for several days. But what commands my admiration was Clifton insisting on driving the horse after it had once bolted and was completely frightened. Not another man that I know would have dared to do such a thing, but Clifton is not an ordinary man. It was fortunate that we were able to drive into that fence as the animal was thoroughly unmanageable by that time. I am sure when we struck that fence the horse jumped sixteen feet into the air. And Clifton just laughed.' '

*   *   *

This year Talbot stayed for four months in San Francisco. Those months moved to the sound of galloping feet of horses and the click of polo stick and ball. Talbot in these spring and summer months was gay. Gay, as when he rode, feeling his eye 'as keen as a hawk's'. Gay, as when driving a Gaiety Girl behind the Crown Prince she cried out: 'I've never been so fast before, darling!'

"I'm surprised at that from you," he said, amused by her expression. Then he touched up the horse.

There were crazy scenes in San Francisco. At such a one the judges of a race were hissed by a set of rogues, at another Colonel C., and Harry Simpkins, nicknamed sometimes the Duke, sometimes the Earl, sat up all night trying with empty cartridges to shoot out the light of a candle. Colonel C. going home fell over the Embankment and the Earl took him back to the club and had him put to bed. The Earl after that was melancholy for he knew that he would have to pay the Colonel's bills; the Colonel never drank anything except champagne, and now he complained that his mouth had been too much bruised for him to eat anything but *pâté de foie gras*.

Polo and riding, steeplechasing and driving a coach filled the days. The horse, Ormond, was bought "looking finer than silk," but the jockeys had been bribed: "So no one even with a string of Ormonds can win unless he be of the corrupters."

Talbot got a fast, neat, small pony, grey-coloured; and then, from the Earl, "A clinking little broncho buck called 'Jumping

11

Jack', not less than fourteen years old. The Earl told me he is about the best pony here." Jumping Jack was at the height of his perfection and from this pony Talbot gained another view of horses' ages. The broncho had been caught one spring, trained and used, and then, each year, freed to go back to the plains and hills until late spring, when it would be caught again. It had made its growth, slow and strong, and had not been too much fed, or cleaned, or pampered, nor broken too young. The creature had grown in accordance with its nature, and in its fourteenth year was still at its best, not having, like many of the racehorses, been worn out before it had fulfilled its promise.

The diary gives two lively presentments. The first: of Talbot teaching Miss Wheeler to drive four horses in his drag, and finding her a quick learner. But his pleasure in her was spoilt because she looked on horses as so much mechanism, creatures that all day and all night should go on, wound up by the mere click of a whip.

The other: that of a long drive on a rainy day that cleared at noon. Talbot went in his coach and four to a ranch in the country, taking with him some friends. The roads were very heavy for the horses, and up-country they came on two men who were perhaps drunk, perhaps merely insolent. They would not, by drawing to the side of the road, give the coach room to pass. So, after calling an unheeded warning, Talbot drove straight at them and forced them to give way. One man jumped out and levelled a gun at him, but did not fire.

But in his diary Talbot did not record what befell one night at dinner; his friend Tobin, in a letter (2) to the Duke told the tale this wise:

'My recollection of the incident that you refer to is as follows: I was present at the dinner that you gave to celebrate the steeplechase which you had won. There was a large party present, racing men and others. Among them were Talbot Clifton and Jack Chinn—the latter I remember as one of the most formidable-looking men I have ever seen. He had piercing black eyes and his dark, menacing countenance was rendered even more alarming by powder burns, the evidences of his narrow escape from someone who had tried to kill him. He bore the reputation of being one of the most dangerous men in the

country, was known to be ready to shoot on the slightest pro-
vocation and to be at all times heavily armed.

'I remember that we discovered on that occasion that he was
carrying a pistol in his trouser pocket and a large knife up his
sleeve.

'My attention was suddenly attracted to Talbot Clifton who
said to Chinn across the table, in a loud clear tone, "You are a
liar." We all knew enough of Chinn to feel that he was almost
certain to meet this uncompromising challenge in the way that
he had always been accustomed to, namely with his pistol, and
quite expected to see him shoot Talbot Clifton dead.

'Clifton must have realized his danger. He was not armed,
and he knew enough of Chinn and of his record to be aware
that he was likely to kill any man who insulted him.

'I think that the fact that Clifton was not killed was due to
two things—I think Chinn, himself, was impressed by Clifton's
extraordinary courage and that he knew Clifton was unarmed.
If he had known that he was armed, and especially if he had
made any movement to draw a pistol, I feel confident Chinn
would have killed him. Much was due also to your intervention
in getting between them.

'I remember the incident as a most impressive display of courage and nerve. I do not think there is anybody in the country
who would have dared to challenge Chinn the way that Clifton
did. It was the more impressive because Clifton had come to the
defence of an absent friend, a picturesque adventurer by the
name of McCarty.

'Clifton was undoubtedly one of the most courageous men I
had ever seen. He did not know what fear was (3).'

Into the diary come a few words which show that in July
Talbot was beginning to get tired of all the fun and the folly
of the picnicking girls and of the horse-besotted men: "Went
for a picnic by the sea. Very pretty but most of the best places
had been taken up. Went along to a cove on the beach and
watched the sea-gulls. In spite of them the afternoon was tame."

Tame, in spite of the sea-gulls: over the page, next day,
"Alaska" is written. Then came the fourth of July and a "polo
match, fireworks display, buffoonery and every imaginable vice
which I believe is thought befitting to the day".

On the morrow he was sailing towards Alaska; the Earl and Talbot's manservant, Betts, and the dog Bob, accompanied him. Bob liked being on board—was indeed happy anywhere with Talbot, notwithstanding he was a moody dog and independent. On land he would run off on amorous mischief and be gone for hours or for days. But on his good days: "Look after it, Bob," Talbot would say, and put his books, or pipe, or flute, before the dog, and all day Bob watched the things and no one would be so foolish as to near the growling animal. Or—"Look after him," Talbot would say, and leave Bob alone with a man in a room. Bob would be gentle enough, but if the man went towards the door then Bob sprang at him and by his clothes held him captive.

"What sort of weather is it, Bob?" Talbot in the morning would ask his dog, and Bob, leaping off the bed would go to the window—always open—always with curtains drawn back. Were the day to be fine he would wag his tail and show joy, were it wet he would slink back. To please his master, at a word he yawned, or sneezed, or rolled over on the floor, danced, or trod along a table laid for dinner. Master and pupil these such as made people gape: but the tricks were in fact nothing; it was rather the rare quality of Bob's understanding, of Bob's heart, that mattered.

CHAPTER III

* * *

THE CAPTAIN WAS a JOLLY MAN, AND HE ALLOWED BOB to sleep in Talbot's cabin. His only evident fault was the love he had for a fiddle on which he tried to play 'Annie Laurie' and many another tune. All the first day the sea was calm and everybody was on deck. They passed many whales, and from the ship, sailing near the shore, the beauty of the coast was seen to be bewitching. At Port Lamont they found a "hotel like a barber's shop with food fit only for pigs". The steamer *Quebec* came in, but she was so full of passengers that Talbot and the Earl slept in one of the ship's boats, which "the Earl thought was an awful discomfort". Next day they were both black with smoke, and there was no cabin in which to wash. "The Earl and I seem to do the drinking for the rest of the sardines on board!"

Past lovely mountainous scenery and past Vancouver they sailed. Black bear-skins costing about forty dollars apiece were put on board. Next night Talbot "sat up half the night singing", and the following morning he saw with pleasure the fine forms and faces of Indians of this country. They made their canoes from the trunk of a tree, scooped out; boiling water and hot bricks served them to stretch the wood.

In heavy mist Talbot, the Earl, and Betts the manservant, landed at Juneau. They walked down streets miry as bogs, and went to the hotel built of pasteboard. Juneau was enveloped in fog and rain, and smoke from the Treadwell Mines. Every second week a ship sailed in, but here was no telegraph or telephone office. Yet Juneau boasted three newspapers a week: "But I think the editors must be very small men or else very bad shots for they are not at all aggressive!" A man called Maas befriended Talbot and gave him written directions as to how to go down the Yukon River. Talbot hoped that the directions were exact; but, in spite of what Maas said, Talbot did not believe that he had been down the river. "People seem to fight shy of him, but he is small and can do me no harm as my purse is very carefully guarded." The next day passed in fishing and shooting and Maas, getting out of a boat, "shot a bit off his foot with his rifle." "Very careless," is the laconic comment, "I hear that he is always doing something like that."

In the creeks up-country, men were washing out gold dust; working so all day, a man might earn two and a half dollars. Juneau now was lamentable; in the days when miners only had reached it the place had been pleasant, but this year a lot of adventurers and tenderfoots ruined the town. Every man carried a 'sack' of gold dust. The dust was the town's currency.

The customs in the town were based on the supposition that men are honest. A miner going into a store with his sack of gold dust would not watch the weighing of the price of his purchases, for did he do so he was 'no gentleman'. The miners till now had enforced their own laws (4) and lately, for cheating, a salesman had been shot.

There was trout and salmon fishing in the country, and cod could be caught from the end of the pier at Juneau. Talbot found it difficult to keep the low newcomers from asking impertinent questions. When they could not be prevented from doing so it was difficult to resist fighting the lot.

Some days later he and Betts and Bob started for Dyea. Here Simpkins said good-bye to them. To reach Dyea by river they took two boats, two guides, and packed a load that weighed twelve hundred pounds. The scenery was dismal but grand. They passed a rich mine where worked some two hundred men, and also a salmon cannery where in five years its owner had made a fortune. To this factory fish were sold at five cents each. The price did not depend on the weight of the fish. Five cents was paid for a twenty-pound salmon or for a small one.

The travellers spent twenty-one hours wayfaring ninety miles. They loaded the boats, but afterwards unloaded them whilst they waited for the tide. Finally they took four hours to go a bare mile to the village. Talbot and the Indians arrived at the place exhausted. One store and six Indian huts—that was Dyea, yet it was very pretty. The steamer now and again brought fresh meat, for in Dyea no cattle could live, the place was a swamp. Cranberries and bilberries grew and but little else: the Indians were fevered and sickly—only the streams were benefi-cent, rich in trout and salmon.

For two days the men rested whilst awaiting pack Indians to come from Chilcoot. They would leave their boats at Dyea and travel to Sheep's Camp and to Lake Lindeman.

Talbot watched the Indians playing blind poker; the best of their players gambled with white men. The Indians cheated a great deal, the white men cheated more. "I think it hardly right for white men to play for money with Indians." Later, with surprise, Talbot watched the red men playing harmless hunt-the-slipper, which they had changed into a gambling game.

Early next day an Indian squaw beckoned to Talbot, for in the net, which she had set overnight, she found six salmon-trout. Talbot gave her a quarter for one of the fish, and he was as pleased with the fish as she with the money. By the water an old Indian "sat eating a ground-hog with all its hairs on, just singed, and guts not taken out".

Talbot had to leave his boats at Dyea and obtain others. On July 24th, the Indian, Ajibnee, started for Sheep's Camp, taking four thousand pounds' weight of goods in three canoes. That same day Talbot broke camp and sent his things a mile up-river whilst he remained dining and sleeping in a store. "At half-past six in the morning 'good-bye to Dyea'. Started for Sheep's Camp on horseback, crossed the River to my Camp. All the horses swam, awful current. (Place where Frenchman got drowned.) Loaded packs, off at 10 a.m. after crossing river twenty times, very deep and dangerous, arrived at Sheep's Camp 4.30 p.m." Now and then Bob, in front of Talbot, had balanced on the saddle; before they plunged into the river, at a given word, he would jump on to Talbot's shoulder and from there would envisage the heavy swim.

After ten hours of travel they reached Sheep's Camp and supped on salmon and bacon and marmalade. The pack Indians with Ajibnee afterwards came in. Then they all pitched camp. There were in Sheep's Camp about seven miners and twenty Indians.

"Two inches of water lying in the blankets"—so observed Talbot when he was awakened early by the miners who, in the next tent, were singing 'God save the Queen'. As Talbot changed the clothes that had been drenched whilst he slept, he wished that the miners would propitiate, instead, the god of the weather. All that day the rain fell, and at night the blankets were still wet.

In the evening Talbot and Ajibnee saw a glacier break off the cliff before them. The cliff was nature's calendar, the ice a used sheet which had recorded winter. On this, almost the last day of July, the winter's record, the great green slab of ice, was torn away. It broke off and slipped down the rock, and was shivered on the stones in the water.

★   ★   ★

Talbot was now making for Lake Lindeman where he would build a boat and go to the Yukon; but hours of trial were between the man and the Lake. "God forbid that I should ever try again such a desperate feat," he wrote when he had reached the Lake; "if I had known what the last ten miles were to be I should have stopped." At ten in the morning they started up the awful Chilcoot Pass. Sixteen Indians carried the twelve hundred pounds of goods that Talbot was taking; the gun, the rifle, the tent, and blankets, and the food. Men, women, children and dogs had burdens tied to them, and according to the weight carried so was the charge exacted. "Words cannot express what the pass was like. Climbing over torrents, scrambling through trees over huge rocks, sliding down a hill one hour, balancing along a precipice the next." Two hours after noon they reached the summit of a range of hills; between the travellers and Timber Camp, towards which place they were pressing, lay five miles "over rocks innumerable and mountains. Did not arrive till half-past ten at night, more dead than alive. Twelve and a half hours of the hardest walking a man can do."

CHAPTER IV

★   ★   ★

TALBOT WALKED IN THE HILLS SEEKING FOR TREES TO fell: below him lay Lake Lindeman. Grayling jumped in the water and now and again a pack of grouse flew across the Lake. No breeze blew, and with the advancing day the bite of the mosquitos became an anguish.

For eighteen days Talbot and Betts camped by Lake Lindeman. Two miners, Jock and Jim, unable to pan gold in this the summer, helped him to build a boat in which they would all go to Forty Mile Town. Grain of men's flesh against this obdurate grain of the fir wood; first the felling, then the lugging—dogs sometimes helping—and the sawing of the trunks, plank by plank. The sweat running down his body, Talbot liked to think how the woodenness of these dull evergreen trees, by nature rooted and fixed, was being changed by whip-saw and by hatchet, into something which should be, a body moving, responsive to hand and to sail—mistress of the water.

As the men fingered the resin of the fir wood Jock explained that the resin was protection to the fir tree against the saw-flies that sought to burrow into the tree-trunks when all else around would be covered by snow—an Indian, coming into camp, with a haunch of wild-sheep, had just been bitten in the face by such a fly, of which the cruel fangs had nipped out a quarter of an inch of flesh.

One day Ajibnee, with his canoes, paddled away under a blue sky. "Seven boats have left us since we came here. We were rather mournful as we saw the last three go off. No one has any idea of the meaning of loneliness unless he travel where the high road ends." Close to Talbot's tent an Indian squaw was dying of consumption. He tried to ease her misery—"many Indians die that way from exposure."

A miner named Antelope Dock arrived alone in a canvas

boat. He went always alone—he was a hermit. In the evening, with a pack, another lone man came; the camp that had been isolated filled up with men staying here to make their boats. Three boats were being built, a scow, a skiff, and Talbot's boat. Four of the newcomers had a boat apiece, of which they carried the pieces and screws, and now on Lake Lindeman they built them up. Other men brought in timber from as far as three miles, carrying it upon their shoulders or dragging it with dogs. The miners were sick men, tortured by the mosquitos. Although the wind, when it rose, blew icily cold, yet every man preferred its flail to the tease of the flies. Half an inch beneath the earth's surface water lay.

"Miners' camps are very peaceful till worthless men, adventuring, come in and spoil these new countries. A blackguard came in yesterday with a bear. He tried to escape from paying his Indians but was forced to do so. Had he refused we should have sent him back to Dyea. Afterwards he played cards with the Indians and won back the wages he had paid them." The next day the ruffian was off in his boat.

On the twelfth of August the scow departed. Talbot had watched her being built, and some of his provisions were put on the flat ferry-like boat. She was called the *Negress* and she weighed six tons. The men could hardly steer the unwieldy thing; she had no sail. She went off at midday "in an awful blue fit of fear". Half a dozen times she veered round to the wind because she could not be steered, but at last went yawing out of sight. At four o'clock the skiff, which also Talbot had helped to build, danced off under a trysail. Talbot's own boat was still unfinished; but on the thirteenth of August, after eighteen days of labour, the last strake laid, the last seam caulked, the mast and stays and rigging set, away they went.

CHAPTER V

*   *   *

FOUR DAYS IN THE BOAT, DAYS OF SAILING, OF ROWING, and sometimes of rolling the boat overland. Talbot, Jim and Jock seem to have been at strife; Talbot was ever for pushing on, beyond all endurance, but by eight at night or it might be later the men insisted on stopping. "Jock is trying to make himself captain, to this I disagree. At eight o'clock we camped in a very pretty place. They refused to go on any later—poor babies."

The next night they did not camp till eleven, having started at seven in the morning—"almost got beat", Talbot owned. The wind all day had been high, and of Jock and Jim was written: "They are both frightened of the water, and the water by night has an awful aspect to them."

Next day, the sixteenth of August, there was no wind, so for twelve hours they rowed.

"*Saturday, 17 August*, 1895. (Thirteen hours rowing.) Started at seven in the morning. Other boat just ahead. Reached end of Lake Marsh at two in the afternoon. Ten hours—doing twenty miles—very hot. Then started down river, four-mile current, for Grand Canyon. At times we went twelve miles an hour; at others caught in eddy and completely stopped for a couple of minutes. All the time we were listening for the noise of the waters in the Canyon and looking out for a danger post the book says it has. It was getting dark and we were looking for a camp ground when we saw smoke and made for it. By this time we were going like a racehorse. Turned a narrow corner. There in front of us was the Miles Canyon. Our rudder lost its power and the boat went stern first, but two of us pulled like hell and we got into the backwater. Very exciting. The steersman, Jock, got whiter than snow.

"*Sunday, 18 August*, 1895. Up at eight in the morning. Took boat by overland—four and a half hours; awful pull one mile.

21

Rained a little, then very hot. Worked all day carrying packs up and down steep places. The Canyon is five-eighths of a mile; very narrow except in the middle where there is a whirlpool. There is an old fellow with a boat here and I offered to go with him through it. After six hours' deliberation he said 'Yes', so to-morrow at five in the morning we will go through. I don't look at the water much as it makes my nerves shaky. It is about eight in the evening; am still packing. The sand-flies and mosquitos are awful.

"*Monday, 19 August*, 1895. (Eight hours' rowing.) Went over to the old man and to my surprise he had packed. We started our own boat between the Canyon and went on to White Horse Rapids which is worse than Canyon. Jock, a stranger and myself took it through twice. The people on shore thought we were gone. The last few leaps turned our boat broadside. In a moment we were almost full of water. Curious experience. Sometimes the boat would stop a quarter of a second, then shoot on faster than ever—one mile in two and a half minutes was the pace. Wet through. We then rowed to the end of the Lewes River, twenty-six miles, camped on an island and am fairly bitten all over. Shot a widgeon."

Although the diary does not record it, yet Betts used to tell a tale of the White Horse Rapids. Talbot had determined that he would not again endure the toil of carrying packs up and down over the rocks that rose from the rapids, and because, overnight, Jim and Jock had refused to take the boat over the White Horse Rapids, Talbot prevailed upon the old man to say a long-deferred 'Yes'. But the elder slunk off in the dawn, grey as his fears. He did not dare to meet the mock in Talbot's eyes nor the great waters. Then Talbot laughed Jock and the stranger into going; the twinkle in his eye and his gibes spurred to assent. Jock did frown, though he half laughed too, when Talbot beckoned to Betts to pull the dog Bob out of the boat.

"Go back, old manny, it's too risky for you," said Talbot to the spaniel; and Bob was led away to do the dangerous part of the journey on foot in company with Betts, Jim and some miners.

* * *

After that for six days they sailed and rowed or dragged the boat overland until they reached Forty Mile Town. The chart

22

had been faulty, and the men were joyfully surprised when Ninety Mile River (5) was reached, with a current running at a five- or six-mile speed, and the Lakes were left behind. To bake bread, and to fry with bacon the dried bean—the 'Alaskan strawberry', to catch trout, to shoot a goose, a duck, to see the splendour of the country—all this was good.

Then came Five Finger Rapids (6) which Talbot's boat took first, the scow followed and both shipped water. Rink Rapids came next, and the men took them clumsily. After were islands innumerable amongst which the boats lost their way, and then came fourteen hours of rowing, with all the felicity of excitement.

The next day they passed a place of wreckage—the wrecks of miners' boats, and they thought sadly of the drowned men. Just then a wind rose up and blew away the fog so that was revealed country magnificent with leaf of red and gold, whilst in earth, and in river-bed, lay the alluring gold.

Through Talbot's mind flashed apprehension of the strange quality of gold. The being of God, the worth of man, of woman, the right to war, and a thousand things beside disputed throughout time, but the preciousness, the value, of this rare, pure, strong and uncorroding metal, ever agreed upon by all people under the golden sun.

In the evening of the twenty-fifth of August, the five canoes of the surveying party stopped where Talbot and his men had struck camp, so they all put up their tents among the trees, pine, and spruce, and birch, with here and there bushes of red currants. How silent were the woods! No song of birds; once the croak of a raven, and twice seen, but not heard at all, a grey bird—the Canadian jay, the whisky-jack.

'That is the camp robber, a thieving pest,' someone said. On the evening air sounded the inharmonious voices of the miners. 'Pay-streak' . . . 'Low-grade diggings' . . . 'Gold pan' and 'Strike it rich': such fragments of talk moved the air; the air that was goodly with the smell of four loaves being baked and of the goose which, after boiling for an hour, was now being fried in fat.

Next day they passed the *Negress*—her crew was so disheartened at being passed that she would not race again. Then

came a very hard pull, and a race with the small boat—her of
the trysail. Three hours after noon they reached Forty Mile
Town, winning the race against the small boat by eighty yards.
For seven hundred and fifty miles, during sixteen days they had
raced her. She had left a day before they had left, so also indeed
had the *Negress*—it was good to have beaten her.

. Talbot showed some letters of introduction that he had been
given, and he was put into a hut "with a very nice fellow and a
bar-owner". The bar-owner's name was Bob Miley.

Standing by the side of the water that evening of his arrival
Talbot, in thought, went over the course of his travel. His mind
recalled the great effort to surmount the Chilcoot Pass: the
building of his boat on Lake Lindeman: the two hundred miles
of lake, and river, and of rapids. The portaging from one lake to
another, each man burdened by heavy weights, a hundred
pounds or more upon his back; the cutting down of trees to use
as rollers for the overland passage of the boat. Then, unseen of any other, Talbot took leave of his boat.

He stooped down and caressed her—the
boat that he had built, and that
ill-built would have been
his doom.

CHAPTER VI

★ ★ ★

TALBOT STAYED FOR NINE DAYS IN FORTY MILE TOWN, because the steamer which he awaited was long delayed. The shack was built of logs, one lying on another. The rifts between the logs were filled with moss, a mud roof was piled upon the top. The windows of this shack were of glass, though in some shacks linen steeped in oil served for panes. "Three of us and a squaw had meals together." At dusk another Indian woman would come in and the two talked together in "their very ugly language". So seemed to him the speech of these Indians whilst he listened only; but he thought otherwise when afterwards, from squaws and from hunters, he learned a little of the language.

During this time of waiting, Talbot went sometimes to Fort Cudahy, a small place standing where Forty Mile River joins the River Yukon. Whether it belonged to the United States or to Canada was debated. The Mounted Police, "nice fellows", had lately arrived and were building barracks. Uncommon leisure was the portion of an Englishman, who all and every day fished for pleasure. He sent to Talbot a basket of fine grayling. To fill the time of waiting Talbot started a newspaper: "We are working hard at it. We are all disappointed because we cannot find any scandal. Twenty-five copies are to be issued at five dollars each. It is not too dear as the papers will all be written by hand."

Forty Mile Town, this early autumn, was wildly disordered. A year before Bob Miley, Englishman, had arrived with fifteen dollars in his pocket. In four days he had paid five hundred dollars for a year's outfit. He bought a saloon; gambling, he won a gold-mine and from it panned ten thousand dollars. Now a new saloon was being opened by him; this was the base of the town's excitement. Prosperous too was the bar-keeper, for in his claim a seventeen-ounce gold nugget had been found. A dance was given to celebrate the open doors of the new saloon. Miners, storekeepers and Indians came. Twelve o'clock struck somewhere; just then Talbot danced a waltz with an Indian girl. He could feel that this was more to her than just a waltz. Her feet, her body, all of her moved as a bird's throat moves in song. Generations of people, who by firelight had danced to show the hunters' joy and the warriors' delight, a whole past of such a people, quiet now in their graves, a whole line of such forefathers, had been needed to produce the joyful easiness of this midnight waltz.

Mrs. ——, full of sudden pomp and wealth, debarred Indians from her private dance given a few days later. That she should be so eclectic aroused comment.

The wife of the storekeeper, Mrs. Healy, of a like mind, had amused Talbot ten days before the dance in the saloon. He had called on the wife of Captain Constantine and "Mrs. Healy was there, but when the representatives of the other store came in she took up her cloak and hat and bundled out of the room—an absurd phase of rudeness."

The steamer *Weir* had just come in. She brought miners, but no stores. She had had a collision with the *Arctic*, which ship, long overdue, was eagerly awaited by miners and Indians. Medicine stores and spirits were getting scarce. The *Arctic*, hampered by the damage done, would be yet later than had been feared.

'Whose fault was the mishap?' every man questioned, and though none vouched for the truth of the surmise, yet suspicion sneaked around Healy, the store-owner.

'There has been foul play,' was whispered, for a chain of events could be foreseen. Soon indeed, just as had been expected, prices in the store surged up. The tongues that scandalized the store-owner grew sharper. One day Healy had no butter; the next day it was salable, at a price. Healy had no medicines but, the need sharpening and the price rising, an odd bottle could be found. Healy was an affliction-monger. The town was full of miners who had arrived in the *Weir*—nearly everyone was drunk.

Antelope Dock is judged

A miners' meeting was held in the saloon. 'Whose wife is she?' was the case tried, and on an immediate scandal some judgment was passed.

A dance was started in Bob's saloon—at three hours after midnight every dancer was rolling over another, and it lasted till eleven o'clock next morning. "One man was wounded with a knife, that was all." Talbot had left soon after midnight. He had watched a game of poker that had been going on for thirty-six hours. Bob Miley and Barker went back to the hut late next afternoon, but did not, till eight in the evening, seek their beds, to which for forty hours they had been strangers. There was another dance on the following night, but none of the women went to it, so the men danced with one another.

The talk of the town was of one Curly who, coming up in his boat, had smashed a man over the head with his six-shooter. The wounded ruffian sought the police and Curly was looked for in his hut, but he had gone away by two o'clock in the morning. "Both men were in the wrong, but I am on Curly's side, as miners are the most damnably irritating beings under the sun," wrote Talbot.

In a canvas boat "the absolute hermit, Antelope Dock", arrived from Lake Lindeman and the coast. He carried a mail, but he had been about three months coming. "He expected to collect a dollar a letter, which was absurd. Because he was not paid anything he called a meeting in the Alaskan Store, but instead of being paid he was rebuked by all for not having come here in good time. His delay has been a catastrophe to several men who had expected remittances and who, not being able to buy provisions, have left the country. Antelope Dock was nearly fined; he was almost sent out of the country, but for some reason he was dealt with gently."

For no clear reason that day, "all the dogs seem to be mad; any amount of fights. One Manuas squaw was nearly pulled down, but threw a bucket of water over the two fighters which had a good effect. Men here talk about dogs as elsewhere about horses. Whether strength or speed is best, raises many discussions."

Often in the streets by day Talbot, of necessity, carried Bob upon his shoulders—otherwise the dogs would have torn him to

27

pieces. At night, as soon as the sun set, "they howled like wolves, from which they are descended". Up and down the Yukon the dogs had many uses: they hauled the wood to be burned in the stoves, they ploughed, they were beasts of all burdens. Men travelled in sleighs drawn by the creatures. The dogs were fed only at night, to be hungry made them zealous—so thought their masters. They were always penned outside the 'shacks'; every time the door of a hut was opened, fighting each other, they would rush to look for food. A dog would snatch a bag of food from under a sleeping man's head; they ate even one another.

Learning Indian from two squaws; gambling at faro; watching money endlessly changing hands at poker—so the days passed.

"This place will soon kill me; the muck we get to drink plays havoc with me," sighed Talbot in his diary. The ship not coming caused whisky to be scarce, and drink called hooch was taken instead. It was made of molasses, and of spirit of various berries; even old leather was thrown into the cauldrons; the whole was fermented and was drunk hot. The talk turned often upon drink. One man would boast that he had gone all day without having paid for a drink. 'Tossed double or quits and won each time', he would laugh. Another would complain that he 'had dropped in for a chink and that had cost him one hundred dollars'. A 'chink' entailed paying for a drink for every man within sight in the whole saloon. "A drunkard has been following me all day to give him a drink. The saloon-keepers will not sell him any more, so he got a box of cigars at two dollars each and gave me one. Then he tried to start a fight; not allowed. Then he said he wanted to talk over the Home Rule question. He was at once turned out of the saloon for naming the subject."

One night, the night before Ajibnee left for Dyea, he and Barker and the doctor and Talbot found some good whisky in the store. "The glasses all cracked afterwards without being touched—unused to such a quality."

On the night before Talbot went off to hunt, the Indians gave a 'potlash', a dance with an exchange, between themselves, of presents. Rifles, blankets and lesser goods

28

changed hands; each man trying to get the better of his
neighbour, but fortunes were even when the dawn broke.
There was still no sign of the boat. On the sixth of
September, after nine days of waiting for
the ship, with men of the tribe of
Tinné (7), Talbot, intent on
hunting, left Forty
Mile Town.

CHAPTER VII

*   *   *

IN THE DIARY THE PENCIL RECORDS OF THE HUNTING
days have been blotted out by rain or by sea-spray. But this is
known, that Talbot, hunting with the Indians, was diverted by
watching a mink. It was feeding upon frogs near some water.
From it came an oppressive smell at variance with the sweet
evening. Lustrous was the soft glossy coat that made the creature the prey of the trapper; its bushy tail was comely.

He caught a heavy silver fish, and shot a bear, and with the
Indians for hours went thirsty in the fierce sun; at night the
frost set in. The caribou, the fat small caribou of the woodlands,
grazed on the high grounds above the blue-berries; moose
browsed on the lowlands and ate the leaves of willows. The
hunters watched a bull-moose wallowing in a pool, seeking
escape from the besetting flies. They heard the hornlike challenge of a far bull; they listened to the moose of the pool grunting back to the call. Then they saw him rush recklessly towards
the rival beast. 'We could kill him now; he is blind with anger,'
whispered an Indian; but Talbot was set on watching the moose.
At evening they heard against the trees the banging of a bull-
moose, ridding himself of the velvet on his antlers. They heard
in the woods a cow answering a bull. They saw the young
spruce trees ridden down, straddled over and broken by the moose
that were hungry for the green food. They saw, too, last winter's 'parks', where the beasts had herded together, in places of
trampled snow. (On the untrampled snow their feet slipped, and
their weight endangered them in drifts. Herded together
amongst the trees they could feed in safety; could defy the
wolves.) Talbot delighted in the primal look of the creatures, in
their noble elklike horns, in the great solid over-lip. What acute
scent endowed those wide nostrils; what acute hearing endowed
those upright ears!

30

But, that he might have a trophy, he killed a beast and sent its head to England.

On the last night in the woods Talbot was surprised by the moon-dogs—five luminous circles hung in the figure of a cross above him: they were the fivefold image of the moon, reflected in the sky. Not having heard that such appearances sometimes distract the Northern skies, Talbot was the more perplexed.

Pity it was that he did not regard the five moons as heralds of fortune; emboldened by the image in the sky he should have snatched bravely at his chance. Instead, next day, he let go a life's occasion, and that, when on the river bank, at morning he met two miners. It seemed that they were at their fag-end; travelling wearily to Forty Mile.

'We have been on the pups of the Klondyke River; heard of Hayne being there; we're certain that miners there will soon strike it rich.' But the wife of one of the two men was dying, so he must travel by the next steamer down the Yukon; the other miner was crippled by rheumatism.

'It is a commanding illness,' he said. Both men had staked big claims; they were certain the Klondyke was rich; all the same they wished to sell their claims. Talbot could see they were sincere. Unless these were low-grade diggings, the claims were bound to be worth more than the men were asking. Talbot got up and walked away to think: he decided that the men were honest and that they knew their claims were good; he decided that here was the chance of a fortune. He could not afford to buy the men out by himself; he could afford a third share. In London he would see B—, who might be able to raise the remaining two-thirds of the money. Talbot would return straight to London, and would cable to the men refusing or assenting. He told the miners of his decision; then the three men smoked a pipe before rowing to Forty Mile. Through Talbot's mind chased thoughts and feelings somewhat thus: that by his travel and the hard living he had saved money; that he must travel again, and often, where he could pay for his living in work and sheer muscle rather than with money. In the green of his youth he had abused wealth; now he would try to regain, by living hard and poor, some of what he had lavished on races and on foolery.

31

Talbot remembers the lands in Amounderness

Though he left his heritage often, yet he never quite forgot that
—according to tradition—it was William Rufus who had bestowed on a Clifton knight 'ten carucates of land in Amounder-
ness'. His farmers might, did indeed, complain that John Talbot
—bluntly naming him so—too seldom 'had a look at them', yet
Talbot knew there was not a faulty window or a leaking ship-
pon in the hundred or more, solid, red-brick farms that stood
upon his lands.

When, later, he returned to London he tried vainly to interest business friends, but 'who has ever heard of the Klondyke?'
they laughed. Regretfully then, though partly unaware, Talbot signed away in a cable his chance
of a fortune. Next year the Klondyke
was discovered to the
world.

CHAPTER VIII

*   *   *

AT LAST TALBOT SAILED "THROUGH A LUXURIANT STORM", and "after struggling with the night and its gloomy surface", after "another wild senseless intoxicating night of horrors", came this entry: "The weather grew hot, the stars were in all glory. There are things to think about at sea which a man ashore does not consider—why that should be I don't know, but so it is. Thinking takes the place of reading."

Talbot read Shakespeare. One morning he was reading, but left the book and, going aloft, he watched the sea-birds. A miner picked up the book, glanced, then read. At school he had heard of Shakespeare, and had thought that he was a writer acclaimed by schoolteachers—one whom the learned might enjoy, but who was beyond the understanding of the simple. Clifton was reputed reckless, was the builder of a boat, hale huntsman and pioneer— what Clifton read might have meaning. The miner read and was convinced. When Talbot went back to his book he was surprised to see the man lost in the poetry and to hear him, in the language of his calling, acclaim the passage he was reading as though it were a seam of gold, a rich streak that he had come upon. In terms of nuggets found, and of ore panned, he praised the book. Talbot gave him the volume. It was bound in red and gold; many of the passages were pencil-marked. The book was battered, a little, by the roughness of river travel.

On October the twenty-first the journey was ended:
"Sighted land northward of Point Orena.
The stars in their glory are making the
heavens blush. Point Orena itself
was sighted at midnight.
Alas, my journey to
Alaska is over."

II
THE BOOK OF
THE BARREN LANDS

*   *   *

CHAPTER I

*   *   *

AT THE END OF FEBRUARY, 1897, TALBOT CLIFTON, THEN aged twenty-eight, wrote in his diary, "Left Liverpool for the Barren Lands". He hoped to go by the unmapped tracts near Chesterfield Inlet, hoped too, that in spite of searchers, and explorers, and whalers, some further trace of Franklin might be found, for after all endeavour the body of the hero had never been come upon. Talbot's provision was belief in himself, and in his aim, besides some knowledge of travel. Afterwards he wrote: "How little did I think as we walked over the wet slippery quay to the Cunarder that was to carry us three thousand miles towards our goal, how little did I think what scant new knowledge regarding Franklin would accrue to me (if indeed any). . . . My quest was to find if possible where the great Northern explorer had his last resting-place. I so much admired his intrepid courage that I felt I must pay this tribute to his name." Talbot hoped also to capture some musk-ox, because none had yet been brought alive to England.

He sailed off in a storm that destroyed two of the ship's lifeboats and so harassed the steamer that she arrived at New York three days late. One of his brothers, Arthur, was with him and the same man, Betts, who had been with Talbot in the Yukon: thin and quick, the outward and the inward man very upright. But to Bob he said good-bye. "I miss Bob very much and keep thinking of him. We have never been separated for more than one week in a period of eight years. It seems wicked to leave the old chap behind." But now Bob was too old for a journey such as this might be, so he was left in Scotland. Then the dog ran fifty miles from Elgin to Ross-shire looking for Talbot in his home in the deer forest, led back there by his loving instinct over all the way he had covered by train. He was sent back to Elgin and he died there before Talbot returned from the Barren Lands.

From New York they went to Winnipeg, carrying letters to the heads of the Hudson Bay Company, and the men of the Company advised him as to his necessities: from matches to a muzzle-loader or even a breech-loader, the Company would supply everything—so bacon, salted pork, beans, flour, and other things were bought. "I move here: tailor, bootmaker, gunmaker, cartridges out of Customs, watchmaker, cards to leave at Club, bills to pay, clothes to try on, good-byes to say."

At Winnipeg, Mr. Chipman helping him, Talbot studied maps and charts, and deliberated whether to go east or west. Then he decided to go to Norway House, Oxford House, and York Factory, stations of the Hudson Bay Company, and thence to Fort Churchill. Farther than that he could not now foresee. There were nine hundred miles to cover between Winnipeg and Fort Churchill, so there would be time for thought.

On the twentieth of March they left Selkirk and spent twelve days going thence to a Hudson Bay Company settlement, called Norway House. Their way was four hundred miles long. At first they travelled with sleighs and horses; they ran too on snow-shoes. Later, they changed horses for dogs with sleighs. By night the Aurora Borealis flashed in the sky as though angel combatants unsheathed celestial swords. By day sometimes they passed other sleighs and met Indians, and now and then a Scotsman, travelling. They slept in tents, and ate moose and caribou. On the third day they saw a wolf, a cave that had just been dug out of the snow by a bear, and, on the lake, a broad fissure (1) spreading for about a hundred miles. One of the men told how these clefts sometimes went to the bottom of the lake, and so were dangerous. They unharnessed the horses, pushed the sleighs over, and then jumped the horses, but the take-off was bad. The drivers were in mortal terror; nevertheless the danger was surmounted. Later, in a snowdrift, the horses were up to the girths in snow and were spent when, at Berens River, the first Hudson Bay post was reached.

One day: "The track is a foot and a half broad. Go off it and you will be up to your middle in snow; crawl out as best you can. Moccasins take hours to dry and it is necessary to be dry-shod." Thus they travelled, sometimes on the great lake, sometimes near it. When they stopped for the night the Indians cut the fir trees down for fuel, but so wastefully that Talbot twice prevented this destruction.

As they neared Norway House an Indian went ahead to test the ice with a pole. Once the pole went through. In the deep water of the ice-holes a man could be drowned (2). "Thank God no fog came on last night, for I was long by myself with unmanageable dogs. I thought the Indian ahead had been drowned in a hole and Betts behind was clean out of sight. The night grew darker, clouds came up, with dogs tired and the track lost—not much fun."

The radiance of the snow dazzled Talbot into snow-blindness (3), "a slight attack—which is hell". After a day's rest they went on again and now Talbot wore glasses. Instead of horses they had five teams of dogs. 'Norway House is a hundred and sixty miles by our way,' said William of the Company: he was half white, half Indian, and spoke with a strong Scots accent. That part of the journey lasted seven days.

On the second day of April William said: 'In an hour we should reach Norway House,' and Talbot was glad for the sake of the dogs.

A flock of buntings flew past him. They were sharp-winged and white as snow. After them came a raven; strong-winged and swift he needed no cover, and on his sable no cover was bestowed. In a just balance his strength had been weighed against the weakness of the smaller birds; it had been found sufficient; in a world of white the raven remained black, pointing the care that encompassed the ptarmigan and the snowbirds. Quick and new, although Talbot long had known of the merciful colouring of the Northern creatures, quick and new then came, with the immediate seeing of these buntings, the sureness that God is good. 'The buntings know some gay songs,' said William, but Talbot did not heed what was said of their singing because, with their silent passage, had glittered a faith that was gay enough.

39

CHAPTER II

★   ★   ★

''REACHED NORWAY HOUSE, DOGS' FEET LEAVING A TRAIL of blood upon the snow.'' Twelve days had passed since the travellers had left Selkirk.

It was early in the morning when they arrived, but not too early for Chute, who was in charge, to receive them hospitably. "Found Chute in bed, woke him up; he kindly gave us breakfast and beds and a much-needed bath. I had the itch badly." For some days they rested; the thaw added delay. Indians who had tried to reach Oxford House came back unable to pursue the trail, for in such a thaw a man might, in a treacherous place, be waist-deep in water.

The feet of the sleigh dogs must be healed before there could be further travel, so moccasins were made for them to wear. There was gear that must be bought in the store. Talbot bought snow-shoes five feet long, the hunting shoes of the Cree Indians. To every tribe its own shoe. Three-foot shoes would suffice for the trail, but for chasing deer over unbeaten snow these were made five feet long, sometimes six, with narrow frames of hickory filled in with thongs of plaited hide. The tribal enemies of the Crees had dreaded the speed of these shoes. He also bought isinglass goggles.

The days were sunny, at night there was frost. Often the traders played football and, in the evening, tales were told by the fireside. The store of whisky was broached in celebration of the arrival of the visitors. 'I was starving, just about to die, when I got a shot at a pike in the river, killed it, and so am here.' Such a tale a man would tell, and another would match it with equal adventure.

One of them who talked and drank was a 'free-trader', that is, not a member of the great Hudson Bay Company, but a trader buying and selling for himself. Anathema in former days, such men now, with the opening of the Western country, found access to the interior less difficult and, with custom, had become tolerable to the servants of the Company.

Then from Behring's River came MacDonald, the head of the station. He had done the journey in four days. 'Good,' said the other Scotsmen. On the day of departure MacDonald gave Talbot a pair of sleeping-boots and a rabbit-skin rug. 'Safe journey,' he called out as the two brothers and Betts started for Oxford House—that was the sixth of April.

They travelled five days, at an average of forty miles per day, over portages hard and long, in some places dangerous. They shot rabbits and woodland caribou for food. In many parts there was deep snow; always there was frost.

One night they slept round a fire that burned away all too quickly, but not before their blankets had been set on fire by the sparks. Another night, because of the snow, they put up a tent.

But the night of comfort was one passed in the hut of an Indian. Eight Indians, some of them Talbot's men, and two Indian women and the three white men slept in a little house the length of which Talbot covered in eight strides, its breadth in seven.

Oxford House is one hundred and eighty miles by the trail from Norway House, and the day that they reached it they had run for hours with the dogs.

Campbell, the head of the station, saw them nearing Oxford House but, when they hailed him, he could hardly hide his disappointment because he had been hoping that the approaching sleighs were bringing flour, of which his need was great.

'There is our little father,' said an Indian as they passed the Company store.

From the mirror on the wall of his bedroom, Talbot saw the reflection of his face which was burned and blistered by sun and snow; the whites of his eyes seemed strangely white, like those of a negro gleaming out from the dark skin. Running with dogs had made him hard, strong and swift. "I can run three and a half miles in sixteen and a half minutes," he wrote. "In a week I have gained eleven pounds."

At Oxford House all the clocks and the watches had stopped,

yet the meals were served to a set time. Talbot's four watches all told different hours. A man, Simpson, arrived and he had a watch with yet a fifth variant of the time.

Indians came in to the settlement, bringing fox-skins and lynx-skins. Soon would come the spring, thinning out the winter coats of the creatures and putting an end to the bartering in furs. Busy too were the Indians catching fish in their nets, and white fish and heavy trout were brought in to the settlement. The dogs were fed upon fish—the troublesome noisy dogs. They were thin and quarrelsome; some of them had just killed one of the few cats of Oxford House.

'I'm glad to see those beggars going away,' said Campbell one morning as he watched his own team of dogs being led in the direction of Goslake, a place where fish abounded more than at Oxford House and where the husky dogs would pass the summer.

Snow-birds going north sang a few notes of sweetness. 'They are of the finches,' one of the Scotsmen said. Next the badger woke up and was seen, and put forth on to the south wind its smell so loathsome to man, to its own kind so alluring. William took Talbot to its earth and this was a great place—such a dwelling as only a brock with its high courage and its strong paws will make. Then, in his own tongue but with many a deviation, with English sentences and with Scottish words, William told Talbot about the badgers, and this was the gist of his talk: A fox, he said, shares that earth with the badger; his hole is an offshoot of the brock's tunnel. Each has his own dwelling, though the badger alone made the mansion. The fox—and William laughed—knows well enough that he will not get mange if he shares the badger's earth, for the badger three times a week cleans out his own as also the fox's earth; he puts fresh bedding for the fox and for himself. The badger asks of the fox only that his vixen shall not let the cubs disgust him by droppings at the mouth of the earth, nor by foolish play with him if he passes near them. If they get in his way he will kill them with one bite across the breast.

William and Talbot spent hours watching the musk-rats that now went abroad, after their winter concealment in the common dwelling which also was a storeroom, and which had been built under the water. The creatures were akin to voles and to water-rats, but they had their own ways. William knew where, on the bank, was the vent. By suddenly breaking it open and letting the light in I could dazzle and then kill them and that is what I am going to do; their pelt is of value, brown shaded from blue-grey. This was the sum of William's talk. But Talbot would not allow him to kill the musk-rats. He liked to watch the small creatures roll off with sailor gait as though a life spent so much in, and beneath, the water ill fitted them for terrestrial journeying. He liked to smell the coming of the spring in the amorous message which the cloying scent of the musk conveyed—liked to wonder at this elastic beast, smaller than grown rabbit, bigger than rat, made with such suppleness that it could squeeze its way into a hole smaller than itself.

Talbot took upon himself to provision the station with food; he went about always with his Indian. They lay in wait for wild-geese coming up from the south, and for duck which were late that year. Ruffled grouse he shot, and a snipe which he long remembered because he had to run over not very solid ice so as to snatch it up before the crows could sweep down upon it. Always this race with the hungry crows when anything was shot.

William taught him to make pemmican from wild-duck. They skinned the bird, and cut it into small pieces that were boiled so that the meat should lose its fishy taste. Then the pieces were mashed with boiled potato on which was heaped pepper and salt. When the mess was cold they fried it with bacon—and it was good.

The fishy taste that the duck had at this season proved that they too must be hard pressed for food, and must eat fish instead of the weed of their seeking.

Talbot learned many other things from William the half-Indian. He learned to speak Cree. He saw it as the perfect quickness of a man's expression: a way of saying that constantly surprised him. He saw the verbs unfolded into sense upon sense, into meaning after meaning. He delighted in those Indian verbs, so many times richer and ampler than his own. Little by little he understood how pliant and enfolding are the Cree words, and how a single one might compass a meaning where the English

43

speech would demand upwards of seven. It pleased him, as a game of skill would please, to puzzle out the many meanings that one root-word could mother (4). Oratory and courage, these, of every chieftain, of every brave had been demanded. No written language had the Cree, but the spoken word was conserved with piety; heirloom of the warriors. Perfection of the spoken word; perfection in the mastery of the body; these the two wings of their ascendance.

Talbot learned to track down the ruffled grouse and to follow a spoor as though the snow were a book. The Aurora Borealis too he must see with a difference, not only as beautiful, but as harbinger of wind.

Talbot now held in his memory long poems of Byron, and Tennyson, and passages from Shakespeare. Sixty lines a day he set himself to learn, and this with a double purpose. He must strengthen his memory so as to learn quickly the Eskimo tongue —if once he should reach that people—also he must carry in his mind spiritual provision against the emptiness of the Barren

Lands. A harvest gathered, a harvest garnered would
be his store of poetry; though his body
might go hungry, he would be
provisioned with nourish-
ment for thought.

CHAPTER III

*   *   *

CUNNINGLY WILLIAM MADE SOME DECOYS, THE BEST that Talbot had seen. He shaped a piece of burned wood into a rough ellipse and to each of these he nailed two wings—ducks' wings. The decoy floated, the incoming duck were deceived, and so the hunger of the station was appeased.

It was, for the brothers, the last Sunday to be spent at Oxford House; the pemmican, what little was left of it, was being cleared away, the Scotsmen were praising it and talking of one thing and another; but Talbot could not talk much because he was hoarse with grunting, for all Saturday he had hidden in sedges and grunted to attract passing geese.

After smoking a clay pipe, and learning various tricks for colouring it, Talbot in spite of his sore throat recited poetry: 'for we don't play cards on the Sabbath,' said Campbell, and dropped into silence—thinking perhaps of Sunday in his native island of Skye.

'Soon we'll sit in darkness, for the oil is nearly finished, and there are only ten more candles in the house,' said Simpson.

'The thaw, the geese, the duck, everything is late this year,' they grumbled, as they settled down to drink the last few drams of the whisky.

The talk hinged awhile on Scottish Sabbaths. One of the Company said that the gloom of the Sabbath, the only free day in the week, was the cause of his being in Canada. 'Same here,' came the answer. Talbot remembered being sent to bed in the afternoon one Sunday, because, at Locknaw as a boy, he had whistled. "But I would never shoot anything on Sunday unless I were really hungry," he said.

Whatever the five contrary watches might prove, the time passed pleasantly at Oxford House. For fifty days the brothers stayed there. If, sometimes at night, a man dozed off after a game of poker, leaving the talk to languish, Talbot would rouse the

45

trader into wakefulness by defaming the Company, for at that its most lethargic servant awoke to defend it.

The weather propitious, there came the day of good-byes and of kindly farewells to the Scotsmen. It was the last day of May. Thirty Indians went to the waterside to wish the Englishmen godspeed, so thirty times must Talbot shake hands.

Then came the long good-byes between the Indians going to York Factory, the Kitchi Waskahgon, or Big Fort by the sea, and their kin who would stay behind. There was about a thousand pounds of dead weight in the big boat. One of the men stood at the stern and steered with a great sweep. Two Indians on a seat had each a scull. Talbot had an oar clumsy as a barge-pole. His brother was in a canoe made of birchwood. The many rapids kept the Indians watchful.

They rowed and sailed, and here and there a pike was caught with a spoon-bait. Then they had to portage the boat, but at the horseshoe-shaped Trout Falls they lowered her and made their way on the outer edge of the whirlpool—nice work. They could not but remember the Hudson Bay trading boat that just there had been sucked down. One man had lived through that fatality, but nine had been drowned.

Farther on they gaily took a rapid, but in the middle of the next one the boat stuck. The water swept round them. "The noble red men bellowed like oxen."

Talbot saw later a rock and on it 'A. L. MacDonald, 1797'. That turned his thoughts to the history of the Honourable Company, its first president a prince, its early traders men of valour. He liked its motto *Pro pelle cutum*—'a skin for a skin'. Idly he thought that had he sprung of a new family he would have tried his fortune as miner or as trader; would have caused a coat of arms to be blazoned supported by strange animals, hard to hunt and mortal in their anger; dexter, a musk-ox. . . . But at that his thought broke off, for William had been talking of musk-ox just before they left Oxford House. 'You must hunt them with the Eskimo in the Barren Lands'—and Talbot, son of Sagittarius, was filled with desire to hunt in their remoteness the only beasts begotten of those unmapped wastes, to bring back alive to England beasts of this species, "for they will be the first that ever were seen there," he thought.

46

Oxford House to York Factory

At night, sheltered on an island in Knee Lake, they heard the broken ice impelled against the shore, the wind wailing through the trees, and the roaring of a rampant fir fire.

In four days and a half of rowing, of shooting rapids, of wet clothes and of hardships, they put behind them some ninety miles and gained the main waterway for York Factory. Those four and a half days were heavy. Hardest of the men's trials were the portages. There the boats and the goods were carried and hauled overland because the rapids were impassable. Two hundred easier miles now lay before the travellers. For three and a half days they went along the deeper, slower river and made their way through the flat country to the sea.

On the night before they reached York, over their camp came a flight of wild-duck, flying low. "Like the sound of an express train rushing through a station"—so was this sound of the many duck speeding north. Then with Betts very ill, and his brother some way behind in the bark made of birchwood, Talbot arrived at York Factory.

CHAPTER IV

★　　★　　★

BALLANTYNE HAD CALLED IT 'A SPOT IN A SWAMP'. "A bed of roses"—this was Talbot's praise of York Factory. "Here are books to read and clocks that agree as to the hour. Doctor Milne did everything for me—he and his clerk McAlpine."

'Our boats are not ready,' said the Indian to whom would be given the command of the boats, 'and on the sea is still too much brash-ice.' So for the month of June and into July the travellers delayed their journey to Fort Churchill. During that time Talbot's determination took shape—he would go far North and explore; his brother (5) and Betts would leave him at Fort Churchill—no matter, he could go on alone. A barrier of ice was in the bay, yet the summer had come leaping in on the retreating spring. After the snow came the mosquitos.

Talbot, living close to nature, was aware of the rush and the hurry of the growing plants. In less than three months the fruiting bushes and the marsh-grown flowers must finish with their blossoming and their fruiting and their seeding. "Amazing that the frail leaves should bear a pressure that would drive a ship across an ocean (6)." In three months the winter would again set in. No wonder that some of the terrestrial flowers pushed domes beneath the snow and waited, ready in beauty, till a thaw should free them. The snow once melted, the bees and the flies would find the flowers ready to receive their gift of fertility.

Talbot saw in the threefold endeavour of the plants—in the effort crowned by the leaf, by the flower, and by the seed—an augury that he too would find a way to bend events to his purpose. If the marsh flowers, and the fruit bushes, could gain their ends by overcoming the accustomed slow unfolding elsewhere imposed upon them, so could he resist being bound to the wheel of custom.

York Factory spread its wooden houses, shops and offices

48

over six acres or more. A stockade surrounded it, and some buildings were raised on piles to escape the floods. It was a place full of character, more like a person than a place. It was good to look at the harbour and to remember the princely ships, *Prince Rupert* and a succeeding *Prince Rupert, Duke of York* and *Prince of Wales*, sailing to and fro for over two hundred years with cargoes of fur. Good to remember the patience of the merchants of Lime Street and of Leadenhall, and their long vision. They had sent out goods to far places of the Company and had known, that for seven years, nine years even, they could have no profit of that merchandise. On the outward journey the ships carried great variety of trade goods, on the homeward journey they carried precious pelts gathered from the natives of half a continent. The nature of the Company's business was such that it did not sap the soul of the Indians. They were not ruined by cities springing up, nor heartbroken by the plough and the harrow. They continued to be that which from all time they had been, wanderers and hunters. The silent Scotsmen whom they served asked no better of them.

Talbot was fretted (7) by the delay, and therefore Doctor Milne allowed two of his Indians to go with him to the Nelson River; geese, duck, deer and bear, all these might be hoped for. "Arranged with Indians to start in the morning, their names respectively being Charles and John Thomas. Charles can talk English, or rather Scotch, John Thomas is a pure unsophisticated Indian with no knowledge of any language excepting his own, and probably leaves the H's out of that." This hunting was not fortunate. They sailed in a beam wind; and even Talbot wrote of the sail as "rather nervous work". John Thomas "is a most arrant coward when faced by cold water. At each curling wave he jumped with fear"—that was on the first day, whilst paddling over shallows with plenty of stones (8). The next day, "We sailed until the square sail (wretched) would not hold. I wanted to paddle the canoe out into the other side to get the right wind, but was told it was full of shoals. Pure funk on Charlie's part, he would not venture in the deep. We never would have sailed at all had I not insisted on having a mast cut. Well, we had dinner—the tide changed—Charlie got rebellious—finally, against an awful stream made one mile and a half in five hours, then the wind came. John Thomas yelled with fear; next, rowing was adopted. Soon after, Charlie said he saw a bear above a house near the water. We landed and went up the hill to spy, sent John Thomas to look for tracks, then Charlie. They signalled, having found tracks. With my spy-glass I saw the beggars making them. They must think I am an awful mooniass as they put seven toes on the bear."

The hunting over, after some days they returned.

On Sunday in the chapel, the Indians sang with sweet voices. A Cree preacher, becoming full of zeal, shouted at the people "and morally scalped them". After supper: "Doctor Milne played a broken-winded organ, I the flute, and we plodded through many hymns, McAlpine coming in every now and then. Our throats finally became dry, so a bottle of whisky was brought out . . . that is the way Sunday is kept in the N. Everyone slept in the afternoon."

As he took farewell of York Factory, there was given to Talbot a chart drawn by Ballantyne. "It will help me greatly." And, too—beautiful gift of valediction—on a slip of paper Franklin's name, written by Franklin himself.

Early in July the *Black Prince* and *La Pérouse* sailed from York, and with them the three Englishmen. An Indian had brought the news that ice still beset the way to Churchill. They must risk that and also must risk "that the boats were manned by Indians who were not deep-sea sailors".

They sailed along merrily till, after noon, clouds rose up and then grew very black, lying all along the horizon. "When the gallant crew saw that, instantly the sails were taken down and all the anchors were put out." No wind came, but thunder and lightning and rain. Afterwards, the storm over, they sailed on.

Although the night was nearly clear as day, yet at ten o'clock the frightened rascals chose to anchor again. Before them was an ice floe. Talbot, lying on the floor of the cabin, went to sleep among the beetles.

The next day Talbot's brother landed, for he wished to walk to Fort Churchill, some thirty miles overland. For three days Talbot saw ice in many presentments. First there had been the floe, in a large space of ice, beyond which could be seen the sea, later to starboard lay a field of ice—so vast this frozen mass that the eye could not see where it ended. If it broke away it would sail, large as a prairie, bearing upon it walrus and polar bear; it would float like a fantastic meadow, harbouring its creatures. Walking away from the boat, Talbot could gauge the awful stillness of arctic places. So profound the silence that it seemed to be an inner silence, such as is suffered by the deaf. Looking away over the ice, Talbot was absorbed, remembering the fate of the arctic explorers. Not far from here the sea had become solid round about Ross and his men—ice that made void their avocation as sailors.

They sailed on, and then 'splash' went the anchor. At eight o'clock in the evening the Indians stopped to say their prayers; afterwards, until midnight, they ran before the wind. They saw sailing ice beautiful and terrible, and they had to beat to windward to avoid its shattered pieces. They bumped into drift ice, and the *Black Prince* shivered from stem to stern. One evening they saw, and heard, a piece of ice thrust up from under the sea, violently ascending into sight. Talbot knew that now he had seen an iceberg calving, throwing up from its entrails this lesser berg, begotten of the summer.

Soon after he saw with amazement, far away, a mountain of ice that leaned suddenly over, quaked, and fell down into the sea. The noise carried for miles, the waters were displaced, the vessel rocked. But Talbot was glad, for he had the fancy that he had seen in the calving—the birth—and in the disappearance— the death—of an iceberg.

When the tide went out from the bays, ice-fields blocked the open sea. Once at night the travellers heard the tearing and rending of the ice that groaned as it moved. Breaks, violent up-heavals, collisions, shattered the air. Very horrible it was to hear mute nature suddenly cry with so strange an utterance. The roll of the sea round English shores, the wail of the wind about a sheltering house, these from childhood had been familiar, but the commotion of the ice was a new and a fearful sound filling Talbot with awe.

Next day, in great heat, they landed on the low flat shore and walked on a carpet of strawberry blossom. Though in terror of quicksands, they waded in the mud to shoot. Many birds were there, curlew and snipe and phalarope and geese. Comfortable seals lay on the ice, and the tracks of a bear were graven in the sand. 'They swim strongly, they move quickly, they never change their coats, but are white or yellow-white always; the young are born under snow,' said the Indians (9). So they spoke of the polar bear.

The men's food was deer and the palatable flesh of a bear; "I eat when I'm hungry, sleep when I'm sleepy and drink lime juice when thirsty." On the third day a sharp wind freed them from an ice-pack, the solid sides whereof rose, it was reckoned, ten feet high.

Afterwards, because no fair wind blew, they ran aground and waited for three hours in the mud till the incoming tide should lift up the *Black Prince* and *La Pérouse*. Talbot knew then the torture inflicted by a myriad of mosquitos. At evening, fevered by their bites, giddy with their buzzing and their plaguing, he landed at Fort Churchill. The last stage of his brother's travel, Fort Churchill, was but the starting-place for the great journey that confronted Talbot.

CHAPTER V

*   *   *

TALBOT REMEMBERED FORT CHURCHILL GRATEFULLY BE-
cause of the friendliness of Captain and Mrs. Hawes, who "have
kindly fitted up a room for me with a carpet—the first I have
seen in this country". Mr. Lofthouse the missionary (10) who,
although no carpenter, had built his own house, Mrs. Lofthouse
with her snowy tea-table cloth (the first that Talbot had seen
for four months), and the chapel with its organ—all these were
pleasant. Of Lofthouse Talbot wrote: "It does me good to talk
to so sincere a man." Lofthouse had been as far as Chesterfield
Inlet, and he gave Talbot a map and told him something of
the Indians and of the Eskimos. The Eskimos living much upon
the product of the sea were free of the white people save for the
little barter that they chose to do (11).

Mary Gray, an Indian woman, was made known to Talbot,
and she cut for him, against his journey, two pairs of mittens
from the skin of deer, and moccasins to match, lined with rabbit fur. These mittens were to be attached to a long string round
the traveller's neck, muff-fashion. This would enable him to
pull his hands quickly in and out of the gloves without losing
them, most necessary provision when a man's hands might, in
a moment, be frostbitten.

At Fort Churchill (12) a half-breed, George Oman, was
brought to Talbot by Alston of the Company, who said,
'Oman (13) will be your interpreter in Barren Lands, for he
speaks Eskimo as well as Chippewayan, and once he went
North with a party in search of Franklin.' An honest-looking
man, alert, short of stature, with clear eyes and a bushy beard,
looked up at Talbot. "He looks soft," thought Talbot; but he
agreed to take the man.

A day was spent in buying trade goods, three double-
barrelled guns and three single, twenty-eight pounds of shot

and ball, eighteen thousand gun-caps, eighteen carats of tobacco, each carat being two and a half pounds in weight. Forty pounds of plug tobacco, three dozen scalping knives, half a dozen Swedish knives, half a dozen roach knives, six fish knives, a dozen butcher's knives, a dozen dog knives, one thousand four hundred and fifty needles, one and three-quarter pounds of seed beads, two kettles, twelve cotton handkerchiefs, three hundred pounds of flour, two kegs of pork weighing sixty-six pounds each, and many boxes of matches. Lofthouse gave him an oil lamp. 'Ten gallons of coal oil will be enough for your needs.' His sextants, and most of his books, he must leave behind.

The days in Fort Churchill were dreary for Talbot who, in his diary, complained of toothache and of indigestion, "to which I am a martyr". Here and there throughout the journey from Winnipeg a day had been marred by "terrible temper". Everything then went awry, such a day would be cankered—"an accursed day". This temper hurt. One entry, after a day so plagued, records, "I woke in a better frame of mind".

On the last Sunday that he spent in Fort Churchill he was ill and did not leave the house. In the chapel, Mr. Lofthouse preached a sermon that was a godspeed to the Englishman and to his guide. After singing a hymn to the music of the organ the people prayed for the two travellers, because they knew a little of the many wants and dangers that would beset them.

Talbot went to bed "feeling lonely and far away"; for a long time he did not sleep. Upon few men is thrust the need to cut adrift and to go where they will be naked in the Hand of God.

Above the page that Sunday night of mid July was written: "Many might think it folly to go.
To me there is an awe and a mysticism that
weighs heavily on the mind, even
though the great change is
in accordance with
my wish."

CHAPTER VI

★ ★ ★

THE 'BLACK PRINCE' LAY AT THE OLD FORT, WHICH WAS four miles distant from Fort Churchill. Bidding good-bye to his brother, who now had gone as far as he wished to go, Talbot walked with Alston and Betts to the Old Fort and the three men rowed out to the boat and there took their farewell of one another—for Alston would return to Churchill and Betts with Talbot's brother to England. At first the smell of thirty Eskimos, with their dogs, bedding and utensils, nearly overpowered Talbot, but he determined not to mind it and he soon overcame his first niceness. Seven Eskimo canoes (kayaks) were pulled on board and the anchor hoisted amid a chorus of howls from the dogs that were left behind.

Passing Seal Island and anchoring at Long Point, fresh salmon were brought on board, but, even as Talbot was admiring them, the Eskimos began to cut them up, and then the men, women and children ate the fish raw. George Oman, seeing Talbot turn away sickened, said: 'It gives them a belly-ache to eat it cooked.'

The Eskimos on their canoes moved to and from the *Black Prince*. Six canoes were joined together by paddles; twelve men boarded them. At night they beat in to the shore to anchor. Talbot then delighted them by playing the flute. He too found that the evening passed away gaily, made pleasant by the simple ways and childlike manners of the Eskimos. He conjured a little to amuse them, but stopped when he found that they accounted the slightest trick to be a manifestation of supreme power.

Then, before following winds they sailed northwards. A whaling-boat manned with Eskimos was sailing behind them. Americans would barter such a boat with oars and sail against a valuable whale. They stopped again and venison was brought on board. This was good to eat—but where was the loaf that

55

Mrs. Hawes so certainly said she had put in with Talbot's things? They looked vainly amongst the baggage—bread and meat would have been a feast, but after nothing but lean meat a man soon again feels hungry. The Eskimos carved great gobbets of meat and ate it raw, but already Talbot was coarsened to such things and hardly minded. After the meal suddenly he thought: "I've looked through all my things for the bread and I've not found it, nor seen my Shakespeare either. Surely I cannot have left it behind, and yet it is not amongst my books— nor with my gear."

Next they came to Eskimo Point, where most of the women and some of the men left the boat. Here Talbot and George Oman went ashore, and after much searching they found an Eskimo named Cattalo who was noted as a hunter of musk-ox. Him Talbot bespoke as follower. The hunter began to make ready to go to Chesterfield Inlet, but would not consent to leave his tent, his wives or any of his possessions. 'I will take them all with me,' he said. 'These will encumber you,' Oman contended. At last the man agreed to take only his tent and one of his sons. At this decision the women burst into loud lamentation, but the outcry was perhaps only a ceremonious keening—for suddenly they stopped and on the instant appeared to be once more happy. But still the hunter made delay, and it was late when they boarded the boat and with much tacking got out into the rough sea—long spits and bars of land delaying them.

In the evening they anchored at a place where stood tents of deer-skin. Into the biggest tent Talbot must not go, for a dance was being prepared, such a dance as is always given when a seal is killed.

Talbot had to go into a small tent which was crowded with children, men and old women. The younger women he supposed were making ready for the festivities. He filled and lit a pipe of tobacco which was passed round from hand to hand, all sharing the pleasure, as is their wont. They asked him where he came from and he, unable to explain, made a gesture towards the sky. From that they understood that his home was the stars, and thought a little in silence; but they gave no sign as to whether or not they believed that he was celestial. He dared not do any conjuring tricks because he feared that they might ask

him to heal sick people or to provide food by miracle. Then he
went back in a leaping boat through the rough sea, "and read
the Bible and the *Strand*", and lay thinking of Franklin, and
wondering if indeed he could live with the Eskimos and hunt for
musk-ox. Enriched by the oil of the walrus and by its flesh, by
the bounty, too, of the seals, the Eskimos living here by the sea
were rich compared with those who lived inland nearer to the
musk-ox. "But how shall I get back once I am five hundred
miles from the nearest timber? This is very rough work," Talbot wrote.

Sunday passed at anchor, the *Black Prince* being by Talbot re-
named the *Black Emperor* because of her much rolling. George
Oman and his brother were sick, but not because of the sea; they
coughed and ached and tossed with fever. Talbot felt seasick
and remained all day in shelter, wrapped in his rabbit-skins,
calling out when he needed food or tea.

Steadily the glass went down; all day the sun was invisible,
and all day his mind—he was sorry it was so—vacillated. "Shall I
go on? Shall I turn back? I shall be hundreds of miles
from wood, in one of the coldest parts of the world,
uncertain of food." George Oman, when-
ever he saw Talbot, murmured: 'No
wood, no wood.' Then Talbot
slept. When he woke up he
wrote: "I will not
go back."

CHAPTER VII

✶ ✶ ✶

THE WIND CHANGED TO SOUTH-EAST; HEAVY RAIN FELL; then came fog. Talbot tried to set his watch, which had stopped. This was gambler's work, for here day and night were one. From his shelter, that was more like a kennel than a cabin, he called for water at an hour that he supposed was eight in the evening, but found afterwards that it must have been nearly two o'clock in the morning, for the moon rose about an hour afterwards. According to the almanac the time for the moon's rising was three in the morning.

Eight days after having left Fort Churchill they arrived at Hell's Gate. By this island—rising at its highest point less than a hundred feet above the sea—Talbot met thirty Eskimos in a great whaleboat. Amongst them was one famed as huntsman. Cattalo, the hunter who had promised to guide Talbot in the Barren Lands, repenting his promise, had taken back his word. So now this other, a fine-looking man, whose name was Atonguela, was brought on board the *Black Prince*. He promised, if his wife did not demur, to go with Talbot. Two hours later he and Talbot, sitting in a tent of skins, saw Atonguela's wife entering, for she had been told to come. She, for the moment amiable, "did not care a straw whether he went or no". So Atonguela assented. Talbot now put up his tent, George Oman and his brother helping, but they were weak with illness and slow. Soon the tent was snug, and amongst the things unpacked was found the loaf of Mrs. Hawes' baking. It had been lost for eight days. "Most opportune," wrote Talbot, not weighing its age against his pleasure.

That night there was a great dance, because, from inland, Eskimos had come to trade with those who had arrived in the whaleboat. In the centre of a circle of people stood a man chanting and beating a small drum. The drum was made of deer parchment.

58

The Market at Hell's Gate

The women took up the lay and in turn droned for half an hour, whereafter a second man entered the circle and continued the intoning. "It was all very strange, but wanting in variety."

Next morning the whaleboat had become a place of brisk marketing. Musk-ox skins there were, and the skins of foxes white and blue, the pelts of wolves, parchments prepared from caribou, raw hide, ropes made from walrus and from sealskin, Eskimo boots, gloves and shoes, and oil, in bags of sealskin. A few walrus tusks lay on deck, and many small teeth of walrus. The great tusks for which these creatures are hunted and massacred are hard to come by, for only at a certain age does the walrus wear them.

The Eskimos living in tents near to the sea had boarded the boat at dawn and when Talbot arrived later, with some Eskimos who came from far inland, all the tobacco had already been paid out and but a few of the meaner knives and axes were left. The disappointed Eskimos were very angry. Having hunted, they expected payment in the provisions that they most needed and this had been promised them by the Eskimos on the whaleboat who, intermedial, had travelled between these people and the white men at Fort Churchill.

It was a wild scene. The wares, wrested with muck-sweat from land and sea, were now flung down upon the deck, while the hunters with dark eager faces crowded round the unsufficing goods displayed for payment.

The Eskimos, whom Talbot always thought to be the best-tempered people in the world, now swallowed their disappointment; they let the hour pass away without revenge; they returned to the tents sadly without the promised goods. Talbot often recorded how gentle are the people, and how good-tempered, in the main, their often-suffering dogs, the useful huskies. True, the dogs fought much; yet their pelt was so thick and their coats so long that generally no great hurt ensued, and the anger of the assailing dogs was usually assuaged by mouthfuls of thick hair.

In the evening there was another dance. Talbot played his flute knowing that the people enjoyed the music, "though they made no sign of like or of dislike". The young men afterwards amused themselves by playing Tom Tiddler.

Next day Atonguela told Talbot that none of the men would go to musk-ox country, they liked better their homes and the grounds that they knew. At that Talbot reflected bitterly on his lost hope of going farther north, but he resolved, that for the present, he would go with those men who would hunt the walrus, "for later Atonguela may find willing men—so I will remain in this part". Therefore he bought a thirty-foot whale-boat with mast and sail and pump, giving, in payment, a double-barrelled gun, fifteen pounds of powder, and ten pounds of shot and ball. He bought also three dogs, giving goods in exchange. The Eskimos were loth to part with their huskies, but feared ill luck would follow on refusal. If they had refused to part with a dog and it died, they would think the misfortune was punishment for having been niggardly.

All the dogs of the settlement were fastened outside Talbot's tent and great was the noise they made. Also thirty men stood there and exchanged for knives and powder their bows and arrows, dolls, and skins and boots.

The days passed. Two boat-loads of Eskimos sailed off to seek their winter quarters. Talbot gradually secured the tackle he wanted from the people. He spent many hours each day learning the language. By dint of a rare attention, of listening, learning and remembering, he could already talk a little with the Eskimos. He found the words difficult to pronounce, but he liked their sound.

He had bought two robes of caribou skin, and needed to have these cut into shirts and coats. 'We do not cut skins at this time of the year, it is ill-fated,' the women said. Talbot then with sleight-of-hand performed two simple tricks foretelling them that they would have plenty of caribou. At that they were willing to do his bidding. Then he tried, but without avail, to be allowed to attach himself to one of the tribes; the men refused to take him in.

To all the Eskimos he met he showed the pictures that he carried of the balloon of André. "Did you, in the air, see such a bird?" he asked. "Or has news come that such a one has been found, fallen on land, or ice, or sea?" But that thing they certainly had not seen.

He observed that the men never did anything alone; hunting,

fishing, trading, always three or four went together. At that time they seemed to him both obstinate and changeable, their word not being a bond.

Talbot still had the coal-oil lamp that Mr. Lofthouse had given him, but the wicks were nearly all burned, and had all caused trouble. To cook the salmon that was his daily fare he had laboriously to feed the flame with lichen and dry mosses. After such a meal would follow the greatest happiness of the day, the smoking of his pipe. It was pleasant, thinking and smoking; pleasant to taste the pipe grow sweeter, and to see it grow more mellow. In his diary he wrote: "I have to mention my pipe, it gives me so much pleasure."

George Oman and his brother still coughed and spat. All day they played with a puzzle that Talbot had given them.

Suddenly Atonguela too fell very ill.

The days passed slowly, no plans were made, events hung in the balance, depending—in the main—on the vain imaginings and ill-founded fears of the people. Such and such an aspect of the decrescent moon would more weigh in their determinations than would a real necessity. But Talbot, man of
action, must do nothing, must smoke his pipe and watch it
grow more mellow. With half-shut eyes that seemed
to notice nothing but that saw everything,
he must watch, so that if ever came
the fit time, the ripe moment,
he would seize upon it—
and enslave it to
his will.

CHAPTER VIII

* * *

ONE MORNING THE WHOOP OF A SWAN HALF WAKED Talbot, and George's voice broke the rest of his sleep. George was smiling. Having wakened Talbot he spoke low, for his news must not be told in the hearing of the Eskimos.

'Atonguela will take you north to his own people, far above Chesterfield Inlet. You shall sail in your whaleboat,' he said.

Afterwards they went on shore to the tent, and then for hours George was silent. Talbot wondered at the silence as he sorted out his things. He threw aside his heavy provision box and the padlocked box, anxious lest, even with these discarded, the thirty-foot whaleboat should fail to hold the gear that he must keep. He must have five tin tubs, weighing about a hundred pounds each, the barrel of powder with ball and shot. He must keep the two bags, each of which held fifty pounds of flour, must keep also the pork and the cartridges. Even now, after giving away many things there was still a weight of about fifteen hundred pounds to be stowed.

At last George had a spasm of coughing and then he spoke. He said that he and his brother Peter did not dare to go farther north. On the *Black Prince* they and Cattalo would return south. Cattalo would disembark at Eskimo Point; the brothers would fare thence to Fort Churchill.

Talbot said little but thought scornfully "that sort of man would have been no good to me; I prefer to go alone with my pagan." But he saw his danger, for in the diary he wrote: "It is rash even for me to go by myself into a bitterly cold country with no interpreter;" then he added, "but I can now speak enough of the language to get what I want."

The wind, that for days had blown strong and not fair, was blowing north-west. The men feasted on the food that had been discarded, and they finished what was left of the jam and of the bread that George had baked.

God to decide which Wind

Atonguela was still sick, so Talbot gave him twenty grains of quinine, and ten grains of phenacetin all at once and covered him up with a blanket. 'He looks as if he will die,' said George Oman. The tent was heaped up with duffle, baggage, guns, tobacco, boxes and much beside. The dogs howled; the glass went up; the night grew cold. Talbot rolled himself up in his furs, then he called Oman: "If the north wind keeps up I will go south with you to Eskimo Point."
He lay still, watching his first candle burn
itself out. In the diary, open by his rough
bed, the last entry that night was:
"Prayed to God to decide
which wind."

CHAPTER IX

*   *   *

WHEN TALBOT WOKE UP THE SOUTH WIND WAS BLOWING.
He put all his things together, leaving out a hundred pounds
of flour, two tins of beef and fifteen pounds of tea and sugar for
George. He wrapped Atonguela in three of his own blankets,
for Atonguela was ill as a man could be. Then some of the
Eskimos carried Atonguela down to the whaleboat. Wondering
what would befall him if Atonguela should die, Talbot slowly
followed the men to the boat. Although leaving him so shabbily, yet when the time came to say good-bye, Oman "could
hardly speak for emotion". Although so shabbily deserted, Talbot saw Oman well provided. In the rain and wind the whaleboat cast off north.

"*August 5*. Alone with the Eskimos. Start. South wind. Put
everything together—fixed them in boat—said good-bye to
George and Cattalo, and went north with a wild husky to an
unknown land: how much in those few words." But again
afterwards he wrote that he was glad to be alone with the
Eskimos—Oman, a man half civilized, would have been but a
barrier between him and the Eskimos.

Thus with his dying savage, bound for the Barren Lands far
beyond wood and civilization, he set sail. That evening in his
diary he wrote: "I do not think that Atonguela will desert me,
but he himself does not know what his tribe will say to my
coming."

Towards Chesterfield Inlet they sailed, passing many new
islands, amongst them Marble Island. The evening star rose
north by east, over a low island. It rose so red that the men
mistook it for the moon. The wind forsook them.

In the calm of the sea they saw a line of breakers; they turned
about; but, because of the current against the boat, the breakers
were getting nearer and nearer astern. The whole night they

64

had to pull away with all their might; what little wind there was came in puffs and was favourable to them.

Having regained their course they felt themselves hungry; therefore, when they reached the mouth of Chesterfield Inlet, they went ashore on the mainland. Soon afterwards they saw a caribou, with branching antlers, feeding on easy stalking ground. Talbot was alone and spied it with his telescope. Two of the dogs had followed him. "Confound them," he said, but even huskies would follow him. These creatures, as he had foreseen, got the wind and pursued the caribou so that it was lost to him. Of the dog Cadge-Eh-hena, and of the stag he saw no more. He was tempted to shoot the dog which did return to him. Though he saw Cadge-Eh-hena looking for him he did not even whistle, so it was lost for ever (as he then thought). A dog could live alone here hunting like a wolf, and Talbot was angry at the loss of the caribou, being meat-hungry; fish alone, though it surfeits a man, does not satisfy him.

The days were very hot, and on the evening of the fifth day, on the mainland at the mouth of Chesterfield Inlet, the men left the whaleboat and pitched their camp where other tents already stood. At first the Eskimos from the tents stared hard at the Englishman, then they put up his tent and got some things from the boat. Atonguela, who by now was well again, had a long talk to the men, which talk Talbot could not understand, but it seemed to be about him, and to content the people.

Now, wanting to prepare a meal, Talbot found that the last wick of his gift-lamp was very bad, burning away fiercely, half an inch of wick being consumed in a minute. He used the fire that an Eskimo lit for him and cooked the salmon which one of the men gave him, but he drank cold water instead of heating some for tea, because cooking over a fire fed with lichen was troublesome on so hot a day.

Encamped, they waited for a few days. At first the men of the tents could not understand Talbot when he spoke, but in some hours this barrier had disappeared. He held a reception that lasted all day. He bought fur-top boots for a knife, and a seal-skin to be used as a gun-case; this also was paid for with a knife. To Atonguela he gave a gun.

On the pebbles inside the tent a ring of Aleutics stood blow-

ing their noses in their hands and wiping their hands on the
blankets near his bed. They all had influenza; Atonguela had
taken the malady from Oman and had infected the tribe. They
coughed and spat continually, the while handling Talbot's
things with great curiosity. When he explained to them how a
spring knife is shut: 'Ah!' they said in chorus, gazed at the knife
and wished to have it. At high tide Talbot swam in the sea; a
crowd of women gazed in wonder at the white giant.

Again they sailed, passing by Marble Island, and pitched their
tents on a point at the mouth of the Inlet. Once more they
hunted, Atonguela and Talbot outwalking the other men. One
day, after four hours of stalking in the sun, the other men refused to go farther, but Atonguela and Talbot pushed on for
two more hours. A splendid caribou rushing towards them got
their wind, for the breeze was changeable and favoured the
caribou, so that it turned and fled from them. Over stony ridges,
very harmful to the feet, and baulked by boggy plains, they
once more returned—steering by compass—south-east by east.

At every mile they sat down to rest. When, exhausted,
they reached the camp, Atonguela cut up half
a twelve-pound salmon. Talbot got
out two biscuits; then without hesitation he ate
the raw fish.

CHAPTER X

★ ★ ★

THE WHALEBOAT SPRANG A LEAK. THERE WAS NO TIMBER or driftwood for its repair, so Talbot had to buy a sled. From the sled would be taken wood for a plank long enough to repair the leak. The old man who was to mend the boat did not for days approach it—he only said: 'It will be mended.'

Worse still, the rain had penetrated one of the tubs so that many needles and knives had been made rusty; also a quantity of matches were spoiled. This was a serious loss.

The day after the deer hunt Talbot remained in camp, for he was stiff with stalking. Near to him a dog was dying of lockjaw. A pair of moleskin trousers that George had given him he cut up into wicks for his gift-lamp. He busied himself, too, with drying the nine coverings that formed his bed, duffle-blankets and his rabbit-skin. That night he snugged thankfully into the comfort of the well-dried bedding. The wind outside roared and whistled; it blew so strong that it mauled his tent.

The next day was very hot, and the little children ran about naked whilst Talbot, watching them, recorded that "the love of these people for their children surpasses all things". Eskimos, standing at the tent door, gazed intently at Talbot who was reading. He knew that they were wondering "why a man should sit with his eyes bent on a white square?" Talbot glancing up and catching their thoughts wondered too, if really this passage of Schopenhauer, out here, rang true. He closed the book of philosophy and sighed again for Shakespeare, for though he had found the bread he had not found the book of poetry.

When he must have air, Talbot got up and walked five yards beyond the tent. The watchers followed; quickly he returned to the tent and they understood that he wanted to be alone. The heat caused the noses of the people to bleed if they carried any heavy thing. The dog that had died the evening before still lay unburied within ten feet of Talbot's tent.

67

Death: delay: death

Men were thoughtful for Talbot. They took the knives and cups and whatsoever he put outside his tent, and washed them for him, bringing him water, and carrying for him. They performed a hundred trifling offices that made his life more easy.

The hunters brought in duck and curlew and snipe, and, most precious of all, sometimes a little wood to cook with. When Talbot had used the last sticks he went out and pulled half a hundredweight of black moss, strapped it to him and brought it to camp. He found that an excellent way of cooking a salmon was to cut it into strips, which strips he laid in moss, and afterwards set fire to the moss.

Every night the nets were put out for salmon, and when the sea was not generous the men stretched the nets across the river five miles away. Once, from a rock they speared salmon; three were killed, but that cost them five hours. The fish weighed about ten pounds each. Talbot was so hungry after spearing that he cooked, and ate, a whole salmon at the evening meal.

"It will be killing work returning to Fort Churchill when the Inlet is frozen," Talbot wrote, for winter was recalled suddenly, and that on a hot day when a high field of ice came drifting down the Bay. 'Bear and walrus may be got,' hoped Atonguela, scanning the white expanse.

'In another sleep we will go on to better hunting ground,' promised Atonguela; for Talbot was now suffering from ringworm and from eczema, and longed for fare other than fish (14). On the night of that promise there was awful clamour and howling, and Talbot was told that one of the sick men had died. In the camp the coughing still increased. The Eskimos would not tell Talbot anything about the burial of the dead, but he learned that they would not now leave that point for six days because this would be the season of their mourning. Talbot, because the light did not guide him, measured time by the tides. Many hours between ebb and flow he passed writing a dictionary. Also he wrote a poem to the place. At the tent door a boy, seeing him write, laughed very heartily.

Outside his tent, two days after its death, a dog lay—still unburied. The living dogs grew more and more fretful with the heat and fought continually, biting each others' vulnerable noses.

The comfort of the wild strawberries

Now the people grew used to Talbot and he saw that they liked him. "My lazy habits please them." They came asking him to play the flute: "These people grow sad and weep when I play soft music on the flute." Unlike the Eskimos in the more southerly camp who showed "neither like nor dislike" these, knowing Talbot, did not hide their feeling. Also they came to him for medicine, and he gave what he thought would help them (15).

The days of mourning passed slowly. By day the people still loudly lamented the dead man; at night the north wind raged. Fearing that his tent might be blown into the sea, Talbot made it fast to the earth with stones. On the fifth day after the death of the Eskimo, a woman, to whom Talbot had given medicine, died. A young man died too. So now in a camp of ten tents lay three dead. He who had died first was still unburied.

The loud howling of the mourners all that day, after a night of blowing wind and fighting dogs, drove Talbot far away over the hills and through swamps. Then he came "to a place thickly studded with wild strawberries. They are not yet ripe but the colour is exquisite, a blushing pink. The fruit is far smaller than the English one. Fruit and blossom lie hidden in their own leaves." Talbot returned comforted to the camp. The wild strawberries, somehow, had cheered him.

CHAPTER XI

★ ★ ★

WHILST THEY WERE MOURNING THE DEAD, STORMS arose. The nets could not be put out for salmon, and save for wild berries there was but little food. Three hunters therefore went out early in the day and in the evening returned carrying as much venison as they had strength for. 'We have killed nine deer and hidden the rest near where we shot the beasts,' said one of the men. For the first time for three weeks Talbot ate meat, for he did not dare to touch the provisions set aside for the winter. His question to one of the hunters: "How many shots did you take to kill your three beasts?" caused the men to laugh shamefacedly. Talbot reckoned that the man had shot thirty times to get the three stags that he had grassed.

Early next morning some of the men, and Talbot, went to bring back the meat that was hidden. As they walked, now and again they spoke, and one of the men said: 'The antlers of the caribou are never free of velvet when the wind is in the east.' "The east wind must blow during the time of the growth of the antlers," conjectured Talbot, "but the Aleutics think that the wind is the cause."

After walking for seven hours they came to the first cache, and taking meat from it they ate it raw. Talbot ate nothing. Atonguela and all the men were very tired, but after eating they rose to go to the next cache, for they must bring in food to the women in the camp. Across bogs, up and down hills, and through a river they went. When they had nearly covered the distance between the two caches, they saw a stag lying down. It was two hundred yards beyond them and a hind was within thirty paces of it.

Talbot, who with Atonguela was leading, now waved the other men to lie down and he too waited. At last the beasts got up and went over a hill. Talbot and Atonguela followed them.

To Talbot is offered a Wife

After a cunning stalk to within ninety yards of the stag, Talbot shot it a little below the heart, and with the left barrel killed the hind. The Eskimos rushed forward and dragged the body of the hind a little way and then cut it open. "The scene at the cutting up I can hardly describe. After shaking it out they ate the tripe, and also great pieces of the fat and lean, raw. Then they made a cache of most of the meat but cut some fat off the back of a stag which with twenty pounds of lean they carried home, and carrying also the skin of the hind."

When they arrived in camp, Talbot, very tired, cooked three great steaks and ate them, for he alone had not eaten the raw meat, necessity—as yet—not having pressed him.

The wood fire was cause of much smoke, but for that there was no remedy. Then Talbot lay down on the skin of the newly shot deer because his rabbit skins and the bedding were damp, the storm of the night before had beaten into the tent.

Next morning Atonguela, smiling, looked in at the tent door, and offered to bring him tea. That day the men went out again for the hidden meat, but Talbot stayed with an old chief and with the women. They brought him wild strawberries to eat and were glad when he spoke to them. They even adopted his accent. One of them went into the tent to mend his clothes and was made happy by a present of steel needles—her own being made of bone. Another woman washed his things, washed them well but brought them back all wet. His white-duck clothes were so dirty and so worn that he threw them away and now had only his underclothing to wear. Feeling cold, he put on a fur coat that the women at Hell's Gate had made for him. The women here were delighted and astonished—to them the weather seemed to be warm. In spite of the water being very cold he bathed, and the women gathered round his clothing so that he had to walk back naked amongst them, but as to them this did not appear to be unbecoming, so neither to him. That night he was offered a wife, but he made excuse.

When the days of mourning were nearly completed, two children and a man died in one day. That he might not hear the lament of the Eskimos, Talbot played sad music on his flute. Mournfully he traced the deaths of the people to the fever that Atonguela had brought to them. Atonguela had taken it from

Peter and George Oman, and from those Indians the sickness could be traced to civilization. "My advent amongst this people has been calamitous," he wrote. It was well for him that the Eskimos did not so view his coming!

Talbot still did not know if any of the dead had been buried. He saw the mourners going round the tents shaking hands with the kinsmen of the dead.

Four days after this day of renewed sorrow all the six dead were buried. The children had died four days before this day of burial, but the man who first had died had, for eleven days, lain not interred. They were buried on a rocky mound. "It was a sad procession, but soon over."

"My sensibility is getting blunted, but it is not nearly the thing yet." The cause of this complaint of himself was the visit, to his tent, of a boy that came to see his father, who was sitting inside with Talbot. The boy's nose was filthy. The father pulled off the mess with his fingers, cleaned them on the stones and then, token of affection, rubbed noses with his son.

Talbot, though the draughty tent was cold, now, like the Eskimos, slept without any clothing. He felt an Athenian's joy in the strength and fitness of his body. He was pleased that when hunting he could stay out all night without sickness, or could, when the storm was raging, sleep in damp skins without afterwards suffering. He more and more felt glad to see how a man's body responds to his necessities. The young men of the camp, killing small birds for food by merely throwing stones at them, were evidence of this—such the quickness of eye, the quickness of hand given by hunger.

The dog, Arois, now became a little friendly with Talbot. This perhaps sharpened his loneliness, for he wrote: "I wonder how my dear old Bob is?"

All this while Talbot was learning the Eskimo language, teaching Atonguela a little English and drawing his picture—which all the men at once knew to be his. Talbot, ready always for vehement effort, owned that the lessons he took from Atonguela were so long that "Atonguela got a headache".

The tally of death was not laid by till an old woman died, the one whom Talbot had liked—the seventh soul to change its state. So again the people, though ready to depart, stayed to

mourn for her during the customary six days. She who had
died was one of those to whom Talbot had given medicine,
and when afterwards her son asked him for some medicine for
a cure, the father forbade the child to receive drugs from the
white man. To this same man Talbot in error had said: "you
are dead." He had meant to say: 'I see you,' but had used a
wrong, perhaps rather similar, word. Errors such as these often
must have put Talbot in jeopardy. Had the Eskimos but once
considered him as ill-starred, or the bringer of misfortune,
they would have driven him away from their tents.
The man was frightened, but was perhaps
disarmed by Talbot's laugh, for Talbot
that day felt merry, because he
had again visited the place
where grew the wild
strawberries.

CHAPTER XII

*   *   *

EIGHTEEN SALMON IN THE NET; BLUEBOTTLES EVERY-
where; and the sun shining.

Talbot and the Eskimos left in three boats. His, the fifteen-
foot whaleboat, was the biggest of the three. In it he had to
stow two sleds, twenty-one dogs and five people besides himself. In the three smaller boats thirty-five people somehow
settled themselves. In this manner, after a stay of twenty-seven
days, they left the place of mourning and of delay. As it was
not marked upon the chart, Talbot named it Dead Man's
Point (16). Later in the journey he thus named places as they
travelled: Nondescript Land, Blowy Harbour, Weatherbound
Port and Disappointment Harbour. And so his chart becomes a
tablet on which the Englishman chronicles his fate.

The sky was black and the south wind blew strong, yet the
men guyed the things to the mast and hauled aloft the sail. Talbot's boat dashed along in fine style, overtaking and passing the
other boats. One of them was running before the wind with a
jib only. After midday they sailed into Chesterfield Inlet, for so
long Talbot's goal. They had passed several tents and now sailed
by a big camp of Eskimos. They rounded a point, and sailed
due west. Off the land ran a heavy beam sea. The wind had
grown stronger. Soon with a crack the boom broke in half, but
that did not make much difference to the sail. Dangerously the
sea serpented about, and broke into the boat. But suddenly there
was peace, as zip, and rip, the sail tore from top to bottom. The
men got out the heavy oars and after two hours at them they
reached land which, when the sail went, had been distant a
quarter of a mile. They landed, and made camp. The on-coming
tide lifted the boats and moved them until they lay in the sand
almost up to the tents; the next tide would drift them back.

Talbot then admired the Inlet with the hills beyond, all
various in height and colour.

Chesterfield Inlet

The men were on what, at high tide, was an island; on the rough chart that Talbot had it was marked as such (17). They stayed there some days because of the wind, because too they needed meat. The dogs also were very hungry, but that they often were. Therefore Atonguela went hunting, but Talbot had a hurt so he stayed in the tent watching Atonguela's wife, who, in the end, had come with her husband. She was patching Talbot's worn-out rubber boots with sealskin. The boots which the Eskimos made for him were never big enough; they judged of his feet by their own. They are proud of the smallness of their feet and could not realize the size of his. The koones, that is the women, had small hands and small feet. This day Atonguela's wife tried to chew the skin boots into a better shape and told him, as she worked, that in winter the Eskimo men have one pair of gloves to three pairs of boots. Again this woman begged of the Englishman to take a wife, saying that so he would more quickly learn the language. But Talbot again refused to rub noses with anyone.

Having thrown away the gift-lamp he built a stand and cooked in a kettle over a wood fire. The morning of the day when he and the Innuits would leave Nondescript Land he was awakened by much noise and wailing. Three boats had arrived and the Eskimos aboard were being told the dolorous news of Dead Man's Point. They remained but for an hour at high tide then sailed away, "a pretty sight". On the other side of the water some cliffs, four miles off, shone white against the sky.

With a spinnaker out, before a breeze that blew them at seven miles an hour, they sailed past islands all day long. The scene was grand and wild, clothed in greys and browns, musk-rat fashion; all violet was the distance. 'Once these islands had deer, now caribou are only found on that one,' said Atonguela pointing to a very big island. Talbot poring over his chart found the chart to be entirely faulty.

Here, near the shelter of the isles, was the little diver, the size of a duck, handsome with its black back chequered with white. It was the little diver, the Eskimos said, that made the outcry at which Talbot elsewhere had wondered. The little diver, and the great diver or ember goose—all these loons made startling sounds. The noise seemed ill-omened to Talbot; werewolf or banshee might in such tones complain. The Eskimos had so often heard the outcry that it was nothing to them. 'Sometimes when it is fine and fish easy to get, the parent birds make happy sounds to the broods, but now they know the weather is going to change and they are scolding the young into leaving the Inlet.' The great diver was less clamorous than the smaller ones, and he was amusing to watch on land with his legs set so far apart that he straddled rather than walked. Swimming and diving, he was at ease, and splendid in his sharp-winged flight.

The whaleboat passed within a foot of a seal asleep in the water, his head thrown back, his air bespeaking repletion. That day they sailed two degrees of longitude; then pitched their tent on a rock. Next day Talbot and the men went far inland. They saw tracks of deer, but the deer had gone because in this wild weather, with falling rain and the north wind blowing, the caribou travelled fast and far. So they gathered blue-berries and ate them instead of meat, and, when they returned, wet and hungry to camp, Atonguela was found to have taken down the tents. He called out: 'We will sail now.' It took Talbot an hour to persuade Atonguela that the wind was too strong and that everything in the boat, as also every man, would be wet. At last the tents were put up again, but as there was not wood enough to boil cocoa Talbot warmed up a flapjack and drank cold tea (18). He had to sit in the dark so as to save burning his candles, for he had not many left.

'The snow cannot be far off,' said Atonguela. Talbot said: "I shall be glad when we reach a place whence we need not remove." 'We shall not get any fish till we reach a lake, and fish through the ice with lines,' Atonguela assured him. Then Talbot ventured, "I wish the snow would fall, we might sleigh to musk-ox country." At that Atonguela was silent. Next day they left Blowy Harbour, and Creek Harbour became their place of sojourn.

Over the comfort of a brushwood fire Talbot set the men to talking about musk-ox. How many of the men would go? Should they take their wives? Thus they debated. 'We shall not start for four moons,' the hunters said; but when they left the tent Atonguela said to Talbot: 'We need not wait for four moons, we shall go sooner.' Then clearly, though quite gently,

The talk about the musk-ox

Atonguela told Talbot that this matter must be left to him, but
that if Talbot meddled the men would not go for musk-ox.
"Atonguela has much authority, he will keep his word
and will go as he says 'kakouwow'—that is, by and by.
First the snow must fall. Nature and the Eskimos are leisurely (19)." That night was very cold. The moon
was bright. The hungry dogs fought till the
morning. Talbot a long time lay wondering: "How many sleeps, how
many moons before we
shall hunt the
musk-ox?"

CHAPTER XIII

*   *   *

COLD—THERE WAS ICE IN THE WATER THAT THEY DRANK before starting—and tired, because the noise of the dogs had hindered sleep—cold therefore and tired, at dawn they left Creek Harbour. They spied deer on an isle and having anchored for one night sailed next day to get them. Some Eskimos in two boats had camped with them the night before, but said that they did not wish to hunt, having meat enough. Yet when Talbot and Atonguela reached the island and had stalked some stags, a shot rang out from the other men who more to westward had stalked the same beasts. Atonguela and Talbot were very angry at the lie, and the men gave them only one haunch. Talbot therefore named this place Disappointment Harbour, and in fog and snow they sailed off. Round some of the points the current was racing and several times they had to take to the oars.

To make the last point took them over two hours against wind and stream. Talbot was convinced that they ought to take down the sail, but the Eskimos obstinately refused. At last they obeyed and after that, by dint of rowing and towing, they made port. At once he spied a stag, and though it was dusk he went after it. A lake, a plain and the hills, were background to the great beast, but the sun went down before the hunter could get near, and he returned sadly to find Atonguela in a black mood.

Next morning Talbot woke with the blanket frozen to his beard. That day the Eskimo men went hunting, and Talbot collected driftwood for the fire. He asked Kinohena to get him some biscuits from the boat, and though there was a high wind he did what was wanted. It was no light work carrying the kayak down the steep bank and up again, but as the kayaks were too light to leave on the stormy water, they were always carried up to the camp.

The word 'Anganting'

The hunters, walking for the first time on ice, got deer, and deer-calves no bigger than dogs, so that next day there was much business carrying skins and drying meat. Talbot sketched the Point and would have drawn the dog Arois, but the creature was too restless, more like a wild beast than a dog.

The Eskimos sat in Talbot's tent, in the corner of which was a girl making him a coat of deer-skin. She had pretty, round eyes, unlike the narrow slant eyes of her people.

'I will give you two dressed skins for a knife,' said a man, and Talbot assented.

He told his guests about the big ships on the Atlantic, and 'Oh' and 'Ah' they cried.

Talbot listening to the talk of the men learnt a new thing, and, by means strange to him, he overcame a difficulty. The thing that he learnt was that these Eskimos called themselves 'Anganting' which means 'I am a little stag'. For Angan is their word for stag. "Is this fact known to white men?" wrote Talbot in his diary. The difficulty overcome was the lighting of his friendly pipe. His matches were packed away on the boat, so hardly, with flint and steel and a piece of bad touchwood, he lit it. At intervals when thus gathered together the Eskimos still wept for their dead.

One of his hands and his fingers were very painful, perhaps from the intense cold which tortured him from the time he got up to when he went to bed, or perhaps—as he thought—from the lack of vegetables. He confessed in his diary that he was in no state to face the cold, but added that he would endure it as long as he could.

The next day, the twenty-sixth of September, the country was white with snow. After they left Sketch Point there were beautiful things to ease Talbot—a herd of caribou, a hundred perhaps, a white weasel speeding through the snow, a pack of ptarmigan, and an arctic fox, and a hare. He had one splendid day after stag at that point, and then five days of sickness.

The stag hunt was thus. Talbot had been thinking of Scotland and how good it would be to lie in heather on a hill in Ross-shire with Sutherland the stalker, and to be spying deer. He had left the camp early, and was thinking this, when he saw deer on the other side of the river. To reach them he must cross the water, so he began to strip off his clothes when suddenly, on this side of the river, on open ground and bad for stalking, he spied caribou. Resolving to hunt the nearer beasts he pulled his clothes on again, but the caribou had been startled and he ·followed them for miles without being able to shoot. Exhausted at last he turned back and made for a small hill there to rest and to spy.

At that moment he saw stags coming slowly towards him. He wriggled down through snow to a good place for a shot but in full sight of the deer. They could not have got his wind and their sight, least faithful of their senses, must have betrayed them into curiosity, for they came on, the four antlered beasts, their breath streaming in clouds. He let them come; when they were but thirty yards away he shot. To the right one, and to the left another, fell. The third stag fell as it ran; the bullet had gone through its heart. A long-distance shot stopped the fourth.

Talbot had never seen such heads, such spread of antler, such shapeliness of attire. Ross-shire was forgotten. One of the beasts he gralloched, but left the others as they had fallen. They would be brought in next day.

After dark, broken with weariness and with cramp, he reached his tent. Ten deer in all had been killed that day, so at last the dogs would be fed. Atonguela ordered that some of the caribou should be buried until the time when they could be brought by sleighs to the winter encampment. Provision must be made for the women against the days when the hunters would be away after musk-ox. Atonguela and the men had guns but not rifles, therefore they often missed or but wounded the beasts that they hunted.

The next day was long with pain. Talbot's tooth, that he knew to be damaged through eating hard biscuits, now gave him such agony that he called for Atonguela and put a pair of nippers in his hand. Thus and thus pull the tooth, he said, "but the man used the instrument like a two-handed sword, and after a few attempts broke off the tooth". Talbot's first feeling was one of rage, but the intense pain brought him to his senses. At night he took twenty drops of laudanum, but he had to seek solace in philosophy in spite of the opiate, because the clamour of the dogs prevented all sleep. All the next day Talbot paced up

and down the camp very ill, sometimes lying on his bed—"that
being another way of feeling the pain". When he asked the
wife of Atonguela to reheat some tea for him, she and an
Eskimo that had just arrived in a kayak laughed together instead of preparing it. He frightened them by ordering that the
tea be brought at once. In his diary he wrote: "A very little
temper shown now and then is useful, but not too much." At
night he took twenty drops of laudanum before supper and ten
afterwards. Then Arois and the other dogs were tied up, and he
slept.

During the next two days his suffering grew less. The good
koone, allotted to him, tended him and dried his furs. The sun
shone—he liked those days. Suddenly the camp was full of life,
men, women and children having arrived in a boat. They
pitched their camp and Talbot made a drawing of their three
tents close together. However the pain was irksome still and
Talbot wrote: "It is dispiriting to be ill so far from even the
slightest comfort. The people are very kind, but if a man falls
ill they get frightened and leave him to recover or to die."

Again he took laudanum—thirty-two drops in one dose.
Atonguela watched with fascination the counting of the
drops. The Eskimo was full of fear when Talbot
said: "the liquid in this bottle is of such power
that you and all your family and a few
more Anganting quickly could
be destroyed." Within an
hour Talbot was
asleep.

CHAPTER XIV

★   ★   ★

AT DAWN ATONGUELA PUSHED HIS HEAD THROUGH THE door of the tent. 'Will you come shooting?' he asked. Murmuring something about shooting anyone who disturbed him, Talbot turned over and slept till late; when he woke the pain had left him.

Glad to be well, Talbot went hunting. Two of the women bore him company. and they were well satisfied with the day. A mighty (20) stag having fallen to Talbot's rifle, the women, as they skinned the beast, measured fully three fingers of fat on its back, and on its haunches. To them, of all foods, fat was the most precious.

"I will give you a knife, boy, to bring in the head," Talbot promised; always he was amazed at the weight of meat that the people could carry. Later with pencil and sketch book he lingered with devoted detail over the beauty of the head of the caribou. He enjoyed, with hand and eye and mind, the creature which as hungry hunter he had pursued and brought to death. Later he took to England the head of this king caribou.

Talbot's loneliness was borne in upon him when he saw the water-birds all going south and when over the inlet the cry of the loons sounded no more. The divers timed their flight well, for twelve hours after they had gone the glass fell and a strong south wind rose up. This was the first day of October.

On Sunday the third of October he wrote: "An awful day. When I got up about midday half the tent inside was over a foot deep in snow, driven through the opening of the door although closed; the hole at the top also made good use of its time as it is to be filled up to-morrow. A raging snowstorm has been going on for twenty-four hours, with no signs of abating; my tent is frozen outside as solid as a wall, so the wind cannot turn it inside out. Twelve weeks to Christmas, where shall I be then? My left lip and jaw have hardly any feeling, which is discomforting."

That cold evening they sat by the light of a candle whilst one of the men sharpened and pointed Talbot's knife that it might be like his own, and fit for cutting deer. Atonguela's wife laid aside a sealskin case that she had just finished. Talbot was to wear this round his neck, for cartridges.

Arois, the only dog bold enough sometimes to come into the tent, crept up to Talbot; the dog Aucalia, in a fight, had nearly bitten off his ear.

Amongst themselves the men were talking thus: 'We could not yet travel by sleigh,' 'the ice must be so thick before it will be safe for us to go into musk-ox country,' Atonguela said, and, designating the ice, he held his hands apart to the measure of four feet. 'It may well be two moons before the world is fit for the musk-ox country', added another, contentedly. That evening Talbot in his diary wrote: "We do not start for musk-ox until the ice is about four feet thick; if my health keeps up it will be all right, I shall wait; but if not, which is likely, as I am cold and wet every day, shall return. Glass at 29°."

"*Oct.* 4. At last this day is over. Woke at about nine in the morning to see an extremely white tablecloth over everything, but closer inspection discovered it to be snow. Inside it was blowing a gale and outside is snowing, so I thought it best to keep in rabbit-skin all day. My koone is anxious to have her portrait drawn; she hops in and out of my tent all day and is useful at times; she put side loops to my husky boots. Had the top hole blocked with deer-skin. It requires six feet of snow on the ground to make a snow-house. Read Tennyson and a criticism on Nordau's 'Degeneration', by Cesare Lombroso. He remarks that, from criticizing, a man is often led on to attack; this is terse. Over two months before we start for musk-ox. A husky is a very stubborn animal, he won't be driven. A lot of matches got wet, which makes me feel wicked. At-koone made me six flapjacks to-day. At managed to find a piece of wood to cook my supper. I concocted breaded deer steak, excellent food; I must have eaten six pounds of venison meat to-day. The glass has gone up—48 hours' snowstorm, not over yet, very cold; everything is frozen in the shape of water or tea at once. If fine will start early after deer to-morrow. Boots frozen.

"*Oct. 5. Stuck.* My boots were thawed this morning somehow by a koone, not by fire, must find out. My hands are covered with chilblains and my bad finger is most painful. Outside and in the tent 12° frost; and a piercing N.W. wind saw me footing it through the snow to my spy-hill—a few hinds far away with no stag drove me back to camp to freeze inside. My boots when I took them off had ice inside as well as outside. I called At and told him I should start back for Churchill. He positively refused to go in the boat as he said the ice would catch it, which I think is a lie. I told him to be hanged—I would get someone else—but as we are one side of a swift river, and the rest of the tents on the other, have had no opportunity to find the some-one. Snowing again this evening—I can hardly write from the cold although just had boiling hot stewed venison and tea. The snow is not deep enough to sleigh back yet, so am in a deuce of a fix. The river will be frozen solid to-morrow, and will fix a plan somehow. At is frightened now of me.

"*Oct.* 6. The swift-running river is frozen solid, and the voice of the rapids is to be heard no more; silence is the elemental way, except where the fruitless jabber of a thing called man disturbs nature's handiwork. I cannot get back by boat."

CHAPTER XV

*   *   *

THE SIGHT OF THE BIRDS GOING SOUTH PERHAPS HAD deflected Talbot's will; just for one half-day he had wavered. After that there was neither talk nor written word about returning.

On the seventh day of October looking out at the tent door he wrote: "Atonguela did not lie, the Inlet is frozen over, although the river is open again." The roar of the ice, breaking and hurled about, shattered the peace of the illumined night. The next day too was bright. It seemed a travesty on his cold self. Talbot and Cuckoo Koone went a mile out to where his things had been cached. "Why has Atonguela cached them so far from the tent?" he wondered.

'Are you tattooed under your beard?' Cuckoo asked as they walked, for she thought that there could not be a cheek or chin in man or woman which was not tattooed. Out of the cache they got vaseline, a candle, condensed milk, lump sugar, writing materials and soap. "I don't know why I don't wash," wrote Talbot. He made a sketch of the country, but found he could not draw the beauty of the snow.

Then they went to the tent of Atonguela—the cold of Talbot's tent was beyond his endurance so that it was to be used for storing deer-skins. He preferred now to face vermin rather than suffer another night of such cold. Atonguela's tent, supported by nine poles, felt warm to Talbot. "By warm I mean not more than four degrees of frost."

The glass was falling, foretelling half a gale. Next day a gale blew from the north. All that day the wind roared, but the river was still, for it was frozen again. The tides of the Inlet prevented the water of the river from being solid as yet.

The snow was storming down. With difficulty a fire of brushwood was kindled in the tent. Talbot, shivering over it,

85

wondered how Atonguela with his brother Illanah, and another Eskimo, could survive the night, out of doors and without a fire. They had gone hunting and they would not, he knew, trouble to kindle one. Atonguela's wife brought a fish into the tent without saying how it had been caught. Talbot did not know its kind. It had a pink skin and white flesh. "That night in the tent everyone lay down stark naked; they look very comfortable (2)."

Late at night two of the hunters came in and sat down to eat a haunch that they had carried in. They had killed eight or nine deer. They ate so lustily that, when still later Atonguela arrived back, the haunch was finished. From the next tent unexpectedly arrived a trencher with yet another haunch, and ribs, and back of venison which had been cooked; this also the thirteen men demolished. Eaten without vegetables or bread, lean meat does not quickly stay a man's hunger—he must be gorged with it before he feels replete. Such fare surfeits a hunter more easily than it satisfies him. Not, therefore, of greed but of necessity the hunters ate mightily.

Arois, brave dog that he was, that evening won a big fight over many husky dogs. Seeing him triumphant, Talbot was reminded of Bob. At the bottom of the page late that night was written: "How is Bob?—love!"

CHAPTER XVI

★　　★　　★

"I SUFFER A NEW MARTYRDOM, THE AGONY OF BEING frozen and then again being thawed." The koones, most often those two called Panaag and Cuckoo, warmed Talbot's hands till the blood crept painfully back into them. Sometimes they held them in their own, or else they laid them against their cheeks, or put them under their breasts. "These women seem to be at fever heat (22)!"

But perhaps suffering was not too high a price for what Talbot saw that day of mid October when, beyond the swift river, its speed not as yet stayed by ice, great bands of deer moved about on the snow: more caribou than ever before he had seen together. Talbot made for a hill, but on the way, crossing a lake, his foot went through the ice, so back and around he had to go. He reached the hill of his intention but the deer trippant had reached it before him and they raced off into the flats.

"I will make for that other hill," he said to himself. He was hunting alone that day. He did not try to stalk the caribou in the plain, for wherever he went some of the thousand deer must have seen him. Nothing was in the snow-waste save the herds of deer. Here and there in places where the ground rose a little Talbot could see, traced against the sky, the branching of their antlers. The wood of their horns put him partly in mind of something that just eluded him. Then he snatched at the scene which this one had evoked, "for so must have looked Birnam moving upon Dunsinane", he thought.

As Talbot found he could not get near the caribou he retraced his own footprints in the snow. Afterwards he wrote: "I am really bad at finding my way about, but the Eskimos are wonderful." (The Eskimos, like birds—guided by some inward monitor—are never lost.) Was it, he wondered, a stone or some curve of higher land that marked a way for them;

87

something so hard to note that only a child of the Barren Lands would mark it? Or was it an inward guiding that led them?

Talbot in Europe seemed, beside other men, to be doglike in the ease with which he found his way; but in this waste of snow, and being as yet unskilled in primal ways, he felt he would have been lost could he not now have retraced his steps.

When he got back he had to wait an hour whilst Atonguela finished building a snow-house that he had promised to make for Talbot. All day and all alone he had built it, and only the testimony of his eyes could have made Talbot believe in such a feat. The house was roofed with deer-skin. 'We shall make the house bigger and then roof it in with snow when more falls,' explained Atonguela.

He led Talbot in. They went crawling on hands and knees through a little tunnel into the kitchen and thence into the main igloo. The walls were about four feet thick; the women had a place apart, twenty-four feet or so for the mending and the making of clothes. The main room was thirty feet in diameter. Half the space was used for the dais that rose two feet or more above the ground. On one side was a ledge to serve as a bed and for his clothes. The building at this time was seven feet high.

The diary tells of the roof dripping, especially one night when all the men came in and ate in the room, causing the ice to thaw and the water to rain down. Another night, after a fearful snowstorm, Talbot waked to find himself "of course wrapped in a white mantle". The snow had fallen between the rifts in the skins that served for roof. In spite of all, the snow-house certainly was warmer than the tent, and this although it was still unfinished. But the faulty roof of skin was left on for two weeks after the house was made.

As the snow fell, so the small house grew. When it had stood for a week the men took off the deerskin roof whilst they added three feet to the height of the house. The house was growing slowly towards its domed completion, but for the present the skin roof must continue to serve, so it was stretched on to the heightened walls. Around this igloo others rose up, the tents, as winter grew apace, being abandoned. Tunnels were run from one end of the village to another, all the houses being thus linked together.

Arois became increasingly daring. That he knew himself to be liked by Talbot perhaps lent him mettle. He started by conquering, in fierce fight, all the other dogs; this being done he determined that he at least would not go hungry. Night after night he broke through the door into the igloo and stole meat. Atonguela, furious, piled up a sack of flour in the entrance. Deprived of filched meat, Arois decided to hunt for food and went out after deer. For days he would be lost. He even followed Talbot and spoiled several stalks. Talbot, also hungry and determined, bound up his front paw; on three feet Arois followed him all day. At last it is recorded that, "Arois now sleeps in the igloo."

There followed some milder days when small comforting things happened to Talbot; his pipe drew well and he records that his bed covers were shaken and that afterwards his bed was made broader. He watched with amusement "Tootaig, aged about four, and his sister, aged two, playing in the igloo absolutely naked. They remind me of the 'brownies'." He gave them two of his blankets for their sleeping ledge.

Watching from his ledge of snow, he learned by what means the women thawed his boots. They slept upon them, thawed them by their bodies, and next day would wear them strung from their necks to dry them. When his socks and shoes of duffle were washed, every woman was given one to sleep upon, and the next day each koone would wear one tied round her neck to dry against her skin, after having chewed it and pulled it into shape. In mid October Talbot wrote: "Spent most of the day strolling about outside. The weather is very pleasant. A small boy has become attached to me."

"*Oct.* 14. After very long hunt arrived igloo one hour after sunset. Felt very faint—much running and walking and no food all day. Found my supper, flapjacks and hot tea, ready—what a treat. But the whole place is swarming with koones in and out of the snow house. Two tents have been pitched close to us. Awful tired. To-morrow must kill.

"*Oct.* 15. *Lost my way.* Quarter to seven in the morning. Started at nine. Killed a fine stag, was shown a new method; 200 deer were together feeding, no means of stalking them. At took me where they all got our wind. We being in full sight of them

89

stood still—some of the stags stood and looked at us—then a general stampede on both sides of us, at about 150 yards off, deer of course going up-wind. When they had all passed I made a long shot, and killed dead one stag, and one hind. Then Illanah pointed the way home. I tramped on and on; the whole country seemed to be the same, could not distinguish any given land-mark. When dusk, saw two huskies far off; made for them. Night came on and I missed them. Made a hole in the ice two feet thick and had a long drink. Moon came up—made a small snow-house, was driven out by the cold; shot occasionally, then steered for where I thought C. Inlet was. Given up all hope. Fired again—was answered, and brought to igloo six hours after dark. Wrist   frozen — no food all day."

CHAPTER XVII

*   *   *

THE BOOTS, THE CLOTHES AND MOST OF HIS OTHER THINGS were found in the morning to be frozen, so Talbot stayed in bed whilst the women smashed them about to soften them. The room was crowded with women. Atonguela's wife was cutting up some of the boots Talbot had worn and turning them into waist-coats since she could but own they were too small for him to wear as boots. She kept coming in from the women's room to reassure her eyes as to Talbot's stature, for it was against her experience and her judgment to cut so long a deer-skin coat, and the shoes that she was making him had often to be refitted. It seemed that now at last she would model her tailoring on him as he was, and no longer upon her idea of how a man should be.

'I wish that you would catch us some fish,' she said. "But how?" asked Talbot. And she: 'If you sat on the lake the fishes would smell your blood and they would come up. Then if you broke the ice quickly enough you would catch one.' She gave Cuckoo and Panaag his gloves to line with deer-skin in place of the duffle which was taken out. Meanwhile Talbot cut off his moustache as, when he had been lost the night before, it had frozen and added a discomfort to the night of bewilderment.

. One of the women called out that deer were close by and soon Atonguela came in, carrying skins from Talbot's tent. 'Come,' he said, 'I will show you again our way of killing deer.' They went out and not far off saw a band of about two hundred caribou feeding together on the mosses beneath the snow. There could be no way of stalking them, the ground was quite flat.

"We had better wait here, they may come near if we keep very still," said Talbot. But Atonguela pulled the string of his gloves. 'Come on,' he muttered. They walked towards the caribou, walked down the wind and stopped. Full in the nostrils of the caribou blew their scent, full in sight of the deer the men waited. The creatures were about a hundred and fifty yards from them, some of the stags stopped feeding, looked at them, and stood a moment undecided. There was a great rush on both sides of the men, the deer racing past, not away from them but past them, tearing up-wind. The men waited till they had passed, then, with long shots, they killed some beasts.

Amongst the great herd Talbot had seen, most beautiful of all the caribou, a white beast that, even in the snow, shone white.

Talbot thought over this way of hunting and understood why the caribou had not fled away long before Atonguela and he had got so close. He reasoned that in a smaller herd the beast on guard over the rest would have given warning and all the deer would have moved away. But in this big herd there was no one beast in charge of the rest—therefore, though all might be uneasy at the nearing scent, each beast would wait for another to give warning.

Atonguela had quickly learnt to spy with Talbot's telescope and he was glad now to show the Englishman a new way of hunting: 'You are a better hunter than most of us, but you are not a better hunter than I am, though your rifle is better than my gun and your glasses stronger than my eyes,' Atonguela had said. Also he asked Talbot: 'In what way are you cleverer than we are?' Talbot did not answer, but he thought that each man to his own world is suited. Though he was sorry for the sufferings of the Eskimos, who, when the deer fail in winter, starve to death, yet he never shared the wish of some white men to see the Eskimos transposed into a tenderer clime. "The good God keeps things fairly even for us all" was the wisdom he found in his travels.

Every day he was learning something in Barren Lands. In such places a man must learn or he will die. One morning he did not shoot at the deer that he had stalked because they were too far, but not till afterwards did he discover that, had he shot, the barrels would have burst, as they were full of snow which had got into the guncase. Another day snow got into the rifle and he could not shut the breech. He saw that a little snow in the breech soon turned to rust, and that if the trigger was not carefully tended it would freeze. Thus he learned to care for his rifle.

The night's entertainment was the passing round of a piece of gold filling that had fallen out of one of Talbot's teeth—he had broken two more on the hard biscuits. The talk circled about metals. To their 'E's' and 'O's' and 'R's' he explained the use of gold to the wondering Angantings. He explained also what iron and steel are, and was in his turn surprised to know that iron was found in their country.

The desolation of the land increased. A few days later he wrote: "Nor wolf nor deer I saw, but yesterday evening crossed the tracks of a fox, ptarmigan and arctic hare. All the deer have gone, others may come from the south. I tried to go in hopes of deer to-day, but was persuaded not to as the snow was being drifted along the ground at a great rate although it was not snowing. I had to go to bed early in the afternoon as my hands and feet were terribly cold. I miss my Shakespeare frightfully. Nothing to shoot, nothing to read, drives me mad almost. My pleasantest occupation is playing with a baby almost eighteen months old."

CHAPTER XVIII

★　　★　　★

IN THE SNOW-HOUSE FOURTEEN DEGREES ABOVE ZERO, outside zero and the glass 29. Talbot shivered and went back to his ledge—he would not hunt that day because it was Sunday. His knuckles were frozen and his fingers out of shape with cold. The koone Panaag laughed, 'for the cold weather has not started yet,' she reminded him. 'On the lakes the ice is not safe; the sleds have not yet been out.' "Cold, or not cold, I shall now wear my fur clothing," and this Talbot did, casting away his Jaeger wear. Clothed in fur he was less cold than before, but the snow melting in his boots often caused his feet to be wet and cold. Over the entry of one day, a day that holds no especial event, Talbot wrote, "Saw a shadow of death," but his writing does not tell what grim threat his dreams had held.

The wall of the snow-house served as a place whereon Talbot might teach Atonguela to write his name. Seven days later he could write his name. Talbot had spent a good deal of time with Tootaig, but found him to be a dullard, unable to learn English words. Worse still, "He does not understand play, but runs away frightened." The babe of eighteen months was after all the best companion. Panaag this Sunday brought in a baby that had been born three days before. The small Aleutic looked like a shrivelled apple.

The walls of the igloo were covered with drawings, and Talbot with his beard was a favourite subject, it being the only beard in the country. Illanah was a good artist and drew scenes of caribou-hunting. Though Atonguela was learning English, Talbot made no headway in mastering the Eskimo pronouns and adverbs, though he supposed the language must contain them. Being tired of study, Atonguela this Sunday said: 'We can use the sled to-day to bring in some of the cache.' Arois was hitched into Talbot's sled together with a new black dog, small and thin but reputed diligent. Henceforth the creature would be called Kallipalick. Atonguela also drove two dogs. Before starting he showed Talbot the newly made dog-whip, with its one-foot handle and ten-foot lash of sealskin.

It was hard work pulling and pushing the sled where the snow was soft, and on the way both Talbot and Atonguela were once upset. Arois raced off after a hare, dragging along Kallipalick and the sled from which Talbot had that moment dismounted. Atonguela's pair followed, for Atonguela was walking with Talbot. After a mile run Arois turned back and Atonguela's dogs followed him. Arois was a hunter, but he never could leave Talbot for long. There was no wind, and without wind the cold seldom seemed to be too great. The light green and the light pink of the sky, reflected on the snow and the ice, were very lovely in the sunlight; after running a man would feel warm.

The cry of the deer roused Atonguela from the igloo when he was cutting up some meat to cache; he ran out to find a lonely stag quite near. It was far gone in rutting, but he killed it to feed the dogs.

The dog Ogilne had run away for four days. This was a heavy loss because Talbot needed dogs for the musk-ox hunt, they were hard to traffic for, and their price was an extortion. Three strangers came into camp and from them he traded for a dog afterwards called Piccy. He paid for it four handfuls of powder, a box of caps, two pieces of plug tobacco, one gaudy pocket handkerchief and two packets of needles. The men went off pleased, the more so that Talbot looked dissatisfied—'We have bettered him in the bargain,' they surmised.

Kinohena had shot a dog in mistake for a wolf, so there again was loss, though the man could not be blamed, so hard it was to tell dog from wolf.

The wolves howled at night, and were seen travelling alone or two or three together—one evening Atonguela saw six wolves go by. A trap was set for a wolf that had run over the roof, but an Eskimo shot the beast by the light of the moon. The skins of the wolves made good clothing, warmer much than the deer-skins.

Illanah had been away for several days, but he arrived home

one evening and the igloo was soon full of men who came to
greet him. He had killed several stags but had not cached any
because hunting made him so hungry that what he did not eat
was not worth the labour of burying. Quite close to the igloo
he had seen a calf with a female caribou, the two creatures had
somehow parted from the herd. He shot the calf and dragged
it in. Within a foot of Talbot's bed it was cut up: "The stench
nearly drove me out of the igloo. And the children had a feast
of lukewarm raw meat whilst the older people picked out little
bits of gut wherever they were seen."

Though the herds of deer had gone, there was business still
among the men. They worked at patching the igloo outside
with snow, and this so much increased the warmth that Talbot
wrote: "Igloo half a degree above freezing, and delightfully
warm for the first time since the frost." The sleds were to be
made ready for the musk-ox hunt; peat had to be found, and
brought in, and soaked in warm water. To ease the going this
turf was laid, three inches deep, on to the runners of the sled.
The frost soon welded the peat to the wood. Industrious, the
women made clothes for the hunt, whilst Illanah drew pictures
on the snow-houses showing the manner of it; the men, the
dogs, and the oxen. His symbol for the igloo was a hollow in
the snow. As they worked, and Illanah drew, they talked about
the ox—'A stupid beast,' said one. Another added that its
sense of smell was not so keen as that of the deer. 'They are
lazy creatures.' 'Yes, but courageous, and dangerous if wounded,
therefore he who kills a musk-ox may be accounted a hunter.'

A wolf howled; Talbot went out hoping to see it in the
moonlight. He slipped in the snow; something scattered on
him like hail; then came the report of a gun. Leaping up
just in time to prevent a second shot, Talbot saw it was the
fool Kinohena shooting at him for a wolf—as though the
dog's death had not been mishap enough. Moaning,
Talbot staggered back to the igloo. He had
forgotten his gloves and his hands were
an agony. The women restored his
hands; gently healing them
in the warmth of
their breasts.

CHAPTER XIX

★   ★   ★

NEXT DAY, THE EIGHTH DAY OF NOVEMBER, THE BLUE
sky invited Talbot to run out and break a trail; he returned,
short of breath but still cold, and noticed that the igloo was
"both cold and stuffy, a horrible combination, the smell in the
house putrid, but generally I do not notice."

Before daybreak Atonguela went off with knives and other
goods as barter for dogs. His family had been in tears for two
days because he would be away for three days. Illanah was looking "as though he had swallowed a red-hot potato—such a kind
of food probably has never passed his lips." In the afternoon he
and his mother fell to quarrelling over some clothes. For hours
they disputed the matter.

Wishing to restore some gaiety to the snow-house Talbot,
that evening, put a girl on to a box and made her sing, so that all
in the igloo were amused. Then he encouraged five boys to sing
and afterwards they all feasted. He ate five venison steaks. "Ye
city men envy me," he wrote. The Eskimo men ate marrow
bones and deer's tongues, six tongues to a man. That caused
them to open a cache, and next day the four stags which had
been shot on the twenty-second day of September, and which
had lain ungralloched, were brought in, on this the last day of
October. The deer were cut up inside the igloo. Talbot had no
fancy for this meat, so he boiled some of the salt pork from the
barrel of pork which he had brought from Winnipeg. He could
not stomach the meat because of its extreme saltness, and therefore he ate some of the unsavoury 'tooktoo' as the Eskimos
called the venison. He found it not unwholesome.

The snow had fallen. 'We can finish building the house,' the
men agreed. Next morning they all rose early and dressed by
the light of burning fat. In place of the roof of skin they crowned
the ten-foot walls with a dome of snow. The house when completed was very lovely.

Talbot visited two smaller igloos differently built from Atonguela's but each exactly like the other. He walked six feet
down into snow and came to a small opening through which
he crawled into the kitchen; this was ten feet across. Beyond
it he crawled on into a broad passage that linked up the two
igloos. This was about twelve feet long, ten feet broad and
seven feet high. It contained a raised dais for caps and sticks.
In the snow wall was a four-foot opening through which Talbot
went into a round chamber eighteen feet in diameter. This
room was light. The sun, as Talbot entered, was shining through
a big slab of ice. On either side of the entrance was raised a dais
on which the people slept. The cold, cleaving to the floor, and
the heat rising, the dais afforded what warmth there was in the
igloo. At the end of the room was a big cavity for storing meat,
and, on the opposite side of the wall, a small kennel was hol-
lowed out of snow to hold a litter of pups.

Walking back, Talbot got his fingers frozen, so "sat down
and put them next my skin and thawed them, very painful."
He got back to find the women had completed his outfit for
the musk-ox hunt. They were resting, and talking, whilst one
of them was catching bugs off another koone, and was eating
them. Then the women spread out before him the clothes that
they had made him for the far hunting. Two fur coats, two
pairs of boots, two waistcoats, two pairs of gloves, two fur
stockings, and a cap of fur to pull over his ears which were now
peeling with the cold, these were his new apparel; his trousers
had been enlarged. He gave the women needles, and beads, and
some matches, and knives, and much besides. Also he gave beads
to ornament the coat they would make for him against his
return to Fort Churchill—after the hunt. Talbot, feeling grateful to the women for their work, was glad to assent when a man
asked him if on the morrow he would pull out his tooth. He
never had pulled out a tooth, but he expected that he could do
so, and the next day he was very successful. The tooth was a
back one; the Eskimo did not flinch.

Cuckoo Koone brought him some more gloves and was
well paid for them, but her mother, a wretched old woman,
cursed Talbot, no one knew why. "I think it is because I do not
return Cuckoo's affections. Curious people."

The snow-house day by day

Next day, "I reciprocated the old lady's couze Koone to-day by addressing her with the same Lord Chesterfield grace." These women would never be famed for their bashfulness—this he noted in his diary—but what especial lack of modesty caused that confession, who can tell?

Talbot noticed now how little tobacco and how few candles were left to him; often he had to write his diary by the light of seal oil. Looking amongst his things he came upon an old magazine and showed it to those gathered in the igloo. Pictures of horses and of fighting they could not understand, but when they came upon a pretty face, "Down went the Huskies' heads and rubbed noses on the portrait."

Suddenly, after a beautiful day, the night turned deadly cold, the thermometer registered thirteen degrees below zero and Talbot, who had just written that with another pair of fur stockings he would be ready for the musk-ox country, or for any other journey, in almost any cold, now added, "I'm a bit nervous of the coming cold, as I stand it badly."

An old man and his wife arrived on that steely night. In spite of all the women sitting round, the man stared hard at Talbot, and this angered him. Then, opportunely, one of the koones brought in a splendid new pair of fur trousers; without demur Talbot changed those he had on for the new ones which caused a pleasant break in the stare of the old man. There was much sobbing in the igloo, for the elders had brought heavy news of the death of an Eskimo who had left two widows. Listening to the talk he found that the stranger needed tobacco; this gave him hope that he might be able to get a dog in exchange for it.

The old couple were untidy and disgusting. When the woman shook out the furs that they slept in she spread bugs and filth over Talbot's clothes and blankets. During the day the aged woman put bones, meat and seal oil on to his blankets; at evening she became very ill and was sick over his things; then he gave her some salts. Her nausea did not prevent her from shrewd bargaining. The old man sold Talbot a big dog for a carat of tobacco. 'Here is a smaller dog of mine, but for it I want such, and such, and such things,' she said between her vomits. Talbot had said "Tobacco is my only payment to you."

The Eskimos watched. They knew how much Talbot wanted dogs, knew that indeed he needed them for his sled. Would he keep to what he had said—or would he change? He did not change; his self-respect lost him the dog. "This unyielding had a good effect on everyone, as all knew how badly I need the dogs, but that I will go without rather than have them get the better of me. Illanah had a fit (23) just before we closed the igloo for the night. He gave me a great fright but I managed to hold him down. He tried to bite. The old untidy koone, who is as black as the ace of spades, went a most curious colour. The little child was hurried out of the igloo. Afterwards I gave Illanah a dose of salts."

Next day into the gay sunshine and out on to the ice Talbot took the men and gave them a prize for a three-legged race. Then he made them try long, and high jumps, and to his surprise surpassed them all, though he was not a good jumper. Another day the boys laughed uproariously when he taught them to leap-frog. Afterwards with a lasso, he caught the boys as in Wyoming he had caught the bronchos.

With Atonguela away, the women became unruly. Panaag was "so untidy she makes more litter than Sam the puppy." Talbot never could discover just who Panaag was, whether or no of the same family as Atonguela. She worked hard, sometimes she "showed nasty temper and reminded me of Betts". She made some garment for Talbot and, having asked for needles in payment, suddenly changed and asked rudely for tobacco. "It was the way she spoke that exasperated me. I frightened her, and gave her very little."

But Atonguela Koone was the worst shrew. When Atonguela was away even Illanah could not keep her in check. It seemed to her amusing to put into Talbot's mouth sharp things that she herself had said against her neighbours; Talbot would not now speak to her, and this angered her. "Illanah and Atonguela both check her harshly, the only way to manage her, for soon she would drive away every respectable husky. One morning she sang her 'Ay-yars' at the top of her voice, panting at times for breath. As the infant was as usual screaming, I got up, dressed hurriedly, and flew out to be received by a snowstorm and a piercing wind from the north, so I went into another igloo."

There he bound up a koone's finger and washed it with per-manganate, for she had cut it badly. It needed soap rather than unguents, he thought. That reminded him that he needed soap too. "I will get it out of the cache and will wash to-morrow," he wrote.

As nearly a week had passed since Atonguela had left, and the weather was very pleasant, Talbot called out to the boy who had become attached to him: "Let us see if Atonguela is in the next encampment." He was not there, but they met him some miles from their own igloo. He was building himself a snow-house. 'I have seen a big wolf,' he said; and went on building his shelter. When it was ready he sat down in it, putting a piece of meat as bait in front of it. 'I will wait here all night with my gun.' Wondering again at the Eskimo's endurance of the cold, Talbot ran back to the igloo.

"*Nov.* 14. (Sunday). Up before breakfast. Illanah went off to search for Ogilne and won't be back till to-morrow. As the dog has been lost three weeks there's little chance of its being found.

"Bought another dog to-day for powder and caps—that makes nine in all. Have been very busy trying to get things together, as we start for musk-ox on Tuesday. 400 Ex. rifle, 80 40.82 cartridges, 150 revolvers. I have four pairs new boots just made, for which I have given needles and tobacco. The Huskies take plenty of boots. Had a pair of fur stockings made and am getting two more boots. Two coats, two pants, two stockings, all fur, that is my outfit. Getting things together has been a fearful job, and the waiting to go a terrible monotony, but to hurry up a Husky would be like trying the same on a Lytham cab-horse. I have been so careful with my matches that I find I have more than enough and to spare, which is satisfac-tory. Harness and whips for dogs being made all day, everyone is quite ready to start. Got some soap out to-day, as I shall wash before I go away. Just going to have some hot tea (by seal oil) and turn in. My feet have been very cold all day. Foggy morn-ing. Weather glass very high."

Illanah returned on Monday, for in another encampment of Eskimos he had found Ogilne—the dog had wandered far and had been found by these other men. That evening was glad-

dened with games and with jests. So as to have the enjoyment
of a fire Talbot sacrificed the tent pole that had served him so
well. The tent had long ago been split by the frost. To burn any
piece of wood marked a day above other days, as elsewhere the
drinking of an old vintage. More so indeed, for it was nobly
festal to see the flames leaping up, and to hear the crackle; to
feel the glow of warmth lapping round the body, cleaning and
warming the air of the igloo. Illanah's joke, this merry evening,
was to get himself a big deer's bladder which he filled with air,
afterwards he made a long tube and put one end down his
throat, the other end he had affixed to the bladder. A friend
squeezed the bladder into Illanah; then took away the tube and
the balloon. For a quarter of an hour after that Illanah belched
up wind—amid the laughter of those that looked on.

Next morning Talbot turned all the surprised, brazen
koones out of the room; then, with the soap that had been
cached, he washed himself—significant, lustral washing, in
preparation of the coming adventure. Because the long wait
was over, and the hunting near at hand, Talbot washed;
put on his new furs; and sang with happiness,
for he saw that all things were nearing
completion, and that soon would
begin — the hunting of
the musk-ox.

CHAPTER XX

★ ★ ★

MID NOVEMBER, THE NORTH WIND BLOWING, AND THE day at the dawn, when, from the encampment, Atonguela and his brother, Acoulah, Illanah, Ahwateer, Kinohena and Talbot, moved away into the wind. They took two sleds—the big one with eight dogs, the smaller with four. Restrained perhaps by some feeling of menace, or made silent by a traditional caution, the men started off without words to their koones; and to their mickies (children) none of them said good-bye.

In the afternoon they saw deer coming towards them and Atonguela and Talbot went in pursuit. Talbot shot well and killed two stags, but Atonguela's rifle got jammed, and he missed a calf, then Kinohena hit it and Arois fought it and brought it down; another Eskimo wounded a beast that went off.

Going over some rocks, several pieces of frozen turf broke away from the bottom of the sled. To freeze turf anew to the runner two days were needed. Atonguela, perplexed, asked Talbot what was to be done. Talbot told him, reasoning out some method; "argument good" can be read in the diary, but what the advice was is blurred and cannot be deciphered. But that, in his own wilderness, in a familiar accident, Atonguela should turn for help, not to his brother, nor to Illanah, but to Clifton of Lytham, that was tribute enough.

They went on as far as the nearest lake and there made a house of snow. Then Illanah and Acoulah scooped a hole a foot deep in the ice and, by thrusting in a handle tied to a thong, the dogs were tethered to the ice. "Very strange and ingenious." Over a basin of seal oil the men fried deer flesh and, though Talbot's hands were burned by his rifle, he ended that day feeling "warm and comfortable".

The next day Illanah sleighed back to the encampment for

103

more seal oil. 'We use too much,' said Atonguela, frowning. Kinohena added a kitchen to the snow-house and the two Atonguelas—that is the chief and his brother—gathered moss for fuel and set about cooking deer's flesh. The stag wounded the day before was found dead, and was hitched on to Arois; the dog quickly dragged it back to the new igloo.

Talbot walked for a while with Tetva and Arois, for Tetva had now grown fond of him. She was a fat small bitch of a nondescript colour, strong and a good worker. An ermine passed near them.

The piercing north wind had turned Talbot's beard and moustache into a block of ice. He had let them grow again, having, perhaps, forgotten the discomfort. For five minutes Atonguela blew upon it to thaw it. Then with a pair of scissors that Talbot had brought he cut it off.

The sled, broken on the rocks two days before, was by now repaired. At evening the other sleigh returned at a gallop bringing the angshaw [seal oil]. With but two Eskimos riding in the sled the weight was nothing to the dogs.

The third day of the journey: "*November 18th.* Started long before daybreak. About the middle of the day changed dogs—put six in each sleigh. We came upon a band of stags; it came on to snow and to blow. I shot well, killed one far off and hit 3 more which lay down close to. We could not stop to finish them off, poor brutes, 4 cartridges. 2 of the huskies shot, but got nothing. The stags have lost their horns. We came across a cache of Ahwateer; while they were getting it out I walked a long way with At's brother. We did not bring in the dead stag I shot and so the dogs have very little to-night. Late we made camp. Although very tired I went to spy, and found deer after a tiring walk. I found they had gone far away—cold I expect. Went back to camp, changed my fur coat for another and had an enormous feed—started with raw flesh. Dead beat."

On the fourth day of travel no breath of wind blew, the air was so still that three bands of deer heard the hunters from a long way off and were seen galloping away into the distance. Although there was no wind the cold was greater than any that Talbot had suffered. The travellers went many miles; they passed lakes, and went by a hill shaped like a cone; at sundown they built their snow-house. The dogs had no food that night, but Talbot and the men "devoured raw flesh with much gusto". 'In four sleeps we shall be in the mountainous country which is the abode of the musk-ox,' said one of the men. Talbot, to add to the festivity, gave them matches.

The next day there was a fog, but the men must hunt and they were lucky. Talbot made a right and left, and then he and Atonguela, who had sent on the sled, saw two more stags coming towards them. The animals smelt the men's tracks and trotted past them quickly. At a hundred and seventy yards Talbot killed the hindmost. Four more beasts were killed by the other hunters, so at night the dogs feasted on meat.

The next day was Sunday. Outside the igloo was a snow-storm, and the wind raged; the Eskimos heaped snow up against the house and so the dreadful wind was barred out. At night this hastily made igloo had been cruelly cold. The twelve dogs looked like barrels after having eaten four deer in two days, but, like their masters', their appetites seemed insatiable, and already they were howling for more food.

"This expedition is capital fun," wrote Talbot, who had been cleaning guns and rifles. "Makes up for all the hardship I have gone through so far, but no weak man could stand it. I had a wretched night. The Eskimos say it will be an easy matter to catch musk-ox, but my difficulties are beginning. To persuade Atonguela not to take his koone to Churchill is one, and to catch and carry to England safe five musk-ox. Ah!"

It must have been to Talbot like saying a word in the creation of a new world to come upon hills unmapped, upon waters unnamed; and travelling to name them. That Monday night, amid very hilly country, summing up the day, Talbot wrote: "Very early start. Came to a big Lake called Lake Carmana, unknown to white men. I christened it Jubilee Lake (24)."

CHAPTER XXI

*   *   *

EIGHT TIMES THEY SAW DEER THAT DAY IN LATE NOVEM-
ber; one lot crossed within a hundred yards of the sled. Talbot
aimed and pulled the triggers; two weak clicks were the whole
result; the cold had frozen the triggers. This was the coldest day
they had had. "We could not, or rather did not, try to get any
more deer, so the dogs went hungry to-night. I ran a great deal
but was soon cold again, sitting on the sleigh."

They travelled for a long way over lakes; the country about
them was hilly. In the evening they camped by a lake, but
hours were spent finding water, for in the lake the ice was solid
to the bottom. They chiselled at it, hoping to reach water. 'We
must find a place of shallow ice,' said Atonguela, and such a
place in the late evening they did find.

Next morning they woke to see everything in the igloo
covered with snow, which had got through the chinks of the
house. Some of the men thickened the snow walls of the igloo.
Atonguela cooked all day and made some rich broth of deer's
meat. Talbot from between his rabbit-skins was contriving a
protection for the muzzle of his gun. He made a covering of
duffle and wrote in his diary: "No food for the dogs when it
snows in this country. Useless going after deer as it is—impossible to see a yard in front of one."

After fasting for two days the dogs, next day, were fed. It
was lucky for them that Talbot was of the hunters, for by his
shooting they survived. On the twenty-fourth day of November Talbot, spying deer, warmed his rifle under his armpit. The
deer had seen the men creeping along the bed of the river.
Suddenly one beast came into view over the top of a hill,
though only its head and chest were shown. Talbot fired quickly and killed the creature—firing uphill was ever his favourite
shot. Going on, the Eskimos saw yet another beast. Atonguela,
imprudent, had not warmed the 40.82 rifle which Talbot had

106

lent him, so it did not fire, and a beast within easy range bounded away. Again warming his rifle under his arm, Talbot clothed it in the duffle cover that he had made; later in the day he shot another caribou.

The north wind blew; for Talbot the cold was very painful. At night the younger men made a snow-house. 'We are now close to musk-ox country,' said Atonguela.

Because Atonguela had cooked the breakfast long before daybreak, Talbot too got up. The day was terrible, with the wind blowing and snow falling. The younger men had made so paltry an igloo that the bitterness of the day pierced the too-thin walls. All the skin was off Talbot's hands as though they had been burned with fire. The supperless dogs howled miserably; the men also had little to eat. Talbot, wishing for fine weather and with a remembrance to Bob, smoked one last pipe to forget how cold and feverish he felt, then slept; and woke to find a day less cold and finer.

That day they followed the course of the River Kaaga. The sleigh bumped and swerved over great boulders of ice formed by the river. Hills stony and rocky were on either side of them. At times they had to climb the frozen waterfalls and the high hills to shorten the way. The dogs were discouraged by their fast, and there was very little game.

About midday stags neared them, but the light was unfavourable. 'You shoot the beasts,' the nearest Eskimo whispered to Talbot. "They have full confidence in me or in my rifle." Talbot shot both stags and later killed a hind that Kinohena had been too slow to kill.

All day they spied for musk-ox but saw none, neither were there any tracks upon the snow.

'Ikke, ikke—it is cold,' the Eskimos said next day, when, in a north-west wind, they struck across the hill, leaving the river. Five hundred and fifty feet it lay below them, so the barometer recorded, and they were eight hundred and sixty feet above Chesterfield Inlet; higher hills towered above them. Atonguela's brother shot a stag that did not fall. But the dogs saw it gallop off and eight of them with the big sleigh tore along in vain pursuit. With his hand Illanah restored to warmth Talbot's nose which was frozen.

New country. An "uneventful year!"

High up in the hills in the evening they built their house in front of a small round lake wherefrom they could draw water. 'This is country that our people do not know,' said the men. New country, that was good. The dogs started to fight. "I swore at the men roundly for never stopping the dogs, they are frightened of getting bitten."

The men whispered and consulted together, for they held it a great offence that a man should lose his temper. Talbot to restore peace made them an offering of tea, then he went to bed. Ahwateer lay on one side of him, Kinohena lay on the other.

The next day was Sunday; Talbot's frozen nose, fingers and knuckles had a respite, for he spent the day in the igloo making a case for his knife because the dogs had eaten up his sealskin pouch. He had tried to go out but the wind caught his throat and nearly paralysed him. "Twelve hundred feet above the sea, in arctic regions in the winter, freeze away all thought of comfort."

Then fell the last day of November, the last day of Talbot's twenty-eighth year: "It has been an uneventful year and things have passed very smoothly for me. Good-bye twenty-eight." All the men had gone out to find trace of musk-ox, but they saw only the tracks of deer and of those not many. "We are in a land of desolation—if we do not find musk-ox, starvation will be the only fare for our dogs and probably ourselves. There are not deer enough in this part of the country, as two a day are required for the dogs and one for ourselves."

After spying vainly all day Talbot again lost himself whilst on his way to rejoin Ahwateer. He yelled. There was no answer. He fired a shot, and heard no sound at all. It was dark now. Suddenly Ahwateer ran to him—he had not been far off but instead of answering had run silently to Talbot. Together they returned to the igloo.

That night the snow-house was full of uneasiness. The men talked quickly in low voices to each other, looked at Talbot, frowned and fell to brooding. Something threatened him. "Oh well, the day will expound it," he thought, then got into his rabbit skins, and slept.

*   *   *

On Talbot's birthday the hunters started early for musk-ox. 'Would you make an offering to Mother Earth, a gift of matches and tobacco?' asked Atonguela. "Oh, yes!" laughed Talbot, "anything to get a musk-ox!" They went on for miles without trace or sight of ox, and as they scanned the distance they saw no form of beast. The faces of the Aleutics darkened, and now they were silent. It seemed that they were waiting for something to happen; they were apart from Talbot and inimical; sundered was the brotherhood of hunting, the kinship of their common peril was made void.

Sullenly, till midday, the men moved onwards—then the tide of their gloom reached its height, and they came all to a standstill. Above them a high hill cleft the sky; other hills half encircled the men. The hills were white with snow, black rocks jutted from their base.

Atonguela beckoned to Talbot. The rest of the Eskimos and the two sleds were a little way off. Atonguela uncovered his head and he prayed with a loud cry. Then he put into Talbot's hand little pieces of bone, of fur, a match and some tobacco. 'Hold these out in the wind and say: *Heaute illeueliah itoro mit, itunga somingane mit* (25)—'Oh Mother Earth, I give you this, give me something and that, musk-ox".

"Whether I have turned heathen or not, don't know, but there was no refusing." Had Talbot withheld the offering, his life would have been the sacrifice made to the earth. After he had done Atonguela's bidding, the faces of the Eskimos lightened; their dark unusual frowns, the unspoken threat that issued from them, were suddenly changed. They bent their steps again upon the northward way.

When, later in the day, Talbot gibed a little at the sacrifice, the men again grew sullen. They would not have him mock. Although the dogs were in need of food, the men, when caribou ran close to them, did not shoot. The musk-ox must not be disturbed by the scattering of the deer.

"The sun will soon be setting, this long day over, and still there is no trace of ox," sighed Talbot. He stopped to look away into the valley and then he saw the bulky forms of two musk-ox. "Exciting birth-day, twenty-nine."

CHAPTER XXII

*　　*　　*

'THE MUSK-OX HAVE HEARD THE DOGS AND HAVE LEFT the valley,' said Kinohena stupidly, and stupidly the other men echoed his gloomy guess. Talbot said that he was certain they had not left. The men looked angry at his contradiction. 'We'll go and see,' said Atonguela. Several of the men, and Talbot, went off at a run through deep snow and they "ran over mountains and lakes all day. The middle of the day I was dead beat." After a rest they went on all together.

'We run when we hunt musk-ox because the dogs do not bark when running,' Illanah explained; then he said: 'When we see the musk-ox we will slip the dogs and we will bay the bulls with them; whilst the attention of the bulls is fixed upon the dogs we shall get close and shoot the musk-ox.'

Talbot learnt that the musk-ox do not go south, but live on the highest coldest grounds where even summer would not thaw the land. They always face danger gathered to one another's aid. 'I have heard that when angry their eyes are red as fire,' said Illanah. 'Their hooves and their horns are a great protection to them, and their pelts are so thick that the older men who have hunted them say that they are hard indeed to wound, either with gun or with arrow.'

Talbot and the brother of Atonguela had no liking one for another and the mutual enmity was increased by what happened on this day. Talbot, guided by Illanah, was running through a long valley when he saw a low hillock from which thirty animals were moving away. The animals were too far for Talbot or the Eskimo to judge what kind of beasts they were. Both of them thought the creatures were musk-ox. When an hour later they were asked by the other men whether they had seen musk-ox the two men answered 'yes!'; later it was proved that the beasts they had seen were deer; (it might have been their flight that had given warning to the musk-ox). The brother of Atonguela mocked long, and rudely, at Talbot and at Illanah, who sorely felt the scorn, for an Eskimo, above all, hates saying that which is not true. "Because they cannot read or write these people are the more careful to observe truly and to report faithfully."

Two Eskimos, who outran the others, now returned with the tidings that, through the spy-glass, they had seen musk-ox. To come on them by stealth the men all went down a steep hill and over a glacier; then ran along a lake four miles long. The sleeves of Talbot's fur coat had, when first he put it on, been frozen inside: later they had been swamped in perspiration, and now sagged down below his hands; soon this was to be troublesome to him. It was evening. A pitiless hill faced the men; the soft drift-snow was hard to overcome.

Talbot, sweating and exhausted, fell behind, but the sudden barking of Agilue and Kallipalick made him, with his last strength, press up the hill.

On the summit, outlined against the sky, a musk-ox with lowered head stood facing the two dogs, which baited him. Talbot snatched his rifle from Atonguela who had carried it for him, and paused a second to watch the ox charge down upon the dogs. Then Talbot went nearer to the bull, and when he was some thirty yards from it, Kallipalick, suddenly frightened, ran back and pressed against his legs. Suddenly the bull charged. "I have never yet been able to say whether it charged me or the dog." Talbot fired. Because of his sagging sleeves he could not get his rifle low enough to hit the brute; both bullets went harmlessly over it. Man and bull looked at one another; then for an instant Talbot glanced behind, hoping to see an Eskimo ready with cartridges, but the men had fled. Talbot reloaded and pulled the trigger; a slight click was the only response because the left barrel of the rifle was frozen. A second later the bullet from the right barrel brought the beast crashing down within ten strides of Talbot.

He ordered that the head of the ox should be cut off, for he wished to make sure that the men did not mishandle so precious a trophy (26). "I ordered the skin to be cut low on the beast's withers and gasket. Of the rest we made a cache so that it should be brought in next day." Four hours after dark they reached the igloo; Talbot was so exhausted that at the entrance he spat forth blood.

Next day they moved some little way to a big river. Atonguela went far to spy, and to shoot, but returned late—and unsuccessful. The body of the musk-ox was brought in, and, on the other sleigh, the head. That night the head served Talbot for a pillow. Now that he was at his ease, Talbot could examine the musk-ox and he saw that it was about the size of an Alderney cow; the thickness of its pelt had made it appear bigger than in fact it was. Against the cold, though that is a need of its being, the ox was twice clothed. Close to its skin was soft woolly hair, and growing beyond this was long dark hair that fell to half-way down its legs. Its teeth were more like those of a sheep than those of an ox. Its feet were miracles of providence; they were shaped into two rims, an outer one and an inner one, and between the two grew hair. Sure of foot it could scale hills and walk on ice, sharp and strong of foot could cut into the snow for the mosses that fed it.

The men before leaving for the south ate the flesh (27), but it was so tough that every one of them, and Talbot, got hiccups; the soup was excellent. The dogs were given four pounds of meat. They were so hungry that they had eaten a whip of sealskin.

Talbot promised the six Eskimos a gun each and they were satisfied, though still troubled at leaving the vale of musk-ox after having travelled so far. As the men were certain that the beasts had left the valley it was useless to remain, but there was hope still of coming upon others on the return journey. Talbot was, as ever, philosophical. "At all events," he wrote, "one musk-ox is worth a hundred of any other animal, and in a few years they will be extinct on this continent as is the buffalo."

Ill-starred, in the snow-house, a few days passed by. The men, long-faced and muttering, thought that the presence of Talbot was the reason for the musk-ox not being in these hills. "Everyone was sulky, notwithstanding I turned heathen to please 'em. The oldest of the men crossed his eyes in a horrible manner." Three days were spent thereabouts, vainly

Five gaunt days

spying for musk-ox and making ready for the return journey,
which the men hoped to accomplish in ten days. To come
had cost them fourteen days. In the hills they collected 'ebu',
rotten wood wherewith to repair the sleighs, but so little was
found that the sleighs remained faulty. In spite of this, in
spite of the men's malevolence, Talbot still glowed—
thinking of the moment when he and the
musk-ox had stood on the heights, looking at one another; that moment
which only one of them
could survive.

CHAPTER XXIII

*   *   *

SAVE FOR THE PORTION OF MUSK-OX, THE DOGS HAD NOT
been fed for four days, yet they went fast and well along a river
frozen and smooth. At sunset deer were seen and Talbot waited
behind to shoot, but his hands had been some minutes out of
the gloves and he missed. Groaning, he found Atonguela who
had gone ahead and built a snow-house. Atonguela warmed
Talbot's hands on his stomach. 'All the men have gone shooting; we should eat to-night,' said the Anganting. But as the
men returned, first two together, then the other three, they
owned to having failed in the hunting. The seven men made a
scanty meal, eking out the biscuits with extract of meat, but the
dogs had nothing. The day had been so calm that the caribou
could hear the hunters far away. Talbot had run all day and was
tired out, but he said: "Atonguela, you and I alone must go to-
morrow to get food for the dogs, otherwise they will not be
able to pull the sleigh." Atonguela agreed.

After that first day follow five gaunt days. "Starvation. Dogs
starve. Dogs and men starved. Starvation. Dogs weak." Such are
the headings over the records of those first days of the return
journey. On December the seventh, Starvation Day, they started
early, having eaten a little biscuit; the dogs went fast and well.
The men separated for deer, and Illanah and Talbot saw some
beasts nearing them, but the creatures, dropping noses on to the
tracks of the sled, ran away terrified. There was not a breath of
wind. Talbot grew desperate as he heard a caribou walking,
half a mile away, perhaps even farther. "If I can hear it so far off
as that, the deer must be able to hear us several miles away,"
he thought. At sunset Atonguela and his brother came up to
Talbot and Illanah; Ahwateer followed them.

A curse be on Kinohena, for the man, always foolish, had
passed along here with a sled and had gone far ahead with

Acoulah. Not a deer had come down from the hills as at evening it was their wont to do. The smell of the dogs in the sled
had stayed the caribou. The folly of Kinohena must sharpen
the hunger of his friends. Long after dark they found the sled;
Kinohena had taken it miles away.

They built a snow-house without a kitchen, and Talbot gave
them a little extract with small pieces of biscuit and tea. "Very
tired and hungry. Poor dogs," ended that day's record.

The following day the dogs starved again, but at evening the
men ate. Talbot and Illanah and the old man had stayed huddled
in their sleeping furs all day whilst Atonguela with Talbot's
four hundred express and Ahwateer with the 40.82 rifle went
out. Illanah, for an intolerable time, moaned 'Ay-yar . . . Ay-
yar . . .' The men talked little, but Illanah finishing his plaint,
repeated foolishly instead: 'Darkoone,' and again 'Darkoone.'

Talbot smoked, and saw that he had only enough tobacco to
fill three more pipes. At last in the evening, after water had been
found and tea drunk, a sound of walking and of lugging was
heard outside the igloo, and Acoulah and Kinohena came in
dragging a calf. Then the men fed.

"Dogs starving!" heads the page of the next day's chronicle.
The men went off at dawn in the bitter cold, all save Atonguela
and Ahwateer who had not returned. Leaving the Coona River
and crossing the last spur of the Maxendigate Hills they spied
for the two hunters, but no tracks could be seen. The cold was
almost unbearable. All day Talbot was cold and ill. More slowly
than usual the men in the evening made camp, for the two
missing men were the most skilled at building in snow and
without them the labour was heavy.

Talbot, though exhausted, had to run and walk about during
the time they were making the igloo, for he knew that if he
stopped moving he would be frozen; during that wait he felt
his reason sicken and knew his self-control to be at breaking
point.

That day many tracks of deer had been seen, but "we are
three days' journey from the nearest cache," he wrote, "and the
deer in this stillness are unapproachable." The dogs, wonderfully hardy as they were, howled their starvation and now they
did not any more fight one another.

"Dogs weak," is written over the story of the next day. Again there was no wind and, though the tracks of deer were very numerous upon the snow, the men did not see any caribou.

As Talbot was resting a little on the sled, Atonguela and Ahwateer came up, empty handed and empty bellied. They had not shot a beast, but had fasted for two nights and for three days. 'It is too still to hunt; we will build the igloo,' said Atonguela, and he and Ahwateer with the other men quickly built a snow-house.

It might seem that starvation was of no moment to them. The men were now near Carmana Lake. Talbot felt strong again, but he suffered, seeing the dogs grow weak. Their gait showed their misery. 'They are lazy,' said Kinohena, and Ahwateer agreed. "Poor devils," thought Talbot. An empty sealskin bag that had held oil was cut up and given them to eat; had they not all day been carefully watched and had the harness at night not been taken into the snow-house they would have devoured the traces and the reins. "I must get food for the dogs to-morrow" —this was Talbot's last entry that night.

The next day, the eleventh of December, was a day very terrible to Talbot. "Dogs and men starving" is the day's title. Snow was falling. "The foolish Eskimos would not continue the journey," but without telling Talbot they went off hunting. Atonguela and Illanah returned without having killed. Talbot was angry. This was no time for bungling. Men fruitlessly pursuing the deer would but drive them farther and farther away. For the first time Atonguela told a lie.

The last piece of biscuit was eaten, for yet the third time the same tea-leaves were boiled. There was no food or tobacco, nor anything at all left in the igloo. Talbot felt sick with cold and hunger. Mindful of the misery of the dogs outside, his pity for them added a barb to his own anguish. He wrote: "Tetva's teeth chattered to-day. Snow or not we start to-morrow."

CHAPTER XXIV

★   ★   ★

SUNDAY CAME. THE MEN STARTED EARLY AND THE DOGS, as long as nobody sat in it, had just strength enough to pull the sled. The men had not eaten for three days. After so long a fast hunger ceased to be painful; the resulting weakness and the poignant cold became the main anguish of the body. The stillness of the day threatened to be a murderous fatality, for the deer could not be neared since every sound carried so far. Talbot had given up all hope of food when, just before making camp, deer were seen. The creatures, far off, stopped and listened uneasily. Talbot took his rifle from Atonguela and prepared to stalk the caribou, Atonguela, thinking that the white man was too weak to carry his rifle, insisted on going with him. Talbot whispered: "Don't come, I'll shoot you if you do," for he felt certain he must be alone to succeed.

Atonguela obeyed him. After creeping along for about half a mile he heard deer walking and saw two stags, so he lay down to await a chance of a shot. He was careful to keep on his gloves until the very moment of firing.

The minutes passed like hours, but when a few had aged him the two stags that he was watching moved broadside to him. They were about a hundred and fifty yards away. Then he slipped his hands out of the gloves, took steady aim and fired. Away went both stags. Talbot supposed that he had missed. Picking up his rifle he ran to a good spying place on a hill that he might watch the beasts moving away. Thence he saw that one of the stags had lain down. Joy filled him; perhaps he had never felt gladder. Leaving it undisturbed he kept out of its sight, and crawling to another hill spoke thence to Atonguela and Acoulah who had remained with the sled. Though they were about half a mile off yet they could hear Talbot when, without raising his voice, he told them that they might hope to sup that night.

117

He crept back where he could watch the wounded beast and soon after with pleasure saw it die. The Eskimos now ran forward, arriving on the instant of its death. The men gouged out the eyes and ate them almost before they had ceased to quiver. Later on the hunters all had their fill of raw meat, giving the dogs just enough to keep life in them.

The next day Atonguela killed a small caribou, so the men were able to go on with their terrible journey.

On Tuesday, Illanah had to help the dogs with the sled for the snow was heavy, and they were so weak that they could hardly move. Even Arois nearly fell in the traces. He had to be taken out of the harness, for he could hardly stagger along. But although slowly dying of hunger the dog kept close to Talbot. Agilue followed gallantly. "That dog will drop before he flags," thought Talbot. Three of the Eskimos, the brother of Atonguela being one of them, branched off across country to their home—a disloyalty—for the heavy work of the sleds and the killing of the caribou now fell upon the few who were left. The men had an enormous supper of boiled and fried meat without bread or biscuit, but, as the lean meat left them unsatisfied, they all ate a lot of raw marrow which made them very ill. Then the deer of the day before was cut up and every dog in turn was led into the igloo to get his share.

The next day the snow was heavy, and though all day long they walked—for running was impossible—they did not cover many miles. There being so few men they took over two hours making the snow-house. The sled also had to be put on a platform of ice, five foot high, as otherwise everything that had to be left in it during the night, such as the sealskin covering for their sleeping furs, the dogs' harness and the rest, would have been devoured by the dogs. Talbot waited in the intense cold, for his hands were so burnt with the cold that he was not able to help, nor was he as yet skilled in the art of building with snow. The cold was so great that the inside of his pipe was frozen. Even when he was in the igloo he could not get the ice off his face. "I did not wait for supper but went straight to bed telling Atonguela to send my corpse to Churchill."

On the seventeenth of December the twelve dogs were put into one sled, the other sled was abandoned, the dog Meetkerrie was let loose, as it was almost dead. They never again saw Meetkerrie. There being so many dogs to one sled they went at a great speed. Talbot travelled for several miles on the sled as the pace through the heavy snow was too fast for him. "I seem to have no strength or vigour left," he wrote.

Talbot got a shot at a running deer, but only one barrel went off. The breech of his rifle was frozen so stiff that it refused to open; so food, needed for the dogs, slipped through his hands. They went on till late at night, unable to find a snow-drift for building the house, or water for drinking. At last they came to a favourable place and Atonguela quickly made a shelter for them.

"Cache," is the heading for the following and thirteenth day, which was the last day of their journey and the sixteenth since they killed the musk-ox. Long before daybreak the men started; the day, full of fog and rain, turned piercingly cold. They came upon three caches which they opened, in the hope of finding fat, but in each they found that the fat had been taken off the meat. At the fourth cache they dug out food fitting for the dogs, and for themselves. Three times, without success, they worked for water with the ice-chisel. On the fourth journey Illanah drew water out of a big lake, carrying it back in the bucket which was used for cooking. The snow was deep and hard, so the igloo was quickly made. Then Atonguela chopped up the frozen meat that had been found in the cache, and scattered it about in the snow. When everything was ready, the dogs were slipped all together, and, without fighting, they ate.

The next day the men reached the homestead. Though mazed by hardships Talbot was so quick of eye that at the entrance to the igloo he noticed a dog as being heretofore unknown to him. He was pleased at this. "Surely I have a good eye for a horse and a dog," he wrote; adding, "I will get that dog."

The women gathered round and fastened to his belt small pieces of deer-skin to show that he was now numbered amongst their hunters. Also they gave him the coat that they had embroidered with beads. It was both curious and beautiful.

It was Atonguela's brother who had enticed to treachery the two other deserting Eskimos. They had arrived at the igloo and had built four feet above the main room another room from whence they could see everything that was happening below; as though from the gods they looked down on the stage of the snow-house (28). "Most unpleasant," wrote Talbot.

In the maw of so much trouble who but Talbot would have daily written in his diary? Who else would have noted on every page the suffering of the dogs? But now that the strain of the long adventure was over he suffered a violent fever, and during the first night in the igloo fell from shivering to sweating, and from haunted sleep to painful waking. But the early morning restored him; he woke and stretched out his hand and touched the comforting pelt of the musk-ox. Through his mind went the cordial thought: "I've got what I wanted, I've discovered the hills and the rivers and the lakes that lie two hundred and fifty miles north of Chesterfield Inlet. And certainly no white man, and probably no Eskimo, has ever been there before me!"

CHAPTER XXV

★　　★　　★

ALL NIGHT ATONGUELA SAT UP EATING. NEXT DAY, LONG
before daybreak, Eskimo men came crowding in and stood
silently looking at the musk-ox head, and at the Englishman.
Afterwards Talbot gave to the men who had hunted with him
a gun each, according to his promise, and to the three faithful
Angantings he gave beside, as free-gift, powder and shot and
caps. Then he set aside a measure of powder, shot and caps—
things vital to the dwellers in Barren Lands—and he showed it
to the brother of Atonguela, and to the other two deserters. As
much as he would have given the three men just so much he
measured out; then, with deliberation, he took up the threefold
pile and put it into a box.

The Eskimos who were watching him were puzzled by the
fierce, silent way in which Talbot moved. He carried the box
some distance from the igloo; he signed to the three deserters;
then he piled moss round the box. Then he set the moss on fire.

The shattering noise of the explosion drew all the Eskimos
out of the igloo. They talked amongst themselves; were scandalized at the act. In their eyes the waste of the precious metal
was as evil an act as to murder a man. The anger of the Eskimos
flared up against Talbot; it was checked by his calm. They
must have understood that he had not destroyed the goods in
levity; they must have acknowledged the justice of the violent
deed.

Talbot was determined to return, as soon as might be, to Fort
Churchill. He felt, that having seen an unknown tract of country, named an uncharted lake, and shot—in its own remotest
wilds—a musk-ox, he had no more to gain, and he could hardly
bear, any longer, the filth of the life; the stench in the igloo when
the stags were disembowelled; the vermin. "I feel like a Briton
before the coming of the Romans, without an iota of self-

respect, dressed in deer-skins and unwashed." Then, too, he was sickened by the unending barter and exchange; he saw gifts made to Atonguela, and to others, handed on as payment, until at last, disgusted, he wrote: "I barter now so strictly that they cringe." One evening the account of the day ends with: "I gave two little girls some presents, it was good to give away something without bargaining. These people will drive me mad if I stay here much longer."

Though this unending state of barter was provoking to Talbot, yet he ever acknowledged the fundamental unselfishness of the Eskimos. In times of famine, and of stress, this spirit of trade was entirely absorbed by a selfless sharing of the ultimate necessities; then a man would count all those of the encampment dear to him as his children, and would share, with each one, that on which his very life depended.

Talbot felt his strength sapped by the cold, and though he was well he could not sleep at night, so he knew he must return now, for later his endurance might not be equal to that hardship. He had learned to work with a panna, cutting snow to build with, for he was determined to try to do his share of this work. His hands were so raw with cold and with repeated frostbites that they were nearly useless. "No one could imagine the effect on my hands of the cold."

He studied the chart that he had, dividing it into sixteen parts, for he wished to avoid the first lot of trees which were not directly on the way. Illanah went off, three days' journey, to fetch the things left behind, and to bring in food that had been hidden. The question arose as to who should go with Talbot to Churchill; Atonguela and Illanah assented, but a third man was necessary for the building of the snow-houses. No other man offered to go. The journey was too uncertain, too hazardous for any to wish to undertake it. Talbot promised to give rifles as the reward, and the men, having seen him so fiercely true to his word, trusted him entirely. Now he said: "Atonguela, I will give you the rifles as I promised, but unless you get a third man I will not give you the cartridges for the rifles." Atonguela had foreseen no such pressure. "I think the someone will now be found."

Strange that, though far removed in time and place, yet the

snow-house became like one noted in Padua. The shrew of Atonguela daily grew more scolding and more greedy and, because of this, some beads that she wanted were given to Panaag. Atonguela's koone burst into tears—so great was her fury. Talbot was angry; more so than ever he had been in Eskimoland. Atonguela said nothing.

The next morning Atonguela sent everyone out of the igloo. Then he came back, looked at Talbot—and closed the door of ice. Talbot wondered, and was anxious. Atonguela turned to him and quietly told him a third person had been found for the journey to Churchill. The two men talked together discussing this and that. 'We shall start in six sleeps,' said Atonguela.

Yuletide was drawing near. Talbot had looked forward to Christmas Day, and had kept a plum-pudding in a tin ever since he had left Winnipeg. On Christmas Eve he hung up his stocking; "but Santa Claus found this region too cold, I suppose, for the stocking was bare."

The sunrise was beautiful; Talbot told the people that this was a great feast. They gave him a breakfast of deer's meat and a lump of fat, and later Talbot and Atonguela and his family ate together boiled deer's tongue, and marrow, and the Christmas pudding, which was as good as Talbot had hoped it would be. The other men, to enter into the spirit of cheer, boiled reindeer heads and split the skulls, each man walking about during the day chewing and munching his half-skull. The young men came in again to admire the musk-ox head, and they played games and sang. The next day brought the rue for the feasting.

As George Oman had cried 'no wood, no wood,' so now Atonguela, to every Eskimo he saw, complained: 'so far off, so far off.' He showed the utmost dismay and fear of the journey to Churchill. Talbot made light of fear, though in his mind he shared Atonguela's foreboding, and knew the end of the way to be, indeed, far off.

Talbot wrote on the twenty-ninth of December: "Thank heaven, my last night here; the igloo has been crowded this evening staring at me. Gave Tetva to Kinohena. Have three musk-ox cups. Very busy all day—am leaving everything behind except what is absolutely necessary, one tin boiler and two bags, the latter only fur. Nine dogs, meat for dogs and men, 8 lbs. flour and 3 lbs. tea—four men, nine dogs and one sleigh over a trackless wild no white man ever traversed in winter. Dogs had a great feed, and most of them are looking well and fat. I wish this journey was over; all the same twenty days may do it or die of starvation—pleasant thought. Wound up watch, going all right; shall be able to judge distance by pace and time to-morrow. Thank goodness I'm good at that. My two charts are seventy miles different or about three days. I think the journey will be barely three hundred and fifty miles. Put angshaw in coal-oil can. Found pipe. Shall I get my musk-ox to England in safety? "I fear at least two of the dogs will be unable to endure the journey and we shall have to shoot them. Atonguela himself has never been to Churchill by land and does not know the way."

CHAPTER XXVI

* * *

AS A PRESENT OF FAREWELL TALBOT GAVE TO KINOHENA
the fat bitch Tetva. It was the thirtieth day of December—in
the igloo was a wild scramble for the things that Talbot was
leaving behind. There was envy, and scrambling, and fighting,
like the all-day, all-night fighting of the dogs outside. It took
some time to get the bed arranged, and to pack the sled for the
long journey. At last all was ready. The head and the skin of
the musk-ox were tied on to the sled. Before leaving, Atonguela
said: 'Cuckoo Koone is coming with us.' Talbot was amused at
this, guessing her reason.

The men and women who stood at the igloo to see them go
called out: 'Eskimos living south, where you are going, died of
starvation two winters ago. Nearly all of them died. You will
have no food, the deer are scarce out there. Here we shall have
plenty to eat.'

Atonguela Koone was furious at seeing her man go off,
furious too at seeing Cuckoo go. She stood at the entrance of
the now familiar snow-house. She gave them no word of well-
wishing; instead screeched at them, "calling forth plague, destruction, fire or some ghastly curse". Talbot heartened his men
and away they sped, leaving the petulant crowd. Before them
went another sled that was bound for a cache. Food was to be
taken back to the women, and on the following day this sled
fared back with the deer's meat. The sleds crossed some part of
Chesterfield Inlet—which course they would follow next day,
and then strike south-south-east. That evening the three men
with Talbot had dark faces and slow feet, and just before they
went to sleep Atonguela said: 'On this journey I will not travel
by your compass. If I go I travel as I think.' The Eskimo had
never been this journey and he was loth to go, but had determined that instinct, and advice from Eskimos whom they were

125

sure to come across, should be his only guides. The white man's
pride in the metal disc was to Atonguela foolishness. Talbot felt
his decision was shattering but he knew he must accept it.

"*31st December*. Well, the last day of 1897 was spent bowling
along Chesterfield Inlet. We are now below Latitude 64. Atonguela to-day said within fifteen days we may reach Churchill
(29). We now go south, then due east, so as to catch the west
wind. We shall then put up our sail (30).

"The other sleigh left us and returned to the igloo and I
parted from Ancolar. The morning was wretched with fog and
snow, the evening clear. Small gloves kept my hands warm.
Am beginning to understand how to work with a panna. Dogs
had a good meal at night, self also, two frying pans full. How
different to the comfort and luxury that civilization produces to
cheer the heart of man against the coming year. Well, this is a
nice warm igloo. To-night I hope to dream of bells. Love to
Bob."

The new year dawned bitterly cold. The sun was covered.
The dogs went bravely over hilly country, that was heavy with
snow, and Talbot in his chart marked eighteen miles as the day's
journey. Atonguela said little and when he spoke it was but to
repeat: 'How far away Churchill is!' Talbot took out his compass to find the lie of the south. Then he asked Atonguela to
point south. "Atonguela and the compass agreed exactly. Wonderful." In the evening deer were seen; the beasts got the men's
wind and galloped away.

The igloo that night was very cold; the ice did not thaw
off Talbot's beard. Twice that day his nose had been
frozen; without hurry Illanah had warmed it with his hand.
Illanah was sulky, and afraid of the long way. The dogs had
food enough, and the men. After supping, Talbot stripped,
and lay down in his fur skins. The night grew late. He did
not sleep, but lay thinking. The Eskimos imagined that he
was asleep. In low voices they began to talk together,
mooting the point whether they should kill him. 'We should
thus immediately possess the rifles and cartridges he has with
him.' 'We could return at once to our igloo and to our koones.'
'We should not have to go this menacing journey.' But something like this Atonguela said: 'We shall gain more if we take

him to Churchill, his word has never failed, and we shall then be rich in rifles and cartridges. It would not be well if we alone of all our tribe owned rifles, for the other men would be jealous of us, but if we go to Fort Churchill he will give rifles enough for us and for some of the hunters whom we have left behind. He is, besides, a generous giver. The man has been good to my koone and to me, giving us medicines and much else; blankets too he gave to the children. I should fear to kill him.'

Talbot thought: "Shall I shoot the two men and force Atonguela alone to be my guide?" But instead of doing this he, without sitting up, without rudely surprising them, joined easily in their talk, dissuading them from killing him. "You would be fools to kill me. What Atonguela says is true—you will gain more by my life." To that they agreed and said: 'Forget about it,' and themselves forgot. Talbot could not but remember, though, because their reasoning had been— in the main—good, he remembered without bitterness.

CHAPTER XXVII

*   *   *

'FROM THIS LAKE, FISH COULD BE CAUGHT,' SAID ATON-
guela to Talbot; then he went into the igloo to woo Cuckoo.
Talbot too went to the snow-house. He took a line and hook to
the lake, and chiselled a hole in the ice. It was thick, a yard thick,
perhaps, yet a hole was made. "No, that is too near the rock," and
with trouble another hole was pierced. There he waited. Everything was white or grey, the hare that raced past, the ptarmigan, the snow, the clouds. A man might feel himself absorbed
by the lack of colour, by the lack of form in that wilderness of
snow. Three bites, then a haul on the line and a flash of red and
gold: a fine fish—but the clumsy native hook had no lash, and
back into the water sank the fish. Talbot plunged in both arms
but the flame-coloured fish was lost to him. Sleeves and gloves
in a moment were solid ice, so he went back to the igloo.

'The deer are very cunning this moon,' said Atonguela, looking up, 'we were lucky to kill this one.' Then he continued to
disembowel a hind in the enclosed igloo; partly for convenience,
and partly to warm the air of the snow-house, Atonguela cut up
the animal in the igloo—but the Englishman wished that he
would not do so, as the stink gave him a headache that would
last till morning. The igloo here had been hard to build, for on
the rocks there was solid ice and no drift snow.

"Three things lost this day." Talbot's panna—Atonguela had
been angry at the loss—then Chapshoe, a dog—that loss was
bad as it could be; only seven were left—then too, the gleaming
fish, all golden red. Arois had run off after the stag and that was
the reason of their spending a day waiting by the lake, for
among the great bands of deer a dog might go off and live for
weeks hunting. The love of Arois for Talbot later brought the
creature back to his master, and then jealousy nipped him, for
he found Talbot walking with Imoatide, a small bitch, a noble
worker.

Cuckoo wooes Talbot with fat

The sleigh needed mending, the peat being worn off the runners, so the day of staying was not wasted time, and the evening, in spite of the stench, was pleasant, for Atonguela showed Talbot tricks with string which was an art of his and of his people. "If only I can get him past half-way to Churchill he will not wish to return," thought Talbot, "but just now any troublesome accident might turn him back."

Food seldom was short, for the deer were in great herds, and Talbot was shooting well. With his rifle he shot the head off a flying ptarmigan. "We do not need lean meat. Leave the stags and shoot only hinds, yeld-hinds if possible," Talbot ordered. Of late stags had run quite close to the sled. What they saw did not frighten them, only what they smelt or heard. And the beasts of this part did not know the form of a man, nor fear it. But the smell of man terrified them. The wind blowing on the deer told them to fly: 'beware the smell of blood, beware the beast of prey—eater of flesh, drinker of blood—beware; be gone.' That the wind's message.

When no one was looking Cuckoo would eat fat greedily, so the men were left always hungry. But when Talbot was angry with her and did not speak to her, she would try to win him back to friendliness by giving him fat enough, though he suspected that she only avoided eating his share. Cuckoo was useful to the men but she served them without graciousness for Atonguela was, as yet, not amorous enough to please her, and Talbot, for whom she had come, remained unenamoured. She had not travelled all this way to be merely useful to the men.

The oil was scanty now and the cocoa and sugar nearly finished. "But oh! above all for a bath!" sighed the Englishman.

Arois having returned, and the sled being mended, they next day breakfasted before dawn and then made up their beds. Atonguela warmed Talbot's coat upon himself—the heavy one with the long unclipped hair—and he tied up his shoes, which were frozen solid. They made a big hole in the side of the igloo and Illanah and Cuckoo went outside. From within, Atonguela handed them the various things whilst Talbot kept the dogs at bay, for, smelling the deer that had been cut up, they fought to come into the igloo. When everything was outside Atonguela and the others made ready the sleigh. Talbot during that time stayed in the igloo, keeping warm the rifle on which depended their food, and wrestling still against the dogs. In about an hour's time all was ready and they started away. After having travelled for an hour they would stop for a few minutes for a smoke, and to right the dogs' harness. That day a ghostly fog enveloped them, the sun shining weakly through it. They lost time stalking some forms that seemed in the mist to be deer but which were only stones.

The snow drifted before an east wind but men and dogs travelled for five hours, going at four miles an hour. At sundown they built their igloo. Talbot, with a spare panna, chopped the snow and Cuckoo piled it up. In just less than two hours this labour was complete, and with the sound of wolves howling, and of Atonguela complaining: 'How far away Churchill is, how far away Churchill is . . . .' Talbot fell asleep.

CHAPTER XXVIII

*   *   *

SOME DAYS MEN AND DOGS WENT HUNGRY. THE DOG Chapshoe ate Talbot's rifle case. Illanah and the third Eskimo were wont to shoot wildly, missing the caribou and frightening them away. 'This journey threatens us, for we have no cache, nor can we burden the sleigh with meat, but day by day we must shoot or starve,' said Illanah.

In spite of the pain of his hands skinned by the cold, and of his face swollen with frostbite, Talbot, when his rifle did not jam with cold, shot well and so kept them in food. One morning Atonguela, whilst pursuing a wolf, met his friend Eenoo and with him went to the Eskimo village of snow. After running and hunting all day with Illanah, Talbot that evening was met by Eenoo driving his own sleigh towards him. 'Get upon my sleigh and return with me,' said Eenoo. The dogs, frightened at the alien smell of the Englishman, bolted all the way to the igloo. Atonguela had built a small cold igloo on to the big one. 'Come to a feast,' he said to Talbot; but, because he had cramp in his legs and stomach, Talbot went instead to his sleeping skins. He lay there, thinking how good it would be to drink fine wines, to eat well-flavoured food when once he had reached home. He came of a line of men who had had pleasure of their palates. His sensibility might be blunted, his senses, he was sure, had been sharpened on the grindstone of loneliness. His eyesight, his hearing were keener much than a year before. "Sutherland could hear the passing of a nightjar; I could not; but now I should be able to hear its flight," he thought. "But the best thing, along with the musk-ox trophy, will be the knowledge I've got of the goodness of primitive man. He'll share his last oil in a flame for another, share his last meal. When I feel sickened by white men I'll remember what I've learned from the barbarous Anganting." Then he slept. The next night he joined the merrymakers. He had a glad sight when, near the igloo, he recognized the dog Cadge-Eh-hena that in August he had lost near the entrance to Chesterfield Inlet. On that day in August when Arois and Cadge-Eh-hena had frightened away the necessary deer. "Cadge-Eh-hena, I'll buy you back, you shall come with me to Churchill." Another happy meeting was with the girl whose fine eyes had lent a beauty to Disappointment Harbour. Her eyes danced now, for he gave her sugar. Then with an older woman he traded with matches for fat. Pleasant was the igloo—big and warm, its great dais covered with skins.

An old man started the festival with the beating of a drum; another, after some time, came into the ring and took the drum from him, and so on and on until a young Eskimo entered the ring, took the drum, and yelled and crowed into the face of the man who had last held it. The other answered—then, putting down the drum, the two men for four minutes wrestled superbly; neither man was thrown. Last of all a boy went into the ring and he was made to dance and to beat the very heavy drum for a long time, the women singing on and on and he not daring to stop. This was a punishment.

Next morning, after Talbot had bound up a woman's hand and given as a present what little he had to give, the four men and Cuckoo said farewell to the friendly Eskimos. They left behind two of the tired dogs and took three fresh ones. Two of the Eskimos crossed with them the great Lake Izheetna, then: 'Stop with us . . . stay and shoot with us . . . do not venture farther,' they begged. But Atonguela was not tempted, his mind was bent on possessing for himself and for his tribe the rifles and cartridges that had been promised him. That night Cadge-Eh-hena ran off back to Eenoo—a dog lost. Talbot's tobacco was finished, so, remembering boyish days and pipes filled with brown paper, he filled his pipe with moss. Sometimes the roughness of the ice made the way seem a switchback. The dogs for a few days had no food. "How would Bob like this?" Often in the diary was a line of love for Bob. One evening they saw three deer closely followed by five wolves. The wolves, seeing the men look at them, stopped; then they went off across the hills. Worse than the lack of food was the lack of water. One day, his mind vacant with thirst, Talbot seized a lump of ice to suck. Atonguela smote it out of his hand but already the skin was burnt off lips and tongue—as though a molten bar had touched them. That evening they found wood, but, being damp, it burnt grudgingly; over the damp wood, slowly, they melted ice to drink. What was left of the water they carried on next day, but it froze again and again. They passed immense lakes and reached the River Coo. According to their hope Coo—from Carmana—lay but four days distant; in reality seven days' suffering for the men divided those rivers. The River Carmana was the mark towards which was bent the travellers' next endeavour.

In a land stony and rocky, with but little food for deer, they found a white fox starved to death. "I hope it is not an omen of ills to come," sighed Talbot. "Ten sleeps may see us close to Churchill, but this is the most indefinite journey I ever made and we can't hurry. We try to, 'but we just kan't', as the Americans say."

The River Carmana was reached. Its width here was two miles, though elsewhere it grew narrow. 'We will follow the river—it will take us to the sea,' said Atonguela.

"But it runs due west, then south and east," said Talbot, looking at the chart with a compass. East and west were one to Atonguela—he would follow the river, though it might, as Talbot said, add five sleeps to the journey. Atonguela would none of the compass. 'Ma-oona? Ma-oona?' Atonguela murmured as he ran, and that, being interpreted: 'Which way . . . which way?'

Couzerawdling, brave dog, was suffering; the sleigh had run over him. After Agilue, he and Arois were the best dogs. The men waited a day in the igloo to rest him. "Atonguela with dirty hands made bread, with slobbering jaws he kneaded it, stopping every now and then to eat marrow out of some bones he kept close to him. Cuckoo finished the loaf by cooking it in fat, and it was good."

A strong wind blew from the west; "That will suit the blanket sail on the sleigh," thought Talbot, for Atonguela had yielded—and now they would travel south-east.

"Piteous all day were the cries of Couzerawdling; in this dismal country very sad to hear." He had travelled with Talbot over six hundred miles in musk-ox country and again on this long journey; he had suffered famine often, yet remained gallant.

Next day the dogs were harnessed, but Couzerawdling staggered into the igloo where three days' food was left beside him. "I fancy he will never be seen again by mortal eyes."

The day was full of pain for Talbot, for though often he ran, yet, when he stopped for a little, he was bitten by the frost— and the cries of Couzerawdling echoed in his thoughts. Waiting for the igloo to be made, his body shivered dreadfully.

From sunrise to sunset they had sailed before a
gale from the west, the gay striped
blanket the only colour in the
dead and shrouded
country.

CHAPTER XXIX

*   *   *

THE AGLONARTO RIVER AND THE COOZLOO RIVER WERE marked on the chart and towards them the men now travelled. The chart was faulty, neither could Atonguela say if this river with steep banks and zigzag course was, or was not, the Aglonarto. The men caught glimpses of the sea but Atonguela was always drawn west. "Shall we ever reach Churchill?" Talbot wondered, but he never said so aloud, nor did he allow Atonguela further to repine, though the man still whispered to himself 'Ma-oona?' and 'Ma-oona?'

'Start to-day?' Atonguela asked Talbot when the first day of February came raging in. "Why not, when all is ready?" Talbot answered. He went outside and could just see the sled. The snow-house was banked with snow newly fallen; the wind shrieked round the rigging of the sled and shook the gay blanket. The snow whirled in myriad directions. The men started and went on for over two hours; at the end of that time Talbot could hardly breathe. His vest had worked up and let in the wind and the snow. The sled ran away from the dogs. Ten times or more it was overturned; the crossbar in front was broken. At last they stopped and made an igloo, but having covered ten miles Talbot was glad that they had journeyed.

The cold was so intense that he lay long shivering in the furs before sleeping—shivering and thinking. "How unlucky that Illanah should have broken his panna to-day. How good stags' kidneys are, cooked, as to-night, in ashes. Those stags looked fine that came so near, but was it near? In this country, in this weather, I cannot judge distance. That hind had seemed a hundred yards off, she was over two hundred and forty yards when I came to pace the snow where she had fallen. How damnable that she had no fat on her, and had to be given to the dogs!" Talbot would never forget how the hind had come with the wind, and had stood at gaze; he had seen only her head and neck

135

over a drift of snow. He had made a brilliant shot at the centre of her neck and killed her outright—the lean creature. To-morrow they ought to reach Coozloo River since the Aglonarto was passed (so they thought). There would be almost seventy miles to go to Churchill. Would he find letters there? It was a year since he had had news from England.

He acknowledged thankfully that his stars had been favourable; so easily might he have made some mistake, have flinched or failed, or have misunderstood the Eskimos. With but small cause they would surely have deserted him, either on the muskox journey, or on this present one. His guns and rifles were to them a sore temptation. He felt glad he had been alone with these heathen; he respected them and they honoured him. A white man, or even the Indian guide, might have brought about disaster. It was good to have been dependent on himself; alone in the Barren Lands; to live or to die as might be, and the margin in favour of life so narrow. "The uncivilized brain is confused by the civilized, and as I learned their language quickly . the Angantings came to respect me and at least I have never abused their confidence or their respect." Then his ponderings jerked off into dreams.

Next day, unexpectedly, they came upon the sea; in a fog they nearly ran into it. The chart showed a river and no sea, but the chart was often wrong. "In three days we should reach Churchill," wrote Talbot. 'In ten days you will still be seeking Churchill,' mocked the Fates. The next day's entry was: "*Feb. 4. Disappointment.* All my hopes of reaching Churchill in two days were shattered. After crossing an endless plain came to field-ice. In the distance were two small rocks. Atonguela recognized them as belonging to Aglonarto. My rage and despair were truly justifiable. Atonguela said he knew the way, and so led us W. 150 miles out of the way, when my compass would have brought us to the sea and Churchill long ago. Very sad we went on till sunset amongst hummocks of ice that looked like tombstones to me, and with much difficulty made snowhouse— very little snow when finished. So cold I turned in at once. We cut up the sail spars, and made tea. My thirst all day fearful and melting ice took a long time. We brought it with us. About three miles of ice to the sea.

The agony of thirst

"*February 5. Long Point.* Started early and went on till sunset on field-ice and hummocks; passed Coozloo R. and made camp on Long Point. Saw a few deer feeding there as camp was being made. We found water under the snow, and I am very grateful to Providence but hope we don't sink during the night. Dogs not fed yesterday but had a good feed to-night. We have about sixty-six miles to go—how long it will take us I dare not speculate. Very cold afternoon, west wind and drift with sun. Everyone very tired: they wanted to stop three miles back, but I urged them forward. Hope to start very early to-morrow as without a sail the sled is very heavy; am almost deadbeat. One pice of baccy left."

For nine days they struggled, sometimes hungry, sometimes fed; often they were thirsty. With driftwood they melted snow or ice to drink. "Boiled snow on arriving as my throat was bleeding from over-smoking. The water was filthy, thousands of deer hairs, and the taste so foul. We had not gone far when I vomited the water."

To wait—when they were in an agony of thirst for snow or ice to be melted, this tested and tried the men above all the rest. Each morning, because they had cramp in their legs and in their stomachs, they could hardly leave their sleeping-skins. Illanah had often to be pulled up on to his feet. Always Talbot urged the men forward, and helped them to drag the sled over the great hummocks. Three or four miles he would add to each day's journey; compelling the men. Agilue would lend his courage to the other dogs—Talbot and Agilue always were the leaders.

A day came when trees were reached. They were spruce trees. The tortuous forms of the trees bore mute witness to the rigour of the earth, to the harshness of the winds. The lowest branch of each tree pushed out from just above the ground, it was thick, almost, as the trunk of the tree. This big branch and the smaller branches all tended in the same direction, growing from one side only of the stem. They sought the sun, they thrust out away from the prevailing winds. A man seeing these trees might fancy that he saw, mile upon mile, the graven images of supplication.

'How much wood!' exclaimed Atonguela, who never had

137

seen trees. Cuckoo and the others also were amazed. They could not make the point where they thought Churchill lay, because great boulders of ice were forcing them to the west.

One morning the fields of ice were full of movement, herds of caribou were going by; over a thousand beasts passed the men. After that, each day grew in rigour; the trees were left behind, and on stony plains and in fields of ice the travellers found increasing difficulty in building their igloos.

On the evening of the twelfth of February they all were parched with thirst. 'We must melt ice; what shall we burn?' asked Atonguela. Talbot looked round. What indeed? Here was no moss or lichen, nothing at all but ice. "The crossbar of the sleigh must be cut into faggots for fuel," answered Talbot. The Angantings cut the crossbar and kindled it, but the wood was damp and smouldered too feebly to melt the ice. The men were maddened with thirst; one of them wrenched a piece off the sled and thrust it into the flicker.

"I shall leave nearly everything here and shall make a dash for Churchill," wrote Talbot. The night fell; the men slept. Next day Talbot early woke the camp. Mending the broken sled as best they could, taking the few things on which their lives depended, casting away necessities barely less vital, taking the head of the musk-ox and of the king caribou, the men started off. Men and dogs followed, wearily, the intolerable way. Now rough; now smooth; now again beset with hummocks, the awful scene mocked them—'Ma-oona? Ma-oona?'

With joy at evening, the mist lifting, they saw the coast not far off. With a last exertion they pushed over the ice and just before the sun went down they marked the Old Fort. After nightfall they arrived at Churchill.

★   ★   ★

Talbot ran from Fort Churchill with the Hudson Bay Company's mails nine hundred miles south to Winnipeg. He stopped at various ports and reached Winnipeg accompanied by Atonguela and the faithful dogs Arois, Agilue and another that had travelled with him over two thousand miles. The dog Agilue he always looked upon as the saviour of his life, because the creature had never lost courage and had led on Arois and the others. Agilue and Arois ended their days in Scotland.

"I have to thank Providence"

In Winnipeg Atonguela suffered many things from the heat of the hotel. He slept in a passage but vomited and bled at the nose and said that he would die of the heat. He received the goods that had been promised to him and then he went back, not having shown any emotion at things seen in the city. A boy passing on a bicycle was the only sight that affected him. Looking at it he fell on the roadside a huddled mass, shaken with laughter (31). Talbot thus summed up the total of his mighty hazard (32): "I have to thank Providence and my 400 Express rifle that I did not die of starvation in the fearful Barren Lands of Hudson's frozen Bay."

III
THE BURDEN OF AFRICA
1898 to 1901
★　　★　　★

THE BURDEN OF AFRICA
1898 to 1901

★   ★   ★

FROM BARREN LANDS, FROM DARKNESS, AND ICE,
From the nearness of death by starvation,
Talbot went into the furnace of Africa;
Into such clarity, such harshness of light,
That, to keep them hidden and unseen,
God clothes the creatures, the zebra and the giraffe,
With stripes of gold and of sable
That they may look like the sunlight broken upon by blackest
    shadow.
Talbot saw great herds of sun-illumined creatures,
And, once, women as naked as the creatures.
How did these—almost alone on earth—escape the early herit-
    age of shame?
Thereafter, on the shores of the Arctic Ocean,
In the rigour of the Delta of the Lena,
He completed the round of his northern adventures.

Only torn pages of the diary,
And barely remembered talk,
But because it runs like a burden in the heart of one who must
    chronicle,
This form is chosen.
One who asked: 'If ever I write of your travels,
What shall I say about those years in Africa?'
Talbot had answered: "Say that I treated my boys
With kindness and with the kiboko.
People who knew my Africa will know that I understood."

The Burden of Africa

Sagittarius goading him, Talbot during these years
Explored, and hunted through days smitten with the sun,
Fever-stricken, sun-stricken, walking an unknown way,
Where had walked the children of Ham,
But never the children of Japhet,
Nor even the sons of Shem.

At Beira he hunted, and sometime
He trekked in a wagon with Rhodes.
The two men, each square to the world,
Bore a fellow-liking for one another;
And that because of a loathing common to each,
And that because life is so very quotidian,
That even friendships are founded on little foolish things.
So, when the first night the bullock wagon was stayed,
Each was thankful to find that the other,
Like to himself,
Away from the caravan—
Pissed under the stars.

In a month of May he was following the spoor of a lion.
He took Bill Upcher and thirty-six carriers,
And they went from Fontesvilla towards Blantyre.

> "Very much rain fell; on through swamps.
> At evening came to a morass up to our shoulders.
> Camped in pouring rain."

Next day:

> "Up early. Raining. Made niggers go through morass and
>   finally got through in safety. No one drowned. After-
>   wards we missed the trail."

Waiting by the drinking-hole; a breath on his neck,
A stealthy nearness;
Looking behind
Talbot's eyes met the golden eyes of a lioness.
Talbot leapt up, towered above the creature,
And she crept away into the scrub.

The Burden of Africa

But for danger to the hunter
The buffalo outstrips the lion,
Its anger greater, and greater its courage.

Talbot, hunting awhile with Bill Upcher,
In the great speargrass, higher than their heads,
Came upon a buffalo. It charged;
Running before it, Talbot turned suddenly,
Faced it, fired with both eyes open as was his wont—
The creature disappeared into the great speargrass.
For a quarter of a mile they traced it by its blood;
By the drip of the scarlet blood from a flesh wound,
By heavy crimson blood from a deeper hurt.
They tracked it with fear lest it be in hiding,
Waiting—as is the habit of its kind—
To bear down upon them.

But Talbot must go on alone, so good-bye to Bill Upcher.
"He had tears in his eyes. Poor old man."

Once, for a time, he hunted with Jimmy Sutherland.
But the killer of elephants said: "I won't play second fiddle to
    anyone."
So each went his way. "Excellent fellow" is scrawled in the
    diary.

Before he started up the River Zambezi
Talbot had seen and had hunted
Sable antelope, wart-hog. rhinoceros and impala,
Had come upon "a herd of blue wildebeeste
Surrounded by zebras."
Had seen the brave negroes of the Matabele
And had hunted the puku-kob, the hartebeest and the brindled
    gnu.
Once the baboons drove off a herd of impala,
And the great adjutant-cranes took flight.

Upon a time he tried to go with carriers from Capetown to
    Cairo.
Nearly died close to the Mountains of the Moon of the deadly
    blackwater fever.
With Belgians he fought against hostile tribes;
The Belgians made him their Captain.

On the Zambezi River, seen with fevered eyes,
A mountain, and high trees, and many hippopotami,
Geese and duck, pelican and fishing-eagles,
And, in the sand, crocodiles.

Somewhere hunting rhinoceros, and great roan antelope,
Talbot rested on a Sunday.
   "My men fired the grass where the tents would be put up.
   Two miles away were other men, setting fire to grass.
   The wind blowing hard in our direction,
   We saw the flames racing towards us.
   We had just time to get our things (about fifteen hundred
      pounds' weight)
   On to the oasis. Then we fired the grass
   In front of the advancing flames;
   We were enveloped in blinding smoke,
   Flames all round us,
   But ourselves safe."
When, fire having fought fire,
The crackling was quieted, and the flames and the smoke no
    more;
On that torrid July Sunday
Talbot saw, by the waterhole of that oasis,
The starry, cool loveliness
Of a refreshing jessamine.

Sometimes carried in the machela,
Often wet through because of the towering speargrass,
Taking poncho; and stuffs to trade with in the villages,
But relying much on the rifle to feed the carriers,
So Talbot travelled.
When meat of eland or of impala was plenty,
Talbot walked in front and put the boys behind him

Because of the meaty stink of their sweating bodies.
But when they had eaten corn and fruit
Then they went carrying their burdens before him.

One August, seventy boys, and Talbot, pressing them on.
Twenty-five miles a day, from six in the morning
Walking till ten of the morning,
Only then breaking their fast.

    "Went very fast, just getting out of forest country
    And going into open plains with mountains all about us.
    Made camp in a village. All the country round
    Roaring in fires.
    For a little time the village was in danger,
    But the green sown-stuff round the village kept the fire off....
    My boy Zambory could not get the boys to fetch water.
    One man ran when I got up to the river;
    (They were making him the inciter) so I ordered the boys to
        catch him.
    I then baptized his tail,
    And made fetch water, also blood."

Near Urneneuzo.
    "Met Crode a great elephant-shooter.
    Had a raving night, whisky and beer.
    During night hell's own delight in next room.
    Woke up, and oh! the pain of fever sores."
Later on, in error, Talbot into his sores
Put mercury instead of soothing ointment.
    "Phew—the agony."

    "I have decided to go to Bakari near to Uganda.
    All my seventy boys refused to go that way
    So I have got another headman and hope, in two or three
        days, to get off.
    Fever sores very painful.
    The Germans tell me the way to Bakari is dangerous.
    (Trash)."

The seventy boys of the safari were summoned.
    "Tell them," Talbot said to the headman,
    "That if any of them steal chickens, or rape the women,

The Burden of Africa

In any village that we pass through
I myself will give them fifty strokes with the chicate."

Then they went through an untravelled country
Marching forty miles in the day—sometimes farther,
And the men would be carrying sixty pounds' weight.
Talbot went through the villages of the chiefs.
They would give him a goat for amity,
And he, a return gift
Of gaily coloured fabrics.
    "One chief failed in this act of friendship.
    I understood what this lack purported.
    The dark-skinned chieftain said he would come
    When the sun was high, to the white man's camp.
    I understood fully
    That they would try to overcome us
    And to kill me and my carriers.
    So I shinned up a tree
    And I hung a bottle
    Over the place where I knew the chief and his men
    Would squat to parley.
    We talked. The upshot was not to my satisfaction.
    He wished me, at once, to go on with my journey,
    And to leave behind my goods and all my native porters.
    I refused his impatient demands;
    Then I reached for my elephant-gun,
    And, when the moment demanded the action,
    I shot at the bottle.
    It smashed into fragments—down amongst the natives.
    Fear entered the heart of the chief and of his followers,
    And by good fortune
    The chief cut his foot with the shivered glass.
    Later he sent me a goat, and he asked me for ointment.
    I sent him only a little every day
    Until I got safely through his country."

A sheet with a date in a month of October.
    "I went to the house of the Greek
    And by force took the Arab half-caste;
    Putting the fear of God into several Arabs.

The Burden of Africa

I had to carry the girl four miles through much sand,
Wrist and arm aching.
So I say good-bye to the great inland Lake Tanganyika."

"*December* 31*st*, 1899. Zanzibar.
So good-bye, old year, old, old century,
And the next bring me better luck,
As it will bring me peace—the grave."

One place that he passed by
Was surrounded by barricades.
All the nubile boys and girls
At night herded like sheep in a fold.
  'We used to keep the untouched women
  Apart, but we have learnt that, for a time, to leave them all
  thus together
  Is the easier custom.'

In some places the people accepted the cowrie-shell,
That polished, porcelain-like money-shell.
So pleasant a tender.

Fevered one midday, and scorched with thirst,
Lying down to drink of a well,
Talbot saw, in the shallow water,
His own face reflected, and below it
The ragged black face of a man, newly murdered.
But in spite of the thing the hunter must drink,
And thankfully he did drink.

Somewhere in the wilds Talbot met with a German
Who was maddened by the lack of morphia.
Talbot—in case of need—carried the drug always.
The German, aware of that, tried to kill him
In the tent at night.
But because Talbot saw everything,
He was forewarned by his own observations,
And laid a trap for the murderous German,
Caught him, bound him up, and so left him.

Hunting buffalo on the River Pungwe, a Portuguese,
Greedy for Talbot's rifles,
Went with him for a buffalo, but with treacherous purpose,
When the beast was nearing Talbot
He withheld the loaded weapon,
Left Talbot defenceless.
But a faithful Swahili
Hurled a spear and stayed the onslaught of the terrible bull.

Juno, his dog, went everywhere with him.
So brave a bitch that she overcame a hyena,
The deadly foe of the dogs.

Talbot was terrible in justice and in anger;
And that indeed was needful.
Once, to quell a revolt,
He gave the offending boys
Into the hands of the loyal
To work their own way upon those
Who would not abide by their word,
And who endangered the others,
By bringing division amongst them.
But he never again did that,
For the Hamitic justice
Meted out by the riverside was so very awful.
It lasted from dawn, till the night
Encircled them; and the roaring of lions
Shook the darkness;
Only then was the fate of the rebels made better by death.

The name of Talbot whispered from carrier to carrier—
Their own secret name for him, their northern master—
Was Simba—which being interpreted
Is 'the Lion'.

The Swahili boy Makahuli
When first he carried for Talbot,
Stole bread: that was on a Wednesday.
Now before this the boys had eaten food beyond the day's
    measure,

The Burden of Africa

So Talbot, in their sight, put arsenic into the morrow's portion.
For if, having stolen food, they had gone all unpunished,
The meat would never suffice, the boys would desert the hunter
(Whom they followed well because, with his rifle he kept them
    feasting).
He among these many was alone.
He must think for all,
And must be the absolute master.

For weeks after the theft of Makahuli
Every Wednesday he suffered the kiboko.
'Why so, Master?' he cried, 'for I am good now, I do not steal.'
Talbot said, "You must be whipped to keep you good."

Makahuli so worshipped Talbot
That before the white man boarded the vessel
That was bound for England,
'Take me too, Master,' cried Makahuli.
Clifton said "No;"
But just as the ship up-anchored, two miles away from shore,
Makahuli swam out to the vessel through waters beset by sharks.
Yet even then—for the good of Makahuli—
Talbot refused again to let him follow to England.

Fevered, exhausted, so Talbot had sailed for England;
But hardly there when, because of the Boer war,
He returned to serve.
He followed Carrington's column,
And worked as a war correspondent.
At Elands Kop one in command called out
'You are a hunter Clifton, see with your telescope
Who to damnation is sniping.
Two pom-poms out of action
And my men wounded,
But we cannot spot the sniper.'
Talbot lay down, knee up, to steady his stalker's glass—
Slowly scanned the distance, whilst the determined sniper
Shot at his horse, at himself.
Then Talbot discovered

151

The Burden of Africa

A boy—a lad of twelve—
Whom the joking soldiers arrested.

* * *

After mapless marches, ooze of mud, far Mountains of the
    Moon,
Speargrass, sores, Shakespeare and the sun,
Murderous mood of men and mutineers,
Wraths and warriors, and wilder beasts,
Flare, and fear of the flaming tracts,
Is ended now the Burden of Africa
Wailing away
Into War of white man upon white man.

IV
THE BOOK OF BOREAS

★　　★　　★

CHAPTER I

★   ★   ★

THE HEAT OF THE BOER WAR WAS OVER WHEN, EARLY IN
1901, Talbot sailed for England.

There he was stung by a touch of March madness, and a hurt—
given by a woman, a mysterious 'M'—so with his dog, Sin, he
fled towards Siberia. His diary gives the feeling of a man fleeing
to wild places, seeking to escape some pain and disappointment
put upon him. On the fly-page of his Shakespeare he wrote the
lines from *Twelfth Night*:

> 'For women are as roses, whose fair flower
> Being once display'd, doth fall that very hour.'

But nothing is known of the mysterious 'M'; the troubling
creature; nor what manner of woman this was that had the
power to impinge on Talbot's detachment. Perhaps he hoped
that he had found a being who could be to him a haven; who
was gentle, and would understand; perhaps too he half knew
that 'M' was not in truth that one.

In Paris, stricken with pneumonia, he wrote that the pain in
his lungs was relief in so far as it kept him from thinking of her,
but that he felt "horribly lonely, miserable, and ill". He lay on
a bed cheerlessly facing the angle of a brick wall; lay there, and
listened to the traffic below. Listening, Talbot foreknew the
silences of the places whither he was hastening. He wrote:
"The perpetual sound of motion makes me realize what I am
leaving behind, but it is all for the best. I feel my own special
philosophy gives me great help."

Still in pain, he left Paris four days later: John, trusted servant,
slipped the dog Sin into his master's carriage. Then he took his
leave. On the train Sin, half collie, half terrier, was the cause of
trouble and of money spent, but even annoyances are distrac-
tions, and Talbot was thankful for some escape from the

thoughts besetting him. His guns had been sent on in advance, but the cartridges had arrived late at the hotel in Paris. Talbot therefore was cumbered with them and had to smuggle them over the Russian frontier—"nervous work". With Sin still beside him he arrived at St. Petersburg and was met at the station by his friend Prince Serge Belosselsky, whose welcome made him feel pleased at "dropping on his feet anywhere". Nine years before, in 1892 through Bergen, and through Archangel Talbot had come—sowing tares and cockles. Weeds maybe; but how gay had been the cockles! Rushing wanton days had swept the friends along together. Opposite Naples, on Talbot's yacht the *Soprano*, ("because she can take the high sea") at anchor they had lain until, one morning, Serge, never a good sailor, had waked to feel himself far out at sea; sailing away to Monte Carlo.

Now for seven weeks, Talbot lived brilliantly at St. Petersburg. Though he was neither contented nor well, his pages conjure up a lost and sparkling world. Turning the leaves of the diary, from mid March till early May, this man of the wilds is shown in another guise, moving gaily in the company of courtiers and of ambassadors, but not as easy with them as with the Eskimos and the wild beasts. Only, he wearied quickly of people of the world, and never enough hid his impatience. But his chief suffering in cities, and amongst smooth people, was a shyness, too often disguised by a manner abrupt, even rude. Who, save child or animal, could gauge the misery of that shyness?

He studied and played his flute with one Haigler who was both master and composer; a good enough teacher but plaguy, wishing Talbot to learn only the easy pieces—quite without original art—which he himself had written. Bernhardt, the director of the opera, befriended Talbot, often taking him in state to the Opera. He liked to have the sensitive Englishman at his side in any seat of the two front rows the which were Bernhardt's empire. He liked the island giant to see the singers, when he entered, bow to him, as being the director. Even the tenor, singing of the eternal duration of vows, or the soprano of her love, must pause to bow.

Talbot had the happy accident of saving Bernhardt's life, for, as he walked into a lift, it rose suddenly and Talbot—only just in time—snatched him back to safety. Once, for some cause, a whole opera was sung for solely Talbot's pleasure, he alone, listening, in the great building.

In the ballet too they found diversion. The ballet-dancers were foundlings, doorstep children, some of humble, and some of secret, but exalted birth. The State provided for these children, and the munificence of the Czar and of the Grand Dukes maintained this chosen people, destined for rhythm. As in France the weaving of tapestry (gravely undertaken by men subjected to State punishment should they desert the work) so, by means a little different, was fostered, in aristocratic Russia, a ballet which was the nation's crowning art.

One delightful April Sunday, through the protection of Princess Orloff, Talbot went to the review of the Gardes-à-Cheval, the Czar's own brilliant bodyguard composed of men whose loyalty was certain. Delightfully, the pretty Princess explained how that when Alexander III was about to be crowned, a written threat had been sent to him: 'You must give Russia a constitution or you will be murdered.' Alexander read it and said, 'I will not give Russia a constitution, but I shall be crowned.' He was crowned. Six gentlemen of proven loyalty promised to guard him with their lives if need be. These six men chose six more, and they again chose others. Thus had been formed the strong guard.

Many ladies added lustre to the Sunday's circumstance. None was more charming than the Princess of his open sesame, Princess Orloff. She was the sister of Serge Belosselsky. Talbot had, a little, loved her in earlier years in Petersburg; "a flame of mine before she was married". Talbot saw Nicholas, the Czar, small and sprightly, beset by a nervousness akin to evil temper. The mother of the Czar had eyes which Talbot thought the loveliest he had seen—blue-grey, like some precious stone, never yet worn, nor discovered; but imagined.

He bought horses of the famous Orloff breed, black and beautiful, and drove, with speed and security, the nervous willing creatures. But when his vodka-sodden coachman handled them they became fretful and unmanageable. Talbot was more than once imperilled by this driver who, a rein in each hand, drove tantivy. The horses crashed into other carriages; Talbot at last dismissed the man. "He is rather a scoundrel, a nuisance into the bargain; a man can be one—but not both."

At Kristovsky, the island of the Belosselsky family, men from the British Embassy; some Germans; Austrians; and a Russian or two, played polo. In a riding-school Talbot broke in ponies; with them he was a magician. He governed their speed with his voice, never raising it; he mastered them with tact. He had learned that horses are not controlled through their affections, but through their memories, and by their sense of hearing. Driving a sluggish animal, "Go on", he would say softly, and would cut the horse with a whip. That being twice, or thrice repeated, the softest 'Go on', would make the horse step out, and soon its habitual slowness would be mended. He trained horses with his voice where others needed bit and bridle. Animals that had been despaired of as jumpers he was known so to encourage that they ventured over high jumps—upheld by his assurance which, maybe, they could sense along the reins; which, maybe, they could smell.

Sometimes Talbot went to the Club, rested there and drove back in the morning. "Glorious morning. The drive is worth sitting up for."

The stud-groom of Prince Serge had gone to the Caucasus, and now he returned with about two hundred ponies for the Prince. The best would be kept, the rest would be sold. Some of the ponies had been trained, but most of them were unbroken —and very wild. They had cost about one hundred and twenty-five to one hundred and fifty roubles each. The ewe-necked creatures looked unlike the rest of the polo ponies; they were not unshapely but they lacked speed.

In St. Petersburg, looking for ponies to buy, was a Dutchman, overpoweringly homesick for Holland. He had Eastern blood in his veins, and for companion a wife, so called. To divert him from his yearning, Talbot drove him to the opera, but he began to covet the Englishman's black horses. 'I have twenty thousand pounds lying idle; I want to buy these horses.' And Talbot: "No one better than I could help you to spend your money, but the horses I will not sell." When Talbot again invited him to drive, the Dutchman changed the clothes he wore for other gayer clothes, and that in honour of the animals. He appeared gorgeous, in red and blue, surpassing the sons of Orient.

Amusing was a private theatrical party; actors, actresses, and aristocrats, supped together; somebody at the feast wanted Talbot to make a stay in the country to shoot capercailzie; but he, realizing the inertia of his Russian friends, and how rarely action followed intention, was certain that the plan would be still-born. "The plan will fall to the ground before the capercailzie." Therefore he did not allow himself to be allured.

After seven weeks had brought the year into May, Talbot said adieu to Sir Charles Scott, the British Ambassador, to Beaumont, and Raikes, and to his Russian friends. He paid his bills, left his horses, carriages, and coachman with his friend de Bathe; made notes for the great journey before him; saw to his passports and packed; then left at ten in the morning: "Splendid time, as one can get all things together by that hour."

In a compartment, alone with Sin, he steamed off for Moscow and Siberia. It was time that he went, for, exasperated, he had written: "But when shall I get away from Petersburg, this desperate capital of all the Russias?"

Maybe that Talbot, in his restlessness, was consoled to know that in Russia a longing akin to his own could consume a man. Suddenly someone, peasant or thinker, would be hounded by a mysterious need to travel. To tread the inner path he would need to tread the long highways of the earth. One so beset would forget his children; change his name; don other clothes— and go forth traceless. He would lose himself, to find himself perchance. He would become 'straniki'—a wanderer. So, in some wise, was it with Talbot, who, in travel, reached out beyond himself and, with a kiss, touched the vestment of his ultimate good.

CHAPTER II

*   *   *

MOSCOW WAS REACHED. HERE WERE NEW SCENTS FOR SIN, and for Talbot suppers with the gypsies, he, and the nomads, understanding each other. They sang to him, singly and in choirs, half circled round their guest. One leading, they sang of happenings—sad, passionate and gay. He sealed his amity towards the tribe with a gift to one of the men, for he knew that this gift would be shared by all.

The sound of Moscow, always the ringing of the bells: from every golden cupola they clashed; the sixteen hundred of them. "In Russia they are rung by everyone. It was amusement to many to haul at the bell-ropes. Every passer-by is allowed this extraordinary pleasure." The greatest speaking bell in the world, the bell of Moscow, not so debonairely treated, for only five times in the year the air pulsed with its ponderous ringing. Bigger even than the speaking-bell was the mute cracked bell now used as a chapel; its broken side serving as the entrance.

A telegram from the British Embassy conveyed to Talbot permission to go to Irkutsk, but to go no farther. "I suppose the Russian officials are frightened of me, having heard I was war correspondent in the Transvaal."

After seven days he left Moscow, paying a rouble at the station as the price of having cuffed the porter who demurred at Sin. Taking a compartment for himself and the dog, he started off.

No one on the train knew any language save Russian, "so that when I want food I shake my waistcoat to signify emptiness." They travelled all that day, through country flat and sown; at night they crossed the Volga; by dawn they reached Samara. After that they went by great pastures, sufficing to the fecund mares that bred upon them, amply sustaining wandering droves of cattle. Trees, and water, graced the bountiful country. On the fourth day the train broke down, not far from Zlatoust, in the Ural Mountains; Talbot and Sin were loosed from it to scramble among sycamore, spruce, birch and crowded cowslips. Beside them flowed a trout stream. Afterwards they passed the town of Zlatoust, busy with iron-works, and, during the afternoon, crossed into Siberia.

On the afternoon of the fifth day of journeying they reached Omsk; the mighty steppe surrounded them. Talbot got two droshkies, one for himself and Sin, and the second for his luggage; he directed them to a certain inn. The drivers not understanding his attempted Russian, "galloped wildly through the country and town until they stopped at an inn." The Englishman entered and was stared at with curiosity. He washed himself, played the flute, then went out exploring, whereupon he discovered that he was not the guest of that inn to which he had been advised to go. He packed his belongings, found the right shelter, and was in bed by ten o'clock.

Next day Talbot and Sin walked far, Talbot delighting in the great forests of birch trees. He found a Scotsman doing lively trade by buying Siberian butter and at a small cost shipping it to England as Danish butter. The day ended by dining with two Russian generals and by beating them both at billiards. Into Omsk at morning very many camels came; they were drawing carts led by men of the wandering tribe, the Kirghiz.

Gaily, in a loitering train, passed the next day. There was an American, and a rich trading Frenchman, called Lebaudy, with whom to talk. In this train, that moved more slowly than did the pleasant hours, Talbot met him who afterwards was his friend, Professor Otto Hertz, with whom was travelling "a curator of German extraction named Pfitzenmeyer. I do not like the looks of that man, but I cotton to the Professor. A baby-faced geologist made up the party."

Hertz counselled Talbot to cast his lot with his and join him in search of a mammoth. 'No difficulty with passports shall prevent your going wherever there is hunting or fishing, for to me all is open and all is allowed, and I shall shoot and fish.' Talbot was a little tempted to join the man of science, but he did not assent, for he had the instinct ever to be alone on his travels, not answerable to anyone. Free to be sick, free to die— alone without encumbering any man—free to go on, or to stay, without disloyalty to another.

The train, fated to travel only a few days without mishap, came on the third day to a bridge which had been burned. It was two weeks since fifty feet of it had been eaten by fire, but, although, for that time, men had been working at it, the bridge was still a ruin. The luggage was carried to another train beyond the bridge, then water was brought in small barrels to the engine— time was of no account. The travellers steamed on. The ladies of the passage played the piano whilst Talbot played the flute, and all the while Lebaudy's valet made them merry because he aped the gentleman. With laughter therefore, and with music, Talbot on the sixth day gained the city of Irkutsk.

CHAPTER III

*   *   *

FROM ST. PETERSBURG TALBOT HAD NOW TRAVELLED nearly four thousand miles when, on the evening of May the twenty-seventh, the train jerked up at a platform at Irkutsk. Snatching his hand luggage, and with a word to Sin, he outstripped other passengers who were all going to the Hotel Metropole. The structure was being raised, but with such tardiness, and delay, that it seemed rather to grow—a work of nature—than to be built—a work of man.

There was but one room free, and it was given to Talbot, the other travellers being sent, disappointed, to the old Hotel. Next day he saw the broad streets of Irkutsk, and thought a little upon its history since the middle of the seventeenth century, when, from hewn trees, it grew into a wooden city, with a wooden cathedral. The cathedral had since been burned to ashes and stood now, noble in stone. The River Angara flowed along with Irkutsk stretched upon its eastern bank.

Russians, and Buriats, and other peoples, came and went in the city; with thick lips the Buriats spoke in Mongolian dialects. The Buriats satisfied Talbot's eyes as lovingly they rode their hardy horses. "As once Bob to me, so is his horse to the Buriat." Though these men of Baikal, and of Irkutsk, were generally Buddhists, yet to most of them clung more primitive beliefs. Therefore the Buriat would still claim the traditional death of his horse for the honouring of his grave. It should be tethered at his tomb, and starved into the land of beyond. If the heir, by chance, should bind it with insufficient cord, or if his grief prevented his seeing that the knot of the tether was slack, then the horse might well gallop back to its familiar biding place; but this escape of the horse would be in defiance of the old respect. Talbot looked long at these slant-eyed Mongols. They wore gowns of silk and of cotton, donned in place of fur and sheepskin, for the sun was hot. Horses and drink—these the Buriats' pleasures and pastimes.

A shop window put an end to Talbot's preoccupation with the Buriats, for he needed to buy a rifle; he would get a Mauser, and cartridges, and various tackle for fishing.

Later in the day he paid his deference to the Governor-General. The Governor urged him to travel with Professor Hertz, and to his diary Talbot confided that "everyone in this country thinks that travelling two and three together is the right way. I must say the result is that men become as children."

Yet he warmed to the Professor, a man greedy of life as he. They were freely entertained by the bloods of Irkutsk, and often the jocund company was dispersed only by the sunrise. "The Professor has not been to bed for three nights, but nothing seems to tire him." Hertz went on to Yakutsk after a farewell supper, given only for men. Strange agapē, for it is written that "the Professor is a great hand at kissing. He stops in the middle of dinner to embrace his hirsute neighbour."

Talbot meanwhile went to Lake Baikal, the 'big lake', sickle-shaped. He found interest in its wealth of omul fishing and in "hell blowing from the hills, the wind nearly capsizing our paddle-boat—excitement!"

'Yesterday we had an earthquake, and they are frequent,' said the captain. Then to Talbot's intense surprise he saw a seal put up an earless head and sink again. Before living with the Eskimos he would have doubted his eyes and would not bluntly have asked about it, because, surely, it was impossible that here, in a freshwater lake, seals could be. Gingerly, he would have neared the subject of seals, and their habitations, but now he had seen so many strange things, and had come so to rely upon his eyes that, unabashed, he asked about the seal. 'Who knows how or whence they came or how long ago, but certainly they live here in fresh water, being akin to the ringed seal. Unluckily for them they are of the kind that nozzle breathing-holes through the ice when it is new, and into these holes cunning men put nets and the seals rising for air are entangled.' So explained a Russian standing near by.

They saw a glass factory, a worn-out gold mine, and the River Angara burdened with cargoes of tea-leaves from China.

The road

Somewhere near here Talbot shot a Siberian roe-deer with long, rugose horns. He shot also a maral, the Eastern red deer, attired with noble antlers.

He left Irkutsk after thirteen nights spent somehow, for "they do not provide beds in Siberia, and my coats and things are packed. I have not yet bought bedding." Too impatient of further delay to await a road pass, he went off at nine of the morning in a springless carriage with a hood; a troika took his luggage. From Wednesday morning, until an hour after midnight on Friday, he drove with six hours of tarrying—but none of rest. Only his insistence, his manner of command, the hardship that men felt in withstanding his will, enabled him to continue his long travel, unfurnished with a road pass. Travellers passed him in post carriages with springs; then again he would pass them, himself travelling in varying vehicles, most of them without springs, some of them "with wooden springs—great luxury". The worst horses fell to his lot; the best were in the post carriages. Because Talbot had no pass, it was only here and there that some bold man, possessing his own horses, would dare to serve him. He spoke but a few words of Russian. Three hundred and seventy versts lay between Irkutsk and the point on the Lena River that Talbot wanted to reach.

As each post was neared the driver would say: 'Here we shall find the steamer,' but always it was in front of them. No man seemed to know its hours, or its days.

After being road-racked for forty hours, at one o'clock in the morning, Talbot crossed a ferry and espied a boat. "After a lot of haggling I got three cut-throats to take me one hundred and forty versts for forty roubles, and so at two o'clock in the morning, too weary of the road to pursue it farther, I threw myself into the hand of fate, and with my money, and my boxes, I settled down with Sin, not caring that it rained, but finding on the open deck most necessary sleep. We sailed smoothly along between high hills thickly wooded. An hour before noon we arrived at Gegulaung but the steamer, earlier in the day, had left it. I paid the men, went to an inn and slept." He was awakened by four travellers whose faces were known to him, for they had passed him on the road; one of them was a woman. They agreed together to hire a boat wherewith to pursue the steamer. Afterwards, doing so, they travelled four days and nights—drifting downstream over three hundred versts.

No food save eggs and bread could be bought. "I woke up feeling very hungry, but as there is nothing to eat it is a useless feeling." But Talbot shot duck and teal and widgeon, and after plucking he cooked them in the stern of the boat, where foreseeing the need, he had put sand with wood laid upon it.

On the fourth day the rain fell, drenching everyone; the bread was blue and mouldy, and the air was bitterly cold. At night Talbot wrote: "Slowly drifting downstream with the fire on our boat is very weird. The flames send flickering shadows across the water and lighten the pines."

CHAPTER IV

★　　★　　★

AT USTKUTSK THEY CAME UPON THE STEAMER. THE FOUR Russians embarked with second-class tickets, and Talbot, after walking to warm himself, rolled up in his wet blankets and slept in his cabin.

His awakening was genial, for before him stood a man a little drunk, but most wonderfully dressed. 'Look what I have bought with the gift of money you gave me,' he sang rather than said, and showed the shirt which he was wearing. It was gay with fine needlework. He threw a glow upon the coming journey, so absolute was his joy. The other men had been pleased with the pay the Russians had made them; nine roubles for three hundred and fifty versts: but this man, besides the pay, had received from Talbot a present of money.

For five days he sailed, and on the sixth day reached Yakutsk. No one aboard spoke anything but Russian. No one warned the traveller that he need change, and each time he knew only by accident, though once indeed he was awakened at five in the morning and told, instantly, to board another boat. But time enough there always was, for leisurely are the ways of the people of the Lena, and often the ship stopped for an hour or so, merely, it seemed, to pass the time away. The days were hardly long enough for all the staring the people did, open-mouthed, open-eyed, wondering at Talbot. "It is a great nuisance to be stared at but I am getting used to it. Do I look like an unfamiliar beast? This I cannot ascertain." He read Shakespeare; played the flute; and learned the Russian language. The setting of his days——hills, covered with firs, and high cliffs of granite. Sometimes the river was narrow, sometimes sweeping and noble. In a narrow a fine sterlet was caught, and with thankfulness was eaten.

At Olekminsk there came to Talbot some Russian exiles

167

asking news; the news they sought was four years old, but to an exile, as to a soul disembodied, time has no existence. 'What did the papers and the nation say of the Revolution?' they asked; and Talbot answered that he had been at that time with the Eskimos, far from white man's talk, and from white man's writings, so that he did not know. They offered to lend him some books, but these he did not accept.

The town of Olekminsk sheltered some thirteen hundred people, and of these several hundred were eunuchs, for, as they thought, the glory of God. They were exiled in Russia because of their heresy, the heresy of the Skopskys. In Olekminsk they lived apart. Talbot visited their dwellings and, by dint of questions to and about them, explored a little of the minds of these calm, rich, cunning merchants, and tillers of the soil. Some men have seen them as demented, nervous, delirious. To Talbot they seemed rapacious, hardworking, simple, with but one horrible diversion from the normal—their history like a demon's fairy tale. He was told that Peter III, spouse of Catherine the Great, was a natural eunuch, and was assassinated, but these simple tragedies became contorted into a legend and it was said that the Emperor had reappeared, preaching under the name of Selivanoff. Selivanoff's creed spread, and one Mirinow seized upon it. He could read. He read the Bible. His morbid mind fed on virginity and on sexless beings. Purity of body alone was insufficient, chastity a delusion, for none could be pure or chaste unless the body were shorn of sex, and the mind therefore freed from all desire. Mirinow left the army, and was castrated. He evolved a rite by which the eunuchs mounted through two degrees of initiation, the second degree entailed their being entirely deprived of the organs of manhood. They preached also that it is better to reach heaven breastless than have breasts as fuel for hell. So the eunuchs cut off the breasts of the women. Withal were horrible orgies, communions unspeakable, candles blown out, whilst pregnant girls, supposedly virgin, were stripped, and adored, and delivered of children accounted to be Messiahs. Unwilling boys were castrated, the women only spared their powers of reproduction through the surgical ignorance of the Skopskys. Stories true and untrue circled about the Skopskys, and the truth often obscured by the money paid to the police, to keep silence. Money their power; for the Skopskys made the land of their exile into a land bearing harvests, and profitable to themselves. By a sterile people the land was made fertile. Before the coming of the eunuchs, food had been carried by river to Olekminsk; now the Skopskys grew abundant crops, and, in spite of a law forbidding it, they had become merchants and tradesmen. Their horrible faith had spread throughout Russia, it lurked in high places, was taught in mills and factories, and sheltered by nobles and by great ladies.

In Talbot's diary, soon after passing Olekminsk, is written: "*Monday, 17 June, 1901.* Passed some wonderful rocks looking like castles. One was perfect in almost every way. The river here is enormous; if it had not a current of four miles an hour one would think it an inland sea. The Yakut birch-back canoes remind me of the Canadian Indians, and the Yakuts have the same sort of face as the Eskimos, but are not nearly such a fine race. Their eyes have very small irises, giving them a cunning stealthy look. We have now been four hours at a small village. If we did not waste so much time we might have been in Yakutsk this morning."

Passing the summer tents of the Yakuts which are made of birch, cone-shaped and pleasing to the eye, a Russian officer said to Talbot, who was looking at them: 'In the winter these Yakuts have log houses and their window-panes are of ice. The panes are made air-tight by running water on to them. Elsewhere I have seen window-panes made from the intestines of bears.' Also he told Talbot that the Yakut people enslave the native Tungus, binding them with debts. The merchants barter food and traps and the Tungus bring, in exchange, furs of the wild creatures; but the hunters are no longer the masters of their own lives. As they sailed, the Russian would have Talbot play the flute, he following the melodies on the guitar. So, playing, they reached the city of Yakutsk. In the evening light of the eighteenth day of June Talbot saw the city rising above the River Lena.

CHAPTER V

★ ★ ★

YAKUTSK FOR FIVE DAYS—THE SOUND OF THOSE DAYS was the whistling of little steamers plying up and down the great waterway. Yakutsk was alive now, its arteries the busy, flowing, waters. But in the winter the rigour of death would overtake the Lena. Then the news that soonest would reach it would come from Irkutsk, by a post travelling for twenty days or more. Yakutsk lay over a thousand miles from Irkutsk and no rail united the cities.

Talbot's memory of Yakutsk was gay with edelweiss; the meadows were full of the flowers. They grew around the city like a drift of summer snow. For beauty there was also the wooden cathedral, two hundred years old; and the older, timbered fortress, with its five enduring towers of wood. The townspeople, save for sixteen hundred Russians, were Yakuts, sly men of business and rich; eaters of horses, and drinkers of tea, and of mare's milk. Their women jingled about the houses laden with silver, a noisy apparel devised perhaps by jealous husbands. For who, so jingling, could escape her lord? Though hard and prosaic the Yakut merchant, yet the cargoes he handled were strange and far-fetched, for he traded, not only in the pelts of wild animals, but also in the ivory tusks of mammoths. "Awful business, buying these things from the Yakuts in the Bazaar," wrote Talbot, weary with bargaining.

There was a wild little club with a good piano and a small theatre, and here a man could play pyramids, and, for losing, pay penalty in champagne. In Yakutsk Talbot refound Professor Hertz, who said again: 'Let us travel together.' "But this is hardly my idea of travel, so I am thinking out another journey."

The Governor-General helped to form Talbot's plans by telling of wild sheep to be hunted, the *ovis nivicula* and perhaps

170

other sheep, unknown. He told Talbot that he had just returned from a place some forty versts away. He had there asked the Yakuts under his control if they were rich and satisfied. They had answered 'Yes', but that he should send the Cossacks into the woods to kill the bears as they were too numerous. "What price rabbits and sparrows in England?"

The last night at Yakutsk there was revel. A priest invited Talbot to sup with him. At that party the churchmen were seven, and the laymen ten. For two hours they ate zakuska and toasted everyone of the guests. The men were hilarious with wine. These married merchant-priests had reason for good cheer. 'I must enter a monastery soon,' said one of the priests to Talbot, 'for my wife died and that not long ago. To ensure his chastity a priest must be married, but a priest who has lost his wife is bound to ensure himself against temptation by sheltering in a monastery.' To a question of Talbot's he replied: 'We should not think it chaste to remarry; it is indeed forbidden by the Orthodox Church; in the world, the lay-folk may marry three times, but after that—not again.'

By the end of the week Talbot, at midday, was told that the *Lena*, which was the only steamer that sailed north from Yakutsk, would sail at three o'clock in the afternoon for Bulun, a town in the far north. The sun was blazing, the day immensely hot: "at three o'clock the sailors, all drunk, were fighting like demons. The captain forced some into the police barracks, others were bound with ropes—altogether disgraceful." Towing a large boat, and some barges, they hove off at nine at night. "Of course I am the only passenger on board. Russian the only language spoken." Talbot slept on deck. The boat sailed along the Lena, past high hills. Three times that night they went aground. Upon the great Lena river they spent four days. On the second night Talbot learned more of the venom of mosquitos than even the swamps of Africa had taught him. "The knowledge of mosquitos I have acquired here has made my forehead swell considerably." The wind changed aft and the mosquitos went away, but the ship was covered instead with burning cinders. Talbot slept a little, to be wakened by rain, but the shelter of the cabin was impossible because there the mosquitos had taken refuge.

The Lena: "It is all very peaceful"

The next day, the river being rough, one of the smaller barges that was being towed could not have lived in the boisterous water, so, to save it, the men tarried all day ashore. In a swamp the captain and Talbot shot a duck for their evening meal.

Afterwards in praise of wild places he wrote:

"*Tuesday, 25 June,* 1901. Written at midnight by the midnight sun. Latitude 69°, Longitude 130°. Started about ten o'clock last night. Stopped to pick up wood at four in the morning and left again at seven o'clock. Had a most needful good sleep in my cabin. Am writing this at midnight, the sun shining brightly over the horizon. Saw this evening many wild geese. The whole day we have been going through a country uninhabited by any race. The river is miles broad with a number of low-lying islands and with one high island rocky and wooded. Many bears inhabit it. It is all very peaceful. We have just passed two swans.

"*Wednesday, 26 June,* 1901. The river has grown more rapid and condensed. We saw a reindeer and calf to-day, and a great sword of duck. We passed the last of the Yakuts. The tribe that is settled here is not a wandering one and none of the tribesmen have reached the jungle. The Tungus people is nomadic, its wealth consisting of reindeer. A very uncomfortable day, wind due aft sending the cinders in showers over the ship, burning holes everywhere, also a slight drizzle. I do not know what to do with my cheque. I suppose I shall have to risk it in the captain's hands. Am just out of cigarettes. We ought to get to Bulun to-morrow night."

On the twenty-seventh day of June, he wrote: "At four in the morning a violent storm almost blew the roof off the sky. We at once put in for shelter. About ten in the morning our anchor dragged, and the steamer was so badly handled that we bumped against an ice-bound shore, almost running into the barges which were at anchor. The captain left the speaking tube to come down and make an oration, gesticulating violently the while. At last, leaving the deck, he went again to the bridge. Taking a good deal of the banks of the Lena away with us, and leaving a few plates in pawn, we got our anchor out in safety. At ten at night the storm abated."

They reach Bulun—but not so all of them

On Friday, cold and wet, they steamed slowly towards Bulun. Then came tragedy. A sailor, rowing from the moving
steamer to the crazy barges, smashed into a barge. Instantly he
sank into the icy waters of the Lena and was lost for ever.
Those who saw this sharply remembered the unacknow-
ledged, the dolorous closeness of death. But
to Talbot the man was blessed in the manner of his dying; "without dependence upon others, without
sickness, and without
words".

CHAPTER VI

★   ★   ★

THEY ARRIVED AT BULUN. ''AFTER MANŒUVRING ABOUT,
we landed, the captain and myself visiting the grandees who
gave us tea and zakuska. Feeling very tired, and wet through,
after a wet wretched day, and finding no one who could talk
anything but Russian, I turned into my rabbit-skin.''

At Bulun they waited a day and a night. The sailors worked
all the time, snatching at rest but driven to labour. The passengers and townsmen were maddened by vodka and Talbot
alone of them was free from toil or drink. Instead he sought
news of the wild sheep that men said abounded in the hills, the
ovis nivicula he supposed. He gauged the height of the mountains to be about two thousand feet. He learned that "the reindeer were upon the flats of the delta and no longer in the hills.
I think that they have come down to feed upon the rich herbage, and this in spite of the mosquitos." He, walking far that
day, saw on the waste the quick beauty of an arctic hare and, in
the market place, the lovely pelt of an arctic fox for which he
was asked three hundred roubles. He did not buy it, for now he
was hunter and wanderer, who soon would be living on what
he could shoot, or could catch food by fishing, and his clothing
would be the garments of the country people.

"*Sunday, 30 June, 1901.* (Leave Bulun.) About midnight
started. During my walk I managed by great good luck to buy
a tent and a few other things, some from a store on shore and
some from the steamer. The tent is in three pieces and is made
like a turyus. We took with us the priest, doctor and merchant
of the place, all going to Ballagun. It is very hard to keep time
or date on board, as it is day all the time. We passed very fine
scenery, but the cold is great. The shores are lined by hummocks of ice; on the east coast are very high bare hills with

corries exactly like those of the Scottish Highlands." On the moving ship her owner walked—wrapped in dreams, of minerals and of money; the day before on a hill he had picked up pieces of carbon—and perhaps—perhaps!

Talbot had been told: 'Torgensen, a Swede, will sell you a boat for the arctic sea, and would find men to go with you hunting for sheep.' Though Torgensen lived many miles away, yet, in the Tungus villages near which they sailed, it was Torgensen's industry that enlivened the people. They were fishing and trapping for him, who was merchant of fish and furs. 'These Tunguses', so afterwards Torgensen told Talbot, 'are a people less clever in trade than the Yakuts, but theirs are the only feet that dare to tread the marshes in the south-eastern parts of Yakutsk, and they the only men who know the great Vitim plateau, or penetrate the heart of the jungle. In hunting none can outdo them, but they number only one to four of the Yakut race.'

On the first evening in July the steamer stayed at Bulkur. "Plenty of dogs, two huts, but no Torgensen." So Talbot and a Russian sailor looked for Torgensen. The sailor from that day onwards regarded Talbot as a godlike being ;for with his telescope did not the Englishman, though no other could spy it, see a Tungus killing a wild reindeer? Afterwards they all heard of the hunting, and knew that Talbot had spoken truly. Did he not walk eighteen versts through the forest of stunted trees and, not finding trace of Torgensen, turn and walk for hours without clue or guidance straight back to the ship? In Barren Lands the spirit that leads migrating birds had, in him, been freed and fortified, and now, trusting to it, and believing in himself, he was guided and led as surely as the squirrels in their travels, or as the birds of passage, to, and from the north.

Next day the steamer took up the search for Torgensen. He was found on the waters, fishing for sterlet and for salmon. Speaking German, Torgensen agreed to get a boat for Talbot, and to man it with Tunguses.

Salted fish in barrels were taken in to the other steamer, and she then returned to Bulun whilst Torgensen, Talbot and Sin went ashore, and walked to Bulkur. There to Torgensen and his wife Talbot played the flute, and the time drifted. "Heavy

"Heavy clouds and no time"

clouds and no time. I think it is Thursday, but I have not,
for long, seen the sun. My watch has stopped; night and
day are the same here. A great snowstorm with
strong wind prevents my starting away
in my boat. I play the flute, and
sleep when Sin sleeps; he
seems to know the
time better than
I do."

CHAPTER VII

★   ★   ★

QUEENCHY, SON OF A CHIEF AMONG THE PEOPLE, STOOD before Talbot. With quick attentive gaze the men measured one another. "He will do," thought Talbot. 'I will guide him,' thought Queenchy; but guessed perhaps that soon he would follow rather than lead. The day was fine, the sun was shining. 'Let us cross to the other side of the high hills,' said Queenchy, and he motioned to the two other Tunguses. The four men went down to the water. The boat was well made but she was heavy. "We will put up a mast and make a huge sail with these sacks," Talbot ordered and, when they understood, this was done, but before the sail was hoisted the wind fell. Laboriously, therefore, they rowed fifteen versts. In a creek where ran a stream the tent was pitched, and Talbot went to spy. There were many signs of wild sheep, but he saw no beasts, and the mosquitos were painful to him, so he returned to the tent, and supped on teacakes, and on a fish weighing sixty pounds the which he had just caught. All night the wind, and the rain, blew in through the top of the tent.

At three o'clock next morning they sailed, for though it was a wild day they hoped to reach a place more favourable. When the boat was half filled with water, and nearly swamped, they agreed to turn back. This was hard to do because a strong gale blew from the north, and the swift tide, contrariwise, ran at six miles an hour. In the waters of the Lena the four men received the baptism of a common danger—then they returned to the tents, and slept.

At night, the others being encamped, Talbot found delight in going alone to spy. "Although no sheep were visible to me it was very pleasant to look far away into the distance. To the north the midnight sun was shining, the deltas were everywhere green, and there grew flowers of many colours." Talbot, looking at them, marvelled, thinking of All the Russias, with cities golden-domed; and vast steppes; with the great tundras; with primitive meadowlands, where wild flowers grow to the height of a man.

At this time Talbot slept hardly at all; the arctic air, the bliss of being so far north; the space; the solitude—these rested and satisfied him.

For three days the gale hurled towering waves upon the shore. Talbot and the Tunguses climbed fourteen thousand feet into heights nearly perpendicular, but they saw no sheep. It was "almost impossible to walk, or to stand on the summits of the hills against the force of the wind".

In their nets the men caught fine sterlet, and salmon, not as good to eat as the European salmon. In a day and a night the three Tunguses ate over twenty fish, each one weighing more than ten pounds. Talbot made unleavened bread, and ate some meat a Tungus had given him, the first bread that he had eaten for seven days. The giver was in himself a gift to eye and to memory, leading his hundred tame reindeer among the arctic flowers. The bucks and the does both wore attire, and even the young beasts were so adorned. The crowned creatures trampled on aconite, and meadow-rue, and grazed among anemones and gillyflowers (1). They stood fetlock-deep in columbines, marsh betony, and love-in-idleness. The dark-flowered winter-rose grew about the herd, and there was a glacier crow-foot close to a reindeer. Was this pink-of-my-John that intermingled with the grass of Parnassus, and with the marsh marigold? And surely that was the felwort with its gentian blue. Anyway, here at the deer herd's feet was the familiar beauty of the forget-me-not.

The waiting for a better weather, was, perhaps, tedious, and Talbot was invaded by a certain melancholy. He diverted himself by little feats of determination; maybe he would throw pebbles into the air, juggling with three at a time, or the like kind of conjuring; remembered from days with the Eskimos. His quickness of hand had been useful; it might be useful again. He succeeded—as he always succeeded—because he would

not rest till he had done what he wished to do, were the thing
to be small or great.

Also he found another pastime—he watched the grass growing. As by Hudson's Bay, so also here, the time of spring and
summer was so brief that the aspect of the lush lands at evening,
to a watchful eye, would be quite other than at dawn. Grasses
would have grown higher, leaves would have unfurled, buds
would have blossomed. The wealth of the natural pastures astonished Talbot; he lay down, then kneeling over the place
where he had lain he would count the various leaves, and grasses,
and wild flowers that grew in just that length of six foot and four
inches. He could not name more than a few of those little green
or coloured existences, but one day he counted of such forty-five,
each one different from the other. As the wind began to lessen,
Talbot collected many flowers. Suddenly he wondered, "Are
they all built on unchanging numbers? and is the number of the
petals and of the sepals and of the stamens always the same?"
He had no books excepting only his Shakespeare; but, with
study, he learned for himself that the number of the petals and
of the sepals in many flowers was constant, but that the number of the stamens was often variable. The knowledge came
fresh, straight from the flower to him, with no book interven-
ing. He enjoyed the simplicity of those flowers, so often constant in design, which he could order into tribes; each member
of the tribe, in some part of its structure, alike to every other
member (lightly considered), however different in hue, or
size, or semblance.

A week later the wind dropped; the boat was launched, and
with the very rapid current they drifted downstream. After
sailing for some hours they saw, among the sedges, the form of
a grey goose. Being hungry for meat, Talbot went ashore and
shot two of the noble wide-winged birds.

Then remorse bit him, for, as the second bird fell, swooped
down, near by, two hawks. They soared up again into mid
air, each holding a gosling in its talons. Self-loathing filled
Talbot. The geese then were parent birds! They had reared
their young where water-plants sustained them. With his
glass Talbot had many times watched such another pair of
hawks perched on a cliff, waiting for days that they might

pounce down and carry off the young. Long perhaps had these hawks been frustrated by the goose in her piety; by the gander with his warning cackle, or by his louder tone of assurance. "Man and hawks together have proved too strong for even their devotion!"

The Tunguses cast off from the land and drifted downstream. The hills were not very high, but steep; often at their base was a ravine, running to the seashore.

Suddenly a Tungus cried, 'Chibuki!'—(A sheep!) "I could see one was lying under the brow of a hill. We pulled the boat to shore, and climbing a small gully I studied the lie of the land. The sheep proved to be a ram about six years old. Returning to the boat I ordered two Tunguses to stay behind and I went with the third man. It was not a difficult stalk but all the ridges seemed to be alike. At last I got to the ridge I was seeking. Motioning to my Tungus to remain where he was I crept forward and, looking over, saw the ram lying where I had first seen him, more than eighty paces away; but below me I spied, suddenly, another sheep far bigger than the first. He was a magnificent old ram. The wind was blowing from me very close to him. Another minute and he was snorting. He stood a long way off, about two hundred yards, and facing me. I thought that it was useless trying to shoot, so I waited. The old beggar came a few paces forward, looking in every direction. In the meantime the younger ram had got up and by now was not more than forty yards away. I could hear my heart beating. I had no idea what to do. The proverb about a bird in the hand flashed through my head, but I turned once more to look at the nobler animal. He had approached a little. I knew that he would soon be off. There was no time to be lost. I waited a moment or two for him to give me an opportunity, which he did, standing broadside. I fired, but—heavens! Too low. Not knowing where the shot came from he stood still. I fired again, this time hitting him low. Both sheep went off at a rattling pace, and I after them, filling the air with lead but to no purpose. Here, like a fool, I took the advice of my Tungus. Had I risked the wind I might have cut them off at a precipice; instead I followed them. Folly absolute! How could one pair of legs rival two pairs? Later I learned that these sheep, if frightened, will

'Chibuki!'—a sheep!

go without stopping for twenty-four hours. Up hill and down
hill I followed in pursuit, leaving my Tungus far behind. It
must have been for three hours that I kept going,
seeing now and then a drop of blood. Then I
came to a maze of hills. I spied here,
there, and everywhere. No sheep
were to be seen. Silence
cover the rest!"

CHAPTER VIII

*   *   *

THE MEN WERE HUNGRY AND, A FAIR WIND ARISING, THEY
sailed before it northwards, spying the land for sheep. On a
cliff, overhanging the sea, Talbot saw a wolf outlined against the
sky. Farther on they spied four ewes with their young, feeding
on the cliffs. Talbot thought still of the noble ram, but the men
urged the hunting of the sheep. 'We need the meat, and the
fleeces of the ewes will clothe us,' they said. Going first a long
way round about the sheep, Talbot was nearing them, when he
heard the whistle of a watching marmot. At that the sheep
became uneasy; then fled.

The Tunguses gave a frown of impatience, for the marmots
are a wary folk and the cry of the watch-marmot had been
piercing to the ear, although the creatures' other voices are soft
and murmurous. The rodents now took shelter in their holes;
the sentinel waited till the last was safe before it hid itself. Afterwards it came up often to see if the enemy was gone. 'Good
food,' said Queenchy of the marmots; but Talbot knew them
to be unsavoury of smell and of taste, for, though clean in their
habitation, they are rather foul and ratlike in their flesh. 'They
would be hard to shoot,' said Queenchy, 'for they go into their
holes to die. A man could stalk them, and kill them, at the mouth
of the burrow because they do not roam. Our way is to carry
water from the river, and to flood them out of their holes; we
stand by and club them to death as they run from their homes.'
Talbot, with difficulty, followed so long a tale, but Queenchy,
with gestures, made his meaning clear.

The marmots were busy now cutting the grass with their
teeth and drying it for their beds, making provision thus for the
long sleep of winter, but not laying by any food. "I have met
its kind in America—called there the woodchuck," Talbot
remembered.

The marmots. The ewe—ovis nivicula

A ewe, less wary than the others, had remained with her lamb, and for hunger's sake Talbot shot them. Then he strode forward to study the first *ovis nivicula* that ever he had closely seen. The ewe was about five years old, and her colour thundercloud-grey, with a small patch of white fleece on her rump. Her tail was black. She had small straight horns, and her pelt was thicker and coarser, much, than is the wool of the man-handled sheep.

Talbot gave the spoil to the men, keeping back but little for himself, and a few hours later he saw the three Tunguses sleeping—gorged and swollen. In front of them were bones and intestines—all the rest they had eaten.

Next day they drifted to within a few versts of the arctic ocean. They had gone past a range of hills where, in summer, the wild sheep grazed, but now Talbot wanted to hunt—only reindeer.

Climbing a height he saw many antlered beasts feeding. Some of the females were suckling their young. Their udders harboured milk, heavy as oil, and aromatic. Talbot, watching them through the glass, saw a hind stray from the herd—saw too the stag jealously seek her and urgently drive her back, lifting her off her hind legs with his great antlers thrust beneath her buttocks.

Stags and *hinds*—so the wild reindeer. But named *bucks* and *does* when herded. Talbot remembered that in Eskimo country the caribou (creatures like to these), in the core of winter, shed their attire; freed so in the gaunt weeks of that much to sustain. Here also, for a short time, together at the same season, stags and hinds would go crestless.

Returning to the boat, they let her drift to the place of the reindeer. Talbot, and one of the Tunguses landed, and climbed about a hundred feet above the sea on to a plateau of marshy ground. They saw many nests. Among the forget-me-nots the swans delighted in their cygnets, and the geese and snipe were reaping the reward of their faith in the eggs: on the wing guillemots passed him.

Here and there, a later clutch of eggs lay on the cliffs, or on the grasses of the flats. "The beauty of the eggs equals that of the flowers." Thinking back Talbot could remember no poem written to the wild black hieroglyphics traced on the white of

the guillemot's eggs, but he had read in them the tale of the
sea's savagery, and of the bare rocks, the nursery of their young.
Constant, year after year, to the same mate, after many rites of
courtesy, the male would lead the female to that same place on
that same rock, where in other years they had brought to life
the one egg of the year that she will lay. Formed so that it will
not slip and roll away, he and she, one after another, will
stand facing the sea with the egg held between the wings and
pressed close to the underpart of the breast. Turn by turn the
wingèd lovers fly off, and rest, and drink of the sea. Thousands
of guillemots on the rocks, all guardant of their eggs; the birds
rather silent, only giving a soft coo of fear if any man should
near them—how well Talbot could remember it all, as seen
in Isles of Britain. When, from precious egg, precious bird is
born, the tenderness by rudeness will be followed, and the off-
spring will be pushed down to the sea. It cannot yet fly, but it
must swim. Later it will fly with its brethren, all in a long line,
so close one to another that the beak of one will nearly touch
the tail of another.

The hawk's egg, too, how prophetic its cipher, rustily foretelling a life of blood! But the eggs of the small English birds
like minims of music in the nest. Talbot had enjoyed the
shapeliness of eggs, and the feel of them—the smooth lacquer
of the kingfisher's egg, the chalky touch of the gannet's, like
that of a vessel before it is glazed with pattern-ore. "How lovely their colours." The eggs of the owl all moon-white; the eggs
of the gannet the colour of foam; and the doves, all of them,
with eggs of pure white.

Now he looked again for the reindeer, and saw them feeding
away from him in a hollow, and between them and himself was
a marshy flat. The watch-hind was not feeding; she stood and
gazed, dutifully alert.

Over Talbot surged remembrance of Barren Lands, the
'leafless moving forest' of antlered herds, led always by a hind,
the hinds, like the stags, bearing attire. And now, glory of the
arctic, he saw that rare wonder among wild reindeer, a white
stag. Through his mind flashed legends and poems telling of
white deer, of mysterious white stags and hinds into which had
been spirited the souls of human beings; flashed too, the primi-

tive lust to possess, to take back to the ancestral home this prize
of the north, this witness to his wanderings. In spite of the fever
of his desire and admiration, he took a steady aim, but the shot
was low. The beast was wounded but not killed. Talbot with
his telescope followed its flight; the wounded animal went as
strong as the others. Suddenly it dropped behind and climbed a
sharp hill a mile away. Talbot, nothing fearing, plunged after
it, through the swamps up to his knees in mire. Soon he too
was on the hilltop. He saw the stag galloping still, going to the
west, across a broad open space to another high hill. It lay down
once or twice; then stopped, and went no more. The beautiful
white beast lay facing Talbot; between them was a flat waste
and a mass of arctic flowers.

"All I could do now was to wait and trust to an unknown
something that would enable me to get near. In this perplexity,
looking to the north, I saw a fog rising off the ice-pack, slowly
sweeping southward. A little later it had covered the hill where
the white reindeer was lying. Snatching at this help, I raced
across the open, my Tunguses at my heels. Once or twice the
fog lifted, then we lay flat. At last we reached the base of the
hill. Leaving the Tunguses behind and crawling as close to
the ground as I possibly could—neck-aching work—I
got to within sixty yards of the animal. I slowly
raised myself, aimed, and pulled a little
sooner than I intended. The bullet
entered the heart of
the reindeer."

CHAPTER IX

★   ★   ★

FOR MANY DAYS, FAR INTO JULY, TALBOT AWAITED THE blowing of a fair wind, that he might return with his men to Bulkur. While waiting he watched the nesting of birds, and read his much-marked Shakespeare. As in Africa, so here amongst them that dwell with Boreas, Shakespeare was company enough.

Staying thus, he thought much upon the white reindeer, and upon the spread of its antlers, grown to magnificence. The pelt he would wear in winter. Queenchy had prepared and cleaned the head so that it would travel without hurt. This head stood to Talbot as the immediate symbol of the Tunguses, and of his fellowship with them; it summed up the orbit of their lives.

In his mind he scanned their lives, thinking this-wise about them: their name—Tungus—means 'Keeper of Reindeer', for the Tungus shepherds his herds, wandering with them wherever is pasture of moss; guarding them against the wolves. When yet a child he can harness a reindeer, and the smell of the reindeer is upon him, because his covering by day and by night is fashioned of reindeer skins. The Tunguses drive reindeer and they ride them, as their ancestors, in the south, rode horses before the more cunning Yakut, with his Turkish blood, drove the Tungus up north.

At night, looking out on the stars, Queenchy had shown the constellation called 'The Great Bear', by him called 'The Wild Reindeer'. In the 'Milky Way' he saw the sign of the scattered river; to him the Pleiades were a celestial duck's nest.

Strange-looking are the reindeer saddled up. Some are grey, others mauve, black, brown and piebald; at a distance they look like hornèd horses. When he needs a reindeer for his sleigh the Tungus, going into the herd, catches one with his lasso. Unless sorely stressed by hunger he eats none but the wild ones.

186

The Shaman

To this people of the arctic the reindeer is the beginning and the end—beneficent as is the coconut-palm to the children of the coral islands. When devils beset the Tungus, when death fells him, the reindeer serves him still.

It may happen this way. A devil plagues the Tungus, evilly possessing him, and a shaman priest is besought. 'Come and heal us with kamlanie (2).' The yoke of shamanism has been laid upon these priests, these men of magic, by the Spirits of shamans who are dead; so think the Tunguses. The spirit call most often comes to a vexed mind, to a youth who walks dangerously near the dark places, where suffer those whose minds are sick. But none who are quite overcome by madness may be shamans, for they must be masters and victors. Two or three years will be passed in strengthening their initiation and they may not beat the drum till their time has come.

The shaman must be able to dance and to sing for long hours, and must be strong enough unwearyingly to beat the drum and to cast out devils. His outer garment is of hide; it is steeped in the blood of reindeer; on his chest two metal discs picturing maybe the sun and the moon. Scattered over his dress are jingling pendants, iron symbols of man and wolf, of salmon, sterlet and plover, a weight of iron to clash when he dances in frenzy.

A stricken Tungus, sick with devils, suffering from a terrible arctic anguish, faces the shaman (3). The people tell the priest of the sick man's affliction, of his howls and mad dances, of his trances, and of the horrible, all-night singing, and intoning. The sufferer knows nothing of the most of this, his anguish.

The shaman kneels on the skin of a white mare, then leaps up, and madly on his drum plays, till every sound of those wastes is given out again upon the drum; the howling of the wolf, the skirl of the curlew, the whoop of the swan, seem to vibrate upon the night. Horror heaped on horror, and winter darkness on winter darkness, melancholy, and self-sought death, the madness caused by the famine of entire villages—all is spoken by the drum. Then maybe the shaman will bargain with the devils and they will agree to leave the man. They must be housed in flesh, clothed in matter; therefore a reindeer is brought in and the devils are cast into it. The beast is saddled with the pain of the man. Then the creature dashes away, or it seems to be spirited thence. The reindeer is harnessed with human woe; the soft-eyed, serviceable reindeer. The man is delivered. But when, his day having come, he dies, the skin of a reindeer is his enfolding shroud.

So thinking, so looking at the head of the white reindeer
which he, by means of the mist risen off the sea-borne
ice-pack, had wrested from arctic heights, Talbot,
with gladness, knew that he possessed
the immediate symbol of the
Tunguses of the Delta.

CHAPTER X

★   ★   ★

ON A CAPE OF THE MAINLAND TALBOT LAY SPYING.
Sweeping the distance with his glass he saw, to the north-east,
broad swampy land with a few hills, places where the reindeer
delighted to pasture. Beyond the swamp was the sea, with a
small high island that looked like a pyramid. It was the shaman
island, but Queenchy's mouth seemed held by fear, and more
than just its name he would not tell. On its summit were three
sticks, about seven feet high, raised to honour the powers of
evil, and standing in a line from north to south, a board being
laid from one to the other. On the board were bowls filled, as
Talbot later learned, with blood, offered to the spirits. To the
west he saw a cross (4) built of wood; "large, bold and heroic-
ally erect." It stood, on the top of a hill, facing the ice and the
snow of the north pole. It was blown on by tempests; it
was illumined by the northern lights; it rose from a cairn.
Beneath it lay the brave ill-fated men of the ship *Jeanette*; the
ten who had died exploring the arctic.

In his writings is shown how this cross was branded on
Talbot's thoughts. The cross, and the three sticks of the devil,
this same delta enclosed them, but their message was set apart by
the spaces that divide heaven from hell. The cross spoke peace
to Talbot and serenity, yet, from the shaman island he heard, at
night, the contrary wild throbbing of the shaman's drum, and
the opposing jangle of the iron on the leather dress of the devil
doctor as he turned, round and round, in his dance, moving
in circles till he became a foaming man; demented.

"I must go over to the shaman isle," Talbot said to Queenchy,
who made as though he had not heard him. But on a calm day,
though demurring, Queenchy landed there with him. None of
the other men would go, and Queenchy was loth, and fearful
of the place. The island was on that day deserted, and stood a

mere grim altar to the worship of the devil. Talbot, a little disappointed in his quest, returned now to the mainland.

On these calm mornings, rare in arctic seas, Talbot saw icebergs floating. Small boats rounded the cape bound for Bukameer. Here the sailors would stay till winter put an end to their fishing of the sterlet and the nailnar.

Talbot decided to return to Bulkur and to go thence to wheresoever he might hunt the wild sheep, but he and his men still waited for the wind. He could not sleep because of toothache, so he gave himself an injection of morphia; and the needle, not being sterile, poisoned his arm. He made a poultice of biscuits and because the biscuits were mouldy his arm swelled and blackened; then, just when he had decided to get Queenchy to cut it off, it became sound again. This is hardly mentioned in the diary, but he spoke of it years later to a doctor: 'having seen you watch me whilst I put stitches into your leg, from the ankle to half-way up the calf, I can imagine you would have endured Queenchy's surgery without even an oath!'

Then for three days the wind blew and the men went before it to Bulkur. The river was a mass of raging water. The four men had to round a cape where rocks rose steeply. The current was great, a gale blew from the north, but because of the shelter of the rocks the wind did not catch the sail. 'Shall we be broken by the rocks or shall we be drowned?' The men rowed, two of them to an oar, and Talbot steered. The third Tungus pushed with a pole or stayed the boat by snatching at such pieces of rock as jutted out of the too-smooth cliff. Often, instead of going forward, the boat was driven back by the current. Waves dashed over the gunwale. They expended themselves in toil and made a furlong. It took the men half an hour to master the last fifty yards: but now the rocks were past, the wind blew fair on the sail; with lightened hearts they sailed on in safety. For the second time Talbot and the Tunguses had tasted together danger, and the salt of the sea. Sometimes in dreams or in illness Talbot remembered this mighty struggle. It, and another later in the Lena, were perhaps the only perils that a little appalled him, and that left in his memory a haunting uneasiness.

CHAPTER XI

*   ★   ★

IN THE FAR NORTH DROVES OF TAME REINDEER DISTURBED
the peace of the hills. Charged with the care of them, Tungus
herdsmen gathered them from the hills, and led them to pasture,
far as the arctic ocean. The flocks must be protected from the
wolves which sought to harass them; the weakly young reindeer must be nurtured. Because of this business and solicitude, the
wild sheep were disturbed, so that none remained in those heights.

Talbot, as he sailed down the Lena, had considered his future
wanderings. Now from Bulkur he decided to go some way up
the river to Carmagourka, on the western bank of the Lena.
"What time of the day or the night is it?" he asked at Bulkur;
and being told he had set his watches. "What day of the week
is it?" and being told he had corrected the entries in his diary,
for day and night had been so merged in a common light that
he was two days wrong in his writing. He had felt uncertain of
the days, but had relied upon a strange Sunday feeling that beset
him on a day when he was trying to get his diary right. "No
one with as much Scots blood as I have could be mistaken as to
that feeling of Sabbath," he had laughed, and had counted upon
his instinct; but here at Bulkur it was proved to him that his
Lord's Day, in fact, had been a Tuesday. Waiting at Bulkur
for the steamer to sail, towards Carmagourka, he watched the
fishing of the great nailnar. The men used big nets and smaller
ones; at every haul one to two hundred fish were taken. The
nailnar sometimes weighed sixty pounds, and there was a
wealth of freshwater herring. These were as good to eat as the
herring of the sea and only a little different to look at. "A small
added fin near the tail is the only difference I can see."

Then the steamer came. "After exhausting my stock of
Russian words I turned to the main cabin, leaving the Russian
to drink tea and to make cigarettes—whilst I went to sleep and
slept for nine hours."

191

When he reached Carmagourka he saw lying beyond him a range of high hills, soaring to sharp points, hills of Chibuki, the Wild Sheep Mountains. The hills were of smooth shale without verdure. "Hardly enough, one would think, to support one sheep in a hundred acres." Talbot took a little food in his pockets and, with Queenchy, and Anocky, he began to climb. The ascent was not at first painful, but after two or three hours the hills martyred the men. Sharp slate cut their feet, the fossil lichen and the shale drew blood on the pads of Sin.

A peak surmounted, they would spy for sheep. Seeing none, they would go down to the very bottom of the hill, then up another peak, and thus many times over. So during four days they climbed.

There was a place where the stones were loose, and where a narrow ledge of shale overhung a mortal precipice; beyond it was a chasm. Here Talbot turned back, for he alone was not sure of foot. Climbing round about the base of the hill he rejoined his Tunguses. They were asleep and snoring. They had climbed like goats and, with a running jump, had crossed the chasm. After that, they followed a spoor along a narrow rock that led from one height to another, a precipice lay on either side of it. 'We are tired,' said the men. 'Here are tracks of sheep but no sheep are to be seen. Let us return to the flats.' But the Englishman would not have it so. These adamantine hills must harbour sheep.

Talbot thought "there is, perhaps, no quarry so precious to the hunter as the wild sheep." Beasts of the plain and of the jungle are less hard to encompass. By a drinking-pool a man may come upon them; or, with the carcase of an animal, he may allure a beast of prey. But the wild sheep he must follow into its own fastness; with toil and with sweat he must come upon it, he cannot beguile it. He must seek it in the high places, in the hazardous hills.

Spurred by anger—Talbot was angry with the men because they still wished to sleep—he scaled a peak yet sharper than the others. Below him lay a ram, easy to reach if noise did not betray the hunter. So leaving the two men he snaked his way down the hill.

"The wind will veer about the hollow where the sheep lies in shelter." Only a little of its body was exposed but, at the sight of its so shapely head—the hunter held his breath. Then he raised his rifle, and shot.

As Talbot knelt by the dead beast he ran approving hands through its sufficing fleece, grey clouded with brown; he let his fingers linger over the noble crumpled horns. "At last I have a fine ram of the *ovis nivicula*." Talbot knew that he was touching the reward of the untrodden heights—the heights that had fought him at every step as with knives, and which had threatened him with calamity of fall. As Jason from Colchis, so now, from Chibuki, a wanderer had wrested the ram of his seeking.

With his spoil he returned to Bulkur and there he parted with the Tunguses, giving pay to all, and to Queenchy and Anocky presents, but the third man was not deserving of a gift. "I was standing near my hut when a bullet whistled past me. It was shot by the Tungus to whom I had not given a present." As he sailed away from Bulkur Talbot saw the midnight sun. He wrote: "Probably I am looking at it for the last time."

CHAPTER XII

*   *   *

AFTER HAVING SHOT THE RAM TALBOT WALKED BACK TO
Bulkur, and there he awaited the *Lena*, a ship famed for having
crossed the arctic sea. "I will go with her back to Yakutsk," he
wrote.

Leisurely for eighteen days the little steamer followed her
ill-directed way back to Yakutsk. Misadventure overshadowed
her. "To-day we attempted three times to drop our anchor—
the fourth effort was successful!" Twice or more she ran ashore,
so mishandled was the ship. "To let her run ashore is nothing!"
Her propeller cut the rope of the large barge she was towing,
and the great thing, having its sail up sped off alone towards
Yakutsk. Sometimes the *Lena* would take two hours to go a
bare mile and a half, but one day, driven backward by a mighty
storm and by the current, she drifted at ten versts a mile down
river; when righted she returned against the current, rocking
and rolling viciously, the sailors seasick the while. She was
carrying fish destined for the gold mines, for Viteen, and for
Verkhoyansk; but the roads and the means were not good
enough for the merchandise to go farther inland. On board,
fish, rice, bread, and tea, were the only fare. "On musty bread
and fish I live. However, I find that by toasting the bread, and
by boiling the fish, I somehow get through my meals. I practise
the flute; but most of the time I think!"

The entries in the diary kept during this journey lend comedy
to the Siberian memories:

"*Sunday,* 28 *July*, 1901: My flute is out of order which
troubles me, but pleasant for others. It is now ten at night; I
notice that the sun is very low on the horizon. Last night going
to bed, I lit a candle which seemed quite strange. I washed some
pyjamas to-day so I am looking forward to clean things; the
first for six weeks. They are not quite dry—that is nothing.

Five hundred and thirty-six scales

"*Wednesday*, 31 *July*, 1901: I practised five hundred and thirty-six scales, flats and minors. Have not smoked cigarettes for a month and feel better for it. The mosquitos nearly drive me mad; I thought I was mad once. The schoolmaster Vassili Vansibivitch went ashore with the manager to shoot duck. It is disgraceful to see him kill duck which are no bigger than sparrows. I rated him for it. He and the engineer sat up late talking for hours about the duck-shooting; pathetically childish. Probably living with schoolboys makes him as they are."

"*Saturday*, 3 *August*, 1901: On the Island of Agrafina are many bears. On my return north I shall try to get the steamer to stop there. At lunch Sin and the dog of Vassili had a slight difference of opinion. Vassili, trying to kick mine, kicked his by mistake. This made him so angry he threw his plate on the table, went to his cabin and wept on the neck of his faithful Gustav. He is now sulking. This is the most childish performance in a man that ever I have witnessed. Been seedy all day with, I think, a touch of African dysentery. However, I took plenty of chlorodyne and coffee and am better; pain gone. The sailors sound with a long pole day and night. They sing out 'Autoban' when the pole touches the bottom, and 'Nemaiarche' when there is plenty of water."

Then, watching the passengers at meals, he wrote his 'extract' of "How to behave in Polite Society in Siberia".

"It shows bad policy to wipe your mouth as you might be hungry afterwards; your moustache full of grease is an excellent substitute for food.

"If very little of something is brought in, knowing there is no more you must hastily take the lot—this requires a quick eye and sure hand.

"Always place the bones of fish or meat on the tablecloth, as they interfere with food on your plate.

"Eat with your knife as much as possible; it is kept blunt on purpose, but it is considered better etiquette to eat with your fingers.

"To show your appreciation of soup, with your left hand place the plate as close to your chin as possible, and lap up the broth holding the spoon with your right hand and making much noise. Spit out, anywhere, what you don't want.

"To hiccup after a meal is the correct way to express that you have had enough."

Talbot's days passed in a torment of mosquito bites. By night he slept in the one main cabin which, until midnight, was full of men, drinking tea after the evening meal of rice, raw fish, and wild currants gathered by the crew. It was pleasant to jump on shore with Sin, and to see the herds of wild reindeer that came up to look at the dog, which was itching to get at them; pleasant also to need the light of a candle after the former unending daylight.

The engineer of the ship was a barbaric dolt. When sterlet was served up at supper, he ate eyes, gills and all. He would become wildly excited when Talbot, teasing, recited Shakespeare to him—for he thought that he was being insulted—and thumped his breast, and pulled his beard. One day the sailors, after some wild horse-play, lost their tempers and nearly killed a man by throwing him overboard. The captain encouraged them, and the engineer gave loud shouts but lent the suffering man no help. A parson, watching, enjoyed the fight. Another day a black bear was seen near the water, and soon after screams for succour were heard on shore. The engineer went crying up and down the ship but left Talbot the part of taking a gun and going on land to see what was amiss—a Cossack who had lost his way quite near the river's brink was the cause of all the turmoil.

Talbot in his long thoughts was aghast at the horror that runs in Mongolian blood, at the pessimism rampant in Christian and heathen, a very disease. He saw the huge population caught up in a terrible nightmare, saw it turning, foaming, dancing, drinking and devil-possessed, from the shaman ecstatic in the arctic to the Skopsky whirling in the exile of Olekminsk. Among the Boreans he recalled sufferers seized upon by epilepsy, spasms, trances and devils. He frowned, remembering the nervous sickness that plagues the Tunguses and that causes a man stricken by it to sing, 'Nayani, Nayani', in mournful monotony the night through, all unaware, till someone, waking him, finds him emptied of strength. He puzzled over that other sickness(5) which flows in Mongol blood as far as the Malayan Isles, the dread *meriatschenje*. Those who suffer from it are shunned.

Day by day on the Lena

In All the Russias this legion of crazed beings striving to escape self and the darkness of long winters; to escape life. Their means—castrations, voluntary deaths, and crazy worships. Here, incense rising to Napoleon, there, among the Christs (6) and Skopskys, women at once mutilated and adored. The brain of thinkers reeling in mad-making thoughts, some turning eastward away from the things of the west, some turning inward, in search of light.

From out the welter Talbot remembered the fine sad experience of the *Repentant Nobility*, remembered the young noblemen and women who, to expiate as they thought the sins of their parents towards the peasants, gave up all, stripped themselves of all. Many shut their books, left their schools and lived like peasants on the land, seeking to regain the virtue they felt was lost to the powerful, seeking to atone for their parents. Some, shattered and disillusioned, returned to the ancestral home and lived again according to their estate; others made expiation until death.

In his ghastly review he thought with a smile of the pretended illness of the Tungus women. In Yakutsk a doctor had told him that a woman may feign to be possessed, may speak in strange tongues, and then name, as cure, some object long desired. Rather than bear his wife's shrieks and her devil-sent mania the Tungus husband will travel countless versts to bring the ribbon or the garment asked for as cure by the frenzied woman.

One night the engineer went up to Talbot and begged him, in charity, to play something softly on his flute; and when the melody was over he told his tale to the Englishman.

Born in Perm, he remembered, as a lad, hearing one Chadkiur who of a sudden began to preach. His message was the choice between death and damnation. Life, he said, entails sin; sin entails hell; therefore they must choose death with heaven, rather than life with sin and damnation.

He remembered still the horrible days when his father, his elder brothers and all the men and boys of Perm dug galleries by the riverside. His mother, and his sisters, with the women of the hamlet, sewed shrouds. When the third such day had passed, they all went out clothed in shrouds, and in winding-sheets, and by the riverside they renounced the devil. Chadkiur adjured them to fast from food and from water, and he swore that on the twelfth day all of them would enter heaven.

The engineer remembered how, first, the children had cried out, and sucked the grass, and chewed their own arms, and the earth. Upon that the mothers had nearly repented of their folly. On such a night two men, unable longer to bear the horrible thing, had escaped and had taken him with them.

After that he remembered no more for many months, but he had been told what afterwards happened. His uncle and the other man had warned soldiers of the madness by the river, so they had marched there; but had arrived too late. Chadkiur grew frightened when death tarried, and when he discovered the escape of the two men he ordered that the children be massacred. This being done, the women persisted in their fast, and the men said: 'We will not fall into the hands of the servants of antichrist.' Death still delaying, the women then were killed with all the men; only Chadkiur and two others lived. These tried to escape, but were arrested by the soldiers, and exiled to perpetual penal servitude in the darkness of the Siberian mines.

Talbot's gorge rose at the story, the horror of it crowning his reflections. He was glad to go ashore,
and quit the boat when, on August
the thirteenth, the steamer
reached Yakutsk.

CHAPTER XIII

✶　　✶　　✶

YAKUTSK WAS HORRIBLE. TWO MURDERS WERE COMMIT-
ted on the day that the ship sailed in, and the cruelty rampant
in the town made a victim even of Sin. Talbot, driving from
the steamer, heard a howl. Some ruffian must have hurled a
stone at Sin. Some days later, "at midnight, Sin groaned fear-
fully, struggled to his legs, staggered to the door, then staggered
back to me, and died. I think he must have been in great agony
almost up to the end. I am much cut up, being so far away,
having no friends—Good-bye, dear old Sin. May we meet
again. . . ."

Often the loss of Sin is lamented: "Feeling lost and miserable
without my poor old Sin, in this strange country;" and, written
at night: "There is a barbarous man who is already asleep upstairs in the bedroom in which I am just going to sleep. He has
an awful big pistol. As I have over four thousand roubles on
me, it is nervous work; however, I am sleepy. Poor Sin."

Talbot stayed in Yakutsk for nine days. It was mid August.
One day he bought another dog, Nick, a pointer. "He was wild
as hell and thin as a scarecrow." There was the trouble too of
teaching him English.

With difficulty Talbot got his passport and letters of introduction for Verkhoyansk from the Governor. "All given on
condition that I return this way, remaining within his jurisdic-
tion. It is damnable to be so tied by the leg, but Russian auto-
cracy is phenomenally autocratic and bureaucratic."

A smotritel, a district police officer, sent a Cossack, Dmitri,
to be Talbot's servant. "He has the eyes of a coward," was Talbot's instant judgment, but as no other was offered he took this
man and gave him two months' wages in advance to buy
clothing.

On the twenty-first day of August they started by steamer

for Bulkur, which Talbot would use as a place of departure for other hunting grounds. Nick could just lie inside the cabin by leaving his tail or a foot through the chink under the door.

"*Wednesday*, 21 *August*, 1901: Did not sleep a wink. My African sores worry; caught a gigantic musk-bug. At eleven in the morning an enormous amount of cargo and luggage arrived, later came crowds of people and half a dozen priests. They went round with bottles and glasses in their hands; the drunkenness was astonishing; drunk, many of them seem better than sober. After the drunken people were coaxed or carried off—this took at least an hour—we started north. I hope this time to hunt more successfully. The proprietor of the ship told me I could stay at the Island of Agrafina where are bears. He would charge five pounds an hour."

There was on board a Diana, a fat huntress, the wife of a judge. She spoke French and called herself a great lady, "but the marked dexterity with which she uses her knife in place of a fork, besides other small things, makes me feel rather doubtful." Anyone who possessed a rifle was accounted a hunter; the fat lady therefore was regarded as such. She sat on deck, "watching for bears as if for tame sheep", but when later a bear hunt was proposed she was not of those that joined it.

There were students from Jigansk on board who spoke French and German, and who went on shore seeking rare plants and insects. A political exile was also on the ship; he was liked by Talbot. He had forty times more courage than anyone else, for of forty young men he alone went to beat the bushes for bears. 'We do not want to be hugged or chewed up,' the others said, and as Diana also evaded the chase, only Talbot, the Cossack, and the exile, went ashore on Agrafina. They found a hill from which to spy, and Talbot through his telescope could see over seven miles of country. 'My eyes are weak; I can see very little, for I was kept alone and in darkness for a year in a prison in Moscow,' the convict said. He went to sleep. Shivering, for it was early morning, Talbot watched hundreds of geese which stayed their flight, and fed close to him. But bears they did not see though there were many on the island.

Next day Talbot was awakened by the oopravliayooshchyi (captain), "almost crying with rage because my Cossack did not want to have his food with the sailors. The oopravliayooshchyi said he would send him back to Yakutsk; this has made a coolness between us." Five days later Talbot was awakened by his Cossack. 'May I put my knife into the oopravliayooshchyi, master?' he asked. "I said certainly not." The oopravliayooshchyi had refused to sell any food to Dmitri who, therefore, was hungry. "This captain has a most stentorian voice and is clever, but has no more blood in his heart than a flea."

The sailors had a bitter time on board although they were given much vodka to make them work. "There is not a single satisfied person on board." Often the river was rough and the boat bumped at anchor. She had half a verst of chain, and the screech of the windlass, pulling it up, filled the hours. The ship, being at anchor, the winch, for hours, would noisily pull up one anchor, and noisily let down another. "When there is nothing else to be done on board the winch is worked. . . . Two small barges that are towed after us are broken, so we are staying here all day, probably only to look at them, as it is impossible to set to work to mend them, that would be un-Russian." Next day Talbot wrote: "Neither of the boats mended, so left behind."

The pleasantest priest on board drank often. On a rough day he went ashore; he was so glad to get across the gangway that he crossed himself hurriedly several times over, and, pointing back with a bit of broken stick, he blessed everyone.

Nick was learning English, although but slowly. The fat lady also had a dog, hidden on board. It howled all day. The oopravliayooshchyi had forbidden her to bring it on board, but she brought it, and hid it, and every day she and the captain quarrelled about it. "I told her about Eskimo dogs, for in shape and colour the dogs here are exactly like them; I gave her an agate as a peace-offering." And that because, when she had shown him her rifle, which was "an old pipe with a broken piece of wood for a stock", he had laughed with surprise, which laugh had vexed her.

On the third day of September the ship reached Bulkur. Talbot, Nick, and the Cossack landed. The ship steamed off saluting the Englishman six times with the whistle.

"It is pleasant again to approach the far north. For me the

north has a fascination unexplainable. The profound quiet that reigns here spurs up my nerves a little, especially as some of the cut-throats on board may come back here with the steamer when she returns to take in wood. They are bound to know that I have much money on me. Queenchy and Anocky (the two Tunguses who were with me before) and my Cossack are in a hut—but half a mile off. A bad cough and heavy doses of quinine account for my fears. Nevertheless placing myself in voluntary exile gives me that peace which civilization and its currency do not hold for me."

CHAPTER XIV

⋆   ⋆   ⋆

THUS, HAVING SOUGHT BULKUR, TALBOT FOUND PEACE.
Three swans flew south. Talbot saw them before he crossed
the water from Bulkur on his way to the hills for sheep. "That
may augur early winter!" Queenchy was with him, and his
affrighted Cossack, Dmitri, a good servant but a coward, in
fear of the sea, in fear of the rifle, which he could not bear to
shoot, nor to hear shot. To spur him on to follow in dangerous
places, it was, at times, necessary for Talbot to use against him
this very weapon of his fearfulness. Dmitri dreaded the direct
ray of his master's eyes more than the wind or the water. So
was fear conquered by fear. From the boat they spied sheep and
landed; then, after a desperate climb, found that the sheep had
moved. Afterwards the men ventured down a precipice and
neared the creatures grazing. The wild sheep, ewes and lambs
quietly feeding, were close to them now. The hills rose behind
them, the sea stretched out before them; Talbot saw how beautiful this was. Titanic galleons seemed to ride the sea, for the
icebergs moved like ships, with sails outspread. Again Talbot
looked at the sheep.

For those who live in pasture-lands the word 'sheep' contains no image like to that which he saw. Instead of silly meadow sheep were long-legged beasts, of the Kamchatkan race,
their fleeces hidden by shaggy hair. Frighten the creatures, and
they bound off like deer; pursue them, and they leap like wild
goats, undaunted by the clefts that yawn before them. Defended
by their senses, no unfamiliar sound, or sight, escapes their quickness. No wonder Talbot, seeing them, was glad. The hunter in
him, the lover of beauty and of the far places, the lover of wild
beasts, these all rejoiced. He now shot for hunger; a ewe and a
young ram fell to him.

The night was comfortless, the tent covered with dry sand

that blew in. The next day the wind rose from the north and was so strong that Talbot twice was blown down. Nick was a pest: he chewed up the head of the ram; he dashed into the reindeer and scattered them; he spoiled a stalk on geese that were feeding near the sea.

Next day they sailed in Queenchy's fishing skiff. Suddenly the wind rose. The Cossack gave a yelp of extreme terror as he saw the rising waves. Later on, when in a calmer hour he caught a sterlet, the knave fell into an extravagance of delight that equalled his unruly fear. He skipped and waved his arms and called aloud with joy.

For many days Talbot hunted, camping on the delta, pitching his tent by the arctic, walking and rowing and climbing the hills. Whenever he could, the Cossack, because of his terror of the water, would rather tow the boat than row it. In the mountains he followed Talbot well, although hampered by the greatcoat he always wore. His hat was made of skins. Talbot again saw the cross, memorial to the men of the *Jeanette*. Here, so close to the arctic sea that at neap tide the waves might nearly touch it, Talbot found a forget-me-not. He stooped and picked the flower, and laid it in the leaves of his Shakespeare. The flower belonged rather to the Forest of Arden than to the Kingdom of Polarus, and had, with Talbot's flute, a sweet concordance lacking quite with the accursed boom of the shaman's drum.

Over him two ravens flew croaking. The reindeer hearing the birds took warning and fled. So for some weeks he lived hunting the wild sheep. He came upon a noble ram, stalked it for days, and killed it in the end. "I hardly thought to find you here," he wrote, for the ram was an *ovis poli* (7) of the great race of the *argali*. Its horns were deeply grooved; "in the hollow of a fallen horn could be cradled a babe, and the length of the horn is greater much than the length of a man's arm." He killed also other sheep, and they seemed akin to the *nivicula*. "But these are not *nivicula*, their ears are thicker and more hairy"—so he wrote in his diary, and hardly dared to hope that they were virgin spoil.

The delta of the Lena stretched nearly three hundred miles, and the winds blew high across it. Talbot found once on the sands a young goose exhausted by its battle against the wind. He found too a cygnet; its heart was broken with the strain of its long flight from the north.

When they got back to Bulkur the Tunguses were hunting wild geese for food because the fish had left that part of the river. Torgensen was working mightily, filling cartridges, and repairing old guns and rifles. He told Talbot long tales of man's vileness, and he, and the Cossack, spat and spat and spat again, in the little wooden hut. "I shall have to swim out" thought Talbot. Torgensen also told him that the Governor of Yakutsk had thought that Talbot was a spy, so had sent a messenger to Petersburg, and from there had been reassured. "What the devil is there to spy in this godforsaken country?"

Now on the hills was snow; the marmot donned its white habit, and "it is very weird to hear the flighting swans and geese calling. Hundreds of swans and geese going south." The frost set in. The waters of the river being very low, the Tunguses set to work in it. They pulled out large stones wherewith, next year, to weight their fishing nets. Talbot played on his flute the music of Chopin, and began to understand its message. Then suddenly: "Good morning, O snow!" The snow had fallen on the lowlands. It was the twentieth day of September. For the first time Talbot wore a Siberian hat of fur, and coat and gloves of fur.

Talbot faced two realities—One: "If I wanted to hurry back to England it would be impossible to get there before the middle of December." The other: "I am utterly unprovided with clothes for the winter, and if this early cold increases, I shall have to go straight to Bulun and get clothing. For when the full winter is set in I shall make another expedition to the arctic shooting and exploring."

Talbot missed his dog Sin. He wrote that travel like this needed much philosophy.

The prophecy of the three swans was fulfilled, for early the winter had come. How strangely the animal world made answer to the imperious winter that would drive the fish down into the depths of the Lena, and change the living water into a thing immovable as land. Winter, that would blot out the colour from the coats of the animals, from the plumage of the birds, that would add to them, awhile, a further dignity, a stranger beauty. Winter, that with its livery would ennoble the stoat, transfiguring it into the emblem of chastity. But this sudden winter wore the fearful likeness of an incubus—stretching itself along the earth, possessing it, whilst the earth seemed to echo the complaint of the captured witches who, from all time under the stress of torture, have confessed to the icy caresses, to the ghostly cold of their demon-lovers. So Talbot saw the arctic winter.

A few days later Talbot and Torgensen started to row and to walk to Bulun. They crossed a small frozen river: "It is exciting as we are never sure if we shall break through or not." A wicked steel-blue sky overhung their start, and clouds shaped like evil thoughts threatened them with storm; they heard a wolf howl to the dawn. Their talk turning upon wolves, Talbot laughed at the bookish tales of large packs of forest wolves hunting together. He himself had never seen above five wolves together. Torgensen agreed that a pack would be hard set to find food enough to suffice it. "I remember," mused Talbot, "the night when Atonguela the Eskimo saw passing near our snow-house six wolves together." 'The wolves of the prairies sometimes go in packs attacking herds of cattle, for, being more in danger of man than are the forest wolves, they travel together in greater numbers,' said Torgensen.

Some hours later the sun rose. Before reaching Bulun he wrote: "To-day we have walked forty miles and now eat bread and fish. All day we have had nothing to drink. I am nearly impervious to fatigue, hunger and thirst, but this life must be a great strain on the body." At night they slept in a tent, and for days they travelled. The sun of Africa had made Talbot vulnerable to the piercing winds and on the last day, "the sharp stones immovable in the frozen sand" hurt their feet.
But they reached Bulun.

CHAPTER XV

★   ★   ★

AT BULUN, IN A WOODEN HUT, NEAR TO THAT OF TOR-
gensen, Talbot stayed.

He was glad to have arrived. On the other side of the river,
fifteen versts away, lay Cusur, and there Talbot went to buy
clothing for the winter. He bought four reindeer skins, and a
coat made of skins. The wife of Torgensen lived there and
she gave him hospitality. As her sisters moved about the room,
bringing the vodka, preparing the zakuska, Talbot felt the pity
it was that the young women, fair-haired, blue-eyed, should be
spending themselves in this forlorn Cusur. They must look
covetously at their sister's man, so full of energy, so virile,
always endeavouring, always succeeding, even in this hard
country. A man fair of skin as they; the entire contrary of the
brooding exiles.

Torgensen, Talbot, Dmitri and two Tunguses now made
ready to return to Bulun. They faced the east wind and the
great waves. Other men, who had wished to cross, turned from
the river, and went back to Cusur. But Talbot, Torgensen and
their men boarded a boat, and rowed off. Dmitri, dissolved by
fear, moaned and would not pull. The squall struck savagely.
So much water had been shipped that it seemed the boat must
sink. The Cossack cried out in terror, and his fear overtaking
the Tunguses was almost their undoing. They seemed about to
abandon the oars.

Seeing there to be but one way whereby to save them all,
Talbot snatched a rowlock and beat the Cossack on the head;
Dmitri slipped down on to the floor-boards. The Tunguses,
shocked into renewed effort, pulled the boat with their whole
strength; soon the keel grounded on the bank. Dmitri groaned.
—"Glad he's not dead," said Talbot. This was the danger by
water which, with that other, sometimes in dreams and in
fever, afterwards shadowed Talbot.

207

From day to day in Bulun

The smotritel invited them the next day to celebrate his daughter's birthday and several guests toasted the infant born some months before. Failing church feasts, birthdays are created in Siberia that men may drink together. The snow fell, the wind blew, the Cossack tidied up the hut, and Nick bit a Tungus. "I am very pleased to see that he has so much spirit."

Next morning a note came from one Urganoff, bidding Talbot come to a feast in honour of his wife's birthday. Ham and tongue were served, and baked fish and game; cigarettes were smoked between the courses. The meal was long drawn out, and Talbot went back to his hut before it ended. As he neared his door he saw, standing before it, a pretty reindeer. 'It is food for you,' said the Tungus who was leading it. Dmitri nodded. Then the Tungus instantly killed it, never suspecting that the Englishman could dislike the deed.

Slowly, with tap of beating hail, with snow softly falling; slowly, came the winter. A man could not hunt in the treacherous yielding snow, and the river was not fit for boat or for sleigh; so, as before amongst the Eskimos, the hunter waited, imprisoned by the naissant winter. The volume of Shakespeare and the flute—these were Talbot's pastimes. For hours each day he practised flute music, passionately playing scales hundreds of times over till he nearly fainted from the effort. The Tunguses, amazed at the island giant, would come inside his hut and stand staring: "so now I make them hurry out quicker than they came in." He would tower up suddenly and walk straight at them, his eyes like blue flames.

In lighter moments he taught Nick some tricks, and he too learned from Nick. He wondered idly at the clothes hanging out in the street as though to dry. "Hardly think it is to air them, but how strange to dry them in the snow and hard frost." Nick grew fiercer, bit another Tungus, was useful now at keeping them at a distance. The people of Bulun were becoming anxious, because the ship from Yakutsk, due weeks ago, did not arrive. "I want her to come to get oil for my lamp." Most of the other men wanted her for the strong drinks that she would bring them.

Then Torgensen, with what vodka he had left, started to drink. He had five hundred roubles of Talbot's money and the police officer warned Talbot to get the money back from Torgensen; 'and I will set a man apart to guard your throat,' the officer added laconically. Torgensen was afraid of Talbot—which was well, for the Englishman stood alone. His shield and armour were as always the light of power in his eyes, his angers, and the quality in him that quelled men.

"In the mountains during winter it is dangerous to travel, but I am tired of this stuffy little room awaiting more reindeer skins for my clothing. As soon as I get clothes I shall risk everything and go," sighed Talbot. Life in Bulun weighed heavily upon him.

The sailing-boat came in from Yakutsk and the priest compelled the doctor, Talbot, and two others, to drink vodka from a tumbler—"no getting out of it." The day was a noisy one and his head ached, so, for quiet, Talbot went to his hut, but was disturbed by the visit of a woman who came with the doctor saying: 'I have reindeer that I will sell you cheaply.' "But I have promised to trade only with Torgensen." So she left.

The ice floated down the river and Nick must have his foolish part in that—he fell off a block into the river, but was saved by the priest. The diary tells of "men in gorgeous garments" who walked with Talbot; of gifts that he received; of a pipe made of fossil frog or of the talon of a bird.

Now the accursed Cossack took to drink; when he drank vodka a glass was not enough but a bottle must serve. He skipped about in the hut, and the next day, his temper growing worse, he flung open the door and rushed in roaring and swearing. A Tungus helped the Englishman, and the raging Cossack threw both himself and his belongings into the snow. The head of the police had him taken to another house and all Bulun was tense.

Returning to the hut Talbot wrote notes to his friends, some convicts, the smotritel, the doctor and the priest, inviting them to drink tea with him on the morrow. They came, and all went merrily till the ladies left—then there was uproar. Before coming, the doctor had been drinking; now, clumsily postured on the only big chair, he scolded and harangued. The other men with anger suddenly leapt to their feet. 'Everyone will go unless you fling out the doctor.' But Talbot, unable to understand the brawl, stood aside; then the smotritel and the priest left, and took the other guests with them, and Talbot was left alone with Torgensen and the doctor, who were swearing at one another. Angered at last, Talbot drove them out; the doctor as he left kissed Talbot's hands. For an hour noises of dispute continued outside, but Talbot went to bed. The Cossack, Dmitri, was still away.

Next day, Torgensen explained to Talbot that the doctor had named the guests most foully, and that if the smotritel had not seized and held the priest's uplifted arm, the 'pope' would have broken a glass over the doctor's face.

Towards dusk the doctor with disarming humility came, full of penitence, to visit Talbot. He said that he felt as though his head misfitted him, so swollen was it after the blows he had received outside Talbot's hut. He blamed only himself, and the drink that was a key to his vile temper.

A pair of fur socks was brought in finished, with a reindeer coat, and a cap of sealskin.

"It is beautiful to see the reindeer coming in drawing sledges. We are entirely shut in now though the ice is still floating and
several frosts are needed to make the river solid. It is
for a while impossible to travel with reindeer,
impossible to cross the river in the
boat." In his wooden hut in Bulun
Talbot undaunted saw—closing down upon him—
arctic winter.

CHAPTER XVI

★   ★   ★

THE MIDDLE OF OCTOBER, AND THE DAY VERY COLD, WHEN Talbot wrote in his diary that the village of Bulun was being cleansed, house by house. Tables and chairs were pushed through the doors into the street—"that the people in the house may have room the more freely to spit", was Talbot's first surmise. Then he saw the cleaning and scrubbing within, and learned that one of the greatest feasts of the year was drawing near, for on Sunday would be celebrated the Protection of the Virgin.

Beyond the house, the river was slowly freezing, but the ice still floated by in great blocks. Along the village street came many reindeer. The evening closed in whilst yet it was still only a few hours after noon. The doctor summoned the Englishman daily that he might instruct him in the skill of dominoes, and might himself listen to the wanderer's flute, and afterwards pour out the volume of his bile towards the dwellers of Bulun.

So passed the day, and the evening, and the next day was marked by hospitality. A man who had served in the Crimean War sent a messenger to Talbot with 'come to my house'. Talbot went and found "everyone there". Then tea was served and vodka, cold tongue, and macaroni, a roast goose with mincemeat, and a sweet excellent sauce made of strawberries. "What is the occasion of so much cheer?" he asked, and was told that it was the anniversary of the death of the wife of their host. Afterwards, behind four reindeer, Torgensen drove Talbot out of the village. Talbot enjoyed driving behind the gelded, greathorned reindeer, that, glad with bells, trotted along. The bells made a gleeful noise, but Talbot was interested in a queer crackling sound that came from the animals. Puzzled, he asked Torgensen what it was. He said that the noise was caused by the reindeer's knee-joints, foot-joints—who knows what? "Or perhaps by a click in the hooves?" said Talbot. 'Maybe,' answered Torgensen without interest. The sound was like no other and Talbot thought of it, always, as the refrain of that happy drive. The approach of winter had so long imprisoned him in the long street of Bulun that Talbot could have whistled, and sung with joy, to be free of it; to be moving.

The festal Sunday dawned. The sound of bells awakened Talbot who, from his hut, saw everyone going to church. The priest had written inviting him to the Mass but the message had not been delivered and, when later he knew this, Talbot was very angry.

Torgensen gave a midday meal to which all went, but the meat was tough. Talbot was still too angry to be glad. The smotritel that evening at supper entertained every man excepting the doctor; since his outbreak at Talbot's tea-drinking, he had been anathema. Dominoes were played, vodka was consumed and, the talk turning on priests, stories were told, and vouched for, and then—by further stories—were surpassed. 'Until to-day no priest at Bulun has preached for five months,' they agreed, and another told Talbot that every man visiting a priest is expected to buy a bottle of vodka from him at the cost of three or four roubles: 'for in Siberia too many of them are merchants rather than priests.' The village priest, insensible with drink, paid no heed to the talk.

The Monday and the Tuesday, after the feast, were red with blood. The village was a shambles; every Tungus had turned butcher. Along the street, close up to the houses, lay dead reindeer, and other beasts were dragged along and killed. "It is curious that the Russians do not mind the Tunguses slaughtering the animals outside their houses." This slaughter of the animals was because of a weakness in their knees that made them useless for carrying burdens; and also because there was so little food on that side of the river that every animal—not necessary to the village—must be destroyed.

It was at this season impossible to go over to Cusur, the richer town across the water. Food was scarce, and that because the season of fishing had not been favourable.

That Monday the village was very quiet, for the men were fuddled after the drinking of vodka on Sunday. The river, that in the morning had groaned and grumbled with the floating ice, was quiet now, for at last it was frozen. A little snow fell. The river had frozen slowly, so that the ice was rough and full of hummocks. It was not yet solid enough to be safe for a high road.

For many days Talbot had been plagued by his Cossack servant. Seven days ago, as he was drinking tea in the house of the smotritel, Dmitri had come in, his face so changed that he seemed another man. His eyes, and nose, and mouth were swollen with drink, his cheeks puffed up—his very voice was changed. The head of police had driven him out and had told Talbot, that for every day he spent drinking, he should be deprived of his wage. The smotritel gave a written order to strengthen his ruling. For several days Dmitri had not returned, but was heard of as consorting with women, and as buying vodka priced at five roubles a bottle.

Then, one day, he returned very penitent and Talbot said: "I will take you back to-morrow." Next day, his debauch having lasted eight days, he returned. His store of forty-two roubles was spent, he was in debt, and had besides forfeited eight days' wages.

That night when Talbot was in bed he heard a growl from Nick, felt a sharp pain above his heart, a wet mess on his hand. Then there was tumult in the hut. Dmitri and Nick were fighting. Talbot knew himself to have been stabbed. He saw the Cossack's knife upon the floor. Dmitri leaped about the room thrusting at space and crying: 'There are Tunguses and Yakuts in this room.' To cow the wretch Talbot shot into the air—because he was drunk the man did not deserve to die. Then he pushed past Dmitri and, with Nick at his heels, got out. Through a blinding snowstorm, and a gale so mighty that twice he was blown down, Talbot, amid the carcases of the reindeer, made his way to the house of Torgensen. The Swede stayed the blood of his flesh-wound. A little deeper, a little lower, and Talbot must have been killed. As it was the mark never left him. Later the two men went back to the hut where the Cossack was still searching for Tunguses. And now Dmitri rushed out, and tried, so afterwards they heard, to enter every house in Bulun.

After that night no one dared to sleep in his hut with Talbot

The devil into Talbot

—so he slept alone. Nor would they willingly enter to clean it
or to cook, for the Tunguses, who are the workers in Bulun,
said: 'The Cossack is locked up, but his devil has passed into
the Englishman and into his dog.' Even the Russian
women of Bulun believed the hut to be filled
with devils. They thought Talbot brave
to bolt his door and, alone with
Nick, to sleep in the
unholy hut.

CHAPTER XVII

* * *

THE LAST THREE WEEKS OF THE EXPLORER'S SOJOURN AT
Bulun were ill starred—a hurly-burly of trouble and bad temper. In vain the young Englishman, fleeing the world, had gone
where the temperature went often fifty degrees below zero—in
latitude seventy-one. Even here greed pursued him; tripped
him up; nauseated him.

He did not want to keep his money—no one ever set less
store upon wealth—but he was put out of joint by discovering
that Torgensen was a swindler. Torgensen took risks boldly,
"and worked like a horse" Talbot had liked him. They had
shared minutes of common danger, had enjoyed music together. But day by day a little was added to the evidence against
the Swede. 'Out of the money with which you entrusted
me I have paid this much for furs and that much to the Tunguses—also I have helped Dmitri.' Talbot found that the Tunguses had received only half of what was charged for their
wages; all the way down the accounts were false. All Torgensen's dealings had been tainted with fraud. 'If any man called
me a swine, I would kill him,' Torgensen boasted, and now to
Torgensen, stronger, taller, heavier than himself, Talbot said:
"You are a swine." The Swede paled, trembled, and left the
room. 'But now I will kill him,' Torgensen swore to everyone
he met. Talbot went about armed with a stick and a pistol.

Torgensen issued a statement against him, and Bulun was
divided between them. The doctor and the priest espoused
Talbot's cause; the smotritel remained lukewarm. He owed
Torgensen money. No one before had ever dared to oppose
Torgensen, though many of those that were in his power hated
the man. Talbot now made public his counter-statement, insisting upon the repayment of the money due to him by Torgensen, promising this money to the smotritel for the poor of
Bulun. Most of what was due finally was paid.

215

Fraud, wrath, darkness

The strain on Talbot's nerves was hard; his disappointment in Torgensen, and his own shattering anger, prevented him from eating or playing the flute. So sore was his anger that, as though it were a sickness, he must calm it with medicine.

Added to this was the madness of the Cossack Dmitri who had returned repentant. Talbot forgave him—drunkards he always forgave. But now the Cossack was again drinking. At night Talbot bolted his door against the inebriated fellow. When, at about ten o'clock of the morning the sun at last shone into his bedroom Talbot would wake, and light the fire, and melt the ice to make tea, but for four hours, or more, the room remained deadly cold.

How gloomy were the long dark hours! The Tungus people slept from four in the afternoon till late into the morning. Already, at half-past one in the afternoon the light of the lamp was needed. "How can I hope in three and a half hours of light to spy, stalk, and kill a beast?" Talbot wondered. Now in the darkness he understood the melancholia, the madness, the fear of devils that beset alike the Russians and the Boreans. Queenchy, son of a chief, for love of Talbot had left the winter care of his reindeer, and his winter hunting, and now, in the hour of Talbot's loneliness he arrived, smiling, at the hut of the Englishman. Encouraged by Queenchy the other Tunguses talked freely to Talbot, telling him of the devils that haunted their everyday lives.

'The fish, dead in our nets, have devils, and though with gifts of butter or of flesh left in the nets we pacify them, yet no woman with child may cross the river. We have so little, yet we must always be making offerings to devils,' they complained. With the people of the Tchuktchis also he spoke somehow, and knew them to be quite heathen, and riddled with fear of the shaman devil-priest. If a Tungus died in a hut it was instantly inhabited by the evil ones, and no man could any more make it his home.

Talbot wrote: "The last of the oxen was killed outside my door to-day. It is a pitiless way of living, at the same meal to eat the flesh, and to drink the milk of a cow just killed. But the people are hungry."

Nick at this time was the best thing in Talbot's days. A bag

216

of reindeer skins was given him, and each night he leaped into it gaily. He had learned to 'look after' his master, and at these words, given as an order, he would fly growling at any man.

One day Talbot hunted, riding in the deep snow on a reindeer. On that day he shot a wild sheep.

On nearly the last of his mornings at Bulun, he was wakened by the singing of a funeral procession going past his window; "and as I had been asked by the priest to go, I jumped up, threw my clothing on, and in the worst storm that I have ever seen here I went to the church. The ceremony was long. At the end of it, the priest kissed the dead man's forehead, and after that everyone came and did likewise. The coffin was then taken to the grave and holy oil was poured out over the winding sheet. Then the coffin was closed. Airgouroff, the dead man, had fought in the Crimean War."

The mail came in from Verkhoyansk, and when the ice was safe, and the wind had fallen, Talbot wrote: "I will give up hunting for the nonce, and I will go straight to Verkhoyansk." Dmitri, crumpled up in a corner of the hut, drank tea the while, and did not help him at all in his resolution.

It was always on the very day of departing that Talbot packed his things. Now, in the little daylight, was a wild rush. His friends came in to work with him. Talbot had hired sleighs from the priest, and from him had bought vodka. He bestowed a rifle, and cartridges, on the doctor in remembrance of their hours of dominoes, of flute and concertina. Someone gave Talbot a paper-cutter made from the ivory of a mammoth, and a fur-covering, of foxes' skins. The priest and the doctor crossed the Lena with him. Along the banks, in some places, the ice rose twice—and more—the height of a man.

'Safe journey,' said the doctor, and the priest blessed Talbot. The three men drank together for the last time. A godspeed to the Englishman; a "God stay with you" to the Russians who slowly, then, turned again towards Bulun.

Talbot gathered up the reins of the
deer and, glad to be moving,
he sped into the
night.

CHAPTER XVIII

*   *   *

A FEW THOUSAND VERSTS BEHIND TALBOT LAY THE border of the civilized; a thousand versts before him to the south-east lay his road to Verkhoyansk. By moonlight he parted from the Lena River that was subdued by ice.

The mounds of ice threw undefined shadows along the erstwhile waters; the shores loomed black through the veil of the night. The only sounds were the sigh of the wind over the broad surface of the ice and, on the moonlit snow, the crisp trot of the reindeer, carefully treading their way, and the grating of the sleigh on the uneven ice.

Talbot and his friends had taken a seemingly careless farewell of each other, but now he felt a pang. "For many pleasant hours these winter months enclosed, when the storm of arctic winter beat on the hamlet of Bulun." Between the Russian doctor and the Anglo-Saxon wanderer friendship had grown close. Yet the joy of independence sang in that solitary being. Sang in him too, the delight of the nomad—travelling alone over the earth. Such pleasure outweighed all the explorer's sentiment for any one person; or for any one place.

"We glided through the deep pine trees, keeping the undecided tenor of our way, then steeply down a pitch, where the reindeers' loose harness could not hold back the sleigh, the sudden rush dispersing wandering thoughts." Forty versts were covered in five hours of bitter cold. The cold brought to Talbot's mind confirmation of the doctor's conjecture that the passions of the Tunguses are frozen by the winter desolation, and that the Tungus is as a man in armour, encased body and mind by the steel of the wind, and the ice; his whole being made proof against life till he accepts, with equal calm, lust, starvation, darkness, and the rigours of the arctic.

On the way to Verkhoyansk

Talbot, in Petersburg, had—half jestingly—attributed to the painful winter cold some of the frenzied thinking of the Russians. "A man whose forehead aches after eating an ice-cream too fast cannot tackle a problem; and, in the same way, a man's thinking may be damaged by the ache of the winter cold."

The travellers reached a deserted 'povarnia' (8); that having been a house of evil. The Englishman could not rest, the bitter cold preventing. After five hours he woke the Tunguses. "We will go on again," he said. The head-man refused to go. Then Talbot pulled off the man's clothes "and the fellow was furious". In revenge, and that he might rest the longer, the head-man made a feint of two of the reindeer being lost. The delay was great, and the start tardy.

The day, bright and cruelly cold, saw them in a gorge following the course of a little river. Here was danger, for hot unexpected springs had broken through the surface. "Some care and a good deal more dash" carried them past the frail place. Though the way grew harder, the enduring reindeer kept up a steady trot. Then, having passed through the deep gorge, the travellers reached a more mountainous region. Snow barely covered the ground and, in the way of the sage beasts that nimbly avoided them, great boulders lay.

Now was a long succession of hills, with no vegetation—save a scanty lichen—no tracks of wolves, fox or hare, but only the small spoor of the ermine. They ascended the steep short hills; and having reached the top they rested the reindeer. The grateful beasts galloped downhill so fast that it seemed the sleighs must meet misadventure.

After some hours of semi-darkness, they came to a povarnia, and here one of the Tunguses lit a fire, whilst the other man freed the reindeer. Afterwards they ate, and drank. Covered by his furs, Talbot slept on a wooden bench. His nose being frozen, he awoke. The reindeer were fed. Three hours after midnight the wayfarers journeyed on; for five hours they had rested. Talbot, wrapped in a coat of bearskin, felt sick with the uneasy motion of the sleigh, the lack of sleep, and the smoke of the wood contributing.

Having travelled thus for four days, at a povarnia they came upon the post although it had started twelve hours before they had left Bulun. Going with it was the drunkard Dmitri. His friend, another Cossack, was in charge of the mail. They frowned heavily, and Talbot wished that his luck had been otherwise. Dmitri had had so much forgiven him that Talbot, versed in ungratefulness, knew that the Cossack would bear him a grudge. Talbot rested as well as he could, pistol in hand. "I dozed—a wretched night."

At this stantzia Talbot made a change of reindeer. His sixteen beasts had gone four hundred versts in four days. Up to the moment of changing they had sustained their gallant trot, though with difficulty.

East of them lay three hundred versts of travel. Most of the way was through a broad valley without sign of vegetation. In this wilderness they overtook the caravan of a merchant, with his family, and goods, more than a hundred and fifty reindeer served it. As the povarnia was entirely filled with the merchant's family, Talbot hurried to the next, forty versts farther on. He had drunk from the samovar and had eaten biscuits with the merchant, so that it was hard to go away again into the cold. The snow of the plateau was deep; the reindeer were tired; it seemed that they had lost their way. Talbot could spy no track, and the pace was now but a walk. For hours and hours they stumbled on; stupid with weariness. Suddenly a volume of sparks, belching out on the darkness, was for the travellers a glad sight. In the povarnia, which now they reached, were two Tunguses, who had made a fire, so that with the Cossacks, the Englishman, and the Tunguses, the hut was soon warm.

The next day, at a stantzia near by, they waited for fourteen hours whilst reindeer were sought, and driven in. The beasts were deer that had been tamed, and freed, not creatures wholly wild, and unused to men. During that delay a girl, with sick eyes, came to Talbot. He had, as ever, a medicine-case, and took from it a lotion, bathing and bandaging her eyes, so as to teach her to care for herself after he had gone. She would not wear the bandage over her eyes, but bound it instead round her forehead. Talbot reproached her sharply—but in vain. Then he slept, and woke to find the reindeer being driven into the yard.

On and on with the reindeer

At the corner of the stockade, like a ghastly decoy, was a reindeer leaning on the fence, frozen solid. A man, at the resting place, watered in the snow, then he sprang quickly aside, for, in a moment, a reindeer bounded forward to lick up the salt, and almost trampled him down. Now the men took lassoes to capture the deer in the stockade, and Talbot used the lasso as he had learnt to do in Wyoming. Catching the beasts by the horns he captured more than did the Tunguses, but they would not learn his way—theirs was to trip the reindeer with their lasso, and to catch the beast when it had fallen. During this business an old stag leaped on the roof of the stantzia, whence he looked down at the enslaving of his comrades. Verkhoyansk was now about two hundred and seventy versts distant.

For three days more they travelled, going sometimes through wastes of snow; sometimes through snow, falling fine as flour and warming the air; sometimes through staggering cold. Comforting moments were those when Talbot met Anocky with a returning post. His jolly face gave cheer on this cold journey. Kind also was someone's offering of a mammoth's skull, weighing half a ton; but the reindeer were tired, and Talbot therefore said "No."

Danger again from hot springs—this time in the River Temur, upon which they came at night. The two leading reindeer were up to their bellies in water before their speed was checked. Their light was "only stars, and the Aurora Borealis". The travellers turned back and went round by another way.

The last day's journey made the blood leap. The weather was mild, three ranges of hills had to be driven over. The reindeer galloped wildly in every direction. Talbot dropped his leader's reins, and the animals dashed along, until a tree, a sleigh, or a collision with another reindeer should stop the rush. Nick's mischance that night was to have one of his paws frozen, and Talbot suffered a hurt. With pleasure he had been driving two reindeer, rushing through small tracks in the woods, climbing steep pitches and shooting down them. The Tunguses in front stopped suddenly, and caused Talbot's beasts to fall back on him, their great horns bruising him. With an effort, somehow, they regained their stand, but Talbot was hurt.

221

The last days

There were several breakdowns, but the night's rest was reached without gross accident. It was shared with two Jews, two Yemshicks, and the two Cossacks, besides the faithful Tunguses. Next day — that was mid November—having covered about a thousand miles, Talbot reached Verkhoyansk, "the coldest town in the world".

CHAPTER XIX

★　　★　　★

HERE, AT LAST, WAS VERKHOYANSK, A PLACE SMALL
enough, but with a strangely different meaning to all those that
lived there. It stood, to the Yakuts, just for home and daily life,
with (as pleasure) dried horse-flesh, or flesh of colts fatted and
killed in their second year. To the Cossack soldiers, and police-
men, it was a place of duty, like any other, with vodka for
paradise. To the prisoners it was exile. They were given no
work; the mosquitos in the summer, the awful cold of winter,
were punishment enough. Since one of them, Serge D—, had
used a bullet as full stop to his nineteenth year, the convicts
were carefully watched, because self-murder was forbidden. To
Serge D—, however, Verkhoyansk had meant an end. The new
doctor and his wife saw the place as spelling a big salary from
the Crown, but he must remain there for seven years. For a
year Verkhoyansk had had no doctor, but it had not made
much odds, for the late Aesculapius had given himself over
wholly to vodka, a drink so engrossing that it left him no time
for the sick. Anyway, definitely to them all, Verkhoyansk was
the coldest place in the world, and for three weeks in the year
the sun was hidden.

To Talbot, Verkhoyansk at once meant comfort. He was
taken to a warm house kept by a Cossack. It was good to be in
the shelter of a place that did not rock on runners, or collide.
Good to eat even black bread when the daughter of the hut
sweetened it by her beauty. Good, above all, to rid himself of
the furs and to wash.

For four days he was warm, and clean, in Verkhoyansk. Bugs,
it is true, fell from the ceiling on to his bed, but he was given
powder to kill the insects. The friendly Governor lent him his
sleigh, drawn by the only horse used so far north in Siberia.

At this time the town boasted one blessing, its government
by the kindest ispravnik in Siberia. He was a little old Pole who

spoke no language but Russian, and had won the affection of
the prisoners, and of the Cossacks. The first time that Talbot
dined with him, he was entertained to such a vast zakuska that,
after an hour of eating plentifully of fish, and venison, and the
rest, he made as to go. 'But we are going to dine now,' said the
governor. Then followed a dinner of soup with chopped meat
in balls of dough, of fine young capercailzie with sweet carrot
sauce, and of dry compressed fruit. Even if the ispravnik spoke
too fast for Talbot to understand, they had a better understanding than language, in the hospitality, in the music of the
flute. Talbot, as a parting present, gave the Pole his precious
medicine-chest—a charity that might have been his undoing.

In Verkhoyansk he made a friend, one Martin, an exile.
The manner of their meeting was strange. 'In this town is a
political prisoner who knows English,' said the governor. 'He
reads and knows by heart long passages from your greatest
poet.' "From Shakespeare?" 'Yes.' Could it be that in Verkhoyansk was a fellow-worshipper of Shakespeare? Impulsively
Talbot went to his house. The first few minutes were dangerous, for after attempted greeting Martin flung out in Russian:
'You are no Englishman. You are a spy!' Talbot's hand
went up to strike the man. Then temper changed to sparkle
in his eyes, and his laughter pealed out—in a flash he had
understood. Martin, in exile, had taught himself English, but
had never heard it spoken. He could read the language, he had
learnt by heart long passages of verse, but when Talbot spoke
the prisoner could not understand, and Talbot, hearing Martin
speak, had asked himself: "What language is this?" All the
accents were wrong; the whole was a new tongue. Martin's
failure was a bitter sorrow to the exile; and he cried.

This exile would soon have served his sentence, but he did not
know if he would be free to return to Russia, and he was certain
that he would be forbidden to live in a big town, or in any
centre of industry. He was not unhappy, for he had in himself
some sources of pastime, also the governor was his friend. 'But
I have suffered. For two years I was in prison without speaking
to anyone; I nearly went mad,' he told Talbot.

Talbot wrote, when he left Siberia, that certainly he had
known men who were wrongly exiled, yet he felt that most of

the convicts that he had met were dangerous to their fellow-men; ill-balanced, or murderous. In spasms of misdirected energy they sought to bring about unconsidered reforms; if freed, they would but add menace to menace.

One night, when Talbot and Martin the exile were dining with the governor, a Cossack rushed into the house announcing that the town was ablaze. Going out into the night they saw that many of the wooden houses were on fire. The Cossack soldiers were drunk; they stood about shouting at the natives to bring water. Talbot seized a hatchet, and, regardless of the fire that scorched his hands and singed his hair, he hacked down a hut at each end of the fiery block so that the fire did not spread. This act was beyond the courage, beyond the thought of the besotted soldiers.

Talbot had wished to go east to Kamchatka, passing through Collinsk, but as Kamchatka lay out of the dominion of the ispravnik here in command, he could not obtain a passport. Before he was given the necessary passes to return to Yakutsk he had to give the ispravnik his word of honour that he would not try to push on farther east. 'I have heard of your journey in pursuit of the ship on the Lena, and of how you somehow got carriages although you have no road-pass,' laughed the genial Pole.

Soon after deciding to return to Yakutsk a starosta—that is the elder of a Yakutsk village—came into Verkhoyansk to announce a wandering bear some eighty versts away: 'We have long set traps for him, but he is old and cunning, and we cannot get him. He is so daring that he has attacked men and children,' the elder said: 'We know why the bear is so fierce. He has lost his mate, the she-bear. This male saw her entrapped. He knows that men were concerned in her death; he rages because he is lonely; because he is too old to fight for another mate; and he hates men because they caused his loneliness.' No man thereabouts ever shot bears, and the starosta was nearly frantic with fear and excitement when Talbot offered him money if he would guide him to his lair. He consented, and Martin, the exile, said he also would go. With the hope of hunting the great bear Talbot found pleasure—rare enough to his north-loving soul—in writing: "I am now going south."

For the last time the governor, Martin, Talbot, and some

others supped together, Talbot was given strange gifts, a
tapestry made of reindeer fur, and ornaments formed out of the
ivory of mammoths. The talk turned on mammoths. One man
asked: 'Why should Siberia so abundantly have mothered these
monsters?' Another reminded them that parts of western Europe also had borne them.

'Were they creatures that, in a glacial age, could have lived
on lichens?' asked the governor.

'No, they would need more food than, in a cold age, would
be met with.'

'Their remains are found entombed in ice, but that may only
prove that the glacial age fell suddenly upon the earth, killing,
and conserving the mammoths.'

"Then why the thick, brown-red, woolly fur with the long
black hair intermixed? Such a pelt surely showed them to be
arctic, a proof that they lived in great cold?" This view Talbot
now expounded, having often seen how little is yet enough
for beasts to live upon. "In barren lands the musk-ox, and caribou, in great nature's little bands eat only the mosses below the
snow and ice, and desert camels find, in thorny scrub, enough
to feed them," he added. "The glacial age may well have been
hospitable enough to sustain the great creatures."

The talk was broken by the entry of "a merchant from Collinsk who came in with a filthy shirt and the latest news from
there—that of a murder."

Next day Talbot packed the sleighs and, with two Cossacks,
made ready to go. The governor gave as speedwell a bottle of
sherry, and a bottle of brandy.

Martin had wished to follow the hunter, and the governor
had lent him a rifle, but now irresolution shook the exile. Why
after all go on this mad trail? The ispravnik mocked him into
going, and the party set out. They journeyed eighty-five versts,
and arrived at the house of the starosta to find that the brandy
was frozen in the bottle, but that supper in Yakut style, and
warm rest, awaited them. "These grand silent places are a
fitting home for the solitary bear, and the effort
to reach him has dignified the hunt. To-day
has been a long preparation for the
endeavour."

226

CHAPTER XX

* * *

THE REINDEER OF THE STAROSTA HAD WANDERED AWAY, so a day was spent awaiting the men who had gone out to find them; the light of the day lasted but for two hours. 'When you are hunting the bear do not use the reindeer of the post, because I am responsible for their welfare, and they should be used only for purposes of the State,' the governor of Verkhoyansk had said, so perforce Talbot and Martin waited through the day. Early next morning away they started with three sleighs, whilst behind them, on his horned beast, rode the brother of the starosta.

Soon they entered a forest of pine trees and saw there reindeer, statant with curiosity. Deftly the two Yakut brothers caught a pair and, freeing the smaller beasts that were harnessed to Talbot's sleigh, they gave him the stronger ones.

Nevertheless the day was ill fated. No path was in the forest, and the reindeer caught themselves in the trees; were disentangled; galloped forward wildly after those in front of them, only to be jerked to a standstill by the sleighs becoming wedged between the tree-stumps. Harness and sleighs in turn were broken. The four men had but one knife between them, and the repairs were slow.

Darkness fell, the stars shone, there rose half a moon. The stillness was that of a frozen sleep stirred, now and again, by the crash of a sleigh into a pine tree, whereupon a silver shower of snow would fall from the branches. Often, along the narrow ledges that overhung deep ravines, the animals had to be guided. In steep gullies the sleighs ran on to the hocks of the plunging reindeer, and the drivers again must help the frenzied creatures. Thus for ten hours they travelled. In those ten hours they covered twenty miles.

The Yakuts all this way had never for a moment missed their

direction. Without a path, in the half-light, they went forward, not hesitating. At last the forest was crossed. The reindeer were rested for a quarter of an hour; then for a few miles they sped along a smooth, level, valley until a hamlet was reached, and the reindeer were halted before the wooden house of the starosta and his Yakut servants, who came out, and carried the beds and food into the hut, laying them on wooden ledges where later the travellers would sleep.

Soon, by the leaping fire, meat was fried and bread was thawed, whilst the ice in the kettle was melted. To the hungry men the smell of cocoa and of reindeer meat was a sweet odour. Within an hour of having eaten they were asleep in their furs, lying on the wooden ledges. Then Talbot dreamt of lands where nature was more tender than in Siberia.

There was no door to the povarnia—a bullock-hide flapped instead in the entrance space—so the men woke up chilled. The Yakut went out to catch the reindeer, whilst the hunters ate as best they might. Then they boarded the sleighs to travel sixteen versts to the haunt of the bear. A motley party it was, armed with flint-lock rifles, "and the livers of the Yakuts grew white as they neared the place of the bear." As for Talbot, the whole man was intent on his purpose, and he was stripped of every other thought, or feeling, his whole self summed up in the being of a hunter.

CHAPTER XXI

★　　★　　★

AT THE EDGE OF THE FOREST THE MEN TIED UP THE REIN-deer. "No one must go near the den unless I order him to do so," Talbot said. The Yakuts assented, indeed the very wealth of Solomon would not have tempted them to the place where the bear was sleeping. The Yakut is neither a nomad nor a hunter, but he is of those that fear.

Nick the dog was left with Martin the exile. "Let him off the leash when I whistle," said Talbot. The dwelling of the bear had been pointed out to Talbot, and now he went to look at it.

"The bear's winter abode was in a small mound, heavily wooded at the back, but in front, and to the east and west lay an open space of about twenty yards. I went up and shouted "medvied!" (bear) to no purpose; all was still as before. Having shouted several times without result, I called for my dog Nick, and picking him up I put him in the den. He gave two or three sniffs, but not liking the smell he walked off and tried to make himself comfortable on a little moss a few yards away. Now the natives had told me that this was a wandering bear, more savage, therefore, than most of the bears. I began to think that the beast had gone from here. My fears were soon set at rest. Going to the top of the mound I traced his clear spoor, nearly fresh. He had gone into the den, no newer spoor showed as coming from the den. I wanted to take counsel with Martin. I called him and he came. None of the Yakuts would have dared so closely to approach the den. "We need a long pole," I said, and when this had been fetched I told the Russian to thrust it into the hole with all his strength. I stood at the entrance, my rifle ready at my shoulder. After a third push, came three low growls at which Martin dropped, not only the pole but his rifle too. He hurried to a safer place. When he saw that the bear did not come out, he asked me for his rifle, which I picked up

229

and gave him. Again we consulted together. "The only way to move the sullen brute is to smoke him out," I said. I told the Yakuts to make a fire opposite the den, but this they refused to do. "Make one a hundred yards away and I will carry it to the cave." They obeyed, and Martin and I carried the burning faggots up to the mouth of the den, and putting moss on it a scarf of smoke drifted into the hole. This aroused the bear, and savagely seizing in his mouth one or two of the burning brands he strode out, rising on his hind legs. Then he dropped the brands and ground his teeth with rage. In his fury he was magnificent."

Then, to the hunter, the beast must have seemed bullet proof, for though he hit the bear twice in vital places, it did not fall. The bear was now towering up above Talbot who, kneeling, sent a third bullet up through its jaw into its brain. Towering, taller than a man, the beast swayed. Then it fell, mightily (9).

The Yakuts came up, each man in his turn telling of what had befallen when he, and he, had shot a bear. Strange that none of them had told any such tales on the long night before the hunt. The starosta smiled and was silent. He always had said that he and his men stood in great fear of bears, and that they never tried to kill any save with traps.

Now from the sleigh they fetched a bottle of brandy, and by sitting on it thawed it, and then toasted: 'Good health—*Vashe Zdorovie!*'

Afterwards, putting the bear upon one of the sleighs, they returned to where the other sleighs had been left. Martin, seeing that all was nearing readiness, now wandered away, and when the reindeer were harnessed he could not be found. Having called, but heard no answer, Talbot sent a Yakut mounted on a reindeer to seek him. A quarter of an hour later the man came back, saying: 'I cannot find him.' Talbot sent three more men "to bring Martin back, alive or dead," for he remembered the suicide of the convict boy Serge D—. It being very cold the hunter returned to the povarnia, and prepared a meal. Half an hour after that Martin came in saying: 'I lost my way.' Seven men had made a track from the bear's den to the caravan, so that to have lost his way was strange.

Now came the moment of farewell between the two men.

The praise of the children

Talbot felt emotion because Martin had been a good companion and had helped to drive the bear from its den. Martin turned towards Verkhoyansk, and Talbot towards the house of the head-man, the track that was longer, but supposedly better, than the one they had followed the day before. Longer it was, and only a very little better than the other.

A strange procession moved away from the povarnia towards the house of the starosta. In front a young Yakut, without bridle, or harness, rode on a reindeer. The starosta followed in a sleigh, he sat on Talbot's cooking pans and blankets. Last of all, driving his reindeer, and balanced on the body of the huge bear, came Talbot. The men had put the carcase on to the sleigh without having gralloched it, and now, by its blood, the bear was frozen solidly to the sleigh. The strange caravan struggled through the dense forest! Here and there starlight and moonlight cast long shadows through the trees. Now and again, the northern lights glimmered.

Four hours after midnight, the men reached the house of the starosta, whose people, kind and attentive, fed and warmed the hunter. Hospitable was the Yakut, hospitable perhaps as the Tungus—but with a difference. Food, drink, and warmth bountifully were bestowed, but the Yakut wife was withheld. Even, it was said, like Rose of Lima, she wore a belt of chastity. In a Tungus home the hunter would—willy nilly—have found the housewife in his bed—a part of the host's entertainment.

Thereafter, in the long hours of the winter darkness, the Yakuts told heroic tales of Talbot. No one that they knew had ever before shot a bear. Long afterwards, the children in the houses near the forest praised God, each night before they fell asleep, because a blue-eyed man from a far country had rid them of the terror of the lonely, wandering bear.

CHAPTER XXII

*   *   *

AFTER LEAVING THE HOUSE OF THE STAROSTA, FOUR DAYS, overlapping into night, were passed in almost incessant travel, with brief rests of four or five hours. At the povarnias, distant from each other some thirty versts, the reindeer were changed. The beasts were fat, and in fettle to travel. When the snow was soft they made great bounds forward. On the hard snow they kept uneven gait; their strength was great. The Tunguses said: 'They can be bogged up to their antlers and then escape. The reindeer fear jumping and would rather creep under a bough than leap over it, but on this soft snow they must leap to cover the ground.' They needed strength even to come by their food when they were freed from the sleighs, because with their forefeet they must paw in the snow to uncover the buried mosses.

Often the Tunguses talked of the beasts that they drove; Talbot encouraged them to do so. He learned of the provision made for their eyes against the glare of the snow. The men, in the spring sunshine, might be blinded with the glare if they left their delicate eyes too long unshielded by net of reindeer-hair. But the reindeer were endowed with a third eyelid, a filmy guardian shield that could be raised across the eye like the third lid of a bird. This saved the beasts from blindness.

Soon after leaving the starosta they travelled through the country of the Lamont people, and the povarnias were so dirty and so cold that often the Englishman pushed past them or rested briefly four or five hours at most. In these four days Talbot put behind him four hundred and ten versts.

One night he found two Russian exiles, evil-looking fellows, seeking escape. 'We are hungry,' they said, and Talbot gave them food. In a spasm of self-pity they told him that they were Christs, or Khlystys, that is they belonged to the heresy of the Flagellants, who seek so great a purity that they account marriage to be a sully. For a Christ must not be bound to any other creature, neither to a home, nor to children. But lest, with perfection, they should grow spiritually proud, they commit sin so that they may be humbled. To this end they practise rituals seared with abominations, and debauch themselves in the name of the High God. There had been, in old times, Talbot remembered, priests who, disobedient to Rome, had persisted in seeking the occasions of sin. 'Our virtue is without merit unless it be proved by temptation,' they had said. Talbot, as he drove from the inn, mused upon these strange wrong thoughts.

Talbot could not keep warm; more than once his nose was frozen. How did he tend the frostbite? No mention is made in the Siberian record of whether he put snow upon it, or whether his servant, by the warmth of his hand, restored the heat, as in Barren Lands the Eskimo women, beneath their breasts, had restored the blood to his hands. He may, whenever he could do so, have bathed the place in cold water which afterwards would show a thin film of ice; ice drawn out of his very flesh. Once he had somewhere seen a youth come into the camp with hands destroyed by gangrene—'he warmed his frostbitten hands at a fire' an old man had said. He had seen, too, another boy, breathing still, but whose feet were frozen, hard and white as marble.

Talbot pitied the exhausted reindeer, struggling along to the stantzias, the second stage that day being fifty versts. There, for six hours, they waited for fresh reindeer, and "in the meantime the yearly post to Verkhoyansk, Collinsk and Oceansk arrived".

The travellers risked being drowned when crossing the River Yarra, because the waters were not hard frozen. The harnessed deer, plunging into unexpected water, had to be whipped up; they barely struggled to the shore. They got through; excited, but safe. Of all deer, the reindeer are the strongest swimmers, buoyed up by air entangled in their pelts.

On the third day they neared the hills, and on the fourth were in the Krebiart Mountains. In the full moon, Talbot saw with joy the magnificence of the heights, and wondered at the prodigal beauty that was piled up where so few could see the glory. And of those few, perhaps not one that would perceive the loveliness. For to the Lamont people the mountains are places where the wild sheep live; to exiles, fleeing in escape, they are but types of hell. "Yet"—his body reminded him—"who could envy me my Siberian beauty? Bumped over boulders, too cold to light a pipe."

On the fifth day raged a hurricane, so Talbot waited at the povarnia, and bought an old silver belt, and a silver cross. Because of smoke and dirt, he coughed all day, whilst a babe cried, and the wind roared. By dint of anger he succeeded in getting water heated, for after such a journey an Englishman must wash. Troublesome though, to have to summon up wrath, but that alone could stir the solid Lamont apathy. Darkness, and poverty, heavily riding the people, only the flare of angry northern eyes could shock such brooding into action. He played the flute in that wilderness and, without speaking, the women got up from the bench, danced a little alone; and silently sat down again. Talbot thought anew of the shaman dance, the Christ dance of fornication, and the mute Siberian dances of the povarnias. On the third day, the storm having abated, he and the Lamont, and the Lamont's dog, went forth.

Stars and the moon lit the mountains that towered up, four or five thousand feet of sheer white height. Before the day broke the men had already gone far, and they wandered spying, and again spying; they saw many spoor but no sheep. Then looking up, set high like a constellation—almost it seemed as out of reach as Aries—they saw a great ram; dark-pelted, magnificent. In the deep snow, stalking they ascended. Talbot, the better to breathe, had his mouth open, but more than once he feared that his tongue was frozen. When they reached the summit they were very near the sheep, but not close enough to shoot. 'May I slip the dog?' whispered the Lamont, and Talbot, hardly understanding him, assented. The dog, sniffing a little, neared the sheep. At the same instant the two creatures saw each other. To the very edge of the precipice the great sheep was bayed; and now it was nearer to the men. Hoping that it would fall dead where it stood, and would not roll down the precipice, Talbot shot. It was standing so close to the edge that it fell over—many hundreds of feet down. Talbot descended into the gulf; he found its beauty not destroyed, the generous horns unbroken. Storms and heights had guarded it; the over-coming of them was its price. He, so long a hunter, knew this to be his great prize, worthy to be given to England. It was of a new kind which would, he hoped, bear his name.

"To-day is my thirty-third birthday." He looked gaily back on his years and knew—that having wrought with the hardships of the world and having seen its narrow ways—he would carry pastime always in his thoughts.

Face to face with his completed year, Talbot, half guessing, understood, that because wonder had been the keystone of his life, he had fulfilled a measure of man's destiny.

He was full of wonder: at man; at strange places; at beauty hidden, unknown, and remote; wonder goaded him on through the earth, regardless of his body. Of that quality—vision of the saint—word of the poet; and, by its power, is straitened the explorer that cannot take, from another, the tale of the earth's grandeur, but must, himself, go forth, marvelling at the un-known.

Talbot had killed the ram (10); now he paused a little to won-der at it. To wonder at its strength, its form, the grand decora-tion of its horns; to wonder at the great strength of those hollow unbroken horns. To feel glad that the beauty of the ram had doubly existed—once in the mind of God, and once in the mind of a man. Its death had followed swiftly on the recog-nition of its beauty, had indeed been caused by it; but the creature had been thought beautiful. Such meditations went dancing through his mind. For a moment more he stooped over the ram. Then he got up, and made ready to return to the hut.

CHAPTER XXIII

★　　★　　★

A FEW NIGHTS LATER THE MOON HAD WANED; ONLY THE stars lit the travellers—stars and the snowlight; for the soft reflected radiance of stars on snow made a twilight. Talbot went on towards Yakutsk. 'The way is too rough and steep,' said the Lamonts, after they had been thrown more than once from the sleighs. 'We must walk.' Talbot held the ropes tied on to the sleigh, and up they went, stopping often for breath. He dared not look down the giddy heights. Awful was the ascent. He wrote: "As far as I could discern in the dim light we left the valley, wide perhaps by half a verst, and ascended high mountains. I stopped sometimes to take breath, and saw the two Lamont drivers standing weirdly among the reindeer sheer above me. I was reminded of old pictures, of prints of people in wrong perspective. A little over half an hour saw us safely at the top on a narrow passage between two peaks. After a rest the sleighs were tied together, three of them in front and two behind and the reindeer were hitched all round but not in front."

Off galloped the reindeer. Talbot and a Lamont sat merely on the slope, let themselves go and so slid down the first incline. To overcome the second slope they got on the sleigh. Again the animals were urged downwards. The flight was tremendous, the ensuing medley at the bottom of the hill makes description halt; the reindeer sat in the sleighs, men, deer and harness—intermixed. Somehow the mess was straightened out again. The whole of the front part of Talbot's sleigh had been pulled away by the reindeer and he left in the snow. A Lamont put him on another sleigh; they reached a povarnia; freed the reindeer; and went in.

Next day the men travelled along the bend of the river, the mountains called Verkhoyansk towered above them. Talbot walked a little then, stopping, saw in a hollow in the snow a sleeping marmot. The golden-red of its fur had turned to grey and white, flecked with black. Not now could be lavished on it the summer wonder of those Russian travellers, who, discovering a marmot, praised it, saying that from a little way off its pelt looked like the several-coloured plumage of a bird. This small, imprudent marmot had been overtaken with sleep ere it had dug itself deeply into the snow. Looking down at it Talbot thought how strange is the protection of the winter sleep which puts upon the creatures a half-suspended life; like the life of the trees in winter. Strange this slow pulse of the heart, this cooling of the blood. The marmot was almost as cold as the snow. Strange the winter immunity that protects the sleepers, so that accidents, which in their waking state would be mortal, can befall them without stopping the slow gait of their hearts. "How small the marmot is," thought Talbot, and because it seemed to him different to others he had seen, he gave it, though loth, to a Lamont to kill: "I will take its skin to England, for this marmot may be of a kind unknown." Indeed the marmot differed from all other known kinds; so that afterwards it was given his name (11).

Talbot had taken upon him the burden of the mails from Verkhoyansk. "My reindeer are better than those of the post and we will hasten," he said. Hasten he did, till suddenly he fell ill and had to be carried back to the stantzia, where he broke into a sweat—and the pain passed. "Half an hour later I started again, feeling very ill. As it was night I could not see the mountains to say good-bye to them."

When in daylight he again scanned the country, the mountains had been left behind—instead, forest trees surrounded the travellers. The next evening Talbot, his senses sharpened by hunger, smelt a strange smell: "Hullo, that reminds me of a stable!" When, having gone some way farther, he reached the stopping place, he found that here indeed were horses. Next day he patted good-bye to the reindeer, and travelled on with the ponies. He was now in Yakut country. The resting-places here had more of comfort than those of the Lamont country, but the Yakut peasants robbed him as the poorer stranger people had not done. In the hamlets, crowds

Bear and sheep

peered and whispered at him—because he was the killer of a
bear. They jostled each other to see the beast, and to see
the great sheep. Having travelled a thousand
miles, having travelled for half a
month, Talbot thus, with chequered passage, reached
Yakutsk.

CHAPTER XXIV

★　　★　　★

TALBOT WAS SO OTHERGATES THAN STILL PEOPLE that some part of what he wrote reads like the tale of a man from a far planet. 'The man from the Stars', as the Eskimos had called him.

At Yakutsk in mid December he fell ill. The Governor of Yakutsk sent a messenger to Irkutsk with the news that he was likely to die of double pneumonia. From there to Petersburg, and from Petersburg to Lytham, the news was telegraphed, and therefore John Green was sent to Irkutsk to meet him. Yet his diary was written each day, and at the top of the pages was noted his temperature taken by himself, 103°, 104°, and back to 103°, and after some days of agony the chance remark: "Did not spit much blood to-day." On the ninth day he was up and playing the flute. On the tenth day he dined out.

Before he fell ill, all Yakutsk was magnifying the Feast of the Holy Innocents; day oddly beloved in this settlement of convicts. The chief spy left his card on Talbot, and there were the usual invitations from the governor, the colonel of the guard, and the captain of police. The guests at the dinners were—for the most part—convicts. At the governor's dinner a vast zakuska lasting for three hours was given. Raw sterlet followed, and sucking pig, and other great dishes. The dinner ended with toasts and with songs. To Talbot "it was good to hear again the frou-frou of women's dresses." Among the twenty guests was one woman who spoke English, and a man who the year before had been chewed by a bear. Another was a convict who had been a doctor. He and his wife languished in Yakutsk, but no hint of why he was thus exiled ever reached Talbot's ears. A great reserve always encompassed that subject. The banquet given by the captain of police was a little barbaric, for all the men supped in one room, and the ladies in another. 'Verest-

239

chagin is dead and Verestchagin was our greatest painter, the next greatest is Rapin,' was the theme of the conversation.

All were kind, but he who entertained Talbot as never before he had been entertained was a convict named Alliani. When the Englishman arrived at Yakutsk, this Russian accompanied him to a real Russian bath, a great wooden tub full of very hot water. 'My grandfather is going to share the bath with you,' Alliani said, but the old man did not arrive. When Talbot prepared to pay for the delight that he had enjoyed, he was told that it had already been paid for.

The Englishman was given a sitting-room for bedroom, and here, of a sudden, he was stricken. He lay in a room gay with wild-sheep's heads, musk-deer skins, reindeer harness and a mammoth tusk. A spear, a gun, a cartridge bag, and a northern diver (half stuffed), decorated the walls. Alliani, seeing him ill, stayed with him day and night, easing his pain by gently rubbing him over with oil, and by laying wet rags on his chest. To the gentle constant friction of the palm of Alliani's hand, Talbot afterwards attributed his life. Alliani made the room as comfortable as could be, and slept on the floor beside him, but he slept so soundly that Talbot's handbell did not wake him. But Nasha, a Yakut maid from below, would hear it and come. A year-old babe cried in the neighbouring room. To this was added the doctor's annoying feat of procuring, with difficulty, a nurse for Talbot. "A woman with eyes like a cat to whom I showed much temper." Medicine bottles half deliriously thrown at her caused her to leave. On the third day of his great fever Talbot recorded: "I found it hard to walk across the room." The Yakut housewife could only make soup, boil meat, and cook some kind of rice pudding.

Then came a saint's feast-day. The Yakut people in holiday dress entered his room, to parade before the slayer of a bear. The women came with long chains of silver falling from their head-dresses of fur, and with silver on their coats of fur and scarlet.

"They arrived at eleven in the morning and sat in the chief room where I lay, playing cards till eleven at night." The pillows that Talbot had bought they plagued him to lend them, for pillows were rare and would add to their entertainment.

ALLIANI AND TALBOT

IN YAKUTSK, 1901

The loosened tongue of Alliani

The mistress of the house now joined her lamentations to the continual crying of her child, because she suffered from an abscess that she would not let the doctor lance. Hoping to soothe her pain, her husband put a petroleum compress on her face. A few days hence he was to be ordained priest. "He is quiet and innocent, but is a superstitious and ignorant man."

Saturday came, and Talbot was turned out of the chief room to pass a sleepless night in the smaller one next to it. He drank a bottle full of bromide but still he could not sleep. It seemed to him that the walls were moving. In the morning Alliani came and saw that the bed had bugs. He put a candle in a corner of the room and twelve bugs dropped into the flame. 'No, you are not mad to think that the walls are moving, for they do ripple, curtained with insects,' Alliani said.

Next day the landlord, twenty years old, was ordained by the bishop, who came attended by six priests. Later the bishop went in and talked to Talbot whilst a girl stood staring down on him because he was ill, and the slayer of a bear. After the bishop left, the company drank vodka and, till two o'clock in the afternoon, no one went near Talbot or brought him food. Then he raised his voice and they rushed to him with food because they feared that all the guests might leave; for the anger of Talbot was known. The day finished with charades and puzzles.

Then Alliani put the Englishman back into the sitting-room. Alliani was in despair. And that, because of some evil news he had received out of Russia. Grief unloosening his tongue, he told Talbot "terrible stories of revenge and betrayal". In this hour Alliani gloated over the scarlet revenge that some of the convicts in Siberia had taken upon their guards. 'With my anger at being a convict I fanned the flames of their crimes,' he said. Also he told Talbot of the vengeance he was planning upon his brother in Russia, whenever he should be free to return there. 'I nearly killed him, but he still has life whilst I am here,' said Alliani.

Talbot, though not squeamish, could only shudder and hope that Alliani spoke in excitement, and not in truth.

After that day Talbot took morphia, but the wooden clappers of the watchman woke him, and he found that he had a new anguish. "I could not turn my head or move my right arm, and in Verkhoyansk I had given away my medicine-chest. How I am to do two thousand seven hundred versts to Irkutsk in my present state of health rather puzzles me."

CHAPTER XXV

★   ★   ★

"FROM THE SOUTH, DE WINDT, AND FROM COLLINSK, Professor Hertz are coming." That was the news—but neither arrived. As among the Eskimos, in the snow-house, he had hung his fur boot, as in Africa a sock, as in Lytham years before a stocking, so when came Christmas Eve in Yakutsk, Talbot hung up, behind his pillow, a boot of reindeer leather. He himself put in some trifle, so as not next day to feel it empty.

Then on his Christmas Day—the Russian feast fell thirteen days later—Talbot gave a supper. Such a supper as never before, nor since, in any place, or time, has been given. The soup was made from the great bear that Talbot had killed; and the paws of the bear (12) were served (for they are like jelly and are accounted a dainty). 'All the winter they subsist on their paws, sucking them,' said one guest. Another gainsaid this: 'The bear sleeps in winter, he needs no food.' 'But the she-bear in the winter gives birth to her cubs, and she must need sustenance,' took up another. "How curious to awake and behold her young!" mused Talbot.

The roasted meat was the wild sheep to be called Cliftoni. In spite of its great fall down the precipice it was good. As a gift Professor Hertz had sent some of the flesh of the mammoth that he had found. They ate it thoughtfully, for was it not about eight thousand years old? There were also young capercailzie brought by Talbot from Verkhoyansk, and the plum-pudding was as odd as the rest of the dinner, for it was of Talbot's own making, and from a receipt he but half remembered. 'For this banquet we need wine of Pompeii,' said one of the guests, but instead they made merry on vodka and brandy. All were glad; all excepting the dog Nick, which had been hurt in a fight.

Professor Hertz arrived before Talbot left, and he filled Yakutsk with his quarrels and his exuberance. He embraced the men, and sometimes too the colonel's pretty wife. With great

243

joy he saw Talbot's sheep, and realized that it was of a kind hitherto unknown. With joy he knew that Talbot would write, to the English papers, news of the discovery of the mammoth.

Inebriated by a like passion for nature these men measured and marvelled together. The following words are their paean to the mammoth:

"This mammoth was found by the River Barazoffka. It must have lain there eight thousand years. It fell down a steep place and broke its neck—we traced the break. Some of the hair of its back had been scraped away by ice and the wolves, or the bears had eaten a little of the flesh. Otherwise it was perfect and entire. Its mane was from four to five inches long, and the beast was clothed with under and with outer hair. The under close woolly covering is dirty yellow, thirty centimetres long, and the coarser outer hair red-brown in colour is six centimetres longer, but the ends are mostly broken. On its tail it has long black strong hair like an elephant's—indeed the mammoth was a kind of elephant. It is about the size of an African elephant, but its tusks are more curved and are two and a half metres long. Its flesh was sound, without a smell (13), red, and very like stone. It is a male, its great organ not destroyed. When it died it must have been about twenty-five years old. In its mouth and in its stomach was herbage, undigested and still green, and thus we can look on flora of another age."

Butterfly, mammoth, and man, beings of the same day of creation. Strange that frail man, and frailer fly, survive, albeit the mighty mammoth is no longer!

Now came the Russian Christmas. Talbot wrote: "The bells do not cease from jangling; the discords jar, for every man rings the bells without harmony—untunable result."

'As far as Kirensk,' said the chief of police to Talbot, 'this good Cossack soldier shall accompany you.' The Yakut clothes and saddles were packed in naphthaline and, in a great case, the bear and the sheep. "Impossible," Talbot said to the pretty Russian girl who begged to go with him. Flotsam of the penal settlement, in Yakutsk, she had been pleasing.

'In no stantzia will you get more than five horses,' he was told. He wondered how the professor would fare with his huge treasure destined for Moscow.

Away and away

"Nick is not well enough to travel," but Talbot did not
pause to wonder how he, Nick's master, would fare. It was but
five weeks since the day of his highest fever. Racked by bodily
pain he now took leave of Yakutsk, and, with a wrench gave
Nick to Alliani. The head of the police said to Talbot: 'Alliani
will never be allowed to go back to Russia, for, though his freedom has twice been offered to him, he averred that if he returned to Russia he would kill his brother! So he must remain
in Siberia—indeed he would choose to stay. Already he has
maimed his brother: for that, and for another sin, he came
here.'

Talbot's going was delayed for hours, so that it was ten
o'clock at night when his two sleighs sped off.

He, with the driver, went in front, and behind came the
kibitka with the great box of bear and sheep, and the head of
the white reindeer, Eja, the soldier, perched perilously on the
case. The horses were harnessed three abreast—the centre one
trotted and the outside horses cantered. Talbot, because he felt
most ill, travelled like one pursued, night and day with hardly a
pause. If once he rested, his will to go on might fail him; the
cold and his pain might overcome him. And before him lay
fifteen hundred miles, or more. So away and away into the
night, and for twenty-four hours they went, stopping
only to change horses. At eight in the morning
a pause for food, and again at eight in the
evening. At past ten o'clock on the night
of leaving, the sleighs will stop, the
horses will be changed, and
then Talbot will write a
page of his diary.

CHAPTER XXVI

* * *

WHAT OF THE OUTER WORLD, AND WHAT OF THE INNER world of thought during these twenty-four hours of travel? The outer world was cold, hurtingly cold; fifty degrees below zero.

There was, too, a haze that lifted; and the night shone, not only with stars and moon, as in lands more southern, but with the glow of the snow-light—that brilliance of the ultimate north.

Fir trees showed forth. The travellers drove along the River Lena, the winter highway; its breadth here two and three versts of ice. By moonlight the high cliffs on either side loomed solemn black; by daylight they gleamed fierce and red, as though still harbouring volcanic fires.

The stantzias were strange to see, built high above the Lena, and raised on wooden piles, as on ungainly legs. Long staircases ran up them—hard places these to climb in heavy furs; to descend them the travellers slid their lengths. So much for the world of the outer eye.

There were also the things heard. There were the sounds of the sleigh bells, the jangle that helped the horses by its jollity, and that varied, for the bells were changed with the horses. There was, too, the sound of the bells in the sleigh behind Talbot. He, who marked everything, heard how one set of bells differed from another—some deeper, some more shrill. Heard too the sound of the horses' hooves, by which sound might be gauged the hardness, or the softness, of the snow. Now and then came the long-drawn howl of the solitary wolf. Then his own voice asking: "How many versts to the next stantzia?" 'Sem, barin.' ('Seven, sir.') Silent calculations followed. "How many versts can be done in an hour; in half an hour; in a quarter of an hour?" Then a dissatisfied, "Skorey!" ("Hurry!").

The road and the stantzias

Then came the swish of the kibitka sliding more rapidly over the frozen surface of the snow in obedience to the urging of the yamshchik. For thirty yards the pace would be increased, then the driver would fall back into his former torpor. The horses would feel the numbness all along the reins; they too would lose zeal. The promise of more vodka money might hasten the pace, but enough had already been promised. Talbot would offer no more; but ever sank back into a silence—not philosophical.

So much for the world of the outer ear. The man from the stars lay back in the kibitka and his thoughts travelled faster than the horses. "Faster than they ought to, for it is no good to dream. Air castles founded on nothing fall back to nothing. Drearily I am left to feel miserably dwarfed in this great world of ice and snow."

He is beset by the magnitude of the cold; by the death of the Lena. Amongst rivers one of the mightiest, he had known it rough and powerful as the sea, had sailed upon it; lived upon it; nearly died because of it. He had seen it a mainspring of movement, the livelihood of a legion; he had watched it slowly freezing, the jags of ice crushing and crowding together, till, over the surface of the river, they had looked like the upturned wings of giant terns. Now it had come to a dead stop in its search for the sea, had been paralysed by an unseen force. It lay motionless and soundless. Millions of workmen would have been impotent to hold back the vast waters that in the summer he had known. The cold of the winter had performed the wonder.

Then jubilantly 'Loo, ah loo!' cries the yamshchik, and he cracks his whip. Signs these that the kibitkas are nearing the habitations of man. At a great pace they climb the steep road from the river's bed. Talbot, for a moment, feels as though he is standing on his head. A swift gallop along a straggling street; a sudden jerk; they pull up.

The yamshchik dismounts saying: 'Priekhali'—'We have arrived.' With aching limbs and face frostbitten Talbot lurches out of the sleigh. After groping, he finds the door, pulls it open, and on the threshold shakes his big dokha as a dog would shake water from its coat. He is in a small room lit by a lamp that smells. No one is there. "Storozh!"—"Innkeeper!" Talbot calls, and there is no answer. He bangs heavily on the door. 'Sey chas!'—'Immediately!' (Everlasting Russian word that means so little). A villainous-looking fellow comes out sleepily asking what is wanted. The Englishman shows his pass. 'How many horses?' "Six," Talbot answers, and taking off his dokha, waits for the horses to be made ready.

The horses are harnessed before the pass is ratified. Talbot, waiting, writes his diary: "We have been going for twenty-four hours and will continue straight on to Olekminsk, about five hundred versts farther on. At first this journey was very uncomfortable, but one settles down to it. I miss my Nick greatly. We are just starting on a twenty-four-verst stage."

Now the bill is handed to him; the charge is small, four and a half kopeks a verst for each horse. At every stantzia the bill is wrongly added up, and always the charge is greater than it should be, but Talbot will not haggle over a few kopeks. He promises this yamshchik fifty kopeks if he drives fast, but no reward if he loiters. If the driver wishes to go fast he will gallop his horses from the start until they can gallop no longer, then he will allow the horses to trot slowly, and for the last few versts he will again insist upon their galloping their utmost. Talbot is once more carefully tucked up in his kibitka and, with a violent jerk, off they go again. They descend the steep banks of the river to regain their road of ice.

"Climbing down into the bed of a river is nervous work; one man leads the horses, another behind hangs on to the kibitka, then away we go for a couple of versts as far as the ponies are able. I hear the bells of a sleigh behind ringing violently. When one is warm and comfortable after a stantzia, the first half-hour passes quickly. There is no wind. The stars are coming out one by one, and the deep gloom of the early night is dispersed. I can see the tops of the fir trees against the starlit sky."

CHAPTER XXVII

★　　★　　★

ALL THE WAY THE BELLS JANGLED. TALBOT WROTE AFTER-wards that "it was like going for a drive that never would end". At the last stopping place before reaching Olekminsk, the driver must have had much strong drink for they started off at a furious pace, and the man, forgetting the cold, took off his hat and gloves. When they came to travel amid trees he nearly fell off the seat, whether because of drink, or because of sleep, who knows? In spite of complete darkness the pace was not lessened. Often Talbot thought that they must have lost the way. A fog enshrouded them. The postilion fell, and the driver dropped the reins. As though he knew the weakness of the men, the leading horse wonderfully took charge over them, and almost unguided he brought the troika in safety through the forest.

At Olekminsk Talbot slept. Eighty-four hours of speed had put more than six hundred versts behind them. He slept for eleven hours and carried thence memories of the hospitality of the ispravnik, who, taking him to his house fed him and talked with him.

Then the drive swept on again. According to the unevenness of the river bed, or some forest path, so were the horses various-ly harnessed. Sometimes three horses, more seldom, four, would face the long way. In places where the ice on the Lena was rough, two horses were hitched to the sleighs, and in front of them was roped a leader ridden by the postilion. In easier places the three beasts were abreast.

Nearing a stantzia, this, or its like, would befall them: "We are now near the next stantzia. Up the steep incline we go, the horses keeping their pace almost to the top; they cannot quite do it. The driver jumps down, easing the weight of the kibitka, and with tired legs and heaving flanks the gallant little Siberian ponies have brought me to another change." The horses were always gallant, but the men varied. Those of the small villages had quality, those in the bigger hamlets were vile, but when they found Russians instead of Yakuts they fared badly.

Here and there the way was lightened; once by a Jewess. "She was combing magnificent hair in a stantzia." Wordless, touchless encounter, but the unforgettable moment stamped with her splendour. Another meeting was with a girl hungering for news of the world. Her mother was shredding the tea that had come to them packed in brick shape. The girl, pretty and rapt, asked Talbot question after question; mammoths, bears, exiles—her interest embraced them all. He told her of Verkho-yansk, the coldest town in the world, and of the wild great-horned sheep. He gave her her fill of tales before he went out of her life.

At another stantzia, a mother begged that her boy might stare at him. The boy gazed at him and saw—what? Saw in him the traveller from afar: the slayer of a bear; a man chastised by the north, by winds and by weathers. Saw him straitened by the earth's forces, disciplined by them—a man courageous.

Talbot, knowing himself unwashed, suddenly broke the boy's long looking. He must on again with the journey.

Talbot dozed a little, to be awakened by the sharp burr of the yamshchik stopping his horses. "What has happened?" and the answer 'Vadi' (water). They paused for some minutes, then circled round for half an hour before returning to the beaten track near the centre of the river. "I am lucky in my driver," thought Talbot.

A part of the road was so bad that in an hour only twenty-five versts were covered. Some merchants passed Talbot, then he passed them, and each time they ate something together.

Farther on Talbot and his men came near to drowning in the Lena. At full gallop they sped into a break in the ice. God knows how many fathoms of water threatened death. This was the very middle of the river. The horses floundered breast high and were whipped, and lashed, till by dint of stout hearts the little beasts, undaunted, struggled into safety. When they had come upon the dangerous place the ice had cracked with a loud noise. Ever since winter had fallen on the Lena Talbot had not heard its silence broken; the shivering of the ice was a very dreadful sound. Now the driver from the sleigh behind, leaving his beasts on the far side of the danger, joined Talbot's yamshchik, and for nearly an hour the men sounded and tested the ice. 'I prefer to return and join you by another way,' at last the second driver decided. Full of thanksgiving, in that they were alive, Talbot and his man continued the journey; at the next inn the second sleigh rejoined them.

At this stantzia, Talbot left a letter for de Windt, telling him to beware of this part of the Lena, for surely de Windt must soon come this way down the river. "Where can de Windt be and how will Hertz with his mammoth manage this journey?" Talbot wondered.

Then on the walls of the inn, surprised, he saw hanging an old bill showing the picture of a balloon. The bill instructed the villagers to tell their head-man if such a celestial visitant were seen, because André, searcher for the pole, might pass in such a thing. This took Talbot's thoughts back to the pictures of André which he had shown the Eskimos, and he thought regretfully of his failure to find any relic of Franklin. The torture of his chest—he was barely rid of his illness—and the added teasing of the bugs caught from Eja the soldier, these shattered Talbot's reflections.

The road was heavy, and the horses were hitched up at random; but somehow they reached Vitinsk. Two men were in this stantzia as Talbot staggered in from the snowstorm and bent over the box that had been lifted out of his sleigh. Looking up he saw that one of the men was de Windt: "Well, I'm damned! —if it isn't Harry de Windt!" De Windt even then did not recognize his friend, although they had been long acquainted. Talbot was clothed in his enormous dokha made of reindeer skin and lined with the forelegs of white foxes; a cap made of the fleece of a wild sheep pulled down well over his ears. So gaunt was Talbot after his sickness and the long privations, so tense lest this drive should prove too much for his will, that de Windt wrote in his book (14) that 'even his mother would not have recognized her son at the post house at Vitinsk'. Talbot recorded: "de Windt was there, looking an unkempt ruffian."

They talked. It was pleasant after nine months to talk English again. Talbot put in his diary: "I told him all I thought most useful, but I was with him only three hours, and part of that time I put down much food. De Windt was taking things too much at his ease. I told him what wretched condition the reindeer were in, and persuaded him to hurry." The Vicomte de Clinchamps was with de Windt. In his book of this journey to the Behring Strait de Windt says that at this junction he would almost rather not have met Talbot because 'his gloomy predictions seemed to sink into the hearts of my companions and to remain there.' He added that they enjoyed some hours together, and that they drank a strong potion of vodka and wild berries that Talbot made for them.

The next day the sun was shining. Talbot felt its warmth for the first time for many cold months. He saw the snow falling prettily from the pine trees, like little jets of steam.

On the day following the wind howled and, having reached Kirensk, Eja, the soldier, left him: "He was very stupid, but the first honest man I have met in this country. He shed tears at our parting." Then Talbot went on by himself: "This is almost reckless as I had to change five hundred roubles here and the people are brigands. As I have not yet had food I feel rather nervous." At Jegelawz he met Russians whom he had known when, in the summer, he had arrived there by boat. They were full of surprise, for then he had hardly spoken any Russian, but now he spoke as one of them.

Afterwards he said his good-bye to the Lena. "One is always sorry to say good-bye to a place or to a river after a long acquaintance, whether or not one has liked it."

Surviving accidents, being gaped at, and gazed upon, in every village, after fifteen days and nights of driving, Talbot neared Irkutsk. Two thousand miles lay behind him. The last strange thing he saw was a Buriat speeding past in a light sleigh and behind him, pulling empty sleighs, a string of wildly galloping horses.

Then, having endured ten months of perpetual hardship he arrived at the borderland of civilization—he reached Irkutsk. He found there his servant John Green who had been sent out in the expectation of bringing back his body, because the

Irkutsk and England

Governor of Irkutsk had cabled that he would surely die upon
this journey to Irkutsk. Thinking over his purpose,
thinking over his achievement, Talbot wrote:
"I feel more or less satisfied with what
has been accomplished." Talbot
rested at Irkutsk, then he
turned again towards
England (15).

V

BURDEN OF TIBET
AND
RHYTHM OF BURMA

1903 ⁄ 1904

★　　★　　★

BURDEN OF TIBET

★　　★　　★

HOW TO GET THROUGH SIKKIM
One, who later in Gallipoli
Would be dubbed Fighting Mac,
Debated together with Talbot.

The heaven-born had denied them passes,
And had angered the two men
By trying to gull them by tales such as this:
'Younghusband is soon going to Tibet to collect moths.'

Darjeeling in the moonlight
Riding they left behind them;
They promised the guide money
And he understood the hazard.
They sneaked through Rhenok
No police on watch,
At Ari the police came for their passes:
'We are Prime Ministers,
We write our own' they said,
And lordly signed a name.

Perhaps they cut the telegraph wire.
Then five miles down hill and five miles up again.
"The latter part of the journey
Paved with stone flags terrible for the horses.

Decrees everywhere that no man without authority
Might pass beyond Natang,
Which place was some miles farther.
Wading in snow, riding up hill,
But walking the declivities.

Over narrow snow-ledges,
Threatened by the abyssal,
So they reached Natang and again wrote out their passes.

No sleep that night and before daybreak
They travelled on a frozen road.
To rise out of the valley
They struggled breast-high in snow,
And that for many miles.

"The rising sun lit up magnificent peaks
With the Sacred Mountain towering beyond Yatung."

In his pocket a volume of Schopenhauer;
Thought lit by the East and shining into the west;
Thought towering up, gleaming in Talbot's mind
Like the Sacred Mountain towering beyond Yatung.

Over the Jelep La they crossed on a path of snow—hardly a
  foot broad.
Death lay, crouching and waiting, sheer a thousand feet below.

Mist in the Chumbi valley;
Snow on the ruins they passed
As they pushed into Tibet.
Over a page in the diary is written one word
SNOW-BLINDNESS
And it tells how "the Sirdar,
Three Coolies and the two syces
Who had crossed the pass with me are dead snow-blinded
And in great pain."
So the packs were divided,
The unhappy blind ones
Staggered on as best they might.

Horror therefore of blindness;
Horror too at a pass
Where another man, whose eyes, or mind, were blighted
Suddenly, over a ravine, which Talbot was crossing before him,

Burden of Tibet

Shrilled, with peal after peal
Of horrible, mirthless laughter
Unrestrained, shocking the echoes
Into a wild repetition
Of peal upon peal of laughter.
Talbot, not looking back, walked the slippery swinging bridge
With tightened mouth.

This the ballad of Talbot;
The ballad of brave MacNaughton;
When they took the forbidden journey
Into Tibet.

RHYTHM OF BURMA

★   ★   ★

TRAVELLING UP THE IRRAWADDY RIVER
Talbot had joy in seeing
The delicate-strong balance of the Burmen
Poised, steering their canoes.
Had joy in seeing the women walk.
"The easy swing of the hips and the swinging of their arms
Like the sensuous tarantella—
Is it something in their minds, their lives,
That lends this balance, this easiness?"

The dusk falling on two remembered scenes,
That of a young man training a bull to the cart
And half the villagers put to flight
By the angry frightened creature.
And that of a young man,
In yellow garments, expounding the thought of Buddha
To a group of pensive hearers.

Beyond Bhamo, on the way to Moguk
Was a white man, bent upon going to the ruby-mines.
An ill-conditioned man, buying mules for the journey.
"Keep me company on this road," said Talbot,
For the fellow was travelling sparsely:
"I can add to his comfort," Talbot thought.

Next day, at the time of the false dawn,
The baggage-mules were sent on
Whilst Talbot and the Australian
Waited in the cold empty bungalow,
So as to find food and fire
Ready at the next dak-bungalow
When this day's journey should be over.

260

Rhythm of Burma

"Then I knew
This was the strangest man I ever had met,
For most men acquire villainy through stress of occasion,
But this man was a born, a natural blackguard.
His almost diabolical talk
Of cold-blooded, melancholy deeds—
Excused in words which made the deeds more foul—
Made me glad to see by my watch
That we could start
To tramp, tramp through the mist until the sunrise."

Talbot walked thinking:
"In my wandering
In the many pockets of the globe
I have been given, unasked, even more confessions
And more confidences than to priest in confessional.
I would like to know—is solitude good for man?"

The road wound upwards. The scent of many flowers
Brought back other scenes, and his memory
Stirred suddenly with a remembrance of roses,
So that his mind held for a little
The fragrance of an Eastern saying:
That one rose is the sign of the sweetness of life;
That two roses blazon the delightfulness of death.

These thoughts, and a canter soon lifted up Talbot's spirits,
Then he remembered: "To-day is my birthday!"
And was glad of his dog Gyp
To lick his hand and give a friendly yawn,
"For dogs yawn with affection."
Afterwards the strange man galloped up,
He had started later but found a shorter way.
"As clever with a Burmese jungle as in the Australian bush."
That evening the man drank deeply to Talbot,
'Let us sit up till the sky is blue in the morning.'
"No—no. My birthday present from nature is sleep."

The next day the ill-conditioned man
Left the rest-house earlier than did Talbot.

Rhythm of Burma

At the summit of a path in the rocks,
Amid the blunt-headed peaks
Talbot saw, spread out,
A sudden flat place
Rich with crops.
Seated on the brilliant grass
Was the scoundrel creature
Encircled by Burmese girls.
"Leaving them I jogged on."

"My dog Gyp would not tackle the stream
Which was rapid,
But once he had plunged in he found that the swim was easy."
Which set Talbot thinking
Of the folly of those
Who make sure they cannot encompass
That which they have never attempted.
Like a sorry superstition
This insidious *cannot* sucking away their will.

At Moguk: "the road we walk on is the very substance
In which are found the purest rubies."
In the country about women digging and using the sluices—
Which the old law of the Kings of Burma
Allowed them—no man might hold a ruby
But the woman might come by them thus, though not by the
    use of explosives.

"Have taken 8 mules to go back,
At one ruby each per day."

One evening: "A lovely sunset,
Played flute,
Wrote to my mother,
And received a gift of a small stone Buddha
Nearly two thousand years old."
Dug up from the earth by Captain Lawrie, the giver.
In Gupta was inscribed:
"The three most excellent things:
God, the law and the priesthood."

VI

THE BOOK OF BARUCHIAL*

* * *

*According to a tradition, Baruchial is the Archangel of the
Sacrament of Marriage.

CHAPTER I

★ ★ ★

DURING THE YEARS WHEN, IN THE YUKON AND IN THE
Barren Lands, Talbot was hardening his body and was forging
the strength of his will, there was, in England, a girl growing—
her name was Violet Beauclerk. Born in Rome, because of
fever she had been nurtured on the strong milk of goats, and
then, whilst yet an infant, on wine instead of on milk.

As she grew older destiny whispered to her: 'Your body
must be the slave of your will.' 'I shall be the wife of an officer
and follow him in wars,' she thought. Then she would creep
out of bed, and sleep on the floor, so as to become hardy.
Her little friends must play 'The Game of Bearing'; they must
stand in a row before a boy who would whip their legs till they
jumped away from the line. Whoever longest bore the pain
had won the game; Violet wished that it might be as easy to
harden the heart. She thought of her heart as if kept in an ebony
box. There were birds of mother-of-pearl upon the lid. Sometimes at night she looked within the box. Because older people
were careless she often found a scratch upon her heart, sometimes even there were cuts and bruises. For hurts to the heart
there was but one remedy, and that was to hurt the body. 'The
cure for a burn is the fire,' her peasant nurse had told her. 'If I
scald my hand I cure the smart in a flame.' So it was with
sorrow. After the bitter parting with her nurse it had helped
Violet to sting herself with nettles; and another time, parted
from someone dearer, to bite her lip till the blood came, and to
write with the blood: 'Come back, come back.'

Beloved older people often did things that hurt; they would
speak harshly to beggars, and they could not understand that it
mattered drawing the curtain when the stars were shining near
to the bedroom window. Nor did they understand how fearful
it was to hear the newspaper-boy calling out news of murder.

So long had they known all evil, so used were they to things that shocked, that they laughed at that which caused her to go white with the fear of life. They came crashing down from the heights where she had throned them, but they could not understand how it was that their fall should hurt her.

Alone flowers never failed Violet. The Travellers' Joy told her many things. She was sure it had been a part of the Milky Way that had fallen out of the sky into the Wiltshire hedge, where she saw it grow as a flowering spray. She had wondered once, 'Do the daisies eat grass?' and her nurse had been angry with her for not knowing about such a simple thing; but the flowers never were angry.

Violet wished that her mother had not died. She wished that she were alive, and were a tree; so Violet could have grown upheld in her arms, which would have been branches. She would have grown slowly in the sun and the air from blossom into fruit; and then to seed; and on to sapling tree.

Lessons learnt from books were precious to her because she learnt for the stranger that would come. Now he came in dreams, wanting her to be learnèd as well as to be hard of body. Nevertheless flowers and toys were better than books, because they talked to her of distant places. The swallows told the flowers of the lands where they had wintered; and when Violet held a flower to her ear it retold to her the tale of the swallows' migration.

On the ceiling of the nursery was nailed a toy stork; it carried her mind on its wings. Her rocking-horse rocked her to the east, and with her picture-bricks she built up Rome and Venice. 'Could Venice really grow out of the sea like a lily out of a lake?' The only human being that was as good as a flower, or a toy, was a particular actor (1); to Violet he was the 'Ghost'. He slept by day; at dusk he came downstairs. She would give him both her hands. 'Send me far away,' she begged. He would tell her she was far away, in an ice country, or in a country of sand. With her eyes shut she would see everything until some elder person rasped out: 'Oh, stop, Arthur! You are hypnotizing the child.'

A stepmother came suddenly into her life, and Violet was sent to school in Brussels. There she forgot about the man of her dreams. For her to be at school was like being one of those sick people who lack a skin and bleed at a scratch; at school her lack was the need for solitude. But sometimes her spirit fled away in prayer—into prayers high and remote, mountain-tops of escape.

Violet hardly knew her father, because, being in the Diplomatic Service, he was always abroad. She remembered best the smell of his cigarettes—the only cigarettes ever smoked in her nursery. When she was seventeen years old her father left Budapest and, as his wife must stay a little time in Europe, he took Violet in her stead to accompany him in Peru.

Sailing away, intoxicated with freedom, with the spaces of the sea, no day, for this girl, dawned early enough; no twilight enough tarded. Before the day broke she was forward and aft, and she would gladly have sacrificed sleep to the stars.

Aboard the ship were negroes; they sang, and danced, and prayed until the day when, touching Jamaica, the news broke out on the ship that Queen Victoria is dead. Then up from the steerage came an old negress; she flung herself at Nelthorpe Beauclerk's feet and asked: Would the black people be enslaved again, sold as cattle? Would all that happen over again now that Queen Victoria was dead?

The travellers arrived at Colon, then at Panama, and then at Guayaquil. The ship lay in the turgid river Guayas. 'Strange River,' Violet thought, 'the coming and going of the ships dependent on its tides that run so swiftly. The high tide being here the time of the passing for those who must die, so the people think.' Her mind rambled to what she had heard of the Guayas, of the seasons when it is flooded by melted snow, when from the mountains of Huigra come torrents of water, and boulders grind along their way. At flood-time floating masses of vegetation menace the boats on the Guayas.

The air was hot and damp and the smell of the mud flats was heavy. Violet's senses grew giddy with new things. On her palate was the cloying taste of the custard-apple, in her nostrils the sweet heavy smell of the mangrove swamps, in her ears the strange new sound of Spanish song, and the trump of the bullfrogs. In her eyes was the smart of the sun, the torrid sun so new to her. In her eyes the sight of men as brown as the river,

267

working in the hold, and at the side of the ship, running over with sweat. They were the first human beings half naked that ever she had seen.

Afterwards father and daughter reached Peru. 'Oh really it is the land of gold,' she cried when she saw the hedgerows flaming golden with broom.

*   *   *

The year that Violet went to live in Peru, Talbot, on the Lena, was hunting, was playing the flute. She must go as far as India, and return again to Peru; he must travel in India; dash into Tibet; must live in Burmah; and see the warfare of Russia against Japan. Coming, and going, with sickness, and war, be-sides a hundred enjoyments, all this lay between them. But, when
five years have passed, star-favoured they will meet. Seek-
ing buried treasure, Talbot will sail west; in Ecuador he will hear a man talking about Violet
and, because of what is said, he will
sail onwards to Peru.

CHAPTER II

★   ★   ★

FROM THE BRITISH LEGATION IN LIMA, VIOLET WROTE A
letter to her sister; she summed up the happenings of each
day. 'Do you remember, Flora, that when I was a clumsy
schoolgirl in Brussels I was so ashamed of my looks that I did
not wish the Belgians to know I was English, therefore I always
spoke German in the shops and trams, hoping, by this ruse, to
avoid bringing shame on England? Well, here with the British
flag run up at sunrise, floating all day above our house, and hauled
down at sunset, people, seeing me, think they see England. That
is dreadful because I do not know how to hold up my long dresses,
my hair never stays pinned to my head, and on reception days
I have no idea whom I am receiving. I do everything wrong.
The Papal Nuncio came; he is the doyen of the Corps Diplo-
matique. Because he was in purple and had a silk cap I thought
he was the Chinese Minister, and talked to him as though indeed he were. Some Peruvian girls came in and, kneeling, kissed
his ring; when he had gone I asked who he was. Imagine my
embarrassment!

'At the street corners groups of young Peruvians stand talking,
I think, about politics. They always say: 'Que bella!' when any
other girl passes. When I pass: 'How big are the feet of the Englishwoman!' When I have to return calls father comes with me,
for I cannot yet speak Spanish. The drawing-rooms are rather
dark and, the first visit we paid, I walked into a spittoon. Then
I sat on the sofa next to the hostess, and stayed there, which I
ought not to have done, because, being a girl, the sofa is no place
for me. I should have sat on one of the chairs in a semicircle
and faced the sofa, where the hostess and the grandest married
lady sit.

'I have not enough to do. I mend the house-linen and learn
Spanish, and I arrange the flowers in the English church, but

the Indian menservants, and the chef, and the housekeeping are managed by father. He eats very little, but the food must be well cooked. At a big Government banquet he clearly showed his scorn of the food—there was too much of it. Because of convention, I cannot go for long walks alone, and father is too ill to take me, but sometimes I ride with the French officers. I love that. One of them told me, that when he gets Indian recruits to train, he first bangs them on the back and yells at them: 'You are men as we are; you are not animals; you are men.' After that they become good soldiers.

'On King Edward's birthday, and on my birthday, floral offerings are sent around to us. Great harps, and butterflies, and open books, made out of flowers. The scent is lovely; but the flowers soon die, short-stemmed, and wired into these alien forms.

'I hate Lima because hens are carried tied by their legs to a pole swung over the Chinamen's shoulders, great bunches of them, head downwards; also because starving horses go round and round the cobble-paved town, pulling heavy trams. They are jerked to a standstill, and whipped on again; they even fall exhausted in the traces. We have telephones and trams and the 'Z Y X' of civilization, but none of the 'A B C'.

'The prison seems model and yet it is said that the falling of a drop of water on just one place on the prisoners' heads is still practised as a torture.

'I am not trying to write good English as I am tired of it. Father gets so very angry when I use double negatives, or make mistakes of grammar.

'I love the evenings here, for I walk on the flat roof of our mud-house and watch the sun setting. Sometimes the English mother-superior of a convent near here, sends me Madonna lilies from her enclosed garden. The moon shines full into the open square verandah of the upper part of our house. It lightens the lilies that I put in vases along the balustrade. Then, again, I am happy.

'I am frightened of father because he is sarcastic when I do stupid things, and because he has times of melancholy. He thinks I have no feelings because I am too shy of him to show them. During a dinner which he gave there was an earthquake.

'Tant de courage'

It was not very violent and I was not frightened, but when the French Minister congratulated him on Mademoiselle having 'tant de courage' he answered, 'It would take more than an earthquake to cause any emotion in my daughter.' And yet there are lots of things I think so lovely that tears come to my eyes, but I dare not tell him so. There is the hibiscus that is pink in the morning and that dies away in crimson, like the finished day. There is too the wild amancaes, sometimes called the Lily of the Incas. It so loves life that, even uprooted, it will, for a time, grow, and flower, and flourish out of the earth, though according to its nature it should grow deep in soil. It is not in fact a lily, for there are no lilies native to Peru.

'Then there is father's character. He denies himself books and wine and lots of things because he would like to save money for all of us. Yet he will take a bottle of wine to a poor sick Englishman or to a negro (British subject, sir!) and carry it in his pocket, which the Peruvians think is very undignified in a British Minister.' And so the letter rambled on, but Violet did not say that she was trying, by sheer starvation, to wear down her young animal need of walks, and of work, nor did she stress her father's melancholy. In this manner, in the city of Lima, she lived for about a year—and then came a change.

CHAPTER III

*   *   *

'THE MOON WAXING, MY FATHER'S MELANCHOLY GROWS
to desperation; the moon waning, the desperation sinks again
into a flat deadly sadness.' So Violet said to herself as she looked
from the square balcony up to the full moon. Although the
library doors were closed, locked too, she could hear her
father drawing his nails up and down the writing-table. Over-
whelmed by a melancholy that verged on madness he moaned:
'*taedium vitae, taedium vitae!*' His body suffered with his mind.
He would sit there for hours, then perhaps would go and sit in
silence near her, irked by a listlessness so great that, if he coughed
or if the clock struck, she would feel glad, because, for a moment, he would be distracted from his brooding.

By a sudden mutual pity they had come to know each
other and to love each other; therefore Beauclerk's torment
was torment for Violet, for at last she understood the man
with his quick brain and his quick hand. He told her about
the years during which they had been parted, and about the
earlier years when she was an infant. She could follow in mind
his happy life in Rome with her auburn-haired mother; his
lessons in sculpture, his success in works of bronze, and could
follow his fear at the rapid increase in his family. His lands
yielded no wealth at all, his pay was small. After her mother
had died he had gone to Peking, as First Secretary of Legation,
acting afterwards as Minister. He learnt Chinese; made drawings of the flowers, and people; and wrested for British trade a
concession on a certain river. The Russian Minister was set
upon obtaining the same concession. 'No doubt every man has
his price, but you have yet to reach mine,' thought Beauclerk,
as with contempt he tore up the signed open cheque which he
found amongst his papers. Promotion and ennoblement should
have followed this success, but Beauclerk had a tongue which

darted openly against the great. He failed to abide by the wisdom of his own saying: 'patience is not a virtue, it is a necessity.' What his brain did for his advancement was undone by his liver. A New Year's Honours List drew from him a lampoon, which, although its wit amused the powerful at the Foreign Office, yet arrested his career. Later, also, was remembered against him an answer which cost him dear: 'Why were receipts not demanded from the Indians who, at the stages between Guayaquil and Quito, hired you their mules?' 'Because Indians do not write, because my word should suffice. If it does not, let me toss you double or quits for my official expenses.'

In Peru, soon after the new mutual love of father and daughter, the tenor of their days was succeeded by another change in their lives. It lay in their struggle to escape his besetting despair. They read and worked together, they gathered musicians about them, they put forth all their strength and through his efforts and hers Beauclerk for some years was healed. To ease the burden of their exile they studied together. He took a thesaurus of words, and expounding word after word, he opened to her all his lore. Seeing few people they invented friends: French, German, and Spanish companions. In foreign talk they acted the parts of these phantasmal people. Someone said: 'You two are a match for one another.' 'A match? Then Violet is the stick and I the head,' said Beauclerk. In gardens they walked together, and for a few pence, cut flowers. 'Oh, do not cut so long a stalk,' sometimes would wail the Indian gardener, 'it takes a year for these gardenias to grow an inch of stalk.' In a garden there were marble statues that showed the signs of the zodiac. There Beauclerk acquainted Violet with the fables of the heavens. Because of flowers, because of stars, she would return so gay that her thoughts must dance into verse.

Sometimes Beauclerk's duty would take him to farther places in Peru, even to Ecuador and to Bolivia; these journeys were a delight to father and daughter. Once they travelled to Arequipa, and stayed there in a house surrounded by a garden. Easily solaced by simple lovely things, he regained appetite for food, appetite for life. Everything gave them pleasure. They enjoyed the shapeliness of the mountain called Misti, and the look of the pretty donkeys, the noses of which were slit to enable them the better to breathe the thin air of the high lands; the llamas, creatures of the mountains, needed no such help to breathe.

Round about Arequipa were many gardens in which were grown the flowers necessary to betoken the courtesy, the condolence, or the congratulations of one townsman to another. Violet wrote: 'Because of all the flowers grown to be cut so ruthlessly into formal offerings, we move in a maze of scent, in the especial fragrance of violets. Now and again, a loitering heavy-breasted woman hiring herself as wet-nurse calls out her ware in the open courtyard of a stone house: 'Arma de leche! Arma de leche!' Indians, wrapped in gay blankets; eager astronomers from the New World, come to watch this heaven from a mountain tower, all these people move in fragrance, as the people in an opera move to music.'

Near Arequipa were bushes and hedges of heliotrope. Above the hedges, upheld on quivering wings, humming-birds hovered, and, so hovering, they drank from the calix of the flowers. In the flashing manner whereby she knew whatever things were necessary to her, Violet, watching them, knew that she also was beautiful. 'All these things are lovely, and I am lovely; the heliotrope and the humming-birds might be as glad of me as I am of them—the glory be to God! Yet the humming-bird goes to the flower, not for beauty, but for honey. Therewith her mind moved on to the other kinds of beauty necessary to completeness; necessary to her a woman as are honey and scent and pollen to the graceful heliotrope. 'How much is demanded of every creature; flower and bird, and man,' she thought. So passed the days, redolent of violets; the clear nights, gay with stars.

CHAPTER IV

★   ★   ★

'HERE IS THE CAPITAL WHICH QUEEN VICTORIA STRUCK off the map' said Beauclerk as he and his daughter stood to look down at the stately pile of stone in the hollow of the mountains. Beauclerk felt a great content because he was nearing La Paz to renew the diplomatic relations between Great Britain and Bolivia. They had been sundered for close on thirty years. 'Why was it that the Queen drew her pen through La Paz?' asked Violet. 'Was our last Minister really tied to an ass, and so sent through the streets; and why?' 'That', Beauclerk said, 'is a tale not for the young. . . . I never saw so beautiful a lake as this high Titicaca.'

They drove steeply down to La Paz; Violet sat straight. She thought of the desert they had crossed after leaving Arequipa. How strange had looked the crescent-shaped dunes of sand, the medinas, the waves of the desert, caused by the winds blowing, nearly always, from the north-west! She thought of the happy Indian peasants, dancing from one lakeside church to another dancing in the churches; dressed in pleated clothes with jackets of fur, and wearing hats, big as canopies. They blew on flutes and banged on drums. The cause of their gaiety was the Virgin.

In La Paz was rejoicing because of the coming of the British Envoy. There was a procession lit by torches; there was eating, and drinking, and amity.

The next day, Violet, with a Frenchman and his wife, rode to distant tin-mines. Vast grassy spaces swept up into the hills where roamed wild vicuñas. Upon their pacing horses the travellers rode and marvelled at the blue above them. Only in such an altitude can such azure be.

In Peru, black people came often into the lives of Beauclerk, and of his daughter. From sugar fields, from the railway in

275

Ecuador, from the prison in Lima, came their plaints. Beauclerk would go to a plantation on the coast, or to an Ecuadorian
height, to see if these children of Britain were being unjustly
dealt with.

On her twenty-first birthday Violet gave to them, and to all
King Edward's subjects, a feast in a garden, and she waited on
her guests. 'Dis is de feast of de gospel, never we sat at a table,
with flowers; waited upon,' said one of them.

In the small English Chapel, Violet striving after charity,
after humility, would kneel in the lowest place below an old,
ragged negress. The chalice, drunk of by the praying purple
lips, afterwards was set to the lips of the girl.

When three years of life had passed in South America, because of an accident, Violet fell ill. Of necessity her father took
her to England. When she sailed from Peru, a line of wistful,
smiling, sable faces, looked out to her from the wharf at Callao.
Leaving her in England, her father returned with his wife to
Peru. Torment to the girl to see him go back to where his mind
would starve and rust, his energies be wasted. Whatever now
her pleasures, they were stabbed through by the pain of knowing that he had returned to desolation. Indeed upon him desolation fell and when, a year later, Violet returned to Lima she
could not wrest her father from his gloom.   Because of the
guidance of a man of science, Violet had lost her faith in Christ.

*   *   *

Tentative young loves came to Violet. In a jungle in Ecuador,
among orchids and toucans, her heart had gone from her to a
man she knew hardly at all. The vision she had of him was in a
tangle of sunlight, and he had a share in the wonder she felt at
the glory of the forest. In India, whither, after her illness, she
had gone from England, again she felt that fever. She saw red-
walled Delhi in a cloud of blossoming fruit trees; saw the Taj
Mahal at earliest dawn. She, and the sky-clad ascetics with
their offerings of marigolds, alone in the garden. She saw the
Taj again, at merciless midday, not a whit less beautiful than
when the sun was setting, or when the moon arose. Ravelled
into that cycle of loveliness was this other, might-be, love. But
when the man spoke of marriage a warning thought urged: 'Is

there on the earth perhaps another, who if he came, might
shatter this happy love, half due to sylvan gods?' Later, in a flash,
suddenly persuaded, Violet answered: 'I could marry you, but
yet I am afraid, because I think that somewhere there is a man
I was born to follow; when I meet him I shall be certain that he is my lodestar.' Therefore Violet remained heart-whole; and free she returned
to Peru for a few months to wait,
unwitting that she waited, till
Talbot should come.

CHAPTER V

★　　★　　★

EARLY IN THAT YEAR OF 1906 TALBOT, AT COLON, STOOD
admiring a statue of Columbus. The metal showed a stooping
Indian woman and Columbus with his hand laid gently on her.

Something Charles Berry had told him over an old dusty
bottle in St. James's had sent Talbot off to search the Cocos
Isles for buried treasure, for the reputed wealth of a sunken
Spanish galleon. Talbot arranged that Captain X and two
other Englishmen, L— and A—, should meet him at Guayaquil,
the port of Ecuador, and he was now sailing from Colon to
Guayaquil.

As the ship lay in the anchorages of the various ports she
visited, the creaking of her cranes filled the hours of the day
and night. Goods were hoisted aboard or flung ashore to the
wearying ugly sound.

On the ship was General Plaza, once President of Ecuador.
He had been called away from Washington where he had been
representing Ecuador as Minister. He was now ordered to Quito
to help the government against General Alfaro who by force
was trying to make himself President. Eight hundred soldiers
and five thousand Indians, so it was said, were helping Alfaro.

"19 *January*, 1906. (Arrive Guayaquil). Arrived at ten in the
morning. Went ashore with all my baggage at half past-one in
the afternoon. Went customs; everything let out, barring cartridges and rifle; duty paid 6 sucres = 12/-. Went to see the
Governor about cartridges. His son wanted to know if I would
sell my ammunition to the Government. Captain X met me,
but A— and another man are at the coast apparently frightened of yellow fever. The revolution is in full swing, but it
is difficult to find out who is likely to come out top side. Met
Ashton, the British Vice-Consul. Went to bank and got cheque
book.

278

Revolution in Guayaquil

"*Friday*, 19 *January*, 1906. (Revolution). Revolution in full swing. General Alfaro the revolutionist has won, and General Plaza had to bolt to an English vessel in mid stream, hotly chased by the revolutionists who wished to kill him. The streets are crowded with ruffians, many of whom carry weapons. The Indians have opened the late Government arsenals and taken out rifles, which, after the formation of a new Government, will be bought up from these people for about 10 sucres per gun. There is much shooting in the streets; there is a Maxim at work round the corner. People running in every direction 'hell for leather'.

"*Saturday*, 20 *January*, 1906. All night the sound of guns and in the morning the streets were strewn with dead men and horses. Soldiers of the late Government were stripped of their uniforms, coats, trousers and rifles. All business at a standstill. No late Government officials—all resigned. The people are waiting to appoint new ones. The shouts for Alfaro in the streets are thunderous and monotonous. 150 people have been killed. I took photos of one or two dead men. On going for a walk in the evening a bullet came very close to me. Am certain it was intended for me.

"*Sunday*, 21 *January*, 1906. The revolution at an end. 150 killed, 450 wounded. Romero had made me a member of the club here. I had breakfast with Ashton and his wife. A deadly dull hole this place. Have an appointment with Ashton to see the late chief of police about a vessel for the Cocos. The chief is in hiding at the American consul's. We would have been shot at if we had attempted to go near his vessel to-day. I hear that 300 cavalry charged some modern quick-firing guns and took them, although there were only 20 survivors; their dead bodies have been left to rot on the ground or be eaten by dogs. Apparently no Red Cross Society in this country.

"*Monday*, 22 *January*, 1906. Went to interview at eight in the morning in the American consulate and settled that as he is going to the Galapagos Is., he shall take us there and call in two months' time, for a consideration of £200. The chief of police is taking his son with him. Went for a walk, and after dinner took flute to the Ashtons. Mrs. Ashton accompanied me. Heat very oppressive to-day. Hope to get away by end of month."

Earthquake in Guayaquil

The expedition to the Cocos was not to be. After "filling in ten pages of my signature," news came that the Chilean Government would not allow any more expeditions to Los Cocos. Talbot had to pay off his men who were glad to be freed, for they had had their fill of danger. The outbreak of yellow fever and the revolution were followed by more earthquakes. The diary records: "*Wednesday*, 31 *January*, 1906. At nine in the evening had a slight earthquake; at ten in the morning a severe one lasting 4 minutes, everyone bolted out of the hotel except myself. L— with his coat over his back led gallantly."

The diary bears no other record of the earthquake, but Ashton wrote about it to Beauclerk. He reported to his chief the attempt of Talbot to go to Los Cocos, and touched on the newcomer's angers, and generosities. He described how the earthquake, by its awful shaking, had set the bells ringing in the steeples. The people had rushed into the street and, falling on their knees, had cried out: 'Jesus! Maria!' They signed their breasts with the cross. The Consul owned himself to be a timid man, but his sense of duty to the stranger had made him cross the street to the hotel where Talbot was staying. He swayed in at the bedroom door. Sitting up in bed, wrapped in a barbaric many-coloured gown, Talbot was playing the flute.

On the day previous Talbot had offered L— "the opportunity of travelling with me. He can only say he cannot come as he might get fever."

The next day, a very hot day, Talbot was "very ill with fever, doping myself with quinine and phenacetin". The next day, "up at five in the morning with high fever," he and a negro servant travelled to Riobamba, ten thousand feet up in the mountains.

"*Saturday*, 3 *February*, 1906. . . . Just before we reached the summit 10,000 ft. the engine could not pull up train so took us up in detachments. As night came on it turned bitterly cold. Yesterday in Guayaquil 140 degrees of heat were registered outside my room. On arrival at Riobamba had great difficulty in getting rooms. At last I got one. Went straight to bed with high fever. No food, no clothes.

"*Sunday*, 4 *February*, 1906. (Chimborazo mountain). Awful night, eaten by bugs and fleas in a filthy bed. Had a fever all day.

Chimborazo

Got baggage from station at nine in the morning. Had some quinine and soup and had a look at Chimborazo only 8 miles off, with its summit covered with snow. Its summit is so round that it does not give one the idea of being as high as it is in reality. Somewhat disappointing in fact. No bath in the hotel, while the sanitary arrangements are cruder than in any of the countries I have travelled in, which says a mighty lot."

The next day: "The band (military) played from half-past ten last night up to four in the morning. Saw a llama led by a native to-day. It reminded me much of a camel. Went for a walk.... Fever better, feel stronger, but still rather yellow and red."

On February the sixth: "Went for a long walk into the country and passed well-irrigated fields sown with alfalfa. Also came across a bad-tempered sheep with a very angry face, the first I have ever seen in my life. A band is playing new recruits into barracks. The moment they get in, the band stops whether in the middle, or not, of a tune.... Am very yellow after my fever."

CHAPTER VI

*   *   *

TALBOT WAS FOR SIX MONTHS IN QUITO, AND IN PLACES
near about the capital. He rode far with mules into the jungles
wreathed with orchids and rode into mountain places along
paths "which would have been a despair even to goats". To
St. Nicholas, and Talia, and Tandaji, he rode, and, during these
months, somewhere in the heights he came upon the tayra.
"The creature looks like a bear with a tail," he decided, and
presently shot one of these puzzling animals to see indeed what
beast this was that lived in the rocks or sometimes had its nest so
skilfully made in the hollow of a tree. It seemed fierce, sitting
erect and boldly staring and chattering. Afterwards he learned
that it was of the family of the weasels.

In Quito was a Swede who acted as British Consul-General;
his name was Söderstrom. He was known and beloved for his
generosity and for his learning. Every kind of humming-bird
that bejewelled the neighbouring jungles was known to him.
In this land of Tsantsa heads, the ancient compressed heads of
the dead, Talbot found much to observe as well in the habits
of the birds, as in the many races of the Indians.

Although baulked "by men too lazy and women too ignorant to teach me", yet Talbot learnt Spanish.

One Sunday in Quito Talbot went to a bull-fight and wrote
of it: "*Sunday, 25 February*, 1906. . . . Walked to the 'plaza de
toros' and saw the bull-fight. The last I saw was in Mexico. I
went here to see how it was conducted, also to see the matador
kill the bull with a sword, which he did very well. In Mexico
the matador made a sad hash of it, missing 7 times and being
hissed out of the ring. The spectacle here was as barbaric as it
could be. Luckily there were no horses to be gored and only
two bulls were killed. One poor brute was not killed outright
by the sword, so every time it fell on its knees, the matador and

bandilleros tried to put a knife between its horns. After many attempts they finally succeeded in killing it. One bull not being wild enough, had two explosive banderillas placed in its shoulders; about 2 seconds after being stuck in they exploded, making loud reports—awful for the poor animal."

But all the time in Quito, at the back of Talbot's thoughts were some words which had been spoken to him by Ashton in Guayaquil. They had left him somehow haunted: 'Now that you cannot go to Galapagos why not go to Peru?' Unless Ashton had asked him this, unless he had spoken of Violet as he did speak, Talbot would perhaps not ever have gone to Peru. Smoking a pipe, Ashton told Talbot of how with her father she had come to Guayaquil. Of how she had ridden his pacing horse, using, pressed against its neck, the rounded rein which was never to be pulled against the heavy bit. She used a side-saddle from up-country, the leather being decorated with silver; she used a silver shoe for the stirrup. The horse was young and wanton. One day it threw her twice into the dusty road, but she laughed and mounted again.

Shaking the ashes out of his pipe, Ashton said that when Violet had left Guayaquil he had shot the horse she had ridden, because she could not have faced seeing anyone else riding it. Then getting up and turning away to look out over the river he said: 'Perhaps there is your hidden treasure. Anyway, go to Peru and see.'

CHAPTER VII

*   *   *

IT WAS IN THE ANDES THAT TALBOT AND VIOLET FIRST met one another. Her father and she were living in a construction train, on a siding, high up amongst marguerites, goldenrod, and ferns, the fronds of which had backs of silver. 'Go up that steep path and in the valley beyond you will find my daughter,' Beauclerk had said.

So Talbot went, and found Violet, lying along a ledge of rock, absorbed in gazing at the torrent that fell foaming into a gully.

In the blue above, wide-winged, drifted a condor. Looking up, Violet saw Talbot as one having fellowship with the heights, and with the tumultuous water. Any other must have broken the edge of her delight, for she had been saying poetry to the rush of the cascade. But this man might have been the familiar of the mountain, and of the torrent. His inward urgency was expressed by his body; by his clothes; so that he entirely befitted the place.

Then Talbot spoke to her, but he hesitated between his words and forced them harshly out, because he had been ill with fever and was more than ever high-strung. Words seldom served to bridge the distance between Talbot and his fellows, but he was able to bind them to him by other means.

Afterwards he stayed awhile in Lima, at the Legation, or went sometimes to the little mud-built towns neighbouring the ocean. Later he sailed to a southern port—Mollendo—and, from a rowing boat, into a basket, was landed on to the jetty. He travelled to Arequipa and to La Paz. On the sea he wrote: "In spite of a sunset worthy of the Incas am feeling in very low spirits; four weeks will feel like four years."

From Arequipa he wrote to Violet a letter in which was caught the crisp high air of those uplands, the festal ringing of church bells, the jangle of little bells swinging from the 'llama madrina', as, free, she led a long line of burdened llamas. His written words showed that Talbot had been aware of the charm of these things, as also of the brilliance of the stars, and of the dominance of the ever snow-crowned Misti; as having, nevertheless, been tormented by warring thoughts, and by doubts.

It seemed he must have been reading Shakespeare and then, thinking of Violet, had taken up his pen and written the poet's words into his letter: 'Oh God, that man might read the book of fate . . . The happiest youth would shut the book and sit him down and die.' 'Does he love me?' wondered Violet as she folded the letter.

Sailing on Lake Titicaca towards La Paz, Talbot wrote at night: "We weighed anchor and steamed slowly out into the night, gloomy and sad as my thoughts." Next day: "Still plodding on our way through Lake Titicaca whose banks take beautiful sinuous curves, the snow-clad mountains in the distance gleamed like jewels in the morning air, while colours of every hue kissed the landscape to the water's edge." After but a short stay in La Paz he returned to Arequipa and on the high Lake Titicaca wrote: "Good-bye, oh serried chain of peaks, Nevada, adieu—Sorata, and to you, adieu, Illimani of the Andes, and Titicaca Lake."

From Arequipa Talbot rode to Port Mollendo. First his way lay through a fertile valley; then into a ravine, and on to the sandy flats—the pampas, till Mollendo was reached. Here he embarked for Pisco and, loading his Mauser, rode thence nearly two hundred miles to Lima: "I hear there are bandits on the road." The horses paced through fertile country, past wine presses, cellars, and dark-coloured people; through miles of sugar-growing country; and past Cerro Azul, where Talbot passed an evening "watching porpoises racing the incoming tide". He rode on next day: "without a guide. The track led up and down sandhills. Wading through deep sand for six hours. Passing near the ocean we saw innumerable birds. The close season for guano commences 31st October on the near islands. A desolate region we passed through, almost white with skeletons, those of whales and seals—and others. Dragging our endless way over deserts, skeletons, and deep sand, we came to Mala, well watered, growing bananas, vines and maize." Next day again they rode, spending eleven hours in the saddle, "a terrible route for horses and men with scorching sun," till they arrived at Lurin.

As he rode, throughout the long hours Talbot envisaged that which he had in mind. Should he forge for himself the innumerable links of married life, bind himself to society? "I am selfish, often peevish and gubernatorial; perhaps I ought not to marry. Also I am fifteen years older than she, it is unlikely that she could care for me." Back to his past went his mind; he saw how his life swung between great simplicity and hardness of life in travel, and briefer spells of experiment and indulgence. His travels were his means of asceticism and escape. Without money, without a name, divested of everything accidental, almost spirit-wise he had wandered. But when he returned to England came the harass, the overspending. There were new discoveries to further, new powers to use; the temptation to build, to lay out gardens, to buy beautiful things. To and fro raced his thoughts; towards marriage, and away again. The abstinence of the Zulu warrior came to his memory and its counterfeit, the uxoriousness of the Western man: "and yet it would be wonderful to have someone I could tell things to." A mile farther on: "perhaps at last she would make me good." All his life he had been rent between the mischievous and the good. He was compelled to self-restraint by his long paternal descent from Catholic ancestors whose lives and deaths had been rooted in the Sacraments; by his long descent, on his mother's side, from Protestant Scotsmen fearing God. Yet his wild nature hurled him against the laws bred in him; always the serpent trailing after the heel, always that vulnerable heel. So that now he sighed, and urging his horse to a canter: "Oh for a life without regrets on the morrow; for love with peace!"

Then as dusk fell, "travel, exploration, hunting, are my métier." How leave a life for him so completely fitting, a life that called forth the virtues which he delighted to exercise, courage and self-dependence? The *cri de guerre* of his race, the *mortem-aut-triumphum* beat in his blood. Years ago he had taken up the ancient challenge and had flung it against unbroken countries, against the elements. But now—in a supreme defiance—must he fling it against himself?

CHAPTER VIII

*   *   *

WHEN TALBOT RETURNED FROM THE SOUTH HE STAYED at the Legation, going now and then into the Andes because he was restless and because the heights allured him. It did not seem as though he loved Violet, but only that he and she enjoyed being together, yet in one day Talbot was twice shocked by the certainty that indeed he loved her.

· They had got on to a train. 'This goes to Chorillos,' Violet said, for in that desert place by the sea they were to spend the day. The train moved and they heard a man say that it was going to Oroya, high up in the Andes. "Jump off," said Talbot as he jumped out and caught her hands. She jumped, not hesitating. It was a small thing but it warmed Talbot to see her fearless, quick and trusting "like a man".

In the evening they walked near the sea: "making me feel a boy again." They watched the seals and the little red crabs that burrowed into the sand. Vic the terrier was with them, for Talbot had given the bitch to Violet, who never before had owned any animal. From a pile of timbers a rat rushed out on to the sand. Vic bounded after it and killed the rat. Violet was aghast, disgusted: "But that is a dog's nature," Talbot laughed. He laughed at her dismay, which had surprised him; but for the pity that was in her he worshipped the woman.

As they walked back to the train he looked at the tall girl walking before him, of whom her father had said: 'She is Juno rather than Aphrodite.' "She looks like Juno, but now I know, she is partly tomboy and partly dove."

The second day of November was her birthday. "She brings spring in this country," he wrote. The soft Peruvian winter was past. At the evening meal, heaped upon the table before them, were violets and jonquils.

"Circe", Talbot called her (because in this his Odyssey she

287

had made him a dish of fruit and wine.) Now he drank and toasted her: "More lucky than Pericles when he deplored that a spring had been taken out of the year, I, in this year, have found a second spring. In the heart of this new spring centres your birthday. We drink, looking at you." At that Beauclerk sighed to himself:' My sweetmeat will leave me soon.'

Four days later Talbot and Violet went to Miraflores, a little town by the Pacific. The day was blue; the sky and the sea blue; on the rocks, by the sea, the great flowers of the morning-glory trailed their trumpets of azure. Little clumps of maidenhair fern sprung out of the cleft, the rock. The sea leapt and swished on the stones of the beach: "shish, shish, just the way you admonish when I say something you do not like," said Talbot.

He had been telling Violet of his journeys; of his days on the delta of the Lena, but even to her he talked jerkily, and with difficulty, of what was so near to himself. Now they were silent, but he was playing with the stones, throwing them up and juggling with them, as he had done on the Lena.

Then, in a few words he told his love. But Violet said nothing because she could scarcely believe that he had said that he loved her. She feared that, pricked by the spur of impulse, he might be betraying himself. Moreover she was ill at ease, remembering the sayings of one whom she had reverenced. 'A man and woman locked in marriage become, each of them, the keeper of the other's soul,' he had said. She saw how great a thing was asked of her. And, above all, in the secret springs of her being was there grace enough to be—to this world-wanderer—as sweet a mistress as his solitude?

Afterwards, with happy silences between, they talked until the sun was low. But because this was to him no light will-o'-the-wisp of love, and because Talbot never found pleasure in any measure but the fullest measure, or any attainment save the ultimate attainment, and because she was not yet his own, he urged against her quick kiss: "Let us wait."

They talked, and again were silent, until the sun was near to setting. When they rose to go they were pledged to one another. They stood for a few instants facing the orb of fire low-mirrored on the horizon. It may be that they wondered what the spaces of their future held. Surely they might go in hope. In

The sapphire day—and Shakespeare

the amplitude of the Pacific, stretching away at their feet, surely they might find a happy augury.

* * *

The first present that he gave her was the volume of Shakespeare with which he had travelled. On the fly-leaf he wrote:

To the Only One
in the Wanderings of a Wanderer.

Afterwards, when she was his wife, he adorned her with the jewels of his family: with diamond wings to wear in her hair and, from the East, a chain of golden birds. As he chose the loveliest: "this necklace of gold-brown diamonds, because of your eyes." She took her jewels everywhere; wore them always, lost and refound them; they had half a hundred adventures. Dining alone with him she would wear them. So, once a kinsman had surprised her on a racing yacht, with Talbot in the tiny cabin. The kinsman misjudged her; he could not have understood that she thought to be with Talbot was holiday as worthy of gay wear as a court festival. After Talbot died, partly in penance and partly for love, she never again wore any jewel; but she kept his first gift to her, the volume of Shakespeare.

CHAPTER IX

*   *   *

'YOU CANNOT RIDE YOUR POLO PONIES INTO THE INTE-
rior,' Talbot was told. 'Even if you have them sent by train to
Oroya, you would find that they could not endure the altitude;
remember the line ascends to nearly sixteen thousand feet.' "I'll
ride up to Oroya and beyond: you will see that it is possible,"
answered Talbot, and fulfilled his word.

'I shall be sadder to see you return than I am to see you go,'
Violet said when they took leave of one another. Talbot could
not know that she was thinking that when he returned from the
mountains, it would be to take her from her father for ever. He
said nothing, but he winced, and his eyes flashed. Hours later
Violet suddenly understood the look he had worn, and she
wrote to tell him the thought which had lain at the back of her
heedless words. Her messenger followed and found him stayed
at an inn. He wrote back a generous letter but nevertheless he
said: "You told me to wash away your words, but the soul is not
a dish-cloth to wash and wring out." In his diary he wrote of
her: "Cynical, fire and ice, pleasure and pain, despair and joy, a
tangled mixture of humanity." Howbeit they were sure of
their love, for it had been tested; his for her had been put to the
trial, hers also for him. Because of words spoken by her phy-
sician (words mistaken, or perhaps misunderstood,) she feared
that she might be unable to bear children. (She who, in secret,
still nursed a doll.) She told this to him; he sighed but said:
"It is you that I want."

The test of her love was the doubt: 'Will marriage with Talbot mean happiness? Certainly not an easy happiness. But if he
became a leper, still I should follow him, therefore let his angers
be as a leprosy; if, perhaps, I am not to be happy with him, it is
certain that without him I cannot be happy.' Violet pondered
the speed and the hazards of this man's life; the stress of his

nature; the tautness of his entire being; the inward daemon that had him in thrall. Pondered too all that he would demand of her. She would have to be his home-haven, and his speeding ship; house-wife, and jungle-wife; Lady of the Manor. 'In a few years I may die overstrained, exhausted: a bird dies quicker than a tortoise; yet I'd choose wings, and death.'

After receiving the letter he travelled up on terraced heights where trees grew, past American Mormons working in mines, and into a country of grass. Then, beyond the austerity of the Andes, beyond the tiresomeness of the treeless plains, he rode down into the tangle of the forest. There, out of small still pools grew arums; on the margin of the laggard waters flamingos stood, and fished.

On, and on he rode, along a narrow way that serpented between heights, and on again until he reached the country of the Indians.

As, from the branches of the great trees hung the long nests of the weaver-birds, so, upon nature, depended the lives of these people.

The agave grew beside them, green and sober for twenty-five years and more, even till a man might count fifty years, or seventy years maybe; then a soaring stem shot up, magnificent with blossom, decked with the only flowers that ever the plant would show. After that was its instant death. But, concurrent with this fatal flowering, offshoots spring up at the foot of the agave, young vessels of its life. No such rare wonder as this blossoming ever glorified the Indians' pagan lives—however long death tarried.

But Talbot turned back because he was ill at ease about Violet. Unknown to her, he had paid two men to be at hand by night, or by day, should she be in need of help, because her father was so plunged in melancholy that at any time his mind might break. Beauclerk had consented fully to the betrothal, but it was hard for him to bear with the man destined to take away his daughter. 'I am tired with seeing Talbot act the ass to your Titania,' he had said, and again, half laughing: 'Oh! go away soon and marry him, and breed a race of idiotic giants.' On the night before Talbot had left for the mountains she had told him: 'my father is angry with you, so lock your door to-night,' and he knew that she was afraid for him, and that she doubted her father's sanity.

When Talbot returned to Lima, news was at hand that Violet's stepmother would arrive in a few days. The time had come when she must leave her father and sail away to be married in London. Talbot and Violet, accompanied by Mrs. Faraday as duenna, by George the groom, with two golden setters, sailed from Callao for Southampton.

In his diary Talbot wrote: "Thank God the most cruel thing I have ever done in my life—to a man I respect—is over."

CHAPTER X

★ ★ ★

'WHAT WILL YOU DRINK, SIR?' ASKED THE SERVANT ON
the ship which plied between Callao and Colon: 'tea, coffee,
or cocoa?' A Peruvian passenger looked up with lifted brows,
the diamond in his ring, and the gold stopping in his tooth
flashed, as he answered, reproachfully: 'I am a passenger of the
first class and am entitled to all; bring me each in its order.'
Violet laughed; but Talbot missed the saying, because, according to his custom, he was eating alone on deck.

Talbot Clifton's diary of the return journey as far as Colon
shows him as sometimes enjoying his lady's society, her "intelli-
gent dark eyes", her poetry that she gave him to read, her
"waking me up this morning as it happened to be my birthday.
I should like a birthday every day under similar circumstances.
. . . And so the day of my thirty-eighth birthday has passed
with a few more wrinkles and grey hairs." But sometimes he
found this "a devil of a journey. Would give £1000 or more
to have it over. . . . I wonder if most engaged men go through
such a rank time as I am having; my interest in married men is
greatly enhanced." Another day he wrote: "Was damned for not
agreeing that a dismal ocean was beautiful. If I had a navvy's
taste I might have agreed. Escorting ladies is, as I expected, a
nerve-racking affair. I shall be forced to take refuge in the
stoke-hole; will be deuced pleased when the voyage is over."
Violet indeed had said: 'Damn you,' for her temper was quick
and she used the expressions of her father.

Two days later, when the ship reached Colon, the great
rains had destroyed the railway lines. No train would cross the
Isthmus before the sailing of the steamer which now was waiting at Panama. The passengers from the western coast drearily
took up their abode for ten days in the hotel until another ship
should arrive at Panama, by which time the rain would have
abated and the broken way be mended.

Not so Talbot—"We'll go by river," he said. "You won't mind, Vi?" 'Of course I don't mind, but I like better to be called Circe than Vi.' "I shall call you Vi—it means life!"

They took an Indian canoe, a dug-out; two Indians steered. The men were offered a good wage if they arrived before the sailing of the outgoing ship. They grumbled at the danger, for the water was a turbulent, dark mass. From the bank, uprooted jungle trees swept along the river, frail houses of palm shivered in the current. Now and again the horns of a bullock rose above a tangle of wreckage.

By sunset the men were tired. 'We stop and will go on again at sunrise.' They landed at a house where lived an old woman with a girl. Talbot and George were shown a room with the earth for its floor, and a table to sleep upon. The younger woman had wished George to stay outside the house because the golden setters, on their chains, had frightened her. She asked: 'Are they wild beasts? Will they eat me?'—'No, señorita, they are faddy feeders' answered George, annoyed because the setters were misjudged.

The old woman gave Violet, and the friend, some sort of bed in a room upstairs. The night was broken by the sound of the old woman scratching herself—troubled by a disease of the skin, or by vermin.

Before the dawn the travellers were up and away, for their ship was to sail early. As the canoe neared Panama it swung into some rapids: 'Remember I have children!' cried Mrs. Faraday. But it was useless now to remember. Violet pulled down her hair, hoping that, if the canoe sank, Talbot thereby would pull her through the water, for she could not swim. George kept the dogs from moving; the Indians did their part whilst Talbot baled. Very unkempt and wet, with but a bag each, safely they reached the steamer when the Blue Peter was about to be hauled down. Without questioning them the officer-in-charge led them towards the steerage until they proved, by their tickets, their right to a better place.

During three weeks' sailing the ship was strangely out of her listed time and everywhere was late, because of some damage to her engines.

Mrs. Faraday and Violet had so few things with them that

the stewardess and the captain lent them clothes. As well as his jersey the captain gave to Violet a saying that served her all her married life. Leaning over the taffrail, smoking his pipe, he said: 'Never let your husband see you in bedroom slippers. It galls a man's finer feelings; sends a lot of marriages to the bottom.' Violet understood. 'Fatal especially with Talbot,' she thought. 'He has lived like a savage, yet he is full of sensibility. From me he asks the fulfilment of his ideals, great and small, and looks to me for the salve of his disillusions. Terrible in his demand for excellence, yet he made excuse for that demand when he said: "It is not that men deserve women to be good, but in that goodness is their only anchorage." ' She broke her musing to answer the captain.

Talbot and Violet, savagely, and suddenly, sometimes would misunderstand one another. Morosely then, a while, would keep apart. Without knowing what she was doing she overtried him. Might-be she was reading early and would come upon something to tell him, or to ask him. Thoughtless, she would pull on a shawl, run into his cabin, jump into his bunk, and call out to George: 'Bring breakfast here to us both.' At night: 'You hardly kissed me, so I can't sleep. Do kiss me now.' Warmly with heart and flesh she loved him, yet had no understanding of the task she put upon him; because, in fact, she was ignorant of the ultimate embrace, she, and perhaps any unawakened woman, could have lived in virginity with the man she worshipped without suffering more than an ill-defined feeling of lack. Once, sweat breaking on his forehead, Talbot flung on a gown and went on deck. "This is not natural and nature has revenges," he said—but she did not understand.

They arrived in England in the midst of the Christmas week and they were met by Caryl, Talbot's youngest brother, and by John Green. It was agreed that next day they would motor to Wales and stay with Talbot's mother. "We must start early or we shall not get there in one day; I will come for you at five o'clock in the morning," he said. Next day before dawn they started. Caryl and John went with them. Before this day Violet had not been in a car. Through snow they went gaily until they came to a swept place in front of a cottage. Water had been poured out, and had frozen. The car slid, ran up

a bank, overturned. In the snow, face downwards, Talbot and
Violet lay. Caryl thought they were dead. They were only
stunned, but the car being harmed they hired a horse and drove
to the nearest station. "The horse is balling," Talbot said to
Caryl. Violet did not understand that he spoke of snow in the
hooves of the horse, which caused it to go gingerly. She thought
that Talbot's mind was suffering from the fall.

He sent a telegram to the station-master: "Keep train very
important passengers arriving." The train was waiting; Talbot
laughed so delightedly at his own brazenness, that the guard,
who knew him, also laughed. Claude Lowther, kinsman and
friend of Talbot, was in the train. Merry, he made a prophecy
to Violet. 'During your married life,' he said, 'you'll eat when
Talbot's hungry, and you'll sleep when Talbot's tired.'

Long after sunset the travellers arrived at Edwinsford (2). To tease Violet, Talbot made
her known to his stepfather as
"the girl I picked up in
South America".

CHAPTER XI

★   ★   ★

THE WEDDING-RING MUST NOT BE MERELY METAL, BUT
Talbot, before the marriage, must wear it upon him, must fill it
with thoughts. In the signet-ring which Violet was giving him
would be engraved defiantly: 'Love never faileth.'

The night before the wedding Violet, wondering if indeed
there is a God, prayed ardently, clasping the veil she would
take—though with a difference.

'I wish I had not to sign a promise that the children be
Catholics; I should like them to grow up without a creed,' she
had said. Talbot had answered: "If we have boys, they especially
will need to love the Virgin; that devotion will be the installa-
tion of the women who come into their lives." So she made
the promise.

At the rite, the priest speaking low told Violet of fire: of the
vestal flame; of the sanctuary lamp; of the hearth-fire: 'Tend
it' he said. To Talbot he recalled the old fidelities of his race,
true to the Red Rose, true to the Faith—though that had meant
exile—true to the lost cause of the Stuarts—though it had meant
loss of ancestral lands—*mortem aut triumphum*—be true for ever
to this Sacrament.

★   ★   ★

"Do women drop and knock over fifty per cent more things
than men?" Accustomed to being with athletes and savages,
dexterous and true of eye, Talbot in his diary wrote that question. He wondered, with a laugh, at many things about his wife,
who was, in a strange ruthless way, thorough-paced almost as
himself, and with a like fixity of purpose. Once, closing a
door, a stag's head, fastened above it, fell and cut his brow. And
pale and with a bleeding gash, he asked Violet for an ointment.
Intent upon her housekeeping she answered: 'Oh! poor Toby,
I'll come and put some on in a few moments after I have ordered

297

the food.' His laugh cured him: "Well it took a King and an orange girl to generate her."

Because the women who had been in his life had played but small and transient parts, and, too, because he knew how easily provoked he was, Talbot was shy of Violet. "She is too tender a target for my barbs." Therefore he would snatch at strange people to make a third in the house—at one time an old priest, then a scheming Hungarian girl. At last he knew no third was needed. To onlookers this man and woman seemed to conform to one another as by a tally, natural and evident. Maybe they were bound to one another by a determined conjunction, like that of two planets moving in the same degree of the zodiac (3).

The slowness of his speech, counter-battering the quickness of his thoughts, fretted him. He would leave unsaid the orderly succession of his reasoning, and so put a strain on his listener who would likely think his utterances inconsequent. "Oh, you tell him," he would say, and Violet, who knew his mind, would interpret it. She often felt that he stood alone, and that she was the link between him and his fellows.

His pleasure in their far Scottish home was to teach her. "Don't believe all you hear; shut your books and observe for yourself; I should have been killed long ago if I had not been observant." He untaught her things she had been taught as a child. 'Look where you are walking,' her nurse had said. Talbot said: "Do not look at your feet or at the bog; look at the birds, look for the deer." He taught her to know the birds in flight.

'What's sauce for the goose is sauce for the gander,' her nurse had said. Talbot told her that on a woman the law of chastity lies far heavier than on a man. He showed her how a man is set like a seal upon his wife's body, and that if she bear him a child she can never escape him. "If the man dies and the woman has a child by another man, that later child might still be cast in the mould of the first husband."

He warned her that man does not cleave easily to one woman, and nature does not help him to keep his lusts in leash, because the outcome of his desires is without gravity for him. "It's not a case of loving lightly, for love need not come into it," he said. 'Through their greed men lose much,' pondered Violet. 'Be-

298

lieving that Talbot would kill my body were I to be unfaithful, believing that were I unchaste I would shatter an ordered spiritual beauty which is beyond my understanding, this heightens and deepens the ravishment of clinging to him in a nearness that with any other would be ruin.'

Teasingly he taught her to reason, when her spoken thoughts were random: "Socrates is reported to have said that nothing is reasonable unless it can be proved in a reasonable manner"—so he would mock.

He showed her how to use a spy-glass, lying on the hill, and to walk erect like a woman of the desert. If she saw him clouded by some disappointment she would fly to her books and read about some tree, some flower, some word he did not know. She would give him a new fact foreknowing that his pleasure in it would dispel the cloud. She wooed him through his mind. She was glad she could not lure him through her body nor use her flesh as a bait to the wild thing in him. A woman had told her that, once married, she would have that power over him. Violet thought with horror, 'Shall I use my flesh to tame him as a hawk is tamed by meat? Shall I use my sex to allure him as the male snake is lured by the smear of the female laid upon the charmer?' It was not so, and she was glad that she had not to stoop, glad that he must have from her always the dual beatitude of love, and peace. She did not inebriate him more than had other women, but they had been as a heady wine leaving a stale dryness in the mouth. She was a generous, still wine, cordial and mellow, leaving no regret; she was love and peace.

He taught her ample regard for humbler people, and to cherish their feelings. "Wave to the children of the village when we pass," he ordered. His hope tended towards growth in love and peace. Therefore, in the uncurtained softness of each night, on his bed he returned to the little prayers of his childhood, so long unsaid. On the first day of the week he said them in a whisper so that Violet might hear; on those nights he added the wanderer's song, claiming the Lord as Shepherd.

Through bitter remorse Violet learnt Highland hospitality. Talbot had gone with the fishermen to try for a salmon; she was to follow. An east wind was blowing. "So it's hopeless," he had said. But she thought he certainly would catch a fish.

A salmon—a remorse

Amused at her ignorant persistence: "Well, I'll flog the waters," he said. A mile or two from the house a dark-haired, wild-looking man had asked for money. Violet had none with her and curtly said so. When she told Talbot he said: "Surely you told him to go to the house for food?" She shook her head. "No one yet ever travelled hungry past it; luckily he will get food from the stalker's wife if he goes along the lower road." At that moment, passing a dead ewe, Violet asked, 'What did that beast die of, Sutherland?' 'Just poverty, ma'am.' 'Oh, the poor creature.' Then, in a flash, she knew she had pitied the beast though she had scorned the man.

Talbot cast his line. As Violet watched him she nibbled the bog-myrtle that grew upon the bank. Matched against her remorse its bitterness was sweet. Suddenly a salmon rose; her thoughts were shattered, she leapt up to watch. The fish was caught and she was 'blooded'. But all her life she remembered, shamefaced, her rejection of the beggar.

CHAPTER XII

★　　★　　★

"COME AT ONCE—HAVE FOUND A NEW RELIGION:" SO TO
be summoned gave pleasure to Violet. The lure was well
chosen; and, laughing, she raced upstairs to pack. Two days
before, Talbot had gone abroad; because of strife between them
she had stayed in England. Often, in his height, Baruchial must
have trembled because, in the nature of each, a root of ferocity
threatened the flowering of their lives.

More than once Talbot, so gentle with the lowly, was rude
to friends of Violet's youth. This angered her. Only in later
years he explained that he always had the impulse to fell anyone who had known her before he had seen her. "Hateful that
the fellow should have seen you with your hair down." But on
this occasion it was through Violet's fault that strife was between
them. 'My words bit like the teeth of a dog—if my dog had
bitten me I should whip it. That I remember, I will do this.'
With the tongs she snatched a red coal out of the fire and
branded her arm. Talbot had gone abroad without knowing of
her self-punishment. With the burn still sore Violet now followed.

The very height at which the ideal was pitched was a menace,
for, rather than have their common life made waste by lacks in
their love, Talbot would renew his life of wandering in Central
Africa. He warned her that he would do so, and, because she
knew of the awful strength of his word, she put a bit into her
mouth, a prayer into her heart. He himself was appalled at his
wraths. "Don't answer my anger with anger; help me instead."
A contention would pierce his sleep, even his dreams. Once at
dawn, awakening after a disagreement with Violet, he found
the signet-ring thrown into the far corner of the room: "You
see what a danger my temper is," he sighed.

Violet often failed in serenity, but she made atonement. She

301

thought: 'I must break down his hardness, his coldness; I must be like the stone-breaker, the little saxifrage. Its tender green strength can shatter rocks; my love must be as powerful.'

In later years discord seldom set them on edge, she being more restrained and he more easy. But yet in those years there was one time when they might have fallen suddenly apart. It happened that in anger, abruptly, she went away for many days. When she returned, Talbot had moved into a small room at the other end of the house. Fixed in woe she slept on the floor outside his door. When the very number of her nights away from his house had passed, Talbot, touched, re-turned to her room.

CHAPTER XIII

⋆   ⋆   ⋆

RHIDOROCH, THE HOME IN SCOTLAND, A HIRELING HOUSE, and Lytham, where Violet had not yet lived—both were closed. Talbot and his wife were on the sea.

The cutter *Maoona* was their home. She was a fifteen-metre racing boat, steel-framed, and of planked mahogany, built in Scotland, and manned by a crew of eight men. They came from Brightlingsea and Wyvenhoe. Fine men to watch, lean and hard and quick, dressed in white.

The racing season was nearing its end. They had raced on the Clyde in May, and then at Ostend. Now August found them at Le Havre, and September would shine on them, hoisting up their full line of racing flags—one for every win. So the season would end.

During these months Talbot had savoured again the ups and downs of circumstance which in youth had been his welcome portion. An outlay which he could not have foreseen caused him to be without money in Ostend. Shooting pigeons, he had won several prizes, but a Sèvres vase, a silver cup and a medal were not helpful in this particular strait. The day for paying the men's wages was near. Confident in his good fortune at the gaming-table he backed a certain rhythm of numbers, won and paid the hands. But that night a friend asked them to a sumptuous meal to which were invited many guests. At the end of the dinner someone said: 'Let's toss as to whether our host should pay all, or each of us his share.' They tossed, and Talbot had two dinners to pay for, so that the money won at the tables was diminished.

Next day, in a storm, the *Maoona* was the only yacht to sail the course. The prize money sufficed till more money was sent from England.

Another day in a big sea near Ostend, with *Maoona* sailing into the wind, someone shouted 'Man overboard!' Talbot, in a

flash, decided to take a risk. "Bring her back, don't put about!
Gybe her!" he shouted. *Maoona* had swung round to just over
where the man had fallen. A life-buoy thrown to him kept him
afloat until the boat was lowered. Afterwards his captain, Diaper, said: 'Last time I saw a man overboard we tacked back and
found we had left him far behind in the water; he was nearly
drowned when we did reach him.'

But the cry of 'Man overboard' had often failed to stay a
leading yacht; she would race on—a losing boat behind could
save the man. It had been known that the captain would speed
on even though the owner had slipped overboard. A new rule
had changed this by making it a condition of a win that a yacht
should come in with the number of her crew complete.

To-day there was a fresh breeze; the waters of Le Havre
sparkled in the sunlight. "There is nothing in the world as
exciting as this," thought Talbot when the starting gun sounded
over the sea and the *Maoona* surged forward abreast with
Mariska.

He could not think of any other pleasant endeavour which
made as many demands on a man's fixed attention as did this
racing of sail against sail, nor any which as undeniably rewarded
skill, and delicacy of touch. Two or three seconds lost or gained
might mean as many miles of gain or of loss.

With a smaller boat than the *Maoona* the steering was as
delicate a handiwork as driving four horses, the tiller demanding as fine a tact as the mouth of a thoroughbred. To handle the
tiller were too gross a word for this fingering. Being a big boat
the *Maoona* was steered by wheel, so that the skill of the master
lay in watching the sails, the white lovely sails, mainsail and
topsail and foresail.

Right into the wind was lively sailing; it quickened the
pulses to meet the sea. Sometimes the yacht must be luffed and
allowed to run down the troughs of the sea rather than that she
should strain. Sailing off the wind needed greater thought, and
a more solicitous watching of the sheets. The relish of such
racing was increased ninefold because of the zest of the men and
of Diaper, the captain. The crew trimmed *Maoona* well when,
because of the wind blowing on her quarter, she heeled over.
Then they lay clinging to the decks sprayed by the sea.

Maoona—in remembrance

After midday the wind dropped. The *Maoona* had rounded a mark against a foul tide. Diaper had set the spinnaker. *Maoona* ran away before the wind, leaving two of her rivals the wrong side of the mark. The tardy boats would be caught by the tide; the prudent other yacht and *Maoona* lay almost becalmed, but they were miles beyond the two laggards.

Diaper now took over the charge of the race. The stress of Talbot's attention was released; with *Maoona*, his mind drifted. "How angry I was with Vi yesterday because she did not know, or care, which way the wind was blowing. Probably few women do notice that, nor even know north from south."

The wind had always meant much to Talbot; with dominion it had blown through his life. There was the wind to watch whilst stalking red-deer, the talebearing wind that served the beasts by blowing on their nostrils as they fed, always up wind. A blade of grass thrown up would test the wind's direction. The wild-geese and the widgeon had the wind as their ally. The *Maoona* had the wind for servant; the very lightest wind was shown on the face of the sea. In Hudson's Bay Talbot had taken the blowing of the south wind as the sign of God's decision for him. Helping winds had blown on the red blanket which was the sail of his sledge in Barren Lands. Without the helping wind maybe Atonguela, and the dog Agilue, and he, would never have reached Fort Churchill. 'Maoona, Maoona—which way?' How often had Atonguela said that as they pursued their course to Churchill; this speedy boat Talbot had named *Maoona*—in remembrance.

But though Vi was not yet aware of the forces that be outside of books, yet she was game. At some most early hour she had gone on deck because, in his sleep, himself had called out: "is the starting flag up?" and she, imagining him to be awake, had climbed up to look. And on that rough day, when they had sailed out from Ostend, and alone of the racing yachts had made the course, Violet had not demurred—but patiently was seasick—so Talbot mused.

Had Talbot foreseen marriage he would not have built *Maoona*, because a fifteen-metre racing yacht was not a home befitting a woman going in expectation of her first child. He must sell *Maoona*, open Lytham Hall, live bucolically (4). But

no house would be lucky as this white-hulled cutter—this
lively, moving, wingèd, darling place. The wind
rising, Talbot's thoughts turned all upon the
race. Not shivering, or trembling, the sails
of *Maoona* must bear her near the
course. Full of wind her sails
should be; full and by,
full and by—so
must *Maoona*
sail.

CHAPTER XIV

★ ★ ★

"THIS HOUSE LIES FIVE FEET BELOW THE LEVEL OF THE sea. Look at the blanket of damp wrapped about it!" said Talbot as he stood at the front door of Lytham Hall one evening after dusk. He was not fully well here, or happy. Around the house the flat Fylde country lay; here and there were little clumps of trees. A charm, a prosperous dignity about it, but the hunter, the pioneer, the solitary one, he was left to yearn.

The solid red-brick farms, all of them indeed his pride, but his fellowship was not with this kind. True, he enjoyed the volume of things there was to learn about this land; in contrast with the raw countries wherein he had lived was this agèd, this Fylde country. He approved the clause in the farmers' leases protecting the permanent grasslands which, by a heavy penalty, were guarded from the plough. Such grass could not be converted into tillage without the consent of the owner of the land.

Soured townsmen, uprooted themselves, forgetful of tradition and without understanding, would see in this clause an injustice to the farmer. How should such men know the difference between arable grassland and the permanent grassland? They did not know that a hundred years, or more, must enrich the grassland ere it be dubbed permanent grass. They did not know of its sweet accretion of fertility and that, in the language of law, to plough over such land is 'waste'.

Two or more crops would spring up out of such soil, stronger than crops dunged over, and fertilized. Quick return, quick gain for a few years—but at the price of an enduring loss to the land. Such land, now and again, might be conceded to tillage, but not without long thought.

Certain it is that he took pleasure in the age of this Palatinate, in the background of the centuries, in the distances of the past converging on this present. Even in his own Saxon name,

Clyfton—the ton or enclosure of Clyf, the stockaded place. Pleasure there was in holding, once and again, a Manor Court. Of such Courts Baron there were three, till lately four. At Westby, at Marton, for over six hundred years, one of Talbot's name could so preside; but at Lytham for less than three hundred years.

Fifteen or twenty people might attend, they being the chief tenants upon that part of the estate. The foreman of the Courts Jury would be chosen, that being, when he was present, Talbot himself. The oath stood thus: 'I swear by Almighty God that I as foreman of this Jury together with my fellows will well and truly enquire and true presentment make of all such matters and things as shall be given me in charge. I will present no one from envy or malice nor will I refrain from presenting anyone from fear affinity affection or regard. But I will true presentment make of all such matters and things as I shall know to be presentable to the best of my belief and knowledge.' The jurymen afterwards were sworn in and were appointed to some among these: Constable, Afferor, Pinder, By-law man, Game Preserver, Searcher of Weights and Measures, Moss Reeve, Wreck Searcher and Overseer.

Afterwards, cheerfully, the tenants would disburse what small fines might be put upon them for breaches of the common good, guilty perhaps of a dog's trespass or of a watercourse not cleaned. The decision of the Court was sustained by moral force alone, for indeed no other power was acceded to it whereby to enforce its decisions (5).

Talbot smiled, though with understanding, at the "monuments to obstinacy", as he called them, which monuments were all within a few miles of Lytham. There was the church with double towers, double because the two sisters who had built the church wished variously about the tower, and each had to get her way. Then there was the mill closed by day because the master had told his men he would close it if they ceased work. Close it he did, and for ever, and that in spite of their after entreaties. But at night, heartbroken, the master, ghostlike, haunted the mill. Talbot smiled too at another proof of obstinacy, that of the man with the house in the centre of a golf links. He would not move thence nor would he have his windows

TALBOT CLIFTON, OF LYTHAM
AFTER A PAINTING AT LYTHAM HALL
BY F. COPNALL, 1908

broken by balls. 'I will live here like this,' he had said, and round his house had built a wooden palisade; for, though it prevented his seeing earth or sky, the golf balls could never now break his windows.

Close to the park Talbot's forefathers had seen the ruff nesting in the marshes. They had brought over Dutchmen and had drained the land. Round about, Talbot, when a boy, had walked among the sandhills by the sea, snaring rabbits and shooting partridges. Even now, in the demesne, sheldrake nested, choosing, sometimes, the rabbit holes. But the town, dragon-like, was lapping the wild things, the sandhills and the stargrass: was swallowing even the farmlands, along with the laborious, worthy lives of farmers, and of fishermen—these fishermen who went for shrimps away from the mouth of the Ribble to the sea. The town was stomaching the life even of the sea.

Talbot, whilst he lived at Lytham from 1908 to 1922, tried to do his duty. For the good of his heirs he had made himself 'a tenant for life' of the estate and had thereby restricted his own liberty to spend. He worked as County Councillor with zest: he forced himself to speak in public (for this demand was put upon him); he even succeeded, and that in spite of the harry of his impeded utterance; but the wrack of his nerve only he could gauge.

Pity it was that Lytham Hall, so beautiful a dwelling, had not sheltered happy children. Long after the cannons of the Crimean War had been silenced, there still was repeated in the family the earlier harsh words of the mother of Wykeham Clifton, who fought in that war. Wykeham had run to Hetty his mother: 'I've put my sailing boat in a dyke I'd made out there in the park, and she's been sailing,' he said. 'You should not cut up your father's property,' she scolded.

When John Talbot, the grandfather of this Talbot, succeeded Thomas his father, as squire he had married Cecily Lowther (6), and her grief, perhaps, still hung about the walls. She had been forced to marry him, but after her marriage she had closeted herself for three days in her room, weeping alone. She had come out of that room embittered, with darting tongue, and heart of gall. She had never grown to love her teasing witty man. She was beneficent to the poor, but violent in her angers.

Even when he was slowly dying she was harsh to their only son Harry, who never became squire. Harry grew up endowed with a brilliant mind, and cursed with scarlet tempers. He had never felt himself cherished at home.

Talbot once said: "At Lytham I was not happy as a boy excepting when once I was ill and left in the house alone with my nurse Patch." When he was seven years old he ran away, hiding himself in a hay-cart on its way to Preston, and he was not found for many days. All these years without love had blemished the house. Even the children of Violet may have felt sometimes forlorn, for she did not weigh them against her husband and would, at any time, leave them to follow him.

In the first years of marriage Violet had been a strange wife, more befitting 'the man from the stars' than the Lord of the Manor. Since her childhood she had not lived in England. In Bolivia she had seen prisoners penned together in cages like captive animals. In Peru she had seen strange things and had lacked the influence of any woman. Her father, in temper of mind, different from other men, had trained her thoughts; whilst a man of science, righteous but unbelieving, had so directed her later studies that she lost all belief in God.

Therefore, as the wife of the squire she took up her life in a fashion tender, but foreign.

. After her first visit to the hospital which the old John Talbot had founded, she took the matron's hands and, overcome by pity, put money into them. 'Spend this in putting out of their pain people who cannot recover, that agonized child the first.' But the matron told her that the law of England forbade it. Visiting the wife of a vicar, the mother of many children, she urged: 'Dear Mrs. Gilbertson-Pritchard, it is so sad to see women worn out with child-bearing; do come with me to teach them otherwise.' But the gentle lady sweetly spoke refusal.

In later years came change of vision. Violet had struggled out of unbelief in God and, though long mazed, had won her way to beatitude as being now welded into the Spiritual Body which nourished, which nourishes: Dionysius; St. Augustine; him of Aquin; Francis; the Catherines; St. Elizabeth.

"We have too many children," Talbot once said; he wished that the family might remain rooted in the land for nine hun-

310

dred and ninety-nine years, as forecast by the written parchment leases of his lands. The family could only persist, so it
seemed to him, if the younger branches were not over-plenti-
ful, sapping its strength away. 'Five is a blessed number,' comforted Violet, 'a child to harbour in each of the wounds of
Christ.'

In her rejoiced the poet, the maker. To her it was wonderful
to be linked to all mothering creatures—bird in nest, and sheep
in meadow. Her heart beat faster with joy when, in the East, she
saw elephants, and apes, nursing their young at their breasts.

Whenever she was carrying a child she cherished the young
life by brooding on the beautiful, by harnessing her thoughts to
the sublime. From her vision she blotted out the deformed,
whether it was expressed in flesh or was without visible texture.
Quickly: 'Angels wipe it from my thoughts,' she would pray.

She said to Talbot that they should be glad of the children:
'because for all eternity these souls will exist as beings full of
joy and beauty. We should be glad had we written five
poems, or built five pyramids, or five temples, which
for all time would be splendid. These living
souls will be shining—not only for
time, but for eternity.' "We
may hope that," said
Talbot.

CHAPTER XV

VIOLET, WHEN FIRST SHE WAS MARRIED, SO OFTEN ACTED in haste that it was lucky she did not more often do things entirely foolish.

There was the day when she and Talbot went to the house of a painter. He showed them a picture, lovely but not great—Diana hunting. Violet drew Talbot behind a great curtain away from the artist. 'If you will sell your yacht I will sell my diamonds and we can buy the picture,' she urged. The price the artist had named was a high one. Talbot laughed, and the picture was not bought.

In Lima, Violet had been used to seeing children offered in the streets for adoption; stringent laws governed the business, but nevertheless the children were exchanged for money. And so, when soon after her marriage pygmies were brought from Central Africa to England: 'It would be wonderful to have some to study, and we could make them happy,' she said and forthwith wrote to Jamrach for a pygmy man and woman, with child preferred. Talbot said nothing but waited and watched, his dressing-room being arranged suitably for their reception. When Jamrach's answer came his laughter filled the hall. Its purport was that the Law of England forbade the buying of people, but would she instead buy a pygmy pony? To allay her disappointment Talbot bought her a small pony from Iceland, and every night after dinner it was led into the dining-room to be fed with such things as she could train it to eat.

'Kill socialism with love,' Bernard Vaughan once had said to those two, but without any set design they gave a share of their good fortune, and found it multiplied thereby. Through the wrought-iron, wide-open gates of the park came the towns-people, once or twice in the week, and they saw the great hares, the jack-a-pods loping along, and the pigeons circling about the manorial pigeon-cot. 'I'm glad,' thought Violet, 'that because we always spend more, not less, than we can afford, we

are saved from ever feeling complacent or rich.' "Invite him to
the house, nurse him here, make him care for life again," said
Talbot to Violet when in Lytham a man tried to kill himself.
The man stayed with them a long while. "Offer the boy's
father a place in the park where he can bury his son," Talbot
said, when a young man shot himself.

At this time Talbot was unduly given to games—billiards
sometimes and golf. One day, quill pen in hand, Dunsany said
to him: 'If Waterloo was won on the cricket-fields of Eton the
next war will be lost on the putting-greens of the suburbs.'
"All the same it's a good game," said Talbot. And being asked:
'Do you feel loving to-night?' "Oh! no, my golf is far too bad,"
laughed Talbot.

Sometimes the irresponsible, bachelor Talbot would come
uppermost. So once, when they were bound for Berlin, Talbot
said, at the station in Paris: "Come along, Vi, this train looks so
comfortable, we will go by it!" They got into the cheerful
restaurant carriage which had allured Talbot. 'But where does
this train go?' They arrived at Rome.

The things Talbot liked best in their life at Lytham before
the war were the assembling of orchids, and the playing of his
organ. The pipes were all over the house; he put the echo organ
in the best bedroom. The house shook with music: "most
companionable of the arts," Talbot and Violet agreed: "with
us in the cradle and the nursery, in marriage, in war, in victory
and in death": 'and the pastime of Heaven.' Soon after their
marriage he had gone far east with his wife to search for orchids
in Burma, Malaya, the Andaman Islands (7) and in the Nico-
bars. They had brought back many plants to England, raising
seeds from the blossoms. He gave the names of his friends to the
lovely flowers which he had crossed. " Come and help to wash
four hundred orchids, Vi"; and they would work with the
gardener sponging the broad leaves. Freed of dust and smoke
the plants breathed as in the jungle. Violet once took, into
the house of the Cattleyas, a lily, an iris, and a rose. Held up
against the orchids the texture of these other flowers was coarse.
Alone the iris, in its frail perfection, could bear comparison
with the ethereal aspect of the orchids. "Splendid in variety"
thought Talbot as he moved from the lovely phaleonopsis to

The beloved orchids

the gnomelike anguloa, hairy and fleshy, blotched and barred, sanguineous. His phaleonopses were thriving in a small melon house; he had found them in the mangrove swamps of the Andaman Islands. Talbot enjoyed their names, like the words of Mary's litany—Amabilis, nobilis, Aurea, grandiflora. He liked their habit of sweet cleanliness. He knew that they would die if the moss about their roots was wilted, or if their water was defiled. The heart of the plant would perish quickly if within it lay drip of water.

If her children were troublesome or fretted, Violet would put down the fairy tales and pull out some books with pictures of all the orchids. With them she would turn page after page. She would show them the green swan-orchid, each bird-shaped flower thrust from the long stem: 'This is better than a fairy tale.' She would show them another kind, so that they might know that the stars had been made flowers. She would laugh with them at the pixie, greencapped heads of the bulbophyllum; she would shudder with the children at the picture of the catasetum, 'so ugly that it might be the presentment of a sin'.

The children liked to be told of the sweet wild orchids growing in the North of Britain, of the kind that are so established in their own earth that to move them and to plant them, even a little way from where they first grew, kills them.

The blue vanda made them good. As she kissed the children and gave to them, kneeling, the evening blessing, she showed one last picture. It was of the waxy fragrant white orchid which enshrines the semblance of a dove.

If Harry, gone to bed, was still uneasy, she would talk to him in the faint light. She would tell him that the trees stood guardian between him and the town; that the blades of grass were like swords to protect him. Then as a lullaby, again and again, the names of the shining: Jupiter, Venus, Neptune, Mars, Saturn, Mercury, Uranus; Michael, Raphael, Gabriel, Uriel, Baruchial (who holds the lightning), and Jupiter, Venus, Neptune—on and on—till the blue eyes closed, and the black head was quiet on the pillow. Talbot, finding them so one night, said, as he moved away: "How different I should be now had my boyhood been thus."

314

CHAPTER XVI

★　★　★

ON THE FIFTEENTH DAY OF AUGUST, 1914, TALBOT LEFT
Lytham at five in the morning (8). By nine o'clock he was in
London and by ten o'clock at the War Office. Could he serve by
instructing the men in the use of the telescope or act as scout
with the spy-glass? In the Boer War he had seen lives thrown
away which, by means of his telescope, could have been saved.
The Zeiss glass he knew to be good, but at several miles' distance
it was not possible to see fine differences—whether for instance
a man be alive or dead. The War Office had not now time for
any such individual effort; inevitably only mass effort could be
favoured. Talbot's difficult speech debarred him from command, yet surely he would find something to do! He obtained
permission to wear the King's khaki and to hold himself ready.
Then followed the unnerving task of finding useful work; even
while he was seeking, there came the painful loss of a friend who
had crossed over from Canada. The man had left his legion of
workmen and the great business which he had founded. He had
offered himself to England. He had been told there was no need
for him, no work for him at all. That was his death sentence, for
he drowned himself in the sea. Talbot in the past had loved the
man and this waste of his friend was very bitter.

Soon after Talbot went to le Havre, and with him Violet.
The Belgians were in need of cars and of every kind of help.
Le Havre was their base. The Baron de Bassompierre received
them in a lucky hour. He needed a fast car to take Mr. Gibson
(9) to Dunkerque, and as well there were letters to convey to
the King and Queen of the Belgians. Violet, he conceded,
might be useful, so she was given a pass. In those early days of
the war the French children were glad to see the advent of the
English. From the roadside they cheered their passing up towards the front. From the north, miles of homeless people

moved in piteous procession before the oncoming of the enemy.

Talbot and Mr. Gibson passed the night at Abbeville, and here, through her folly, Violet was arrested. Thoughtlessly she had given a French officer a piece of misinformation. Talbot redeemed her. Next morning at four o'clock he woke her. "This is the hour when spies are shot," he teased.

From Dunkerque, along an avenue, they drove towards la Panne, seeking the small house of the King of the Belgians. Coming from the trenches, French and Belgian soldiers staggered towards Dunkerque. The lights of the car blinded the men and forced some of them to move a few paces off the main road. For this added yard of torment one of the men cursed Talbot. Violet shivered, knowing themselves to be indeed accursed for having added a jot to the horrible sum of that day's pain.

Rout of waves roaring, of enemy cannon shelling Belgium— that was what, night and day, the Queen heard in her small house at la Panne, yet serenely she came in to receive from Talbot the letters he had brought. They were from her children, were packed in English autumn leaves—'à papa', 'à maman'. Later the King entered. His brilliant eyes, his height, his whole heroic bearing made the moment of his entrance not to be forgotten.

A few days later Doctor Hector Munro accepted Talbot as a helper. 'Your big car, with room for a stretcher, is just what I need, and with you as driver we shall save many lives.'

This was the third of November, at Ypres, ruined by the shelling of the day before. For weeks after that the two men worked, bringing in the wounded. Munro said: 'I do not care where I put them—in a church, deserted house, or square, or whether I do complicate official records by so doing, for surely anything is better than leaving the men, wounded, and frostbitten, in the radius of that active hell.'

Between Ypres and Abbeville, early one morning, German shells fell on to the high-road in front of a British detachment (10). Sharp rang the order : 'Don't run—walk!' All the men turned and faced Ypres. Talbot drove farther up the road to turn the car. He had just stopped so as to make Violet get down, and turn back with the rest. He laughed to see her ordered into a military wagon, whilst a Tommy on the road called out: 'Who's that prisoner you've got? Is she a spy?'

Most of the time during which Talbot was with Dr. Munro, Violet worked at Dunkerque with a French officer who lodged in the same house. He was in charge of great bales of clothes which came from Paris. To every garment was pinned a note written by the maker, a good wish, a prayer, an encouragement. Mahomed, the son of that Algerian chief who years before had revolted against the French, came into the room and haughtily asked for clothes for his splendid men. They had come of their own will from Africa to fight; some of them he said were now wearing socks of paper. The officer answered: 'I cannot give you any of these clothes as they have been sent out for French soldiers.' 'My men need clothing. It should also be remembered that they are not conscripts,' stormed the departing chieftain.

By night Violet helped Sarah Macnaughton in the kitchen that she had established in the railway station. After sunset, straight from the battlefields, the French wounded soldiers lurched in, and flung themselves into an unwarmed train, there to wait for hours, perhaps even until the morning. When dawn broke the women went to the farm near by to get vegetables and meat, and to search for fresh milk for the men's evening meal. Violet was obsessed by the pain, and by the blood. When she slept she dreamt that the sheets were shrouds, dark with blood.

At the corners of the streets in Dunkerque were pictures of the Stations of the Cross. At one corner was a signpost and past it marched legions of young men. On this cross-board was painted: "TO YPRES".

But the horror of those days was redeemed by one loveliness; by the word 'camarade'. Offer drink to the wounded, or a hand to lead the blinded, the cup is pushed away, and the guiding hand. 'Give it to camarade;' over and over again. It was as though some fabled, splendid love-story were being lived anew; as though the Son of Man made revelation of His Heart. The everyday love of men and women paled quite beside this agonized solicitude, this union through suffering; this wedding made in fire, and sealed in blood.

Dunkerque and England

Several times, on business for Hector Munro, Talbot and Violet went from Dunkerque to England in ships which sailed for grimmest duty only, and at great hazard. Then a letter from the Admiralty instructed Talbot, with his yacht, to serve Admiral Tupper at Stornoway. He felt that now this would be a greater service. So he left Lytham Hall to a Belgian homeless family; he raised, and gave money for the first motor soup-kitchen to be used for the Belgian troops. He returned to Belgium and, withholding his name, gave the kitchen to Doctor Munro, for presentation to the Queen.

As for the last time they sailed this sea, beset with floating mines and submarines, Violet said: 'When we get home I have something wonderful to tell you.' That instant the ship shook. Whistles screamed, the engines were reversed: the ship barely avoided striking a floating mine; even so she had grazed it. This was the second time within the hour that she had escaped that peril. 'I cannot tell you here on this awful death-sea.' Talbot laughed, though gently:

"Don't wait to get home, tell me now.
This place is as good as another,
for wherever you are is
home."

CHAPTER XVII

★　　★　　★

THERE WAS NOT VERY MUCH, NOT INDEED ENOUGH, WORK
for Talbot to do between North Uist and Stornoway, the seas
being tempestuous and mine-sown, and the yacht, the *White
Eagle*, so small that the Admiralty was loth to employ her even
at Talbot's own risk, and expense. But merely to watch the
coast around North Uist was too light a task. Talbot grew
uneasy.

It was early in 1917. The lease of the deer forest in Uist came
to its term; it must be renewed or must lapse. Whilst these
dovetailing circumstances were being considered, Talbot learned
of work to do on the west coast of Ireland. Admiral Barton
needed an R.N.V.R. officer for that part. An officer with a
yacht would be the more valued as, so far, no yacht had been
available, and Q-boats did the work when they were in those
waters. Talbot was given the rank of Lieutenant in the
R.N.V.R. and wore the naval uniform. As though everything
pointed to that work, there came up for sale a fishing lodge, with
shooting and fishing rights. The house stood under the Nine
Pins of Connemara; it would be in the heart of the Coastguard
work; its price was a jest. "I'd like to buy it and work there till
the end of the war," Talbot said. "Come, Vi, and see it, and see
Admiral Barton with me."

Going from Lytham was a venture for her because the baby
Michael was her nurseling, but she put him to be mothered by
a soft-eyed Jersey cow and she risked leaving him for three
days or more. She returned with her heart in the work which
had been offered to Talbot, and Michael went back to her
breast with a grunt of content.

Next time they went from Lytham it was to live in Ireland;
she took the nurseling, and three of their other children; the
eldest, Harry, was at school.

He who sold said to Talbot: 'It is our custom that, when a place such as this is bought, the people on the estate must be compelled to put into the road all that belongs to them. The houses of the tenants must be bare, otherwise it could some day be said that these houses were not yours.'

Therefore, past tripods and cauldrons, past tables, beds, and chairs, and all the humble household gear of the peasants, Talbot and his wife walked along the road to Kylemore House. At the locked door of that house Talbot was given its key. He must unlock the door, and in front of witnesses he must walk across the threshold. To prove his possession of the lands some earth was put into his hands.

★   ★   ★

The *White Eagle* had been sold, and the *Cabar Feidh*—Head of a Stag—was bought instead. She was ketch-rigged with red sails. She was white, and long, and spare. The Canon at Letterfrack said: 'I know the captain for you,' and, although Conboy did not want to serve, for he had boats to build and liked to be free, yet the Canon compelled him. So Conboy and 'the boss', as he named Talbot, with Violet, and now and then a naval officer, sailed to the islands—to Aran, to Bofin, and as far away as Westport. Even when, perforce, Q-boats lay tossed at anchor, the *Cabar Feidh* could take the sea; no waters were too wild for her. Conboy had a voice that carried above the waves and the wind, and he and his master knew no trepidation. Conboy could not read or write but he knew the names of the fish, and the speed at which they swam in the sea. Later in Islay, taking the lobster from the creel he would draw his fingers down its shell of lazulite, so that it lay as though charmed. With the ferocity of an age-long rancour he hated the dog-fish taken in the nets—foul feeders on dead sailors, the kindred of sharks—and he would cut out their ears and fling them back to bleed to death in the sea. He said: 'Without their ears they cannot steer in the water.'

But a female big with young he respected; even though she were dog-fish he would spare her life. Such a one, caught in his net and landed on the jetty, gave birth to seven hoe, and even Conboy smiled at the provision granted to the young. He showed Violet the little gourdlike bags attached to each small shark as it left the belly of its mother—pendent yoke-sacks that would partly nourish the infant spur-dog when their mother had cast them off into the keeping of the sea.

The *Cabar Feidh* with favouring wind and a clean bottom could sail at ten knots an hour. Often Talbot and Conboy sailed, unwitting, over a particular anchored mine. When peace was signed the Germans took up the mines and then this very one, lying beyond the roadstead of the yacht, was revealed.

On these Islands, Inishbofin and Inishturk, the days were empty, but the coastguards and the people were, nevertheless, always up late at night, walking near the sea, as though the day had not been long enough. Talbot taught the men under him the manner in which they should use their spy-glasses; how lying, or sitting, to steady and support the telescope. From the rocks, red-legged choughs flew away screaming; but the peasants, though nearly as shy as the choughs, gathered curiously about the visitor, for such a one was rare.

Once the sea gave up a corked bottle wherein was a sheet of paper covered with writing. Talbot unfolded it and read a piteous story. Day by day a man in an open boat had written a few lines. Three other men had been with him, but he had died the last. Their ship had been torpedoed, and they had escaped from her in an open boat. At first they had hope; then no hope at all. They were consumed by thirst. On one page, in a mad agony, the man had cursed his wife because she was the cause of his having gone to sea. But in the last entry, in a last superb phrase, outsoaring reason and the experience of his parched body, stood the brave words: 'GOD IS LOVE.'

CHAPTER XVIII

* * *

TALBOT HAD HIS WORK TO DO ON THE SEA; HIS PASTIME was in fishing for white-trout and salmon. Violet had a hundred things to do. The war had scattered most of her household, so now, from the mountains, she gathered girls to serve in the house. Barefooted, shawl over head they came, their voices soft, the look of their eyes so modest that in a city men would have gasped, and seen it as strange and beautiful. But they fostered vermin. 'You must never say that they are dirty or without order,' warned the priest, 'because that reproach would reflect on their home, and on their upbringing, and could not be suffered.' Sometimes a whole morning would be spent in just showing a girl how to turn the handle of a door, unfamiliar because the cottage doors had latches. To switch on electric lights seemed terrifying; that also must be taught with gentleness. If any one of the maids was listless or sad she must be given the work of another. For if Kathleen might drive the pony, or Maria take out the setter dogs, then content would be restored. When Maria asked to be free for half a day, it was not to walk the road with a man but to trail seven times on her knees round the holy well, that the vow which her mother had made for her might be fulfilled. The disorder of the house was maddening; there was no feeling of mine and thine nor of anything being used for the purpose for which it had been made. Did Annie need a stick for the fire she would run to the shed where the workmen were preparing a floor for the new room and take away a square of parquetry, a length of oak. Shoes sent to be cleaned were put back without the laces. On the lake the boats were chained to posts—had they been tied the ropes would have been taken.

There was no courting by the lakeside or in the pleasant wood; the spring flowers bloomed unpicked, the hedgerows

322

sheltered no lovers save the birds. And the pent-up, the frustrated fever of youth vented itself as love of country. Instead of whispered trifles between man and woman, man to man would mutter of the enemy—and he was not the German. In the lanes the boys drilled, preparing to fight for Ireland. No lovemaking, no play with football or with cricketball, but instead: 'Up with Ireland! Up with hatred! Up with death!'

The peat in the bog must needs be cut for use in the house, and many laboured at that task. In Connemara men asked for employment as elsewhere they might ask for help. The labourers slept in a loft as free of the need of comfort as men from the deserts of Arabia. Only on Saturdays they must be paid early in the day so as to start homewards over the mountains, to rest at home till Monday. They must be in their cottages before dusk fell, before the fairy hour. It seemed that the fairies all were evil. Every evening the mason, stalwart and mature, was fetched home by his father; the two men walked back by the rambling road to avoid the sombre woods spread about the neighbouring Castle of Kylemore. To go by the narrow way, that was cut through the park, was quicker far than to go by the roundabout road, but the trees in the parkland harboured fairies. A child was dying in a cottage near Kylemore House. 'Go—fetch the doctor,' the mother entreated. But the child's father did not go till morning, and then it was too late. The terror the fairies put on him had power to hold him against the urgency of his wife, against the cry of the child on its deathbed.

Then, soon after the buying of Kylemore House, the young men who were cutting the turf in the bog and working on the farm ceased suddenly to work—some threat, some misunderstanding—who knows what the cause? Violet, the children, the maids, fed the beasts and cleaned the byres; Violet milked the cows. She learnt many things as she milked, and each of her senses was delighted. Her head, covered with a handkerchief, rested on the warm flank of the shorthorn, and peace completely clothed her. How pleasant was the fall of the milk into the can; the sound of the cow chewing the cud; the mild smell of the cow, the sweet smell of the milk; the feel of the soft teat, the feel of the cow's content. Her mind brooded on the communion of each thing with another, on the dependence of a blade of grass on the sun, the grass that was turned to milk in her pail. 'Remember you are drawing blood though it seems milk,' a yeoman had written to her. Since then she fed the cows as though she were paying a debt. Because of the cows she scattered lime to the field, she repaid the milk, the blood. She saw everything in God ordered and just—the giving and the receiving equal. Although the sure return came not always to the hand that gave, yet there was no daring to think that a man might pay short measure; there was no cause to fear that he might receive short return.

So ignorant, when first she came to Ireland, that she had sent to the stable sawdust from a packing-case because she had thought it was bran, Violet now learned many solid things. The value of food, the gravity of bread and of meat heightened her work, hallowing the very feeding of the poultry. At Renvyle in the valley beyond, poets were gathered together, Æ. and Yeats, as guests of Gogarty. But because of the war, of which these poets did not reck, because of the seas sown with mines, Violet knew that the eggs she carried in her basket were of as great worth as the lyrics written in the valley.

The hedges of fuchsia; the nine Pins of Connemara; the three blue lakes clipped by the mountains; the fish jumping; the five happy children; all these made it sometimes hard to remember that across two seas was war. But to-day came the order to search a neighbouring bay for submarines. 'How gay to die with Talbot, how drab to live without him.' To her request the answer: "Be quick then; I am going on this tide."

CHAPTER XIX

*   *   *

LATER ON: RED SAILS SPREAD, MAINSAIL AND JIBSAIL, sailing before a stiff breeze, that was the *Cabar Feidh*. She was making for Inisheer, the most southerly island of the Aran group. Talbot said to his wife: "We'll anchor at the South Island at Inisheer, then, in a day or two, I shall inspect the coast-guard at Inishmore." Judge Ross, stretched out on deck, was entertaining them with merry tales, enchanting them with the poems he recited. "That's a wicked-looking sunset," mused Talbot: "We'll go ashore and sleep somewhere, for I don't like the look of the weather." Soon afterwards, 'Good night, Conboy,' they sang out from the lower boat. 'Safe rest to ye,' he answered. The mate rowed the boat and told them that there was a house where they could stay; it was used by the priest and by the doctor when they visited the island.

When the doors opened to them, the woman of the house welcomed them, but they must fend for themselves. The utmost she could do was to cook—clearly she was near her time. They were given three rooms, one candle, and one looking-glass between them. But they made shift to change into fresh clothes and, carrying up the supper, they feasted on turbot, which was common fare at Inisheer. Having cleared the table and washed the dishes they returned to the big room and then became aware of its treasures. Stacked on the floor, piled against the wall, were many books. The three of them dusted and sorted the volumes. They learnt that the books were the harvest of a man's lifetime. They found books of travel and of history, books in Latin, poems, essays; strangest of all to find the several conflicting causes so well served by these books. No moot, no burning question that racked Ireland, but it was dealt with here, and every opinion had its advocate in a volume on the floor. Till late at night they knelt on the boards putting the

325

books in order; they finished the task next day. Violet asked the woman how she came by such books. She answered that a man who had served in the police had passed his last years in the house. He had arrived with a box of books, and often afterwards he had sailed to Galway and bought more. As he lay dying he had called to the woman and had charged her with these possessions. 'I have gathered these books together so that every man coming here may find his desire. . . . If, however, you sell any of them, my curse will blight you.' Then he had died. More than once men, passing through Inisheer, had offered money for what lay neglected on the floor. The woman had refused to sell—the books might be taken away, or might rot, that was nothing to her, but she dared not accept their price.

At night the storm worsened. The *Cabar Feidh* was battered by billows; Talbot, seeing her so in the morning, could but hope that her anchor would hold, for she was very near the rocks. He and Violet went out into the morning wind, which was crumpling up the sea and flinging about the spume. On this island were no trees for the gale to bend or break. The shores of Inisheer were grey with stones and with boulders. Growing in the clefts of the rocks was maidenhair fern, its tenderness gainsaid the rigour of the crags. The island was made holy and was refreshed by many wishing-wells, and offerings of pence lay on their margins. There was a castle reared on a hilltop above the sea. Women, dressed from head to foot in scarlet, led donkeys up and down the steep places. The men walked lightly, shod with shoes of cowhide; by their women's diligence they were clad in homespun clothes of wool.

A voice behind Violet said: 'Will you buy a dress in the fashion of America?' She turned to the peasant. 'Show it me,' she laughed. He went to a cottage near by and returned carrying a red silk dress. It had a bustle, and red glass buttons all down the back. 'It was my wife's; I ask twelve pounds for it.' Violet shook her head. When they returned she told the woman of the house about the dress from America. The woman frowned. The peasant's bride, she said, had brought it from America; she was married in it. She had died at the birth of her first child; with her last words she entreated to be buried in the red silk gown. The man buried her with the infant, but he could not bring himself to bury the dress. Instead he took it to Galway to sell it. No one would buy it. Wishing to marry again, he promised it, first to this young woman, then to that one, but no one of them would be his wife. From that tale the talk between Violet and the woman turned on burial clothes. 'The habit of St. Francis is the best habit for the dead,' the woman said. 'From purgatory St. Francis will free those who are wearing his colour.' When Violet told her of the white shrouds of the English, surprised she cried: 'Would you not be ashamed, running about naked in glory?'

A few days later, as the *Cabar Feidh*, bound for Inishmore, sailed passed Inishmaan, Judge Ross said: 'Clifton, if you and I landed at the Middle Island there and if, unobserved by me, you went into the cottage, were I to ask any one of the peasants if he knew where you had gone he would say 'No'. In the past, hunted men escaped across the island and from its western shore sailed the Atlantic for the New World. That tradition of bygone loyalty makes secret, even to-day, the whereabouts of any stranger landing on Inishmaan.'

During the storm at the South Island, Conboy and the mate had been for three days imprisoned beneath the hatches, but they were cheerful now. Singing, they let go the anchor at Inishmore. Talbot inspected the coastguard station, but Judge Ross remained aboard. Afterwards Talbot and his wife walked along the road, on either side of which rose ancient columns and crosses. In the flaming sunset, ignorant and unprepared, they came upon the wonder of Dun Angus. They walked the cyclopean walls, and, lying on the edge, they looked down the precipice to the sea. Against sheer cliffs the spent waves lay mangled into foam. Silently, a spell upon them, past graves of saints and hermits, they returned to the quay. Another storm was rising. Two reluctant men, moaning over the oars, took them to where the yacht was riding the ugly open sea. They hardly reached the *Cabar Feidh*, were barely able to board her. The will of Talbot compelled the men; in spite of their reasonable fears they had been driven on to the darkening sea, and that, by the instancy of his eyes.

CHAPTER XX

*   *   *

JOHN BROWN, MENDICANT, SAID: 'IT'S A GRAND SILENT place you have here.' He flung open his cape and sat on the bench near the hall door. 'Yesterday my head was mazed with the storms; here is quiet.' Talbot's children brought him food. He accepted it as one conferring a benefit, for he knew that the Holy One stands on the right hand of the poor. Before eating he said: 'May you always have enough for yourselves and for God's poor.' Soon after their coming to Connemara Talbot gave this instruction to his wife: "From my observation of the people, I feel sure that here any poor man would choose rather to receive five shillings given at the front door, than ten shillings given at the back." So a bench, and a table had been placed near the porch overlooking the lake. John Brown, having eaten, asked for the naval overcoat hanging in the front hall, but as that could not be given, Violet gave instead some other things of Talbot's.

Pilgrims from Croagh Patrick passed this way. One of them came to repay a loan. 'I pay you back so that I may borrow again later on,' he explained, and to Talbot, who was looking at the fruit bushes stripped of berries, he added: 'Your fruit garden is known to be very convenient to the road.'

Another man, Timothy Coneely, gave, as merchandise, talk of all the counties round, and of the quality living within a hundred miles. He was a laughing man, but once he came full of trouble for, at Castlebar, 'the boss' had been shot. The peasants had coveted his acres, harassed his cattle and driven them. Mr. —— would not yield to the clamourers, nor patiently suffer their outrages, so, from the shelter of a hedge, they shot him. The laughing mendicant was scandalized by the lack of wisdom of the boss rather than by the murdering of him. 'Often', he said, 'I told him that if men needs must have my coat or else kill me,

328

then I would give my coat. Better to be alive and naked, than dead, all clothed in your best. But Mr. —— would not listen to me, so now he has neither his lands, nor his cattle, nor his life.'

The gayest of the passers-by was a small man who sold apples and onions. He drove in a cart pulled by a donkey, and one day Michael's English nurse gave him a ten-shilling note. He crushed it up in his hand so roughly that she exclaimed: 'Don't be so careless with that note! It is worth ten silver shillings.' Flourishing his whip, dancing his legs below the board on which he was sitting, he sang back to her: 'Money, money, what is money? Without it we came into the world, and without it we shall leave the world.' The nurse frowned. 'I've heard the shroud has no pockets, but all the same—'

On clear days without breath of wind Pat would row upon the lakes, dapping with grasshoppers. On one such day, when the white-trout would not take even a cricket, Pat sulkily rowed inland, telling Talbot he had just spent seventy pounds on a fence to keep the postman's horse off his grazing. 'My cow trespasses on his land, so he will pay half the fence.' A passer-by was talking to Violet, an old man whom she had not seen before. He asked nothing of her. When they had talked awhile he asked: 'Is that your husband?' and pointed to Talbot in the boat. To her 'Yes' the old man said darkly: 'I have something to tell him.' He went down to the lakeside and awaited the boat. When Talbot landed: 'Your wife's face is a consolation,' he said—then turned and walked away down the rambling high road.

That morning Talbot had received a threatening letter. He was to be shot soon by the man who had penned it, and that because 'in the grey light of dawn' the writer had been dispossessed of a cottage that he loved. The small house had been lent to him by Talbot until it should be needed for workmen at Kylemore. Talbot smiled because it was strange to receive such a letter from a man who, although idle and diseased, yet had a certain weight in the neighbourhood as being the husband of the school teacher. There was in fact no hardship for man or wife in moving to another house, across the lake, and much nearer to the school. In Connemara, Talbot often smiled, as on the day when Martin MacDonagh, a merchant of Galway, entreated him not to fly his heraldic flag—'The people will take it as an insult, they will be certain it's political; they will pull it down, and perhaps raid the house.' "If we ask for help of the police to trace theft, will the people forgive us?" asked Talbot of MacDonagh. 'Yes, yes, you can make known a theft, but not a murder,' he answered, and did not understand why the Englishman laughed.

Talbot mused: "Murder is hallowed in their minds, because it is linked up with causes that they cherish. Their land-hunger fosters slaughter, but land-hunger being a passion understood by the people the crime is easily forgiven. The other fever of this people is love of Ireland, which also crowns with laurels the meanest murder if only it be committed in Ireland's name. But theft is merely theft; unheroic."

So the years went on till the eleventh of November, 1918, when at Westport, on the *Cabar Feidh*, they heard the news of peace. A few days later Admiral Barton visited Kylemore. In brandy of 1810, poured from a glass flagon, hand-fashioned and shapely, they toasted the peace. When the toast had been drunk Talbot filled himself another glass. Going to the window he spilled the spirit into the earth, then, throwing his glass on to the ground so that it was shivered, he whispered: "Here's to those for whom this peace has come too late. O God, give them a better peace!"

CHAPTER XXI

★ ★ ★

IN THE YEAR 1921, THE POLICE, ON BEHALF OF THE BRITISH
Government, had gathered up the guns and the rifles of the
loyalists who lived in various parts of Ireland, so that the Sinn
Feiners looking for arms would not be strengthened by finding
them. "If we are disarmed we ought to be protected, but we
are not given protection," said Talbot, and added, with a twinkle,
"also the woodcock will soon be in." Therefore, on his return
to Lytham, he got his gun and, hugging it under his arm beneath a great fur-lined coat, he landed at Belfast. Many people
were searched at that time, but his haughty ways took him
through, although one policeman remarked to another: 'That
tall man is walking in a stiff way.' 'How is your lumbago this
morning?' Violet loudly asked Talbot; he understood and answered that he felt "mighty stiff".

In those days of trouble often Talbot observed, on the roads,
sticks laid crosswise. "That is not a gypsy's nor a tinker's sign,"
he concluded. "It is probably a signal to ambush. Vi, tell Lord
French of this when you stay at the Viceregal Lodge." Violet
did so. (Talbot would but seldom stay with anyone, so she went
alone.) "Evil sticks these," mused Talbot, "evil as the three sticks
of the shaman, though with a different significance. What a lot
can be done or undone by sticks, here murder designated; on
the Lena, devil-worship; whilst a huntsman can be confounded
by walking on a stick. Zip!—it breaks, the quarry hears the
crack, and the huntsman goes hungry."

Then, later in 1921, Talbot and his wife went to Celebes (11)
to hunt the *Bos Anoa*. Good-bye to the sign of the plough in the
skies—greetings to the Southern Cross! When they returned to
Ireland they found, in Galway, a letter from Michael's nurse
warning them that the roads between Galway and Recess were
dangerous because the rebels had dug deep trenches to wreck

cars and convoys. Men in ambush would wait near by ready to kill the victims of their savagery. The same warfare which formerly had been waged against English force was now being waged against the forces of the provisional government set up by the treaty.

It was night-time when they left Galway to drive to Kylemore. In the moonlight Talbot saw a hare down the road. He forgot the warning and chased it with the car. They rushed upon a trench dug in the road, but the brave length of the Lanchester car just spanned it so that it was not crumpled up in the ambush. As though good fortune were the cause of their being at hand, some wretches heaved the car; they were, indeed, helpful in restarting her upon her homeward way.

Next day a woman at a near cottage was taken in labour. Violet and the nurse went up the hill to help her. 'I must be confined in my work-dress; that is our way,' she said. Painfully she travailed; it seemed that she might die; the doctor was long in coming. Her old mother fetched the great missal and the key of the door from the Chapel near by, and laid them on her. At last she was delivered of twins; the umbilical cord cut with the sheep-shears. 'The boy is dead,' said the old mother, and laid him in the corner of the room. But the nurse beat the infant and warmed it by the hearth and gave it brandy, so that it lived.

At the end of their week a car full of men in uniform stopped in front of Kylemore House. "The Free State to visit us," said Talbot; the last to go uninvited through the house had been the Black and Tans. But these were not Free State men, but Sinn Feiners. 'We want your car,' they said. "You can have the Ford," answered Talbot, but they all went to the glittering Lanchester car. Talbot stooped over her as though to examine the speeds but he was locking the gears. The men, baulked and believing that the car was damaged, said: 'Now we will search the house for guns and rifles as we need them.' They went to the house. They searched about in a dull way so that they did not come upon the gun which had been taken down and hidden in the recesses of an armchair. Meantime Talbot beckoned to Violet and they walked away into the garden. "I want to get off with this key as I've locked the gears of the car," he explained. Just then a knot of men came up. 'We cannot move the car;

Sinn Fein

come and start it for us,' a young man said. Talbot did not answer. He looked into vacancy as though he had not heard. 'Oh! do as they say!' whispered Violet. Then suddenly was glad that he ignored the rebels, for over her swept an angry scorn of them—standing there with their cheap cigarettes in their mouths, with their caps on their heads, the ill-mannered, the upstart gallows-boys. Let them shoot him, let them shoot her, she would not mind; she would die alongside of Talbot, not because he was her husband—but because he was of her class.

The figure of their mechanic appeared. "Go with him," said Talbot to the men, and went back to the house. But some of them followed him, and shut him, and Violet, into a room whilst they searched further through the house for weapons. 'If we find anything it will go badly with you.' They found nothing. When they had freed Talbot, he went up the yard, but the Lanchester had been taken away; the mechanic in fear must have unlocked the gears for the men, although afterwards, to Talbot, he swore that he had not done so. Then the remainder of the men also went away. 'It's their insolence I hate more than the theft of the car. To be rude because they are armed!' Talbot laughed at that. "Their manners are nothing to me, but I will not bear the loss of my car." Days went by. The car was not returned, although the men had promised the mechanic they would bring it back after a day had passed. They were boasting of the car in all County Galway; she was at every market, at every meeting; they drove the young women about in her. "I shall ambush them, or in my small car I shall cut across the road in front of them and upset them. I may be killed, but they shall not make a fool of me!" Two or three days went by. Talbot now was silent—he was bracing himself, and waiting.

CHAPTER XXII

*   *   *

SMOOTHLY, AT THE TOP OF THE TABLE, CLICK-CLICK, gentle kiss of ball on ball, cannons suave as the air of a minuet—thus Talbot playing billiards against his wife. She stood still, waiting whilst he made his break—forty-five, forty-seven. . . . 'Those long skilful hands, queer they should have been so often frostbitten,' and: 'I can do nothing as dexterous as this play, my needlework is less precise; but I did grill the salmon and the chops well to-night'—with a glance at the silver grill. It was built into the room with an ingle-nook on either side of it: 'I hope when I'm old to sit in the deep seat by that grill and think of travel.'

The score continued fifty-two, fifty-four, fifty-seven—then an in-off which was played a jot too hard, and the break was finished.

The door was thrust open, and the mechanic rushed up to the table. 'Coneely has driven the Lanchester down the road to Letterfrack; two men and a woman in it; they must return past here to go to Westport.'

Silence. Talbot pulled on his smoking jacket, put his cue away, and said: "You and Conboy will take the Ford car, I will take the Austin, and we will wait at the bend near Leenaun. You will switch off the lights, and, when the Lanchester comes near, switch them on again to dazzle the driver—I will do the rest. Vi, do you want to come?"

Weakly she opposed him. In revenge the house might be burnt; the car was not worth the risk, she said. She spoke as though she did not know that Talbot took life on his own terms, and without caution. She seemed to expect him to drowse by the fire whilst the potato-boys drove past his house in his car—stolen and abused. "I'm going now." From the recesses of an armchair Talbot pulled out his gun and put it to-

334

gether. A better thought took hold of Violet; she ran upstairs and put on her diamonds under a high dress. They would be safe worn upon her. Then she ran to kiss Michael. From the store-cupboard she took some ropes. 'We'll bind Coneely with these and take him prisoner to Galway.' From a cupboard she took pepper to blind him.

Talbot was ready with his gun and his number-six shot; ready also were the two unarmed men. They drove to the bend; they wedged the cars across the road so that the oncoming car could not pass. Talbot went on to a commanding knoll. They waited. Then, a pest on it, the moon rose, and because of it the electric light would not dazzle or surprise the opposing men. After an hour came the sound, then the silver sheen of the Lanchester car. Violet was dissolved by fear, her bones felt like jelly. In the car were not two men, but six men; five of them were in the livery of the Sinn Fein. In face of this Talbot surely would not pursue his endeavour?

Then came the sound of brakes put hard on so that the Lanchester was brought to a skidding stop in front of the small cars, and the sound of Talbot's voice, compelling the men. "Get out of my car. Leave your rifles in it." Whispered talk and the men obeyed, but though the rifles were left, every man had his pistol. Hands went to pockets; one man stood apart. He was the prisoner Coneely was taking to Westport, guilty in that he dared to oppose Sinn Fein. 'That leaves seven men to be mastered,' thought Violet. Now she felt calm. One of the seven ran back down the road. A little pause, then a shot from Talbot's gun. 'Prelude to the conversation,' thought Violet. 'How glad I am that the Nuns of Perpetual Adoration pray for me at this very hour—eleven o'clock!' None but Talbot knew or guessed that he had shot the man. He had seen the fellow creeping back towards the knoll and, taught by many encounters, he reasoned: "The man means to get behind and shoot me in the back." So Talbot shot; then there was silence.

"Give back my car, Coneely," but the man answered that he needed the Lanchester. The other men whispered entreaties to Coneely. 'Give it back to him; his friends are lying in wait behind the knoll.' Coneely called loudly: 'Gilan, Gilan, are you behind Mr. Clifton? Are you covering him with your revolver?' Gilan did not answer, for the reason that he was lying wounded in the road.

Coneely was nerved with wine and had, besides, some natural courage and a habit of danger, for he had served in the war. 'I will not give it back to-night—we must take our prisoner to Westport.' Talbot had no liking for refusals; he raised his gun. Coneely had out his pistol. Violet thrust herself in front of Coneely. 'They won't shoot me but I'll be in their way like this.' A strange conversation followed between the two men; but Talbot won his point, for Coneely promised he should have his car back the next day. "You must not take revenge on Conboy," Talbot said, and Coneely gave his hand on his promise.

Then Talbot sharply ordered the men to "get in the car and go off before I move". The men must not see that he had no friends in hiding behind the knoll. The men obeyed. "Touch your hats!" ordered Talbot. They gave a shamed salute, and were gone.

"Come on home, Vi," said Talbot. As they drove back she asked what had happened to Gilan. "I shot him." 'Oh no, surely not? The light was too dim. How awful if you did shoot him!' Talbot laughed. "I don't shoot at a fellow without hitting him, and it would have been more awful if he had shot me in the back."

They were back at the house. Conboy spoke now and he, usually so full of easiness, became suddenly forcible. He said that Gilan (12) would be found wounded, that the men would take revenge upon Talbot. 'You put no promise on them for your own safety, but for mine, and all the rest of us. You must go or you'll bring a doom on the lady, and on the house.'

Talbot pondered; saw that Conboy spoke with reason. "Yes then, I'll go. Will you come, Vi?" She would not go, his going would make it safe for them all. With the mechanic he drove right through to Belfast and sailed from there. Happy that he did so, because the next day and for days afterwards, because of Talbot, the boats sailing from Dublin were searched by order of his enemies.

CHAPTER XXIII

*   *   *

VIOLET THOUGHT: 'I'LL GO TO WESTPORT TO SEE THE head brigand and surely be able to make him admit that a man may put up a fight for his own. I'll get him to ratify the truce made upon the road last night.' She felt light of heart, for it was good to be alive. A twist of events, and Talbot and she would be lying now by the roadside; sodden with dew. She wondered: 'did men in the war, after a great peril, feel this delight at not having been killed?' She went to Kylemore Abbey to ask the loan of a car, for Conboy must not be seen on the roads. 'Go and hide in the hills,' she said to him. The nuns dared not help her, so she went to Senator Gogarty at Renvyle. He was without fear, but his car had been damaged and was off the road. 'I'll leave these things with you,' Violet said, and she left her jewels in his custody.

Towards evening she was sitting in the billiard-room, reading fairy tales to the children, when, still absorbed in the tale, she glanced dreamily out of the long window. On the grass slope outside many armed men stood, scowling at the house. A few minutes later some of them entered the room. They ordered everyone out of the house, into the garden. 'We'll search for Mr. Clifton; and we'll shoot him here and now.' Violet laughed. 'You will not find him; and tell me, Coneely, where is your word of last night when he could have shot you?' Coneely explained angrily, and without logic, that his word of last night was empty, because Gilan had been found shot.

Michael, the boy, had run off for his wooden gun and now with blazing eyes he found that it failed him. His sister, Easter, gentler, mollified the men with her birthday cake. At last the search was over; the men went off. The fairy tale, too long interrupted, was read up to the magical, the concluding words: 'And they lived happily ever afterwards.'

Violet wished that she could telegraph to Talbot telling him not to return, but realized that she could not send any telegram. She decided the following day she would go to Galway so as to hire a car to take away the old family racing-cups, and the like.

So she drove the black horse fifteen miles to Recess. A torrent of rain was falling. At Recess she took the train for Galway, and went to one she called 'her mother and her father'—that was Martin MacDonagh, a merchant of Galway. His brother Thomas, more cautious than Martin, thought that the Mac-Donaghs would be wiser to stand clear of this trouble, but Martin asked if Violet had telegraphed to her husband to advise him not to return.

Martin said: 'I'll strengthen your counsel by also telegraphing to him. I'll send you home in this motor-car; it will be followed by a lorry for your goods—clear the house of everything.' 'Most of the things are already packed,' Violet answered. She returned to Kylemore, and soon afterwards the lorry arrived, and the silver was packed into it. She was getting out of her bath, refreshed after the dreadful wetness of her clothes, when a trembling maid knocked and said through the door: 'The armed men are back—you must go to them, they have a letter for you.' 'Give me my long black dress,' she answered, and when she had put it on she walked downstairs to the men waiting in the hall. The lorry was still by the door. Looking on the pictures which hung along the wall of the staircase she reflected: 'Being of to-day, I think it terrible to have armed men waiting for me, yet, had I lived in olden days in a besieged city, the enemy might have been for years about our walls. In spite of them I should have thought it worth while to work at tapestry and to gather books about me.' Now she stood on the bottom step looking down on the men; even on the threshold, because of her height, she looked down, and she felt glad that it was so. She needed such petty support, for her hand almost trembled as she took the letter:—'but it shall not tremble,' she willed. Surely the letter would be her arrest? The men would take her to Westport, Talbot would come to redeem her and would be shot—this she was sure must be the sequence. She read:

Violet is ordered to leave Connemara

To:
    Mrs. Clifton,
    Kylemore,
    Connemara.

Headquarters,
4th Western Division,
Castlebar.
14/4/22.

On the night of the 12th April, 1922, your husband Talbot Clifton with others who are known to me lay in ambush at a point on the main road between Kylemore and Leenaun, and fired at officers of this division who were proceeding to Castlebar.

As a result of the shots fired, Captain Eugene Gilan of the Irish Republican Army is now hovering between life and death in Mr. McKeown's Hotel, Leenaun. I am satisfied, from information received, that you also participated in the ambush, and this is to notify you that an armed guard will be placed on your premises, and that you, Mrs. Clifton, are to leave Connemara before 12 noon Monday, 27th, 1922. Otherwise other steps will be taken.

If you desire to make any statement it will be necessary for you to come to Castlebar, and I promise you a safe conduct.

Signed, Michael Kilroy,
G.O.C. 4th Western Division, I.R.A.

N.B.: The armed guard will remain on your premises pending the return of your husband.

There was no train on Sunday and the Monday train from Recess left after noon, therefore its departure would be outside of the time granted to her. Was this a trap? The chief man said that all now belonged to them—to the Sinn Feiners—Violet must give him the key of the cellar. The men would live in the house from now onwards; the servants would serve them, or go. 'If these men get drunk we are undone,' she thought. She said sharply: 'You must not frighten my children, therefore you will take the servants' rooms in the new building behind this house.' Then she called the children, played a game with them and sent them to bed. But, in spite of her endeavour, the younger children were frightened, because a man with a rifle walked up and down the nursery passage; they were frightened too

339

because the nurse lost her calm and cursed the men in God's name. 'My last mistress was shot before my eyes by men like these,' said Ellen, the maid, as she helped Violet to pack away the old china and the household treasures. 'You may take nothing with you,' said the head-man, but Violet set aside four things to take. Because of its loveliness she took the Japanese Princess, made of gold lacquer and of ivory, carrying a basket with roses of ivory; because it was the trophy of their march through Celebes she took the head of the *Bos Anoa*. Also she hid, and took away, the billiard-cue that was balanced more perfectly than any other Talbot had ever played with. For herself she took the copy of Shakespeare which had been Talbot's first gift. Then the priest from Tully came and supped with her, but the villains burnt his bicycle to point the reality of their displeasure against this woman who had opposed them.

Next day, the Sinn Feiners having consented, she hired a car and went away. She took with her the nurse and an English maid, the four children that were in Ireland, and a dog or two. The ponies, the setter-dogs, the hens, the old silver from Lytham, the pictures and everything in the house was left behind. As she drove along the road to Recess, Violet looked at the children of this unruly people, at the little children playing along the roadside. 'Europe is full of such,' she thought, 'and will these children grow up to fight my children?' Having seen revolution she shuddered. The only person in the countryside who dared to call a blessing on her was the mother of the twins. The other peasants passed the house silently as they went to the Easter Mass. Around the house door the Republicans stood dark, uneasy. They were in fear of the curses which the nurse of Michael called down upon them. She left the house with a shriek. She had lost her reason.

That same year two of these rebels were killed in a fight with Free State men. They died, unshriven, on the running-board of the Lanchester car.

*   *   *

In a friend's house in Lancashire Violet and the children joined Talbot. Till she came he had been as one demented wondering "was she safe?" cursing himself for having brought this upon her. He was restrained from returning by Martin

MacDonagh's telegram. When they did come together, he said: "You might well leave me for ever after this." So used was he to dangers that, at first, the hazard had seemed but small, and he had not reckoned that it would fall so heavily on his wife.

One night in Lancashire he saw Violet knotting sheets together so that if the wretches came to kill him she could let him down from the window. He laughed away her cares, saying: "I'm damned if I will sleep without sheets." But he understood that fear had blasted her; and he again repented.

For a year they were under the special protection of the police, in case a Sinn Feiner might come over and in revenge shoot Talbot. Strange warnings reached them; a barber at Liverpool said to a friend of Violet's: 'A man is coming for the Squire of Lytham.' On Christmas Eve a watchful policeman found an Irishman in hiding close to Lytham Hall, whither the Cliftons had returned.

'God bless the house from roof to floor—the twelve Apostles guard the door.' Every night Violet prayed so for Kylemore, and the nuns too prayed. Talbot said: "the Devil looks after his own." Conboy had been arrested by Coneely and put into prison, but afterwards he was freed.

After a year of vicissitude, suddenly Coneely wrote to Talbot: 'We are beaten by the Free State men. We promised there should be no revenge. All the people here spoke for you; so you can come back. Your goods shall be restored; the people want you to stand as member for Galway'—something like that he wrote. The silver—which had been like litter on the floor of a barracks at the neighbouring town of Clifden and afterwards had been sent back to Kylemore House—the pictures, the books, almost everything was still at Kylemore House—the things had been ill used but not stolen or destroyed.

Later on, the long-lined white-metalled Lanchester was found battered in Dublin. Returned to the Cliftons, it was restored to use. 'She was worth the struggle,' Violet said.

Towards the end of the year 1922, or maybe early in 1923, Talbot, when he had received Coneely's letter, sent some men from Glasgow to pack and bring his goods to Islay from Kylemore. The men took a tramp ship and loaded her with the gear. When the things were unpacked, sticks of gelignite were found laid amongst the beds and the chairs. The placid Scotsmen had found the sticks of gelignite lying about the house in Connemara; not knowing what the stuff was, they packed it in the bedding. When afterwards Talbot returned to Ireland it was as one of 'the guests of the Nation' at the Tailteann Games of 1924 (13).

CHAPTER XXIV

*   *   *

ALL HIS LIFE TALBOT HAD DESIRED TO POSSESS LAND IN
Scotland. In the year 1922 he obtained his desire. He was able to
buy Kildalton Castle, and Estate, in the Island of Islay, the Queen
of the Hebrides. For five years he would enjoy his home in the
north-west. During those years he went with Violet to the
Persian Gulf, and made alone the painful African journey from
west to east. In the spring of 1927, for the sake of Aurea, his
eldest daughter, he leased a house in London. But still those
years in Islay crowned his desires. A strong sense of possession
joyed him; his eyes rested thankfully on the hills that were his.
Never before had he possessed hill country; his eyes swept
gratefully over the sea coast, his own—over the islands and the
Skerries. These seas, in springtime, resounded with the low
loving notes of the pairing, and of the brooding birds, of the
swans, and of the eider-duck. Mated for life were the mute
swans, coupled upon the sea; year after year they returned to the
same nest. Their nests were built of seaweed upon the islands,
upon the sea rocks, among the thrift and the sea campion. Their
eggs were laid among the blade leaves of the flags where, later,
yellow flowers would glisten.

But the cygnets were threatened by the sea, and few escaped
being drowned. Although the pen carried them upon her back,
although the cob showed them where to feed, yet they would
become entangled in the seaweed, and so would perish.

Once Talbot saw, very lovely, a cob and pen guardant above
their eggs—their necks nobly stiffened in anger, their wings
held out like birds of heraldry. Very lovely were the swans
when they swam against each other, defending their allotted
bays against young trespassing swans—white and brave, like
fairy sailing-ships, sailing to battle.

Fearful, though lovely too, Talbot saw one of the cobs in the
bay move through the water towards Aurea, as the girl was

343

bathing in the sea. Quick as the swan to Leda, so swam this bird with head thrown back and wings raised furiously.

The spring in Islay was full of its own sounds. "Come, Vi, and hear the snipe drumming over the bog." They would listen till again came the sound like the beat of a wild heart vibrating. "Come and hear the curlew." They would walk silently to near where the curlew sang his nuptial gladness whilst, on the nest upon the ground, his burning mate quickened the eggs. 'His wild note of alarm; and the other shorter notes of his careless usual call to his kind, even the gay skirling music of a herd of curlew, all give no hint of this rare seasonal song—the love song of the whaups.' So listening Violet mused.

Talbot learnt that, bowed over all the terrestrial nests, is a providence which absorbs the tell-tale smell of the mothering bird. Immune upon her nest the hen may sit whilst under her breast the young within the egg receives the April air. Sharp of nose, a dog, unwarned by any tell-tale scent, would pass the nests of plover or wild pheasant. In spite of the dog's hunting, the wild duck or the snipe might sit on in security, no stir in its feathers.

At dawn, or at dusk, Talbot and Violet would hear sometimes the squeak of the woodcock, tense with passion. 'Apart from the life of the birds, which of all the springtime's marvels seems to you the greatest?' asked Violet; and after thinking a little Talbot said that "on the March winds depends the perfection of the summer leaf". Asked to explain, he told Violet how he thought that the March winds, blowing on the trees, dries out of them the winter wet, and then, to fill the void, the sap rises. "Without wind the sap still would rise but more tardily, and the foliage would not be as perfect," he said. Violet said: 'I like best to know about the sugar that the earth feeds to her young during the spring months, for that is her sweet milk to the infant green things springing out of her.'

Then came the summer. It blotted out the shapely structure of the trees, clothing them with a mantle of colour. In an azure sky the clouds hung like silken banners, their ends frayed by the gentle wind.

But yet the summer was not the jewel of Islay. Therefore Talbot and Violet went to Barvas in the Lewis, for there, together with a friend, Talbot owned many acres, a river, and sea lochs. Landing at night was strange enough, for on the jetty was a crowd of shy young men gathered together in the half-darkness to see those that had come by the boat. None of them spoke, nor moved about, all of them gazed merely till Talbot's spotted Dalmatian dog provoked a whisper. The young men could not believe this to be a natural dog—they thought it wore a painted coat. 'Island of the love of learning' Violet called it when she learned that from the Lewis, in late summer, sails a ship, laden with glowing youth, bound for a mainland university.

On the morning after the coming of Talbot, a pair of swans settled on one of the lochs, and since, for many years, no swans had been seen in that northern part of the Lewis, this was taken by the peasants to be of good augury. Talking of swans, to the sound of the oars dipping in the water, the old boatman told them the tale of the Macleods besieged in Stornoway long ago. The siege was about to be raised; the Macleods would soon be free to come and go. One of the retainers, speaking in Gaelic, treacherously enticed them, half saying half singing the false words: 'The whooper stiff-necked swans are on such and such a loch, shall we not go out to shoot them?' The young laird was agog to go, for he had never shot a swan. 'To be a Highland hunter, Mary,' he told his sister, 'I must shoot a swan, a seal, an otter and a stag, each one by myself alone. I must catch and bring ashore a salmon, and I must kill an eagle too.' In the corner of the hall an old retainer signalled: 'Do not go'. A little later he whispered: 'We must send out bold men, for I never yet saw whooper swans upon that loch.' A party of men went secretly and fell upon the enemy lying hidden by the loch so that the young laird had his baptism of blood—but of blood other than that of a whooper swan.

And as on the sea loch they drifted in the boat, Talbot fishing for salmon, the boatman told them that all along the northern part of this, the Long Island, there was no cove or shelter, no smallest harbour where a boat in safety might lie embayed. 'This coast lies open to the Atlantic, like the soul of a saint swept by God; without harbour for the things that pass,' thought Violet.

The common lands

The pastures of the Lewis were blown upon by gales from the Atlantic, so that the many flowers grew dwarfed. Clovers, vetches and flowers of the tribe of hellebore, grew so plentifully that the shoes of those that walked in these meadows were golden with pollen. The cows, cropping such pasture, gave what was more like cream than milk, although they gave but a little. No trees grew on Barvas; in the autumn was no fall of leaf, but instead, a multitude of stars falling.

Talbot and Violet, walking in a rough place near to the river, some seven miles or more from any crofter's cottage, saw, surprised, a bull and some milch-cows grazing. They were told that the crofters, so as to drink of the evening and of the morning milk, would, towards evening, join the cattle and sleep in shielings. Next day, barefoot, they would return to work in the barley patches which ran, green and gold, to the edge of the sea. Much of the land is held in common, and from a common purse a man is paid to herd the cattle, in summer far inland, in winter on the *machair* near to the sea. The elders of the village direct these matters. Those who grow old in the Lewis have authority, but they that have gone away to the New World, or served on the sea, or with the colours, are allowed but little say when they return to the Long Island. Many have gone, and have returned, for in the Lewis is great content, and there, men, not ambitious, serenely meet old age and death.

Happy in the Lewis were the days of Talbot and Violet, happy in the skill of casting the fly, in the jolly whirr of the reel, in the tug of a salmon up the line and along every nerve.

Just beyond the flowery flat which bordered the sea loch,
only just out of sight of the fishing boat, the
tang of it in their nostrils, the sound of it
in their ears, was the Atlantic. It
swept resistless, unescapable,
along the harbour-
less coast.

CHAPTER XXV

★   ★   ★

"I AM GOING TO BAGDAD TO SEE GERTRUDE BELL, AND ON into Persia. Will you come?" Talbot's words conjured for Violet caravans, and bales of carpets, the rose, the bulbul, and Persepolis. 'Oh yes, I'll go.' It was hard to get a Government pass for her. 'It is not that she is not a fit and proper person for Iraq, but Iraq is hardly a fit and proper place for a woman just now,' was said at the Colonial Office. This was early in 1925.

They left Islay, and the children, and reached Kantara and Lydda. At Kantara on the ferry, in the cold night, the consciousness of the race-age of this people swept over Violet. She felt herself an upstart, quite without background compared with these immemorial Egyptians. She never afterwards forgot the strange overpowering shame of those minutes on the ferry.

At Lydda was a train, upon it was painted the name Jerusalem.

At Nazareth a boy ran out to sell narcissi; 'to look at just such another as He'. Dark-haired Syrians, some of them blue-eyed, bore unknowing witness to the long-ago advent of Crusaders.

At Damascus, up and down the street called Straight, Talbot walked, as much entertained as though he never before had seen a foreign city. Fingering linen and buying silks, testing steel blades, eating sugared fruits, watching the busy feet and the busy hands of the squatting craftsmen in the small shops, so he passed his time.

Afterwards they went to the ruins of Baalbek, and drank wine of the vineyards of Lebanon.

Then came the journey over the desert to Bagdad. An Envoy from the League of Nations went at that same time in a second car. The winter was very cold; snow was on the oranges; in the desert the many skeletons of camels mutely told the long unusual hardship. Over the narrow street of Palmyra the moon was shining. They drank some coffee in the house of an Arab. 'A Frenchwoman passing here when he was a boy took him to France; he lived there for years as her lover, then she sent him back,' they were told.

Because the Envoy was in haste they drove all night and late into the next night, although the danger from marauders on the second night was cause of a guard being sent with them.

In the morning, while the driver was busied with the car, Talbot had walked on alone towards a great camping-place of Arabs. When the driver saw Talbot in the distance, shaken by fear he called out: 'We must go after him at once, these Bedouins will rob him or harm him.'

This was the French route upon which they were travelling, the British cars followed another way, and the drivers of each company had tales of equal horror about the deaths in the desert of travellers going by the other way. The travellers in those cars which, against the law, went one alone, and ill-provisioned (driven by Syrians or Arabs), did, in all likelihood, sometimes suffer horrible fates.

Bagdad was reached; the splendid arch of Ctesiphon, and the lightning-quick presence of Gertrude Bell. Hers were nervous hands, a nose like a tool's sharp end, eyes fine and penetrating. She and Talbot were friends instantly, understanding, enjoying one another. Open her preference for Talbot, fellow-explorer; but yet, writing afterwards to Violet, she said: 'You are one of those few people who should come to the East.' In Violet's mind were lines translated by Gertrude from the *Divan of Hafiz* (14), so Violet sighed that the poetess, the scholar of Persia, should now be involved in the political difficulties of Mesopotamia. Poetess she proved herself to be when, in the museum of Bagdad, she renewed the youth of the world. Taking tablets of stone from out of the great urns, she rekindled the fire of the ancient boast of conquering kings victorious in the lands of Tigris and Euphrates: 'I have conquered the land; I have irrigated it.'

By evening Gertrude Bell became, above all, charming woman and hostess. Her table, set with caviare and with foods well cooked, was surrounded by interesting guests, amongst them Jaafar Pasha (15). 'One of the few men to have been decorated by the opposing nations during the war,' whispered someone. 'What great gashes are on his face!' exclaimed Violet. 'Oh those are not war wounds but were caused by Bagdadi boils bursting,' maliciously replied her neighbour; who seemed not to like Jaafar Pasha.

After having taken them to see Feisal, King of Iraq, Gertrude Bell obtained permission for Talbot and Violet to visit Fields —that is to say, the oilfields of the Anglo-Persian Company. They went from Bagdad to Basra in a smokeless train fed by oil, past the barbed wire, past the sandbag entrenchments which marked places of bloodshed in the rebellion of 1920. At Basra there was trouble with Violet's pass. White women could not go on farther. The matter, by a ruse, was overcome, and meantime her anxiety had been diverted by a hunting scene—Englishmen on Arab ponies; dark-skinned grooms, and hounds, amongst them the saluki. They motored over the desert to where, in groves of date-palms, was Mohammerah.

'A man from Oxford lives in the desert in that oasis with the cluster of palms, to study date-palms,' they were told, and Talbot broke into spoken memories of the manifold uses of the date-palm, the coconut-palm and the reindeer. By each of these a man may, for the most part, live. Talbot and Violet took up one by one the uses: the food, the drink, and so much more beside. Violet was a little glad because the female date-palm was reliant on man's effort for her cultivation. Often she had watched a man high up in the clustered green holding the inflorescence which he has cut from the male palm. He hangs it in the blossoming truss of the female tree, and when the stamens of the male flower be ripened the virgin-sweet flowers of the female will be fertile. Too great a reward in fruit the date-tree gives for her abundance to be dependent on the wanton winds and breezes. 'If you plant a date-stone, see that its heart is always to the south, to the sun,' put in the driver.

Mr. Jacks at Mohammerah gave the travellers comfort and hospitality.

Up the River Karun they went in a paddle steamer, sleeping on the steady boat, and waking at Dorquain, one of the four pumping stations that lie between Fields and the port of Abbadan—a hundred and fifty miles lay between those places—whence the precious oil from Fields travelled down a great pipe to the shipping port of Abbadan.

At each of the pumping stations the oil was sped onward by power of steam, which was produced by an immense boiler fed with oil. Distant ten miles from one another were small stations where was recorded the pressure of the running oil in the pipe. Three Persians in shifts of eight hours read the pressure-gauges, and they telephoned the measure to the next station. The pulse of an only child, the heart-beat of a sovereign, could not be more carefully noted than was the flow of the oil.

Heat and cold, accident and malice, endangered the flow in this pipe, this great artery of the great body of the Company. Of that body are Indians, Armenians, Arabs, Persians, Englishmen, Scotsmen welded in the commonweal of the oil.

Thereafter they travelled by car over the desert to Ahwaz through forty miles of Persian country, past Bedouins living by the river. In the streets of Ahwaz were holes to drain away the liquid dirt—dogs, beetles and kites ridding the town of the rest. The business of the Company in Ahwaz was the repair and the care of the pipe line. The river here was navigable no longer, being full of islands and having a fall; so the cargo for Fields was put upon a light railway.

Next Talbot and his wife went over the roadless desert for forty miles. A slight rain had made the heavy soil to be slippery, and the car slipped and curvetted about. Here and there the soil had been turned with a plough, and a faint green showed between the ploughed wedges. The fat-tailed sheep, grazing the dried scrub of the past year's growing, were very weak; the goats seemed to bite into the earth. 'How terrible for that woman to see her sheep failing, to have to lug along that famished one; to search in such a blue for any cloud, to know that unless rain falls within ten days no rain will fall throughout the long dry season; to look from the sheep to those children in the hut. Oh! I wonder she is not stark mad with terror,' said Violet. Yet the woman looked carefree enough; it may be that like the sheep she suffered only the pains of the immediate day. "The fat-tailed sheep are luckier than she," said Talbot, "she

The flaming hills

should be big-buttocked like the women of the Kalahari, the bushwomen of desert Africa."

Now, as far as eye could see were hills, the substance of the soil mightily creased and undulating, catching sunshine and shade, gold and black and purple.

A flying bridge bore the travellers across the last bend in the river—they had arrived at Dâr-i-Khazinah.

Then for thirty-two miles they followed the triumphing road; firm and broad it went winding past hills of pink sandstone, streaked with lime, shaped like flying buttresses, like great walls, or broken into sheer sharp wedges with green flats between. Englishmen had contrived this road. In spite of torturing heat, and of barren country; in spite of the lack of watersprings, undismayed by the salt and bitter water of the river; by valleys nauseous with the fumes of sulphur, within fifteen years they had built two hundred and fifty miles of such roads, had spun telephone and telegraph wires. Between Wales and Persia sixty oil tankers ploughed the sea. "The whole is more like a nation than a company. Sixty thousand people in this country maintained through the energy of the Oil Company; these at least the threatened drought will not destroy," said Talbot. Through high-railed outposts they issued and saw, in a valley encircled with hills, the place called Fields.

Talbot and Violet visited the workshops, the hospital, the dwellings of this ant-like enclosure called Fields. A few miles away, outside the pale, were places freshly probed for oil. Above such, were derricks seventy feet, or higher. Here a young Scotsman, harnessed with a safety-belt, swung sixty feet in the air; there three Englishmen drilled with ardent concentration, striving to outdo three more-practised Americans, who were at work somewhere not far off. In two and a half months the Englishmen had drilled nearly three thousand feet into the oil-promising earth. Harsh the noise of the drills, the noise of the cranes. In the season of the great heat, what painful work!

At night, after dinner, Violet went out alone on to the verandah which ran round the house set on a height. In the houses were lights, and lamps along the road, only in the sulphurous valley was the river, was no light. The air was charged with fumes, fumes that blackened and corroded all the metal

351

Well F. 7.

things in the house, and in some parts lay so thick and threatening that locked barriers had been raised, and Persian guards were set on watch, to ward off the danger of fire.

But Violet noticed neither fumes, nor home-lights, nor stars, but had a sudden thought of Dante and knew that this that she saw was unforgettable.

The amphitheatre of the hills was alight with flames upward rushing; scarlet, crimson, incarnadine; the waste-gas of the oil flaming away into the night. Some of the flares man-made, but some of those great fires had burnt for all time. Even it was said of these flames that they were the cause of the foretime Persian fire-worship. Violet felt worship to be the only equal return for such a glory.

On the last day Talbot was shown the two wells of destiny— Well B. 1 'closed in' and no oil taken from her now, the well where the first oil was found. Also, enclosed by a fence guarded by a locked gate of which three men only have the key, the Mother of Prosperity, Well F. 7. Men of the Fields touch their hats when they go near to her, because the fortunes of the Company hung in the balance till Well F. 7 'came in'. She gives oil magnificently, it rises from her at high pressure—she is the romance of Fields. Talbot had determined to go to some of the Ports in the Persian Gulf, so he and his wife said a farewell, full of gratitude and of regret, to Mr. Clegg and Dr. Brahms in whose house they had stayed whilst in Fields.

CHAPTER XXVI

★　　★　　★

IT WAS TWO O'CLOCK IN THE MORNING; A HEAVY DEW was falling. A launch rocked in the swell of the bay. She was purposed to carry Talbot and Violet, and some shivering Persians, from the departed steamer to the Port of Bushire. Talbot and Violet lay down upon the deck, as did the other travellers. The engine of the launch was faulty; the vessel got banked upon sand, and then the engine broke down and was silent. The launch now lay motionless on the sandbank. At nine o'clock next morning another boat took ashore the dew-soaked travellers.

The welcome given by the Resident, Colonel Prideaux, and by his wife, made amends to Talbot and Violet for the cold hours of delay. Pleasure awaited Talbot, for in Bushire was an Englishman who traded in carpets. Talbot passed hours learning from him about the tribal mats—the strawberry colour of this one showed it to be an ancient Veramin, the cross in the design of that other proved it to be made by a Christian tribe from Shirvan, now nearly murdered off the earth. 'The greater the number of knots to the square inch the greater the value of the carpet; the stitches can be counted from the underside of the carpet; look, this one has one hundred and sixty-one. The small silk rugs are too fine for the floor, they should go on the wall. They are made by children, their fingers bleed with the work, therefore the making of such as these is to be forbidden. When the rugs are dirty, put them in a burn and let the water run down the pile, not against the pile.' These things the Englishman told Talbot. He showed him that every rug has a flaw in the design; the very piety of the maker of a rug enforces him to blunder, for Allah only is perfect, therefore it were unseemly that a rug be perfect.

"The Oil Company allows us to sail on a tug of theirs to

Ganaveh and to go to Mishun, their new station in the Hills. Will you come, Vi?" Colonel Prideaux said that the shamail, the north wind, was blowing, that the tug was not safe, that the gulf was treacherous. He nearly persuaded Violet not to go with Talbot. But next morning a tap on the door awoke them. 'The tug will leave in a very short time, because of the tide we cannot wait. Come if you wish.' Such was the message called, in Arabic, through the shut door. Violet leapt up and dressed without again thinking of the shamail. Talbot had said nothing more about the matter of Ganaveh, but he had perhaps despised her poor spirit, and he must have been glad now to see her grasp so rare an occasion. When, after eight hours upon the sea, they landed at Ganaveh, she was told that she was the first white woman to have landed there.

The next day, invited by Allah Kerim Khan, they went to his village in the desert. He, and his friends, met them at the gate of a great yard. Around this courtyard hooded hawks, chained to their perches, awaited in darkness the moment of the hunt.

Allah Kerim spoke in English, which had been taught him at Ganaveh by the engineer of the Oil Company. From him Allah Kerim had learnt also some way, better than the ancient way, of bringing water to the oasis where lay his village. He had, besides, made some study of French. His ideal was that this his village should be like the village of the Vicar of Wakefield, because what he had read of that place had moved him. Fat donkeys, cared for and free of sores, and streets sweet and clean, these the outcome of his ideal. In the middle of the chief street an old man sat at his loom—he had sat there for half a century or more. So much he loved his work and his own place, that an open square had been dug just beyond him, and this was to be his grave, so that he should rest, there, where he had worked.

Talbot and Violet and Allah Kerim ate together, and then Allah Kerim took Violet to the inner court. As they went he talked to her of Hafiz the God-thirsty poet, whose song, he said, was all of the mystic wine, the mystic grape that makes the seer reel. Kerim Khan cared nothing for Omar, 'for he sang only tavern songs, of carnal love and of fermented drink'. He gave Violet, wrapped in silk, a Persian book with the poems of

Hafiz, and, besides that, a coat of finest camel's wool, white and lined with silk.

He told Violet that for a year before his marriage he had climbed every palm and every roof, hoping to see in the enclosed court the form of her who was to be his bride. He had not seen her until they were married. He loved her; she was as yet his only wife. She was lovely in pale gauze clothes. Although she was past the thirtieth year of her age she had no lines on her face, but the smiling placid look of one sheltered from the world. True, she said she envied Violet her travels and her much looking, but yet Violet could see that she envied her this freedom as Violet herself might covet the wingèd flight of an angel—a pleasure so remote from experience that the lack of it meant nothing.

A slave came in, a waiting woman, and she sat on the floor near to her mistress; then the two women told Kerim in Persian what questions they wanted him to put to Violet. The thing that most pricked their curiosity was how it came about that, after having had five children and being over forty years of age, Violet had not the sagging breasts of the mature Persian woman. She laughed and perhaps reddened a little, and explained as best she might. Then Kerim said he trusted that his talk was not in any way unbecoming, but that he had never before spoken to a woman from Europe, nor indeed to any man from there—excepting the engineer in Ganaveh. Violet reassured Kerim Khan. For years after that day, the Persian chieftain and she sometimes wrote to one another.

The Khan was full of trouble, because at that time legions of soldiers were marching through Persia and, being a levy on the people, they brought ruin on the countryside.

Then Talbot and Violet left the oasis and went into the hills to Mishun.

A lasso, cast serpentine along the mountain tops by the playful hand of an Olympian, such was the outline of the road which had been cut along the crest of the mountains; sheer precipice was on either side. The driver sweated with fear.

In one stopping place, the barren shaly hills blossomed with narcissi.

Violet remembered that part of Persia always with trepi-

355

dation, for near Mishun was an officer, Persian or Turk. He gave the travellers sherbet and talked to them in French, sitting in a room full of rugs that hung upon the walls. He talked of Paradise and of poetry, and she could hear the stallions moving about in the stable, that was built under this upper room where they sat.

When they left him, they walked through an old archway on either side of which were dark deep hollow places. A fearful stench came from the darkness, and sounds. 'What sounds are those?' and he laughed. "No wonder he laughed," Talbot said, "for those are his money-boxes," and he explained to Violet that this Captain kept miscreants and misfortunates there till they should pay him to free them, hence the smell, the sounds. "In Persia men still suffer the bastinado, are still imprisoned in wells which are so shallow that the imprisoned can nearly climb out—nearly, but never quite."

Next day they went back to Ganaveh, and to Bushire, and then steamed to Bahrein; that was eighteen hours of seafaring. Twice Talbot had cause to wonder at the atmosphere. Once, when at night on this ship *Barpeta* forty miles from Shatt-al-Arab, could be seen shining the twelve-mile light of Shatt-al-Arab. And again, when at morning the captain took his bearings from two hills in Persia distant eighty miles, the bearings were true within a few seconds.

The *Barpeta* anchored, and Talbot and Violet were taken by a sailing boat ashore to stay in the house of the British Advisor, Major Daly. These seas with springs of sweetness; this barely known island of Bahrein; this Persian Gulf, with preciousness of pearl, were, to Talbot, stirring and strange. He moved about silent, with shining eyes; won by their witchery.

CHAPTER XXVII

★　　★　　★

CHANTING OF HELL PREDESTINED, AND OF PREDESTINED gardens of felicity, in the early windless morning, Arabs punted and rowed the heavy pearling vessels towards the fisheries. The sails hung slack, and the chanting put a rhythm to the labour—Koranic promises and consolation hung upon the air.

A man dived with a skin into the sea and came ashore carrying the vessel swollen with sweet water.

> 'As I have heard that,
> Somewhere in the main,
> Freshwater springs come up through bitter brine.'

On the instant both Talbot and Violet remembered the lines. Pearl-giving seas; seas, giving also sweet water to this rainless barren land!

An old Arab talked to Talbot by the seaside, using Arabic and Malay. He told of the pearl-divers; how they would never wear, or allow any of the brotherhood to wear, the diver's dress, 'for that would do away with their livelihood'. He explained 'a diver could never remain below water longer than so long,' and he bowed his head into his hands and recited words from the Koran till Talbot's watch showed that one minute and a half had gone by. 'The men will tell you that they can remain thus long' —and he bent down for a long five minutes. 'But that is not possible. It seems as long as that to them. Their eardrums burst, their eyes suffer, but they can never be under the sea for long. They come up and rest for five times as long as they work below; often they hang on to the boat-side to rest; then they go down again, and so all through the day.' The aged Arab told Talbot that these divers are enslaved by their own necessities. A man may come from far off, and to make certain of the work he will arrive before the season of fishing. 'You must wait, you will need a woman, and food. These I will give you and your

357

work shall be my payment.' The fisher does not take much thought; he drifts deeply into debt; he becomes, in truth, a slave to the owner of a vessel.

Later in the day, in the market Talbot saw some mean pearls, for the best had long since gone to India, and to Paris. Tassels made of the real gold thread were the prettiest of the wares; big white donkeys brought in the merchandise.

On the morrow Major Daly took them into the thirsty country, and he showed them a wonderful place of which as yet nothing was known. From round about them, and going away into the distance, were hundreds of tombs, rounded, low like billows. Their age and history were undiscovered.

From thence they drove to the palace of the Sheik of Bahrein, the owner of the pearl fisheries.

Major Daly was intermediary, and Talbot understood and spoke some Arabic. They sat on cushions on the floor in the carved cool room, until they moved into another place and sat around the feast of rice, and eggs, and of a sheep roasted whole, and various other meats. They ate silently and fast, and Violet, unaccustomed, wished she could have eaten more, but she clumsily wasted time feeding herself with her hands. Talbot was as easy as any man, sitting cross-legged and accepting pieces of the sheep pulled from the dish by the sheik. The remainder of the meal was carried away to the women, and a man came with a ewer and a basin so that they might wash their hands and mouths in the scented water. The sheik, it was easy to see, had much liking for Talbot; he motioned to him to look at his stallions and his mares. He gave Talbot a bay mare, Ayesha, and that was a gift full of honour, for an Arab does not lightly part with a mare. 'I will bring her to you when I visit the King of England.' And he kept his word (16).

Next day the shamail blew and the land looked grey with the flying dust. Talbot and his wife went out to the ship that lay in the Bay; for nearly three hours they were sailing and steaming to join her. Nor was it easy, in the dark of the night, to creep over a chain of barges to reach the steamer's side.

At Kowait, noble Arabian town, they landed. By the great walled entrance was a cluster of sheep and goats. These, in the morning, had been gathered together by a herdsman, he calling

at every man's house for beasts and then leading them to pasture, some miles away. Now, it being evening, he led them
again to the town, and from its northern point they would
scamper back, each to his own place. In the harbour lay
great ships, built at Kowait for the pearling.
They were of wood: "You may
think you are looking at
the ships of Queen
Elizabeth."

CHAPTER XXVIII

*　　*　　*

THE DAY WAS DRAWING NEAR WHEN THE FREEDOM OF
Lytham and St. Anne's was to be conferred upon Talbot. So
good-bye to Gertrude Bell; break this magic of Bagdad;
wrench the eyes from Ctesiphon.

This time they would travel by the British way, the Nairn.

Past palms, blighted by the calamitous frost, and through a
sandstorm they went, as far as Ramadi. Between Ramadi and
the rest-house, where they stayed the night, lightning fell, and
in the desert, English airmen in motors, and an Arab force
mounted on camels caparisoned, loomed into vision from out
the grey of the sandstorm. 'Give me water,' said an Arab, leaping in front of the travellers' car, and the driver nearly ran him
down. "I never went through any country in this spirit; no
wonder there are murders in this desert," Talbot said; and the
driver, his revolver in his hand, answered that there was nothing
an honest man might say to another when dusk has fallen in the
desert. 'We never stop even in the day, or give presents.'

"No wonder there are thefts and murders," Talbot insisted.

For three days and during the last night of the three they
travelled and, on the fourth day, reached Damascus. 'Beware of
Wâdy Hauran,' the Arabs said, and later Talbot discovered that
the armoured cars, the camels caparisoned, the flying machines
in the desert, all had to do with Wâdy Hauran.

A day or two before this crossing of the Syrian desert a car
had been shot at in the Wâdy Hauran, and a young Frenchwoman
had died of wounds. It was supposed that the thieves had intended to stop the car by shooting at the tyres. They were
perhaps starving, for the winter had been very cruel. This
tragedy overhung the journey, and the unusual rain made the
desert like a sheet of ice, elsewhere like a bog. The cars danced
and skidded and near overturned; then they were embedded in

mud, and at Wâdy Han was a sudden unknown overflow of water, big as a river. 'The most aged man cannot remember water here,' they were told. At Qubaissa, a walled small town where a night was spent, the Arabs were all merchants who sold goods to the passing caravans. From the sulphur well and from the sweet-water well in the sand, their women came, walking like goddesses. They left their water-pots, pointed to the sky, named Allah and followed Violet, tormenting her for money. Miss Dawson, a fellow-traveller, said: 'Imagine in England wives of merchants and of farmers begging from us.' Violet laughed, and remembered how, in Bagdad, the beggars pressing round her had keened their need of money. Goats, sheep, and camels, coloured clothes, and the walls and minarets of the little place, made a beauty in the desert, but the fly-devoured, diseased, blinded-eyes of the people gave it a horror. Hardly one in the begging crowd had both eyes whole.

In the moonlight, colonnades of Palmyra, desecrated ruined temple of the Sun; ghost of Soloman, wraith of Zenobia. Damas; Jaffa; sphinx!

'Oh God: thou great sphinx.' Violet had been slapped for praying thus when she was ten years old, and now she stood before the sphinx. She had been told in childhood that only two things in life would not disappoint her; the Taj and the sphinx. The Taj seen by moonlight, and again at sunrise when she and the naked, the 'sky-clad' ascetics had gone with marigolds to the tomb, seen again at burning midday, and in the rosy evening, the Taj in all that cycle of her pilgrimage had never failed to be entirely perfect. But now sphinx! Her heart hurt her, ached quite physically as though it were cramped, for the sphinx looked out over irrigated patches: 'over potato plots' she thought disgustedly. Violet had to turn her back so as not to see the plots and a giant advertisement at which the sphinx gazed. Then she heard two voices, one at her elbow: 'Take a camel Miss, take a camel Miss!' and another—that of an American woman talking to another woman of her advancing age: 'As Robert Browning said, don't mind getting old—only hurry more.'

Talbot and Violet travelled to Rome, and thence to London.

* * *

It was the last day of March, 1925, and Talbot, thinking over the honour this day was to bring to him, reminded Violet of the day after the war when she was overbowed with honour, for she had been charged with the presentation of war-medals to eight men of Lytham. On the greensward near the sea and close to the old windmill stood the eight men. Fearful of troubling the heroes by the emotion that she felt, Violet put upon herself a cuirass of steely coldness. Years afterwards one of the crowd said to her: 'In your crimson dress you were so very white that we thought you would faint, and the Squire stood close by as though to catch you if you did.'

When they got home Talbot said to Violet: "You did not shake hands with the men, or even smile." To make amends he ordered eight gold watches from the nearest city; Violet would give the chains. That evening at a feast given to the valiant, Violet, with a kiss to each man, gave every one his present.

This March was a day for thinking back on the past, and after the great midday meal the Mayor, Mr. Thomas Critchley, spoke of the years behind them and told the guests why this honour had been done to Talbot Clifton. During the lifetime of this Lord of the Manor benefactions to the value of about one hundred and fifty thousand pounds had been made to churches, schools, and the rest (17). Fifty years ago their new Freeman had laid the foundation-stone of St. Anne's, and now Lytham and St. Anne's were the lungs and the loveliness of that part of Lancashire. The Clifton Estate had benefited the whole district; after years of cavilling and rebuke from the shorter-sighted people, the ultimate good done to the district by the Estate was at last recognized. To the sacrifice of Talbot's own immediate wealth was due the comeliness of St. Anne's.

Talbot answered, and wit mingled with his reasoned talk. It seemed that at last he could express and explain himself.

In a casket of gold the citizens presented him with the scroll conveying the freedom of the borough. The casket was embossed and was inlaid with painted ivories showing things that touched his life: a map of the world, and below it, inscribed, the name of the places of his travels: the sandhills as he had seen them when a boy, a shepherd and sheep walking amongst them: and next to it a picture of gay St. Anne's raised where had been the sand. On the casket also was portrayed Cuthbert

Clifton chained to a wall for the Faith. The *Ovis Cliftoni* was imaged at one end, and at the other end was shown the ruff, bird of the moss, which moss-land had been reclaimed by Talbot's forefathers.

Talbot had given the famed Green Drive of Lytham into the care of the infant borough; he himself had been the first to attempt to make the amalgamation between the two towns, leafy Lytham and gay St. Anne's.

After the presentation of the casket, Violet was called upon to speak, and she spoke in verse that she had written for the occasion.

Talbot did not any more live at Lytham, but he took back
to Islay, and he never lost, some sense of attainment
and fulfilment (18) because of the town's
recognition of him on that last day
of March.

CHAPTER XXIX

*   *   *

IN THE YEAR 1926 TALBOT SAILED FROM ISLAY THAT HE
might after many years return to Africa. "*February* 17*th*. The
last gong has sounded for passengers' friends to leave the ship.
Charming telegram from V. Melancholia set in as ship sailed.
Evening beautiful."

*   *   *

In mid March the haramata was blowing upon Kano.
"Instead of a breeze, a fiery blast blowing fine dust from the
Sahara." The dust fell upon the great mud walls of the Hausa
city; it powdered indifferently the fifteen miles of those walls,
it powdered the stark, the unforgettable city, it was shed upon
the fifty thousand dwellers in Kano.

The dust fell into the market place, where to and fro upon
their business moved thousands of people—seven thousand or
more. It fell upon the wares displayed for purchase, upon the
beautiful long-horned cattle called fulani, upon camels and
upon goats. It marred a little the great scarlet patches of pepper-
pods spread out for sale, dimmed a little the brown pods of the
tamarind, pods that enveloped the bitter-sweet food of the
silkworms. It fell upon the red slippers, which someone would
buy. It added dust to the smoke-smirched goods of Lancashire.
The dust fell upon swords in their scabbards, upon an Emir
fingering a Koran from out a leather case. It fell upon a horse-
man handling a saddle from Tripoli. Nostril, tongue, and eye—
each could mark it, that fine hot dust from the Sahara that fell
upon Kano, the extraordinary Hausa city.

Seven hundred miles away from the city rolled the sea; the
railway crept up to the mud walls of Kano, and stopped. Talbot
Clifton was savouring the morning, enjoying the buying and
the selling: "Whimsical that this poor man should salute me by
bending both legs and shaking his fist at me. Wonderful to see
that Arab in snow-white clothes on the high-peaked saddle

saluting me with his mighty long lance; to see the natives with bows and arrows, and with swords the handles of which are like those of the Crusaders."

Next day hot wheels—through hot dust—rolled for three hundred and fifty miles. They turned through the great forest of Bornu, where many fires had stunted the great trees. At last, at Maidugari, the wheels stopped: "In all my wanderings in Central Africa I have never seen anything like this village of Maidugari, laid out in long avenues."

Drinking something—could a man ever drink enough in such a furnace?—Talbot reread and put away in his case the farewell letter of the Governor of the Northern Provinces. Colonel Palmer had written: 'I am only too glad to help in what I think will be an interesting journey—and I like your coming with a toothbrush to cross Africa.'

"I wonder when that boy will come." Then, looking up, Talbot saw Mahomed Noa standing before him. "Can you make tea? Can you make bed?" he asked. He spoke in French to the African, for his country was near Lake Chad. There Mahomed, son of a chief, had kept his father's flocks. He wore a white covering; he was tall and shapely; his eyes were fearless. So scant his instruction in the laws of the Prophet that in truth Mahomed was a pagan. Soon, however, he styled himself Moslem, for he quickly gauged the dignity which Islam conferred upon him; as untaught pagan this was lacking. His mind and his wit were sharp; he was full of desires for clothes, for money, for new things. 'I promised master to trail with him around Africa'—so Mahomed wrote later (19). Now, promising, he gave his allegiance with complete adherence.

White man and black towered together through the market. 'And master laughs about the funny things of the crowd. The big men and all the people were pleased to see him, and he shook the hand of the chief. And the women were some of them with red lips, and some with black lips, and some with white lips. He asked me why? I told him the red is because of the kola nuts they eat, and he said "Oh yes, and with the black lips?" That a kind of leaf in tobacco. "And the white lips?" A powder and rub same on their lips. Then he said he never saw such in his life.'

* * *

In the Ford car the thermometer registered a hundred and forty degrees Fahrenheit: "Go to the Turkish bath and see what that reading means," so Talbot wrote to Violet. Dikoa—the English boundary town—passed, the French Cameroons succeeded. Here were dry mud flats with sparse trees; Talbot shot a cobb, a Jackson hartebeest and a large antelope of a species he did not know. On one of those nights of travel the moon shone. The car had broken down and Talbot was walking. In the pearly light he saw an animal standing near the road. He stalked it so stealthily that it did not see him even when he was within twenty yards of it. Then, wondering what beast it was, Talbot aimed at the looming form. He shot, and when he stooped over the creature he saw that he had killed a bush-cow, a buffalo. He said to himself: "I'm glad I did not know at what I was aiming, as this, I've always thought, is the most dangerous of African animals. I wonder if I should have been fool enough knowingly to shoot at it with only a .202 Holland rifle."

Along that road to Fort Lamy the hot wind blew: "My left arm scorched and blistered by the wind—not by the sun." To what homely thing would Violet liken this heat? Talbot had smiled sometimes at her similitudes. He remembered that sailing an Irish lough upon which the soft wind was tracing long V-shaped lines, she had said, as though to herself: 'Blue watered-satin; miles of it spread about me—whilst other women have to be content with merely a dress or even a yard or two.' And on that other day when she had called out: 'Look at those narrow clouds like silver pennants, their ends just ravelled by the breeze.' This heat grated the throat like a steel rasp. She would liken to a burning pumice this intolerable sandy wind, "which penetrates the nostrils and brings on heavy bleeding," which dried up even the sheltered kidneys. "It is an effort to petit-besoin even twice a day." So his thought ached on.

The car jolted along the way to Fort Lamy. Before Kusseri was reached there was passed a night hideous for master and for man. "A tornado blowing. Cannot see a hundred yards through the sand. One continuous hot blast. No sleep at all in this bush village with drum beating till morning, devoured by mosquitos, horrible night."

To Mahomed it was thus: 'This place there are lots of thieves and many cannibals. During the night they turn into leopards and catch men. They are men-flesh-eaters. Their eyes are always red as fire. When master was on bed I guarded him behind the bed. I never sleep till night-break because I was afraid.'

Talbot did not know of these leopard-men, but Mahomed had known of them always. Mahomed knew also of the brotherhood of the crocodile-men who, living near rivers, assume that horrid shape. He knew that there are men and women who are incorporated in Satan, and that these evil ones prey upon children, and upon others besides. Some years later when he was a travelled man, a Christian clothed in blue serge, Mahomed still retained his assurance in the power of the leopard-men, the power of the crocodile-men and women. Did not the Bible itself bear him out in the belief in witchcraft? Mahomed had known since boyhood of the bag of evil physic, possession of the witch doctor, or might be of the chieftain; dread treasure of the wicked. Rice, the white of an egg, some organ of the human body, these things and more besides, kept in a bag and called physic. Mahomed, and the others of his colour, knew the compound to be a vehicle of satanic power, a conveyance of malediction. To liven the magic power of the content of the bag, human fat and human blood were needed for its anointing.

If the owner would wield good fortune, or did he desire the power to blast his enemy, then, to vivify the power of his foul possession, he must continually enrich it with blood and fat, and for this existed the human leopards, and the human crocodiles. For this the murders in the dark of the night, between the beating of the drums. Children taken for the most part, but virgins and boys too carried off, as the white men might think by the leopards, or by the crocodiles. Always Mahomed will shudder to think of the handshake that reveals one human leopard to another—and how at night. . . . but enough of this thinking! However the white men might explain the mysteries, whatever they might say about the leopard-men being but apparelled in skins, Mahomed was certain that, by means of magic, men did indeed assume the shape of beasts.

367

CHAPTER XXX

* * *

THE TRAVELLERS HAD SPENT TWO NIGHTS ON THE ROAD, although not much over a hundred miles lay between Maidugari and Kusseri. The roads being bad, and the car bad, the hours moved on in heat without their reaching Kusseri. When they did arrive: "*Wednesday, 24 March*. The French officers in charge at Kusseri were charming. They lent me their boat which took me down the Shari river, twenty minutes to Fort Lamy, where I gave official letters I had been carrying to the Governor. He looks exactly like Napoleon. I was then handed over to the police who had fixed up very comfortable quarters for me. I insisted on having a drink as the heat is intense. Finally a carafe of water was brought and a pint of champagne. Oh, what a delectable beverage! I then called on a Greek by name Marco Paulos who kindly gave me food. I had risen at five in the morning and had a biscuit at eight. It was now half-past two. This Greek had learnt English at Lytham. I dined with the clever interesting Governor who spoke English well.

"To-day I am trying to induce the Governor to let me have some petrol so that I may go as far as Bokoro, a hundred and fifty miles farther on my journey. To-night he will give me the answer. This is a most vital vital question, as the journey for the first hundred miles to Bokoro is through level mud flats and very bad fever districts. I shall go on from Bokoro with bullocks and ponies. I bought six bottles of champagne and two of brandy (oh this pestilential heat!) . . .

"The Governor has the petrol. He, Monsieur Coppet, is lending me the car to Bokoro, 150 miles, which will leave me roughly four hundred miles to trek to Adre. This I am told will be my route:

Bokoro to Mongo 120 miles.
Mongo to Am Deban 130 miles.
Am Deban to Adre 140 miles.

"I may have to continue with bullocks or camels from Adre as far as Geneina."

Of this Mahomed later wrote: 'I followed master with luggage on the big river Shari with many of alligators and crocodiles. At Fort Lamy every morning the prisoners have to bring water, sweep the house and do everything that is necessary. And the people thieve, even a man's head if you don't look sharp.

'Then from there we go to Bokoro with the car moving. Master killed six guinea fowls. The driver stopped the car and I took them. On the way soldiers came and saluted master and he asked for the chief. Then came a man playing a musical instrument like violin and other kind. Master took this feast together with the soldiers. At this place there is no river, the people live by well water.

'Near here we see a town, near it are many of leopards and during the night the leopards come down from the mountains to the town to find what to eat. They will be growling along in any parts of the city, here and there many of giraffes, and wolves and a great mountain. The natives of this place whenever one wants to marry they make a string or native line in three colours red blue and black. Then they tie it on the girl's waist and rub red dirts in her face and all over the body. The man who is going to marry her comes with a piece of goathide around him covered his front and his back because there is no English clothes not even piece to see. They are Mahomedans and that is the way they marry by their own system.'

When Talbot reached Bokoro he wrote: "*Bokoro*. Terrible day. Motor broke down one mile beyond Fort Lamy, two wheels broke during the day. Too tired to eat, having been in the open tumbledown Ford all day in the awful sun. Slight touch of dysentery owing to bad water tea is made from. No sleep as boy upset scalding tea over my ankle. The continuous throbbing pain kept me awake. Pitched my bed outside camp."

CHAPTER XXXI

*   *   *

BOKORO TO MONGO—A HUNDRED AND FIFTY MILES TO
go. The way must be spun from the bodies of the travellers as
the spider's line from its belly. Hooves of horses, cloven hooves
of bullocks; feet of men; they would, step by step, cover it.
No bloodless tyres, no unsentient metal to cope with the one
hundred and fifty miles, but instead flesh and blood, monstrous
heat notwithstanding. Three miles an hour would be about their
pace, for always there would be a beast less strong than the
rest to cause delay.

The white bullock was fine; it would go as far as Mongo; the
others would be changed, the ponies too. The owner of the
bullock asked eleven francs for a hundred and fifty miles; he did
not reckon to charge for the journey back, nor for his own
service; eleven francs was the charge for the white bullock, and
the man would tend the creature. The people here asked little
for their goods. Years ago Talbot, in Africa, had carried cowrie
shells for payment, and yards of fabric; now in a rough canvas
bag he carried ochre-yellow, half-franc pieces, singing together as the bag swung. A sheep might cost fourpence; rice
and eggs were cheap; milk was hard to get, but water was even
more scarce. There was no fruit at all, but only crops of guinea-
corn raised for the cattle.

After four hours of travel, the first stage from Bokoro, nine
miles, had been covered.

Afterwards, with flies, with lightning, and with astonishing
heat, Harbat Shatak was reached. Strange that any place was
named, for the whole was but a flat, a vast main of land, with
sea shells here and there—a nightmare for alikeness. If a man
were to shut his eyes, and to open them again a hundred miles
farther on, he would but see the same flat desolation. True, the
manner of the people changed, negroid races and several Arab
tribes showing sharp differences one from another.

A privilege granted to few

Harbat Shatak offered a rough consolation, a great thunder-storm with torrents of rain: "The heavy clouds and wind saved me from heat. When the rain ceased the bed was spread out under the skies. Not so hot, thank God!"

Talbot was roused at four of the morning. Sometimes walk-ing, sometimes riding, he had time to think. A letter written to his wife came back to his thoughts, for on the cold evening in February when he had sailed from Liverpool he had written: "How wonderful it would have been if you had continued your travels and seen Liberia and Nigeria, Sierra Leone, the Gold Coast and Gambia. It would have placed you high up among women travellers. It takes a certain amount of will power at my time of life to leave my native country, but to gain an in-sight into one of God's great worlds is a privilege granted to few. Well good-bye darling.—Yours, T." (20)

The journey was not as he had forethought; on this journey Violet could not have gone; the heat would have killed her. Talbot wondered if it would kill him. He had started from home with blood-poisoning, a doctor crying warning. He had sweated the poison out by now; but, riding along the mud flat, he had to cast out a seed of weakness, for his thought had turned willy nilly to the cool of the Green Hill in Islay. He wondered if Violet would remember that he had told her to bury him there if he died on this journey.

From the forest of Bornu up to where, the night before, the men had lain encamped, were hundreds of miles of scrub; but now, between Harbat Shatak and Matari the travellers came upon a few trees and great boulders of granite. In the pretty village they exchanged their tired ponies for young mettlesome beasts. The one that Talbot tried to mount kicked out at him—then galloped away into the open country. Mahomed flung himself across a capering stallion and rode it by stark balance. They passed giraffes; they passed thousands of dusty-coloured guinea-fowl, all meetly plumaged for this incinerated country. Even the evening breeze was hot.

Because they lacked water the men must push on: "Awful day, marches very tiring on bad pony. The back of one's throat seems to crack a few minutes after sucking the water-bottle (weak tea and muddy water). I dare not smoke."

"In the bush without water"

There was a day of disaster; the mainspring of Talbot's watch broke and it was by the watch that he measured the distance from water to water. Either by a chart given, or by some instructions received, he knew the wells to be so many miles apart the one from the other. But he could gauge the measure of the miles only by time. Two and a half miles to the hour he reckoned, or maybe three miles; but now, with no watch, it was impossible to measure. Without knowing until too late, he passed by water, and that in the centre of Equatorial Africa. Afterwards they came upon an Arab who, for a few francs, sold his watch to Talbot. A shoddy watch, but more to be relied upon than the gold one which had failed. This mean watch hung on a short chain, gay with blue stones; it lay within a case of metal like to that of which it was made. In the front of the case was talc so that, even in the blowing sand, the time could be seen without fear of the powdery dust clogging the works or the hands of the watch.

After midtime of that painful day behind the caravan, two cars were seen approaching. The cars rolled on, but there was no offer of help, no hail from the men within. Mahomed said: 'These not English.' But the men were English. "It was Gray and Co!" Two days later Talbot found the letter which they had left for him at Mongo. They had learned who the khaki-clad figure was. Gray wrote to say he would have stopped had he known that he was passing an Englishman. 'We thought it was a French gentleman on trek.' "Makes it worse," wrote Talbot with disgust. "All the traditions of travellers broken by Gray not asking me if I wanted help. I slept that night in the bush without water." After having travelled during nine days from Bokoro, Talbot reached Mongo.

CHAPTER XXXII

*   *   *

THE NEXT MARCH WAS FROM MONGO TO AM DEBAM, ONE
hundred and thirty miles; this journey was to take them seven
days. At Mongo Talbot cabled to his wife and wrote in his diary
of the kindness of the French people of that place. Then he went
forward with fresh bullocks and horses to a mountain village,
and beyond it to a village off the mapped way. It lay at the foot
of a mountain; cattle, horses and natives were gathered round a
fire. Talbot, enjoying the sight of them, rested awhile.

Of this village Mahomed afterwards spoke thus: 'Then from
there to a town at the foot of a mountain. The natives or in-
habitants of this place, they are not Christians neither are they
Mahomedans, nor believe in true God, but worship the mountains, trees and rivers. They are pagans and savages living in the
bush and the mountains, wearing no clothes neither hides, but
wearing leaves only to cover the front and the back. When they
see a civilized person they kill him with their instruments made
with iron; knives, axes, bows and others, made like sickles.
When one of them is dead they keep the body for over a week,
waiting that if a god will take the dead body. They will come
and look every morning during these days whether god has
taken the death, and throwing stones and quivers in the air,
saying: 'Come down and take the man, we don't want of same.'
Then after seven days have passed, they bury the dead body.'

Mahomed remembered that village with a lasting anger because, beyond it from behind a rock or tree, a hand had hurled
a spear at the travellers. Mahomed could not understand why
his master—so often angered—now only smiled; nor why he
kept the iron point—which fell broken from its staff—as
though it were a thing propitious.

Beyond Melangangi "the sun dimmed—small rains expected—hope we don't get them." The pace now was four miles in

one and a half hours. From Melangangi onwards the map was often faulty. Always was the anxiety as to whether or not water would be found. Talbot's water-bottle got burnt, which accident might have proved fatal had not a Frenchman at Mongo given him an old spare one.

"*Shededi* 8. Sleeping in bush with no water again.

"*Thursday*, 8 *April*. When I called agif, my guide said: 'Bad place for lions.' However I told him I was there to protect him from 'linga' and there the matter ended. Ramid is very stupid, too fat and a eunuch I think. I have fever."

Talbot's bed was put apart as it were an outpost; the men huddled round the fire. Mahomed afterwards wrote of that night: 'I met a lion standing near the bed of master but master was sleeping not knowing anything of the lion. And then I make up the fire and then it ran away because that it fear the fire-flame. The whole night I never sleep because lions were making noise all along the country. But master he not care for lions.'

Next morning: "Must keep going, biscuits and tinned fruit running out. My horse is a real pet." Now they left the mountains and were in flat bush country again. They passed Kirelmi —the map was wrong again—and then amongst hills they came upon Saraf. Here were heights, and rocks formed in great beauty, and here dark antelope and hartebeest were seen.

Mahomed beheld things thus: 'There are many of fierce animals, leopards, lions, unicorns and other kinds all around this place, plenty of range of mountains wood and jungles where live all fierce of animals. There about five o'clock of the morning no man can go out so early because he will be killed by the unicorns and by other fierce animals. The unicorn has only one horn on the forehead and other dangerous creeping animals which are snakes, cobras and so forths. Some live in the river, some on land, some under the ground along the roadside. During the night some go in a hole and head out, but if a person tread on him will bite and in a few minutes the person will die by the poison the creeping animal has in its mouth. Another live in the river called boa, big and long, can kill a man by rolling on him, others black and long when sees a man can send out spit and if the spit goes in eyes of the man he will be blinded.

'In another place there is no river. They dig a well about

twenty-five yards deep before they can see water. The people have no watch neither clock, their time is the sun. They pray and do everything when the sun is in the middle, and when they walk in their shadow it is about twelve o'clock. And when their shadow is about one and a half yards long that is two o'clock. And about three yards long is about four o'clock. And when the sun falls down they know it is about six o'clock in the evening. During the night they know the time by the cock; when it crows, they know it is about two o'clock, and last he crows they know it is about six o'clock in the morning or the rising of the sun from the east. In this place during the month of June they do not eat but keep fast and pray till the evening, then they can eat.

'In travelling in all this places I first go before master to prepare everything before him as cow milk, chickens and so forths. There master see they take milk from the sheep as from cow and goat, but master was unlike of same.'

"*Mongelmi. Saturday, 10 April.* This is an old deserted French part of the country, many villages, good shooting near the hills. The eunuch guide deserted here, but sent his soldier brother. This I arranged with a certain amount of hard ———."

A few drops of rain fell, so when night came the traveller slept in a straw house. The great heat of the house and the worry of the flies gave Talbot fever. After that night the bullocks went more slowly than ever; the men were tired; the guide desired to stop; the map was wrong. But Talbot pressed on towards water.

"*Monday, 12 April.* Went into a strong breeze this morning, the strength of a furnace in it, urrr. Ordered bullocks, only three were brought, so commandeered one donkey and two men. Heard that at Halibar is no water, terribly slow going."

Next day from six in the morning till ten they walked. "*Tuesday, 13 April.* Yesterday afternoon long, long ten miles. Sun fearful, got off my horse to vomit. Had my last pint of pop and water in camp. Back aching. Shot small buck. My lunch and breakfast two biscuits. To-day left at quarter to six in the morning. Reached Maile at half-past ten in the forenoon. Waited alone a long time for water-carriers, dead silence in camp while water was being brought."

The master and the goats

Thus Mahomed: 'Very far from the town there were many
goats, in this place that it was very hard for water, not even a
well as in some places. There were about forty goats, most of
them dying thirsty, and the master was having a water-bottle
filled with tea. And he started to share the tea amongst the
goats. And it finished. And none remained, not even as
a drop for him. Then the men went to find water.
They leave in the morning and they come
back in the evening. And most of
the goats have died.'

CHAPTER XXXIII

* * *

FROM MAILE THE TRAVELLERS MADE THEIR WAY TO AM
Deban. At Am Deban were many lions. The mountainous
country showed granite hills thrown up here and there, "looking from the high ground like islands".

The French administrator was hospitable to Talbot who
reckoned, and reckoned rightly, that in distance only a hundred
and forty miles, and in time only ten days, lay between himself
and Adre. He marked the day by giving himself the treat of
only now opening the box of greengages which his wife had
sent when he had sailed from Liverpool.

One night was spent at Am Deban, and then they went on
again. "Ants and flies, no peace, big marches ahead. Hope I can
last!" There was trouble with the men; there was punishment.
"The guide said: No water for a long way! I had to send twice
for water. Some was brought and some milk." Mahomed told
of the thing thus: 'Far away in the bush we were having no
water to drink, no river neither a well near the place, but far
away about one day's journeying one can get water. I with two
men went to beg water from the people, they told us they have
no water even a drop to spare. Then we returned to master,
I thinking how to get water when I heard men talking a language I know. And I tell these men I am going to get water
from these people. And they say they will not give it. So I went
again and told the people 'Good evening' in their language and
ask them if they know God, and they said, 'Yes', and if they are
Moslem, and they said 'Ila ila, hi'. Then I told them if they are
Moslem and they know God they should give me a bit of
water. Then the chief called to give me water and each of them
give me a little. I am asked how I got it. I said because I know
how to speak the language. That is why they give me water,
though other men never get of same.'

The following day was the sixteenth of April—in England wood-violets, white and fragrant, here the only flower a sulphurous-coloured bloom without scent, pushing up from the sand. "The whole country is an ocean of land with sea shells found along the way—dead level with only a line of hills; bush scattered here and there." Rivers were shown on a map he had seen of the country, but in the dry season flowed only the Shari river.

Farther on was Banden: "A brown hare greeted me; I passed partridges and a species of weasel and many antelope." Here the men wove cloth and the women, all short-haired, made pottery. Two women drove the bullocks of the traveller.

The next village was Am Gereda. The people there had brewed a kind of beer which they gave to Talbot to drink. It was not intoxicating but it caused him agony. At Am Gereda camels were brought in place of bullocks for the carrying of the baggage. The man who brought the camels threw two spears at the guide of the caravan, but then the miscreant escaped. "Ipecacuanha, quinine, and brandy may get me away. Cannot start yet because of dysentery, although fresh horses have arrived." Talbot went on for two miles, and then, unable through sickness to go farther, he stayed the night beside a well.

The next day: "Am writing under a lean-to, flies and natives everywhere. Am better but very weak. Managed to sit my horse for two and a half hours. When we come to the six hours' trek without water I shall collapse. My horse stumbles every step. D—. Rather interesting country. I vomit all the time. Trying a long march to-night—can I?"

Next day, April the twentieth, "Excelsior" was written over the page. Talbot had reached Um Dagig. He and Mahomed rode from five o'clock of the morning until a quarter to ten; they covered thirteen and a half miles, "a feat of endurance after enteric and fever".

The dawn was full of the pain and of the growling of the camels; because of the sores on their backs the creatures groaned and roared as their burdens were put upon them. "Never sun rises without—somewhere—this complaint," thought Talbot with pity. Seeing Talbot astir Mahomed became useful again; when his master at Am Gereda "lay sweltering on the bed too weak to shout, Mahomed did not come near me (21) and his shaven head lost all its English. I do not think I should have attempted to trek across this part of Africa if I had known what pain heat can produce." Talbot fell to thinking of an Englishman he had met before he reached the city of Kano. For a year this man had been making preparation to cross to Khartoum and he was soon to follow along the way Talbot had taken. "And I have not even a filter. I deserve to be ill!" he concluded.

The twenty-first of April held beauty. A Sultan of the Masalit Arabs travelled with Talbot eight miles. The chieftain had met the Englishman the day before, and had accompanied him to the sound of whistles and of drums. They passed dried-up watercourses shaded with trees: there were hills to look upon; there was the pleasure of understanding and of being understood in the consonant language of the Arabs. "Language fine to the ear as to the eye," thought Talbot, thinking of the beauty of the letters, graven or embroidered. This Sultan, the night before, had given a sheep to Talbot; now—at Kungerei—he had grass huts built beneath a hill in the shade of ample trees. "During the night saw a flaming meteor fall to the earth—superb." It had seemed to the traveller to burst into flame just before it fell; indeed the meteor's fires, frustrated in the heights by the screen of the earth's coolness, became revealed as it neared the kindred heat of this too ardent Africa.

And the next day early, looking upon many shooting stars, over a track which led them across hills and dried-up khors, they went their way. Half-way to Sirti another Sultan, the ruler of that country, met Talbot.

Talbot "vomited all the way; seasick from the back of a horse for several hours—most wasting process. However we went quickly and my horse bucked, which did me good." Accompanying them was a flute-player who blew three notes, over and over again, upon his flute. Somehow, at the same time, he shook a rattle merrily.

They camped in the bush. This country was the ancestral home of the imperial Arabs called Masalit, or Geroning—their tribe far-spread throughout Equatorial Africa. The chieftains gave Talbot shelter by night and shade for his rest during the vehement heat of the day. They gave also sheep, and guinea-corn, and milk. In the evening their men carried water into the camp for him. Antelope, guinea-fowl, and the lesser bustard were seen in this part of the country.

But either the night, cooler here, or else the dreadful illness Talbot had suffered, caused such an aching in his back that riding towards Adre was an agony. Masalit chiefs, on their wiry little ponies, could not understand why he rode in silence behind the camels, in trails of fine sand. Thus, cherished by the Arab chiefs, thus, accompanied throughout their country, Talbot arrived at Adre.

CHAPTER XXXIV

★　　★　　★

HIS WIFE'S IMPORTUNITY AT THE COLONIAL OFFICE IN London was the cause of a car being sent for Talbot to Adre from El Obeid, six hundred miles away. El Obeid was at the railhead. Had Talbot trekked from Adre it is likely that he would have died; he was very sick for long afterwards. Formerly in Africa, youth and his daemon had ridden him, spurring him on. Now in his later years his will upheld him—but hardly. 'Do have the car sent as far as Geneina,' Violet pleaded. (But even at the Geographical Society Geneina was not on the map.) The Assistant-Resident at Geneina joined the car and went to Adre to accompany the traveller back to Geneina of the mahogany trees. Talbot rose off his camp bed to get into the car; he was less ill but he was weak. Mahomed went with Talbot. Some of the way was very hard to travel. In a hundred miles they passed: "One hog-deer, one jackal, and two villages. There is really a sense of desolation in this awful bush which has hardly varied its monotony for over a thousand miles— more formation of granite and hills to-day."

Mahomed said: 'Then from there to a big town called El-Fasher, and there they tell master that there was an Arab King called Ali Dinar. That means King of Gold. He was almost built of gold, and they said that long ago a war fell between them and the English. He was in his garden and there was an aeroplane came down and he arrested by English soldiers and carried off till to date they do not know where. The English Government took his house and crowned his son.'

In one day were seen partridges and guinea-fowl, and hares, three kinds of antelope and, within fifty yards, two coveys of ostriches, a hog-deer, a jackal, squirrels and parakeets were seen. The cars—for they now had a second one—went only six miles an hour, so slow a progress because of the sand, the bad road, and the heat bursting the tyres.

Of one town, not named by his master, Mahomed said: 'We pass a town called Suego and the people do not accept King Edward's money. Why? They say that he is death so they will not take his money that has his head. When master sent me to buy bread and I give them this money they do not take of same but of King George because he is alive. And I went and told master. Then he laughs of same and said that should be a naughty people.'

The last hundred and twenty miles took eleven hours. On the sixth day since Talbot had left Adre he reached El Obeid. Of the last day's journey he wrote: "Desolate bush country—the natives hollow out the baobab trees in the rainy season and fill them with water which keeps wonderfully all through the dry season." At El Obeid was a train and so, by Khartoum and along the Nile, Talbot went homewards.

Mahomed, with his white man, went to the Hebrides. He travelled with him long roads, balancing himself on the mud-guard of a racing car as gaily as he had balanced himself on buffalo, horse, or camel. On the 'glorious' day of August when the first grouse fell to his master's gun, he, with a black retriever dog, rushed forward on the heather to bring the fallen bird to Talbot. Once when his master was angry, he nearly took his own life; and once, when his master was pleased, he lay on the carpeted floor of the hall laughing with joy. He lived in the Isle of Islay without a mate, but the loss of his country, and of his people, weighed nothing with Mahomed—so only he might follow Talbot.

CHAPTER XXXV

* * *

IN THE AUTUMN OF THE YEAR 1926, TALBOT FROM AFRICA, and Violet from the south, returned to Islay. Then in him awoke the highlander, and for weeks before the season of stalking Talbot would watch the stags through the spy-glass, for he nursed and cherished the forest. In those long days of watching, of counting the beasts, he decided, the season being come, which creatures should be left as sires, and which should be killed. One might be a 'royal' next year; another was judged to be at its perfection already; the forest would be well rid of this or that head. When the stags were clean of the velvet, and the antlers fully grown, Talbot sent his friends to grass the beasts and he increasingly enjoyed stalking them for friends rather than for himself. He would take a young man up to his first stag—would watch the shot. When the beast was killed, the stalker blooded the man and gralloched the beast.

At night the toast "Gentlemen! Blood, more blood, coupled with the name of ——" would be drunk. Standing, the guests repeated: 'More blood', and would say the name of the killer of the stag. Once a boy, who that day had killed his first stag, felt, as he rose to respond to the toast, that more than words was needed. He went out, and fetched his pipes. Walking up and down the dining-room he piped the praise of his day: of the stalk; of the kill. Talbot, who always had so much rather blown flute notes on the air than words, would have understood and have been glad; but this happened at Kildalton after Talbot had changed his world.

"The antlers are like a book, with the life of the stag that carries them written on the horn," Talbot taught Violet. "If a stag breaks his right leg the left horn will show the hurt." 'But surely only this year, the year of the wound?' "No, next year and always, however often the antlers are shed and grow again."

383

He told her that it was the same with the ostrich, and that a year of famine will be recorded in the feathers with a thin marring line. 'So it is that sorrows sear us, and sins blemish our souls,' thought Violet. He told her that what he most prized in a stag was thickness of antler, horn all rough like pebbles, and springing from a pearly crown; 'horns of ebony tipped with ivory,' as Sutherland used to say. He told her too that, even before the time of Christ, stags so attired roamed in Great Britain. The island stags still grow the thick rough horn, which is the particular glory of the stags of Proaig and of Kildalton. Talbot showed her how the horns of the stags are built for strength and for lightness, and the cells made to fulfil this twofold purpose. He showed her that the structure of the horn is the perfect counterpart of the struts of wood, and of metal, used by the builders of to-day.

In 1926 the most beautiful of all the stags (22) grassed that year in Scotland was killed at Proaig. Talbot had followed into the low ground a solitary stag which he would not kill, but he watched it day after day. Unlike most of its kind, but like the first stags of its far-ago race, it loved to be among trees. Whilst the stalking season lasted it hid in the low wooded ground where no man could spy it or surprise it. Later in the year it went up into the bare heights to pursue the hinds, and to fight other stags.

The stalking season ended, the hills would be filled with the sounds of passionate happenings. Nearly silent now the birds; and not yet to be heard, from the north, the silken sound of the flight of the widgeon, nor the sound of their whistling. The business of the nesting birds quite over, with the most of their singing. The bees are quiet in the hive, the gathering of the honey is finished; the sap in the trees is ebbing, the horns of the stags have come into use. The cradling-song of the birds is over: instead now is the furious mating of the red-deer; the roaring of the stags in the forest, the crash of antlers as they fight for their hinds. From the hills can be heard the sounds of frenzy. The grasses become crimson and gold. Fire and blood, anger and desire—thus the autumn in Islay.

"Come and see the grasses of Parnassus flowering on the *machair*." On the flats by the sea Talbot and Violet came upon the honey-smelling flower. All day it smelt of honey, but in the evening and throughout the night it harboured its scent. 'It declines in sweetness with the sun's decline,' thought Violet; 'spending just so much sweetness as is demanded for its increase, harbouring the reserve of sweetness for the morrow.' They counted the stamens of the flower—five—each one demanding its own separate day wherein to mature. 'Look here too at the arrow-head growing in a tuft, with rush-like leaves; it has three white petals; a poem in terza rima.' Violet had but just put away her Dante to follow Talbot to the *machair*.

Then, slowly as the winter came, day by day was again made visible the beauty of the limbs of the trees as their leaves fell, in a shower of garnet and of topaz. In the evenings Talbot, always coatless, and with him Violet, would go to lie in wait for the wild-geese, the greylag and the bernicle; for the great birds were legion, honking in from the north.

Waiting so, they learnt the roosting time of the birds, and the time of their nocturnal feeding. The pigeon came first, and the pheasant. Later came the blackcock, and these all flew into the branches of the trees. At sundown, the mallard came roding in, and the widgeon to seek in the loch the food which best they like. At dark the peewit came over, with a great swishing sound; they were invisible save for a flash of white which, for a second, showed with the upward stroke of their wings. Then came the curlew; then the geese according to the tide. For, the tide becoming high, there would be left no feeding that they could reach along the water's edge—the green ribbon-weed, the *zostara marina*, being now covered by water. Therefore the clangorous geese came in a gaggle to feed in the stooks of corn which were built up in the fields.

On such an evening the deer would swim away across shallow waters to an island, and the heron would cry a warning if a man but moved.

Talbot, during those years in Islay, knew all this felicity.

CHAPTER XXXVI

* * *

FELICITY IT WAS TO STRAIGHTEN THE GARDEN, TO BESTOW symmetry upon it, to give it apple trees, and flowers from far away. Felicity in the pine woods to cut narrow paths, where a man could walk delighting. Felicity to make a room so small that only Talbot and Violet could sit there, walled in with books and oak—a winter room—the wind raging outside, and comfort within.

Talbot's life of travel, of hardship, flowered now. "Travel is worth while because of the return home," he said.

On the wall a picture by Verestchagin, on the table a box, set with rough jewels—by these Russia would be brought to memory. A god carved in wood, a poisoned arrow—such things would recall some tribe of the jungle.

Bark of a tree, folded book-wise and painted with the lore of a cannibal people; a garment cut from the skins of caribou; the drum of a shaman and his jingling robe—these goods hung about the hall reminded Talbot of his wanderings.

He set most store upon the bronzes of Jomé that he had brought from Japan, as also garments, and Satsuma china, and swords.

He taught Violet that the manner in which a flower is set in a vase may be fraught with meaning. 'Arranging flowers is like singing a song, or writing a lyric. I sometimes understand the mind of the Emperor of Japan who gave up his throne that he might have the more leisure for this joy,' she thought.

Out of a sheath of silk, and out of a scabbard of wood, Talbot would draw a sword of the samurai. He had many such. He told Violet that these swords guarded a special darling-honour known only to the nobles of Japan.

Unsheathing a sword, Talbot would bow, and turn his head so that his breath would not sully the blade. "I was taught to do that in Japan. Such swords as these were made by men, hon-

386

oured throughout the ages; they were forged with fasting and with prayer, and into its owner was said to enter the spirit of the sword. Men, skilled in reading the blades of swords, would see in a flaw in the steel, in a waving line, or in a mark, the symbol of bird, of sky, or of beast. By that means was foretold fortune or disaster to those who owned the weapon."

Felicity, laboriously to list the books which all his life Talbot had gathered and now had assembled at Kildalton—books that told everything, that assuaged the mind's curiosity.

"No one can say I'm not a good laird." It was joyful to build up the byres, and to strengthen the homesteads. Felicity, to fill for guests a great barrel of blended spirits, the whiskies of Islay, made on the island because of the sweetness of the water which carried the flavour of the peat, and of the bog-myrtle. To taste and to choose wines, to bottle the wines of Burgundy and of Spain, to see the robe in the glasses; all this was pleasure: 'like music in our mouths,' Violet said.

Across the steam of the great cauldrons in the outhouse, cauldrons made for boiling food for the cattle, it was felicity to see Violet, high up near the wooden rafters, brewing ale in a copper vat. She thought: 'With this yeast I am doing what is done by the spring when she sets the starch fermenting round the seed which has been dormant; my work is the marvel of fermentation: spring and my beer therefore the same miracle.'

Every smallest thing about this Hebridean home affected Talbot—this home which held no early dark memories, no memories of adolescent suffering. Because in his loveless home his worth had been questioned, he had gone into the wilds to prove himself to himself. Hammered on the anvils of hardship he had proved his power. Now he could rest satisfied. Here his children would grow up, his wines would mature, he would read his books. But, this content notwithstanding: "It's only by going away and coming back to comfort that I can fully enjoy home," Talbot said. So even now his desires turned towards movement, towards the sea. He would buy a boat, take Vi and Easter and the governess, see the glories of Europe and, for much of the year, live moving. How good to sleep in this port and to wake in another, to follow the spring from south to north, to wander according to his wishes. Always, Violet enjoyed the return to Islay. She liked to feel that the waves were a portcullis to draw behind them as they landed; or that the sea was a great moat, dug about their castle. She liked to hear the Gaelic language so rich in love, and to hear the pipes. In such lonely places and at such strange hours were heard the pipes that she and the children wondered if the sound, coming from the old battlegrounds, was, perhaps, not of human breath.

In the past the success of Talbot in some emprise of special daring, even perhaps the actual conservation of his life, had depended on his being able to master those men whose help he needed. He had always loathed lack of purpose, or failure to carry through what had been intended. It seemed to him a want of pluck, of breeding, to be downed by difficulty. To his wife he had said of the firstborn, the son: "Do not hold his hand. He must not grow up soft, let him learn by falling," and to make them hardy Violet would whisper to her sons when as each slept: 'Your body must be the slave of your will—your body must be the slave of your will.' But now he softened his abruptness, he lessened his severities. "Why are you frightened of me, Easter?" 'Because, whenever I am naughty, Mademoiselle says:'I'll take you to your father." "Next time she says that make her bring you, and when you come I will give you a sweet."

The wooing air of the Hebrides, the gay grass, the amethystine mist—in these Talbot found so much content that his moods softened. With his dogs, his books, his children, and Violet, he felt himself ringed about with comfort. But his demands remained always strict. Even of his dogs he asked much. By patient training, by banishing fear, he raised the dogs of his friendship to the utmost degree of their intelligence. If they lacked confidence in him, or were not able for what he asked, he gave them away. His demands on himself, on his body, on his mind and memory, were tense as ever. His journey to Africa had been a rigorous test, the proving to himself that his years had not sapped his endurance. From Violet his expectation was also exacting, for he looked to her for perfectness day by day. He checked her, if she lacked sweetness, by saying: "Violet, you will never become a vintage wine!"

The pioneer in Talbot exulted in the small chapel as in a flag unfurled in a new country. The daily Mass, unsaid for hundreds

of years, said now again; the Sacrifice, the Terrible Victim, offered—beneficent and valid—however little the islanders recked
of it. Like the rising sun, the orb of the Host raised above Its
worshippers.

Felicity, was the loveliness of a sunlit Good Friday. Talbot
played on his golden flute. The seals, tired of fighting and of
thrashing each other, came up near the rock where he was—
with black heads thrust out of water, they listened to the music
that told of the joy of all creatures redeemed.

Afterwards he and Violet walked across the flat ground
hoping to see the mother woodcock carrying her young with
her feet. As they returned by the road, suddenly Violet stopped.
She grew crimson, then as suddenly pale, and that for shame.
She had looked at the keeper's board. Rat; and black-backed
gull; and, nailed with wings stretched out, the peregrine. The
hawk had stooped to kill; the Most Perfect had stooped to save.
Yet she, and all sinners, had nailed Him like vermin to a board.

The days in Islay might seem to be without event, but yet
they were fervid days. A walk by the sea might bring an unforgettable experience, as on that summer day when Violet had
thought: 'I must walk alone near the sea.' She followed the causeway; she was exhilarated by her feeling of unity with nature, of
unity with God. Like a breeze, blowing among the marsh
flowers, so God was the breath of common life—'we living
creatures are all akin.' She rounded a crag; a heron saw her,
sent out a harsh warning and flapped away. A chough echoed
the cry, gulls and curlew took up the chorus of fear; the sand-
erlings and the godwits sped off in a silvery sweep. A red-deer
leapt up from the bracken, a fallow bounded away. She had
given out love, but fear had come back to her, and that so
sharply that she was stunned. She saw herself cut off from the
common breath, like a dead part in a living whole.

Talbot came upon her, past the flooded causeway, but he
never quite understood why, at the moment, she seemed a
being at ebb; nor why she caught hold of his hand and held it
for the brief time he left it to her. He but half heard her say—
something about his being her only friend.

So passed the seasons, every day astonishing in beauty—
astonishing too this privileged, this remote life (23).

Sprites: and spoors: and Shakespeare

The fallow came in from the little wooded hills through the gates now left open for them. Talbot said: "They are more beautiful than the bushes which they will destroy." He accustomed them to his voice so that they heard it unaffrighted. He fed the woodland birds and tamed them. If he was late at the lower window of their assemblance they would fly up and in through the bedroom window to hasten him.

There was a golden spring morning, golden with the young shoots of the yew hedges, with the firstling leaves of the oak, with the flame-bright honey-azaleas that shone from out the grey, mist-born moss which grew along the twigs. A hen-blackbird came that morning to the stone where the birds fed. For some days she had been missing from the banquet of crumbs spread near the door. Shyly she fluttered towards him that fed the birds; behind her came the two fledgelings of her nest; big-eyed and hesitating: "the prettiest presentation I ever saw," said Talbot.

That same morning Violet was affected, suddenly, by the low flight of chaffinches coming towards him, his bounty the purpose of their quick expectant flight. Moved, she said, 'Oh! the lovely flirt of their wings! How joyful that they fly towards us and not away from us!'

At night Talbot liked to lie awake listening to the screech-owls. Their hooting caused him pleasure; it caused his children fear. The nights in Islay seemed to them owl-ridden. None of them were indifferent to the owls, for at some time it had been held that owls were of evil portent, or of good omen to those of this family. Tradition enfolded a half-forgotten legend whereby the owls and the Cliftons were allied.

All this time long-haired Easter gave her father a share in her adventures with the highland fairies; under the trees he left letters which she believed to be elf-written. To the boy, Michael, he taught the spoors of the creatures; he praised him when he killed with the arrow. For these children he gathered together the lines he most prized of Shakespeare, a decoy to draw them to the poet. Sometimes their nights in Islay were silvered by the aurora borealis; and—stormy—or halcyon—those days were enlightened.

390

VII
THE LAST JOURNEY

*   *   *

CHAPTER I

★ ★ ★

OLDEST CAPITAL OF AFRICA, BUILT UPON THE FORETIME
boundary of the summer wanderings of the Tuaregs, city
named after a nurse: Timbuktu! When the advance of the season caused the veiled men to move from their summer station,
the nurse, her tent pitched upon the sand, guarded the tribal
possessions. On the place of her fidelity was built the city.

Timbuktu had long lured Talbot. In Kano in 1926 he had
resolved that he would return to the West Coast and would
enter Africa by Dakar, going to the Niger, and over the desert
to the city of Timbuktu. Now the year 1927 was nearly spent;
next year, Talbot would start; Violet could go with him or
not as she wished; Talbot did not say which he would the
rather. She hardly dared to think that he wanted her with him.
But when she told him of her desire to go he made her
going easy; so joyfully she began to make preparation for
travel.

Now fell the Christmas of 1927, but the story of the wonderful Child hardly at all moved the Gaels in the Island of Islay.
'What more could He have done so as to make this people
smile?' wondered Violet. Only at Kildalton there was rejoicing; a festal tree, a man with his pipes and, at midnight, the
first of the threefold Masses. Whaups and sea-pies flew crying
around the house seeking their meat, and as Talbot and Violet
walked back after the Sacrifice they heard the wings of the
birds, and their crying. Talbot explained—that on the tides the
living of these birds depends, and that they mark the changes
of the ebb and flow of the sea rather than the change of light to
darkness. Now was high tide and they were seeking for food in
the fields, and in the greensward near the house; but at low tide
they would search along the shore for their sustenance. These
birds could see in the dark, and their lives were in concord with
the change of the tides; but the lives of men are in concord with

the day and the night. The wash of the waves; the cry of the curlew, and of the oyster-catchers; the cadenced Latin conjurations—such were the sounds of that Christmas night at Kildalton.

Next night at the Castle a supper was given for all who served, or had commerce with Kildalton; farmers, and tradesfolk, and fishermen. They danced to the music of violin and pipes; the festival was of Talbot's planning: "We have lived here for five years and have made friends of them all."

The captain of the storm-tossed little ship that traffics between Islay and the mainland said that night: 'The laird is full of glee.' Rich in wit, and in goodwill, Talbot delighted in the holiday return of his children, and in the entertainment of his guests. 'What a burning, benevolent bonfire, lit nearly two thousand years ago—warming us still; what a supreme sweetness that sugars this remote to-day.'

On New Year's Eve, Talbot and Violet were together in the Inner Library, a room of oak built for the winter. Big enough for two people only, it lay beyond the other two oak rooms and, like them, it was full of books. As midnight drew near, Talbot threw up the window. He stood aside, with courtesy ushering out the Old Year; and as midnight struck he welcomed in the New.

Violet shuddered, but not with the cold. 'I accept, I do not welcome you,' stabbed through her mind. Talbot drank to the newcomer and she drank from his glass, wondering at her own repugnance to this New Year. But when she and Talbot had kissed one another she forgot the unreasonable aversion. He took up the golden flute that was become the flute of the home, whilst the silver one was the flute of the foreign places. He played an air that he had named "Siberian memories", a music which he had made in the delta of the Lena. Afterwards they stayed talking, whilst the fire licked up the spruce logs, and grew fragrant in the peat that was mixed with the wood.

For the approaching journey to Timbuktu Talbot made almost no preparations. Only just before he and Violet left the Hebrides he chose the bags he would take, the khaki clothes, the rifle, the gun, and a few books, for he liked going fresh to fresh places, to see and to learn for himself, to be surprised.

Abdurrahman and Timbuktu

Violet travelled with a difference. "This book will help you, read it," Talbot said. She steeped herself in books on North West Africa, drove all else from her thoughts, was so absorbed that more than once in error she wrote 'Africa' on some letter, though London was its destination.

'You are going to Africa, you are going to Africa,' rang along her nerves. She wanted to see Jenné, she wanted to be in that outpost of Songhay cities, that throne town of Askia the Great. For thirty-six years Askia had ruled in Jenné; therein he had seen a hundred children leap from his loins. In Jenné perhaps a priestly sage would unroll for her the true scroll of the Tarik el-Soudan.

She wanted to see Timbuktu. 'Oh Talbot, will the city somehow solve the riddle of Abdurrahman's fourteen days of happiness?' She told Talbot of how, at the height of Mohammedan power, of his empire, at the height of his intellect, after half a hundred years of fealty to beauty and to knowledge, Abdurrahman, looking back on all his years, wrote that he had known only fourteen days of happiness. Were these days spread through his fifty years, or did they hang together in one resplendent moon? Was it love or friendship or the joy of a special conquest, or was it a light from God that made these fourteen days shine out from among the years? And were they days that Abdurrahman had passed in Timbuktu?

"Geographia is a hungry goddess," Talbot said. He piled up before Violet his books that showed her the sweat and the sacrifice with which this goddess is gorged. He put Violet in thrall to the explorers of Africa. There was Caillée, the boy, panting for breath, hollow eyes, his tongue hanging out of his mouth for thirst; wedded to Africa, leaving it, and then returning. There was Caillée, the man, leaving El Arawan, taking his departure from the wells of Mornan, that last region of the fertile Soudan, praying before they all set out into the desert. For secretly he prayed to the God of his Christian youth, to the God that was not the Allah whom he seemed to serve, because his very life depended on his disguise as a follower of Mohammed.

On the border of the great northern desert he sent up a prayer and wrote, that with the fertile Soudan behind them, and the great desert before them, the desert they must cross: 'the camels uttered long moans, and the slaves became sullen and silent.'

'There is Laing, and Mungo Park too, and it's worth while knowing something of Africa if only that the courage of such be gauged, for it is beyond the measure of the sheltered, and of the shaded.

Three words in italics danced before Violet's eyes, as she read the book that Talbot gave her of Park's journey. He had ridden through marshy ground to Sego, he was looking for Joliba—the great water—when he saw, 'with infinite pleasure . . . the long-sought-for majestic Niger,' flowing slowly 'to the eastward.' The course of Niger was 'towards the rising sun'—this was Park's discovery—'It runs to the world's end,' the Arabs had said.

'TO THE EASTWARD', danced before Violet's eyes, but they were misted over when she read of 'that small moss in fructification', that met the eye of Mungo Park when five hundred miles from the nearest European settlement, alone and almost dying in the wilderness, in the height of the rainy season, 'surrounded by savage animals and men more savage,' Mungo Park sat down in terror and amazement. Then the small moss saved him from despair, for how could 'that Being that brought it to perfection' forsake a creature 'formed after His own image?' Consoled he rose, pushed on, and lived.

So passed the last days at Kildalton, coloured by the tales of heroes. An immense happiness was about Violet. 'It is wonderful to go away again alone with Talbot, and to go to Africa. To put aside clothes, and jewels, to leave even the children. It is beautiful and terrible. Dying may be like that,' she had thought.

A feeling of newness came on her when they were together away from home. In London there was a sense of adventure. It was gay to eat unfamiliar foods, and to see strange faces, and there was the happy vanity and the pride of going about with Talbot to his club, and his shops. The pride of being seen in company of one who walked in the city like a man come out of an age of giants and heroes. The crowd of London did not engulf him. 'I saw a man like a Viking who walked down Bond Street as though he were breaking a trail; is your husband now in England? Perhaps it was he.' So said a friend of Violet; and another: 'I passed a man who looked like a Russian grand duke, from what I've heard of him I think he must have been John Talbot.' He stood out, magnificent and strange, and she felt the tang of him as fresh to her as it had been twenty years before, like salt for savour, like wine that grows but better. In a half-blinded way Violet knew that this would be their last long journey; only youth should bear great fatigues, and they were past heyday. But his resolution stood in place of meridian and would carry him on. She, too, had her own strength which did not depend on youth.

'I'll take care of your cousin,' was the message she sent to Lelgarde. So they left England to sail from Bordeaux to Dakar. The day of departure was in the middle of January, 1928. Talbot had been ill since the New Year. He was shivering with ague. The ship lay in the estuary delayed by a mutiny of the ship's firemen. The sun, setting beyond the flat banks of the Gironde, went down in gold and scarlet; the evening was very cold. Violet's perception echoed a muffled admonition, insistent as a pain: 'Go back, go ashore, go back.' The counsel came from shadowed spaces, from who knows whence? It was like the warning note of a distant horn sounding through a sea fog.

She touched Talbot's hand, she was about to tell him of this fear that possessed her, but she bit back the words. She bit them back so fiercely there was blood instead of words in her mouth. For if ever the course of his will were to be by his body deflected, then Talbot would not be Talbot.

CHAPTER II

★   ★   ★

TALBOT WAS VERY ILL, SO FOR FIVE DAYS THEY STAYED at Dakar. The three of them stayed there, Talbot, Violet and Mahomed. He, the Ethiopian from Lake Chad, that had followed Talbot from Maidugari to the Hebrides, was still following the white man of his adoration.

At Dakar the days were full of the shamal, the parching dusty wind that blew from the East.

The dry season had fallen early and Talbot now abandoned the journey to Timbuktu. The river being low, he and Violet would have had to travel on a barge drawn by men struggling along the river's bank; after that the crossing of the sand to Timbuktu would have been blinding in the intensity of the heat. Talbot declared that after a few days of rest at Dakar he would be well enough to go to French Soudan. They would travel by train to Bamako, where the railway ended; thence they would circle over hills and through jungles down to Dahomey, city of the last of the Amazons.

Violet began to fear. 'The journey to Dahomey will be hard, the heat very great. Let us return and stay in the Canary Isles or in Madeira,' she urged.

But Talbot's eyes flashed blue. "I do not go back," he said. So she was silent and trusted that his resolve would suffice to uphold his suffering body.

Talbot was put to bed on an unpillowed pallet in one of the many mean rooms of the hotel. Into the stone corridor outside the room the black servants swept the rubbish of the bedrooms. Like mud heaps along an ill-kept street, so all day along the passages these piles of dust, of fruit skins and waste paper, remained —the petty monuments of sloth.

Every night there was noise and music from the great room below where white women danced alone or with each other.

398

The yellow fever

Negroes stared in from the street. Later in the night Frenchmen and women danced together.

For Violet the nights at Dakar were strange. On such a one below their window in the street some Africans contended so noisily that Talbot could not sleep. "Go and silence them," he begged.

When she walked out into the street she saw a black man and a woman standing in a garden full of scarlet hibiscus. They were screaming angry words to another man who leaned upon a garden gate on the other side of the street. She knew that it would be vain to order them to be quiet. So she made her plea to them, speaking in French, and they became quiet.

On another night she went out to buy oranges in Dakar, because only the juice of oranges would allay Talbot's cough. She put money into the hands of the servants and of the cabdrivers, but they returned it, saying that until the morrow when the market should open no fruit could be bought anywhere in the town. Unwilling to be baulked, Violet determind to find oranges in Dakar. Walking, at last she came upon a house where many black and white men sat drinking and dicing and talking of the yellow fever. Having looked through the metal wire of the door, she went in and beckoned to an Italian woman who was serving the men with beer and spirits. The drinkers stared, surprised at the Englishwoman. But the wife of the house was attentive to her need and sent out a servant who, later in the night, came back carrying country oranges in a basket, and these she took back to Talbot.

In the city yellow fever had but lately been subdued; the sap of town life was again rising slowly. For many months doom and misery had weighed heavily upon Dakar. Men and women suddenly had been stricken; often before the third day the sick would be dead. Always the white people were cut down; never the black. During the day men going backwards and forwards to their work had worn gaiters and veils to protect them from mosquitos—this the law had enforced. No one had been able, for a moment, to forget the terror of the times. The dwellers in Dakar had not been allowed in the streets after sunset. With the setting of the sun, with the taking down of the French flags, the windows and the doors of every house were forcibly shut against the death-bringing stegomyia. The French people, whose sole pleasure, after their day of business, had been meeting one another, were slugged with melancholy. Sitting in dark closed houses, deprived of their habitual leisure, of the little round tables under the trees, of the cool drinks, of music, the white men of Dakar languished piteously.

Of the three pilots of Dakar, only one had survived the plague, so that even now ships were delayed, lying in the harbour. Even now, the people might not gather together to dance, or to sup, in lighted rooms unless the house were made safe against gnats.

The things of Dakar that Violet afterwards remembered were, in a garden, an avenue of casuarina trees towering up; and in the sandy country near the town, huge hornbills on the ground. But her pleasure was in the negresses of Dakar. With ornaments of gold and silver upon their ankles and their wrists, upon their hands, and necks and ears; draped and sumptuous, insolent of demeanour, they swung along the streets of the city. Their skins were of the colour of grapes; their white ample garments were scented with sandalwood; along the roadways the women moved superb. Fecundity sealed them; every line of their bodies showed them prolific of children. All the French people spoke ill of them as being vessels of temper and of evilly constraining their men. But to the eye they were magnificent.

* * *

Having ceded some days to the importunity of his sickness, Talbot, a little rested, never doubted but
that he could travel onwards, so, with the
shamal hotly blowing about them,
Talbot and Violet travelled
eastwards to Bam-
ako.

CHAPTER III

★ ★ ★

WHEN TALBOT AND VIOLET IN MID FEBRUARY REACHED Bamako, the place, because of their suffering, seemed to them to be rather a state of nightmare than a town that is marked on a map.

For two days and nights the train had shaken and burned its way through flat and arid country. Baobab trees alone redeemed the complete dreariness of the continuous flats of Senegal. Yellow flowers grew here and there. "That was the loveliest thing I saw when I crossed French Africa in '96," Talbot said, but Violet answered that it looked to her like a flower made of brimstone. Acacias and scrub added thorns to the prick of the earth burning in the sun, but the baobab was magnanimous. Its trunk, greater than the trunk of any other tree, upheld branches themselves as thick as tree-stems, and these, tending upwards, were crowned by a globe of green. Beautiful, of massive sculptural design, the trees—in that smarting country —were the only tokens of a benign intention. Talbot told Violet that, eaten with the daily fare, the bark of the baobab and its leaves are a remedy, and the fruit provides food, and, crushed it yields a drink, allaying fever. How good was the coolness of the trees, and of the fruits! How good their constant inner coolness unchanged by the sun or by the smart of the burning ground! The trees and the palms, in countries such as these, remained the serene, the only guardians of pleasantness.

Ill as he was, Talbot answered to Africa with a traveller's constancy. His aneroid beside him, he wrote: "it has shewed me no elevation for four hundred miles."

Here and there they caught sight of the river Senegal, and then Talbot told Violet all that a river might mean to a man travelling on foot in Africa. The sight of the water deeply moved him. After twenty-four hours they reached the river Niger and ascended abruptly from Senegal to French Soudan.

Violet wondered greatly at the people; suddenly to see a countryside of black people was amazing. It was so abrupt, so flagrant, so unmodern. England, she mused, was all sameness. Its women in outward seeming like the men, the old and the young alike in the fashion of their clothes, the vulgar like the patrician. But here was a trenchant difference. The negro might be a 'coloured gentleman', a black brother, an equal, a superior, what you will, but nature, anyway, had rudely branded him to Ham in a way that could not be gainsaid.

Some of the people seemed beautiful to Violet, sombrely magnificent and eye-sufficing; others were burlesque, a jape, a mockery of man. 'One would expect their lips and tongues to be black,' she thought. The very smell of them was all their own. The skin of the hot fat cook, as he hung over the panful of shark which he was frying, and the skin of the serving-man, smelt pungently.

The train stopped near a little village. It seemed a mock to Violet that insects should outbuild the men, that the mud house of a Senegalese should be no higher, no more shapely than the home of the white ants that rises in its neighbourhood. Side by side stood the buildings so alike—black babies emerging out of the one, white ants out of the other.

On the train Violet met a marabout. At every station he blessed the Africans that came to greet him. In his white robes he looked noble; she invited him into their carriage and gave him lavender water for his frequent ablutions. Talbot gave him fruit, and the marabout said, in French: 'I will pray for your health.' Talbot smiled at Violet because she regarded the marabout as a noble being, but he preferred this regard to the contempt a Parisian woman showed the marabout. 'He is but a rapacious fraud,' she had said.

They arrived at Bamako. It was a stage set for their much suffering. They put up their camp beds in a railway inn; a busy Frenchwoman was in charge of it. She was a cynical noisy woman with a hatred of Africa; her livelihood was the drink that was ruining so many of the young men who sat round the tables in the dusty little garden. The drink was not strong, but it was perpetual, and it was expensive, so that nearly all the money, made amid the miseries of homesickness and of burning heat, went to pay for long cool drinks that for so short a time quenched the dreadful thirst of Bamako.

Violet was astonished at the power of thirst—she felt it for the first time in her life, and it frightened her. At night she would wake, and would creep about looking for water in the red earthen waterpots. She must not wake Talbot. At meals Talbot was shocked at her quick, long, snatched-at drinks—the lack of control shocked him. When Violet knew that, she said to her thirst 'Wait': and found that it could be tamed.

Talbot had promised Mahomed a wife. "If you good you take her back to England," he had said. Now, going to buy fruit and slippers of dyed skin in the red stone market of Bamako, Mahomed was ordered to look for this wife.

One morning a girl was brought to the inn by her father. 'Come and help us to see if she will do as a wife for Mahomed, who has arranged thus far with her father,' said Violet, and the Frenchwoman then questioned the African. 'That girl must cost but a small price for she is not a virgin—her eyes show me that,' the Frenchwoman screamed. 'Do you boys know her as being about the town?' she added to the Soudanese menservants. They did not know the girl, but the Frenchwoman insisted to Talbot: 'Before you buy her for Mahomed you should engage a doctor to see her.' "So it is," wrote Talbot in his diary, "that marriages (for Africa) are made in Heaven!"

Another girl came later. "Mahomed likes them young," said Talbot, when the child came up to be questioned. Mahomed had chosen her and now her parents brought her to be seen by his master. Her father did not wish her to go to unknown England, remoter much to them than France. The quest for a wife for Mahomed proved useless, but he chose, wed or unwed, to follow his master.

The suffering of Talbot increased. He saw that the jungle journey to Dahomey would be impossible.

The evening, and the nights, at Bamako were strange. All day there would be talk among the Frenchmen about 'la Colonie'. 'C'est la Colonie,' the landlady said whenever any man was ruined or was ill; on Talbot's evident suffering her comment was: 'Mais c'est la Colonie.' The Frenchmen talked too always about the sun. Even when the monster was hidden behind grey clouds they dreaded its terrible ray. On the dullest day—and the days often were dark with hot clouds that made Violet think of the smoke of a furnace—on the dullest day no man would go a footstep without his sun-hat.

Talbot, who never before in Africa or the East had worn more than a felt hat, had, on this journey, used a sun-hat, but if for a moment, in the train near a window or walking from under one roof to another, he did not wear it, they cried out warnings to him. Two young men in the inn who had just come from France were struck down by this mortal sun.

The devil that walks at noonday—that, for them, was the sun. When evening came, dinner was served in the little dusty garden lit gloomily by weak electric globes hung in the trees. Generally the light was nearly out; it burnt so dim that those sitting at the tables looked like phantoms, like unhappy querulous ghosts who supped together after the burning day. They were all overtired, long hours they spent in offices and hours at the little tables drinking, but never any hours of sport or of pleasure. Some of the women had but just come from France; most of them had fine stockings of the newest colour. The French doctor who attended Talbot shrugged his shoulders. 'Those silk stockings are the price of most of our women dans la Colonie,' he said. 'They need so many pairs and their husbands are poor. You may take it from me that the price of our women is a pair of stockings.'

To redeem that sordidness there was one group at a table, a cluster both brave and gay. The young father, after the fiery day in his office, sat opposite his wife, an infant sat on the knees of each of them, an infant to feed in the half-dark, and a young child was between them. A tender gathering of poor young people.

After the strange darkened supper hour Talbot and Violet put their camp beds on to the verandah. In the court below them hundreds of negroes laughed, and exclaimed, at a cinema show. A steady roar of talk and of laughter rose from the court. In his diary Talbot wrote of one night: "During the night an Arab brought a girl to a Frenchman's room. Not being certain of the number, he asked Violet, who kindly showed the pimp the correct bedroom."

A quiverful of anguish

One night at supper Talbot said: "Either the glass is crooked or my mouth has been struck." Violet did not pay much heed, because she thought that his sufferings had made him fanciful; and he said no more. The next day, though only at midday, suddenly she saw it—the crooked twist of his mouth, and his eye affected. 'C'est le soleil, c'est la Colonie,' screamed the Frenchwoman. Talbot had not again spoken of this visitation, but early he had written in his diary: "Better; but slight paralysis of the mouth. Settled to go French Guinea, Violet will like it!"

The doctor, when he came, took Violet aside. 'The paralysis may spread down the whole of his side,' he said, and seeing her pale and rigid with horror, 'but you must never let him see you like that. Be gay! Any shock might hasten such a thing. See that he does not lose heart or think gravely of it.'

To divert him she, with the Governor's permission, summoned chieftains from neighbouring villages and they danced, and rode, and sang before them, but all was for payment and not from the gaiety of their nature. Violet must have seemed heartless and metallic, for she urged Talbot to drive out with her, and she laughed at every absurdity, seeming to disregard his suffering. The French Mayor of Bamako said to her: 'Your husband is set upon your seeing French Guinea, so I am arranging the journey. The roads are so rough that I have sent an order to the villages that men are to be ready at the worst places to carry your car. I will go the first hundred miles with you as I fear for you.' But he did not say that his fear was that Talbot might die on the road.

The train returned to Dakar once a week, but only late on the evening of the day before its return did the doctor prevail upon Talbot to abandon the journey to French Guinea, for Talbot felt that he was failing Violet—and that on a journey.

'He does not at all know how ill he is, nor must you tell him,' said the doctor, but in his secret diary Talbot had written on the day that they left: "Still alive and ill. Dr. B— thinks I am better, perhaps I am. Giddy with heat. I shall have done a record if I manage to survive the return journey to Dakar."

Violet had thought that they might fly from Bamako, but that was impossible, though there was one aeroplane. Yet how

again bear that railway journey? The heat had increased greatly
since the upcoming travel.

'Do not let him see this thing just before he starts,' urged the
doctor to Violet next day, when the incoming train on which
they would travel outward from Bamako had jogged to a
standstill in the station. 'This thing' was the body of a man,
lifted out of the train; he had died of the heat. Another man, a
boy almost, was carried dying from the train; in the last station
he had been struck by the sun.

On the return journey the electric fans did not work. Ice was
obtained at various stopping-places but only with insistence
from Violet. The journey was a fifty hours' agony.

Talbot never spoke of his sufferings, but once he fixed his
eyes upon the engraved motto of his signet ring: 'Mortem aut
triumphum'. In the train he wrote in his diary: "*Saturday
25 February*. Nightmare. Oh! Dreamt it was hell and
a voice said: 'It is hell.' The pain, the heat, the
cough, the thirst, the dust, the sleepless-
ness, mouth not functioning, left
eye not closing, and
the dirt."

CHAPTER IV

★　　★　　★

AT DAKAR IT HAD BEEN ARRANGED FOR TALBOT TO GO TO
the French Military Hospital until he could get a ship to take
him—anywhere away from Africa. The doctor, who before had
looked after him in Dakar, met Talbot and Violet, and they went
to the strange hospital where comfort, and kindness, were their
portion.

The next day they sailed, as they thought, for Las Palmas,
but the purpose of the captain was changed, and Santa Cruz
became their destination. Over rough seas they sailed for three
days till they reached the islands that the ancients had thought
were the islands of the blessed.

There, for three weeks, sorrow constricted them, and doom
closed in upon them by day and by night. At first they had hope;
and then, first Violet, and afterwards the doctor despaired. But
Talbot was silent, fighting for life and never saying what he
thought or what he foreknew.

For hours he sat on the sofa or lay on the bed, perhaps half
sleeping, utterly weakened by his long fast. At times his old
energy flashed through him and, with Violet, he would study
Spanish, which both of them had known and forgotten. Now
and again he took up his Shakespeare and reread some passage
marked, or sometimes a gleam of mischief would lighten his
brooding as when the Spanish doctor, to discard his long silence,
asked him to say something: "Hell," he said, with a twinkle.

His lifelong observation of men still served him, for, as his
malady increased, Dr. Z— said: 'We must get the English
doctor from Las Palmas, or else I must consult with another
Spanish doctor here.'

The Spaniard came, and Talbot lay looking as though he
observed nothing, but afterwards he said to Violet: "We need
not get the Englishman. I like the breadth of that man's brow,

407

and by his eyes I can see that he has studied. Curious, that though I've lived so much away from England, yet it takes nerve to leave myself entirely in foreign hands!"

Violet, on the floor by his side, sat reading or sewing—or simply fanning flies away. Pitiful that so much love could only serve to keep the flies away. She remembered a long-ago tale of Spanish warriors in Teneriffe; and of how some were captured by the gauchos, the children of the island. In exchange for certain promises the gauchos restored their enemies to liberty. The Spaniards broke their oaths and fought once more against the islanders. The gauchos recaptured them, but they so much despised the oath-breakers they would not kill them.

'You shall live to ward off the flies that beset us,' they decreed. 'In Teneriffe the race of the gauchos is no more, but here the generation of the flies still flourishes,' thought Violet.

Measured against her passionate desire to serve, and to save him, Violet felt that all she could do was as nothing. Talbot needed her always, and they had no nurse. That they should not be disturbed she took on herself the care of the room—that room full of lilies, and of love—but most of the time all that she could do was just to be near him, wearing gay colours, and smiling when he looked at her; crying her fill when he slept.

Whenever he said "Vi" her heart so leaped to hear him that her tears dried in the fire of her joy and perhaps, seeing her thus, he never knew how she sorrowed for him; perhaps he thought she was hard. Foreseeing the desolate time when he would no longer speak her name she treasured his every call upon her. For the night, to prove love, she made a game. Every time that he woke or turned she would give a little cooing sound to show her wakefulness, but if he had to say her name—then he had won. In those weeks he twice won the game. But every night she struck many matches, for he woke often.

Twice Talbot had to go into the town of Santa Cruz to be photographed by X-rays. He went the first time in a motor, held close to Violet to steady him over the unbuilt road that led into the town. Everyone stared to see them, pale and distraught, clinging so desperately together. But the second descent into the town would hold even more of pity.

The photograph had shown density of the right side, no light at all, just a pall of blackness where light should have shown the ribs. After that the doctors had painfully drawn away, from his back, water fatally mixed with blood. They did also other things to discover his sickness.

A week later they said: 'We will draw away more water, and immediately afterwards we will photograph his side, but if then the picture is dense there will remain no hope.'

They still hoped that the lung's sickness might be the cause of the water, for the lung they could cure. But they now feared that this water might be but the endeavour of the body to preserve itself. It was perhaps building up a liquid barrier against a deadly growth threatening the organs.

Ever since Talbot had left Europe his daily suffering had been borne almost without complaint, but at night in his sleep he groaned and murmured. The floodgates of his will released, the torrent of his pain was let loose.

So on a day, a Wednesday, the two doctors, and an apprentice, came for the second time, and Talbot, astride on a chair and leaning over its back, had the evil water drawn from him. Violet, in a long looking-glass, could see that again blood and water were coming, not water only. She murmured in Spanish: 'Hide that from him.'

She knelt in front of him and held his elbows in her hands watching the sweat break out on his forehead. Now and again the doctor stopped to feel the pulse and to measure his exhaustion or to stimulate him with an injection, and Talbot, never at the limit of his endurance, said always: "Go on, go on, finish the thing."

All through every day, from the great dragon tree in the garden, a bird sang. From early in the morning, until the hour when the frogs started their croaking, almost without ceasing, it sang.

But during this anguish Violet could not bear it: 'Oh!' she sighed, 'that bird sings in spite of everything.' But Talbot—whose heart was always with birds and beasts, hunter though he had been—said: "How charming it is!"

So for an hour the horrible work went on. Violet, in her anguish, broke into bits the crucifix of her rosary without even noticing that she had destroyed it till the fragments fell on the floor. The pain of watching his pain ate into her flesh like poison, like acid; much later, she ached anew with the re-flected anguish. In the place where his pain was seated, there—years hence—her body would ache. 'Oh! Talbot, what self-control you have.' His eyes lit for a moment: "At last, but not in the past."

Kneeling in front of Talbot, Violet saw the face of her hus-band with awe. She seemed to be ministering to a divine stranger. The victory of his will over his suffering was his investiture; was the crowning of his life's attitude towards his body.

The beloved hunter, the son of Sagittarius, is mortally wounded—behind him lie his gay pursuits—but his last arrow he will aim at a high, a luminous target; at a shining prick-spot.

During his ordeal Talbot could hardly bear Violet to move from him, even if but to put on light for the doctors. But the hour was at last over, and he lay exhausted on the bed, feeling no relief, though so much evil humour had been drawn away. Then, nearly an hour later than had been promised, the stretcher-bearers came to take him to the town to be X-rayed.

Enrolled as helpers, the workmen of Teneriffe carry the sick to the ships in the harbour, or to the hospitals. Grotesque, dressed in white and red like mummers, they now came into the room, and put Talbot upon the stretcher. Violet chose to walk by his side, and Mahomed followed, carrying some coverings. The doctor drove behind them. Can the terror of that walk be told? He, himself, taken out like one dead: augury piled on evil augury; men baring their heads as Talbot passes, and making the sign of the cross. From a church, a chance bell, tolling. Children following the procession; whispering and laughing, until Mahomed drives them off. Then is the weariness of the X-ray photographs, the long return uphill, whilst, over the heights, the sun, in glory, setting. And this, the last time that Talbot, alive, is freed from the walls of the house.

* * *

After they had returned Talbot was given an injection, for he could not drink even a sleeping draught. Violet undressed her-self and also went early to bed so as not later to disturb him. This she did each day for, after sunset, Talbot could bear the

410

day no more, and commanded the doctor's apprentice to give him the needle of sleep.

Later in the night—how horrible those frog-fevered nights in Santa Cruz—the doctor knocked softly, and Violet sprang up and went into the passage. He told her that the photograph was completely dense, that only one illness could be the cause of such a picture, that no operation could avail—that Talbot's life was forfeit. Many questions rushed to her lips. Ought Talbot to be told? Would they be able to sail eleven days hence as he had planned to do? And how could they get him confessed? 'He may live a few weeks, but the journey would be agony to him, and before arriving in England you might have to see his body thrown into the sea,' answered the doctor. 'It is hard to tell a man that he must die, when he suffers as much as your husband suffers, and when he has the will to live.' As to confession, there was the saintly Bishop of Teneriffe who spoke English. The doctor and Violet must think how to bring about his visit.

Then the doctor went away and Violet got back into bed, chilled by his words. Coverings did not warm her; ice had entered into her blood. For very long after she felt that winter in her veins.

Lying awake, and thinking, she decided, that unless he asked it of her she must not tell Talbot the truth. On him, innocent, had been passed a judgment than which the extreme rigour of the law is not harsher. He was sentenced to death more certainly than is a murderer who always may hope that the sentence be reprieved—for Talbot there was no hope. Her whole being rose in revolt at this seeming cruelty; at this horror. She would not tell him, for he was fighting for life—he desired to live. He had eight days more to suffer, but Violet did not foreknow the number.

The next day Talbot said nothing, asked nothing about the photograph. But towards nightfall, watching the sea tumbled by the wind, he said as though to himself: "I am in very broken water, but I may yet get through!"

CHAPTER V

★　　★　　★

THE MOON, IN HER LAST QUARTER, HUNG IN THE UN-clouded skies, and with bitterness Violet wondered if Talbot would see the crescent moon to come, or if his life would wane with this one. From the bay the siren calls of the departing ships made her question wildly if he would go hence like a ship piloted, or if he would sail away to eternity trusting to himself alone. 'Oh, Christ! Be Thou his pilot!'

Haunted by the outgoing of the ships, she prayed fervently that he might make the confession of his sins, and be absolved of them. But she had two fears: the one that by speaking to Talbot about confession she might deprive him of the hope of life, which in his increasing agony seemed to be his mainstay: the other, greater fear, was that he might—for weariness—refuse to see a priest. It was certain that Talbot would never revoke a refusal, for his "No" had been no, and his "Yes" had been yes, all the years that Violet had known him. Now, without robbing him of the hope of living, how to get him confessed?

On the third morning, after the doctor had said that Talbot would die, he looked so wasted that Violet felt that now she must ask him if he was willing to be shriven. So, with a piercing prayer to the Holy Ghost, she said: 'If you did get worse, my darling, and did die without absolution, that would haunt the whole of the rest of my life. I should have no peace of mind for ever, and I should have to go into a convent to try and make amends for you.' And he said: "That is silly, isn't it?" To which she answered: 'Silly, it may be, but it's true.'

He thought for an instant, a little space on which hung things immeasurable, then he said: "Well, yes, I will receive the Bishop. What shall I say to him? What sins have I to confess?"

The white-robed Dominican Bishop came to see Talbot, of whose travels he had read. He understood English, but feared to speak it, so Violet had to be mediator and to convey to the priest the sins of Talbot.

She said for him the *Confiteor*, and afterwards Talbot told her to say that he had lived a wild life but that he felt no weight of sin, though he was sorry for what he had done amiss, and for his lacks. Twice he asked for Absolution.

The Bishop did not answer; there was a vital silence. But, like the silence of Talbot, when Violet had asked him to confess, this one also flowered into blessedness.

Seeing that Talbot's will and intention were towards God, the Bishop loosed him of all his sins. Then Violet was so full of joy that, for a few moments, she left her husband, and going out into the sun she talked with the Dominican under the great dragon tree in the garden. When he moved away she fell on to one knee, and kissed the amethyst of his ring, full of blessings. She knew that even death could never wither the laurels of that hour.

CHAPTER VI

*   *   *

AFTER THIS ABSOLUTION THERE FOLLOWED TWO NIGHTS and a day of calm when no one but the doctor might come into the room. Violet trusted that Talbot might die thus in peace, without noticing that the day was very close when the home-going ship was due, without suffering the pain of knowing that she had sailed to England whilst they remained in Teneriffe.

Love was visible in the cabled hopes of friends, and children, and fellow-townsmen, and in gifts of flowers from people in Teneriffe, who knew of their trouble; the room still always full of lilies, and of love. For nearly a month these two had suffered in Teneriffe.

But at the end came two nights, and a day, terrible with pain and sweat; and terrible in silence. Between this man and the woman lay a threefold silence, and a reserve; the reserve of their particular natures, and the reserve of their breed and the reserve of their race. Neither of them dared, by words, perhaps to add an edge of sharpness to the steel of their suffering. Violet felt as though she were being dragged over stones and through briars. God knows what Talbot felt. Then Violet sent for an Irish nurse who was on the island, because she was no longer certain of having, herself, the strength to support him when, hounded by his unrelenting will, Talbot would leave his bed, and walk to the couch between the bay windows. And still he did not give up hope of living, but would compel himself to exertions. In the dappled hours of the horrible day, between those two last nights, hoping for relief, Talbot summoned the doctor and endured a third operation on his back. He choked, and fought for breath, but his strength was still so great that disease could only break him fibre by fibre. Watching him, Violet thought of the slow felling of a forest tree. The doctor said: 'With that will

414

and that superb body there is, I think, no other sickness from which I could not have saved him.'

At six o'clock on that last morning Talbot said to Violet: "I know that I am dying," and she answered: 'Yes, you are dying. There is nothing that could have saved you, because you have another illness that you do not know you have.'

To Talbot open-eyed the knowledge that he was dying came sudden, and stark-naked. At the same moment his body was being wrung with a terrible anguish. After so many weeks of silent suffering Talbot cried out now in a wild pagan passion, beseeching Violet to end this intolerable agony, to shorten it with poison, somehow, anyhow. "I would do that for you," he said. Violet knew that he would have risked vengeance human and divine rather than have stood by, seeing her so tortured. But though never yet had she disobeyed, or refused him, she did now fail him, for though she got up and fetched a lancet from his case, and sought on his wrist the place of the mortal artery—yet, because of Christ, she dared not kill Talbot. 'Be brave as you have always been' she entreated. Later the doctor came, and promised that soon he would give some relief. He sharply told Violet to pray with Talbot, so she recited the psalm about the Valley of the Shadow, Talbot saying after her what he was able. Also after her he said: "Jesus Mercy!" and by himself he called loudly: "God help me"; and once he moaned that he was forsaken.

Because Talbot had always been her master Violet would not now seem to command him, so she whispered to the doctor and he, for her, said to Talbot: 'Offer to God your acceptance of this agony.' "Oh! I offer it," he said, and never spoke again.

Soon afterwards a priest came. Saint after saint the priest called upon—half a hundred holy names or more—and the power of consolation enshrined in the holy oils, and the summoned unseen company soothed Talbot. Violet all that time prayed passionately in silence that lovely girl saints, Lucy and Agnes and Catherine, would come for him, young and welcoming; and St. Hubert the hunter, with St. Francis bringing to Talbot the semblance of the dog 'Bob'.

The priest gave a candle for Violet to hold, but her hand shook too much, and the doctor had to take it from her. Piti-

fully the priest anointed Talbot, purifying his eyes from wrong
things seen, his ears from evil heard, and his lips from the wrong
he had spoken. When he would put the oil in the palms of his
hands to cleanse them from the sins of touch, Violet had to turn
over, and open, the beautiful hands clenched in agony. After he
had anointed the feet of Talbot, Violet begged the priest to pray
fervently that now her husband might quickly die.

After Talbot had received the seventh Sacrament (which
Raphael the archangel guards) Talbot ceased all lament, nor did
he again even moan or speak, though all through the last hour
it was clear that the pain was still wringing him, and that he was
aware of everything.

But even yet Talbot was not defeated by pain; with help he
got up from the bed and went to the couch in silence, there
suffering his last hour.

Violet was so devoured with prayer that she did not weep at
all; perhaps he may have wondered at what seemed hardness in
her. Behind her silent immobility, as she sat on the floor near
his feet, was her strong invocation to the Spirit of Life to leave
Talbot's agonized body, her prayer that he might be delivered
of his soul. For he seemed to her like a woman in bitter travail,
who waits for the relief of birth.

'His pulse is still strong, he may live all through the day,' the
doctor sighed. He had put, at Talbot's sign, a heavy table
against his feet for him to press against (like a woman in travail)
and this table Talbot had now pushed far from him in the
strength of his pain. 'How can such a man die?' murmured the
doctor.

Violet and Talbot did not again speak to one another—there
seemed to be nothing they could say—and then the others were
there, the nurse, and the doctor, and the apprentice, and, as ever,
there was between Talbot and his wife the terrible threefold restraint. The reserve of their particular natures, the restraint in-
born with their traditions, and the reserve of their nation. So
Violet, who never before had watched anyone dying, saw her
beloved gasp away his life which too was her life. She only
whispered to him, at the end, godspeed on his last journey.

Suddenly Talbot sat stark up and looked at a far corner of
the room. All the blue of his eyes was restored, and the bright-

ness of them. Without terror, without pleasure, he looked
fixedly as at some strange and unexpected thing. A few
minutes later, still sitting up, Talbot died—and
Violet, not thinking at all about herself,
was led into another room, her
whole being flooded over
with a torrent of
gladness.

CHAPTER VII

*   *   *

THE GLADNESS SOON WAS CHANGED TO SORROW. FOR fourteen hours Violet bore him company, that being until when at midnight men came to take him away. During all those hours she sat on a stool by the bed holding his hand as, sometimes when he was in pain, he had called on her to hold it. When the nurse begged her to rest, she answered: 'I shall have years and years to sit without him; surely for one day I may do this?' The lady of the house came up with branches of rosemary, and from another woman Violet had a mass of roses and of stocks. On the face of Talbot was peace, and a little half-smile.

Mahomed came and stood long, silently looking at his master, then he saluted him, and went wordless away. Violet let him look, for she understood his simplicity, and his way of having loved and followed his master as though he were his god. When she was alone, Violet took leave of her husband, kissing his forehead, his hands and his feet. She loved his body for its perfection; its beauty was the feast of her eyes. She put back on his finger the ring which she had given him when they were married. 'Love never faileth'—engraved behind the armorial bearings—and love had not failed. She gave him also her crucifix. Unreasonably, for it belonged neither to her culture nor to her faith, unreasonably—looking down on him—she longed that suttee might have been possible—the flaming pyre—it became a need. She did not yet know that sorrow is a fire, and that in a spiritual suttee she would burn.

After midnight had struck there was a heavy noise on the stairs. The nurse came back into the room to take Violet away from it, and she shut the door quickly behind her. But, when they opened the door to leave the room, Violet stood face to face with six or eight dark-skinned men, in sombre clothes, carrying a long black coffin. At that she could not restrain a shuddering cry; but the woman of the house clapped her hand on the widow's mouth, for she did not wish the sleeping, other guests, to be disturbed.

For five days after that night, Violet harboured with the nuns, finding great comfort in them, for their talk was all of heavenly matters. As she watched them, in their purple habits, with veils and cloaks of white, reciting the offices, or, two by two adoring the Sacrament, she knew that they had found a solution to the riddle of life.

She had hours by herself in the gallery of the chapel, feeling the kinship of the sanctuary lamps, and of the burning candles, and the smoking incense—she too was being consumed.

In the chapel, the Stations of the Cross held Violet, but the one that held her most was that which showed the Stripping of Jesus. The beloved now was stripped of his earthly vesture; of his land; of all the dear familiar things; even of his body—he was stripped and left, a bare and naked soul. So to Christ, naked, and exposed to the sun, and to the dust, and to men's looking, she prayed vehemently, asking that He would clothe her belovèd, and cover him.

She too was stripped, her good torn from her, her comfortable wifehood lying about her in the dust. But she asked that she might have courage to stay thus; instead of clothing herself anew with ease, or with a lesser love, to remain, till death, ungarmented. 'Naked and heroic Jesus, make me naked and heroic.'

But at the last Station, the fifteenth, she understood how much less than God's sacrifice is the grief of man. Christ had suffered double darkness, double eclipse; the night of the womb darkening His Godhood, and the night of the tomb engulfing His flesh. 'Oh, Thou who hast known the double darkness, the darkness of birth, and the darkness of death, help me!'

Because she was a Catholic, she feared Purgatory for her husband. She understood, that even if angels straightway took him to Paradise, he must needs be weaned from earthly things before he could enjoy the light. She knew that there was a debt owed to the supreme justice. Yet she might hope that the measureless mercy would accept from her a part of what was owed to the justice.

In the Convent of the Assumption

So the days passed by. The white-robed Bishop of Teneriffe
blessed her widowhood. She had taken her bridal veil with
prayers, and with wonder, meditating before it on the eve of
her wedding. Now with tears, and with wonder, she took her
widow's veil. But when she spoke of taking the other
veil, the veil of the religious, a priestly counsellor
said to her: 'Because of your children you
must remain in the world; for your
children are God.'

CHAPTER VIII

★ ★ ★

SO PASSED THE DAYS. VIOLET SAID: 'I WILL TRAVEL BY any ship whereon the coffin can be put where I am allowed to be near it, and where, too, it will be blessed by winds and the sea.' The vice-consul, full of kind offices for her, said that this would be impossible, for sailors and voyagers alike would account the coffin of evil omen, and wish it to be put aside in darkness, and hiding. Later, he told her that her wish could be fulfilled if she would travel on a little Norwegian vessel trading in fruit, carrying no other woman, nor any passenger but a timber merchant from Finland. She consented, and six days after Talbot's death she sailed for home and landed in London on the tenth day after the ship sailed from Teneriffe.

His last journey befitted the explorer. The coffin was lashed to the taffrail on the boat-deck; sun and moon, wind and spray upon it, an English flag over it. The Spanish firemen, passing the coffin on the way to their stoking, murmured a few words of prayer for Talbot's soul, and, taking the watches on the bridge-deck, a young Spanish apprentice prayed. He was studying navigation under the mate for the captaincy of a Spanish ship, debonairly learning his art instead of lengthily working his way upward, as a northerner must do.

The little ship, *San José*, was full of mettle, overtaking larger ships. In all the journey she never once was passed by any vessel. She shone and sparkled with cleanliness, the darling of the Norwegian crew. The Norse captain loved the sea with passion, and ever regretted the time when he had sailed under canvas, leaving land then for as many weeks as now for days.

He companioned Violet, and gave her welcome to his room which was filled with flowers, and with books in four languages. In return she gave what serenity she could, so that no other should be darkened by her sorrow, but should feel instead that a cherished cargo was on the ship, not anything that could bring gloom, ill luck or ill passage. Violet had resolved to break the tradition of burial in the family vault of Lytham, where for generations had been laid the other squires, the Lords of the Manor. Two years before this spring (when Talbot had sailed alone for West Africa), he had said, one night, that, if Africa killed him, he wished to be buried on the Green Hill of Islay, "where the deer feed, and over which come the birds flighting from the north".

He had survived that former journey, but Violet now, alone, saw from the *San José* the cliffs of England. She remembered that in Teneriffe he had said: "I hope to see England again." She was looking at the land; what seeing had he? Shame came upon her that she should bring him back thus, in his coffin; that in this wise his friends, and his children, must remember his return.

After landing in London there was the journey to the Hebrides, and then the crossing of the sea on the ship that ministers to Islay. Her flag was flown at half-mast; for the seamen knew that in Talbot they had lost a friend. By their handshake and their more serious look, their concern was shown to his widow.

All the time she must wear the mask of serenity, and, in the home in Islay for the children's sake, even the mask of gaiety. Sometimes she was taken off her guard and the rawness of her wound was exposed before she had time to cover it. The birds that he had fed, coming to the door for crumbs—they undid her. He was dead—but they, brief singers, still nested in the home trees.

*   *   *

It was hard to hear the belovèd youngest child crying at night, hard to hear the bloodhound whining and nosing about the rooms looking for Talbot. It was dolorous to know that the other children suffered, and dolorous to listen to the swans whooping together on their nest on the skerry near by, and to hear the flap of their wings as they flew, always a pair, back and fro to their nest built among the yellow iris. It hurt to gather the wild narcissi because Violet never, even when a child, had plucked one flower and left another solitary, or divided in her bunch the flowers that had grown together. Yet he had been

VIOLET CLIFTON

WIDOW, 1929

taken, and she had been left; she, a feeling creature, had been less compassionately dealt with than was her dealing with the silly flowers.

The old Gaelic-speaking man, brushing leaves from the drive, lamented to her: 'I'm missing my good master up and down the paths, for I have seen lairds very plenty, but never such a one —he was a most decent gentleman.' He, the old, old man alive, and Talbot dead—how could she see it and not wish any other dead but he? 'Ah, that he might be back here in his splendour.'

Since her childhood Violet had never seen any beautiful living thing without a secret courtesy and a thanksgiving to God, but now rebellion scorched her thankfulness; even the growing things of the earth did not move her to bless God. Until, love not failing, she suddenly saw that towards the payment of Talbot's debt to the supreme justice, she could offer the acceptance of this mortal sorrow. Even as she had asked Talbot to offer up his acceptance of the pain of his death, so must she, in a supreme effort, offer tranquillity in the will of God. She must agree even to the death of her husband. When this was revealed she bent her will— and assented to the death of Talbot.

CHAPTER IX

★   ★   ★

BROTHERS AND FRIENDS CAME TO SEE TALBOT BURIED ON the Green Hill. Violet waited six days for all to arrive because one of them had far to come.

The coffin lay in the house, and the children went in and out to say a chaplet, or to look at the gifts of crosses, and wreaths, which the ship brought every evening. Their puppies, too, went in and out, and the sun streamed through the windows so there was no hush or chill to repel them; and Talbot was still the centre of the home. One of the children complained: 'Why cannot the coffin stay here always?' So they all looked on his face, for he lay embalmed, and comely. By night, that one who most loved him slept on the floor beside the coffin.

The men of the Isle had resolved on a Highland funeral. Twelve of them offered themselves as carriers of the coffin when it should leave the cart to be carried the steepest part of the way. About a hundred men followed. The women of Islay are never present at the burial of the dead, but to-day, because they knew that the widow and children would follow the dead, some of them had gone to a knoll over the grave and there awaited the coming of the mourners. The piper, who had come from far away, also waited among the short trees, piping the lament, *The Flowers of the Forest*, whilst fell the soft Scots mist. Once again, just as after Talbot's death, but now for the last time, Violet felt an enveloping beatitude, an invading sweetness.

The monk said: 'Come to his assistance, all ye Saints of God! Meet him, all ye Angels of God!' A little later, although the Green Hill is not the hunting ground of eagles, and although they shun the nearness of men, yet there fell a wingèd shadow over the grave. And those who looked up saw a golden eagle that twice soared, and twice stooped, and then swung away out of sight. Violet thought, 'is this to tell me that his youth is renewed like the eagle's?'

424

Good-bye and good-bye

One child gave the censer to the priest, and he incensed the grave; another with a sprig of yew sprinkled the tomb with holy water; the others threw into the grave earth that had been blessed. On the foot of the coffin Violet pressed a last fervent kiss, and then must see it lowered into the pit lined with daffodils. The body might be but a mask, but this was the person of her husband from which had sprung the bodies of her children. Even it had grieved her to see dead flowers thrown out into a heap of rubbish; and no letters, no envelopes inscribed by anyone she loved, ever were thrown by her into the dust. Yet she must bear to see Talbot lowered into the soil. She threw in a wild violet and, as emblem of their travel days together, a bunch of orchids. Good-bye to him, and good-bye to the North, and to the West, and to the East; to the import they had held for her. They had been to her but painted scenery against which he was outlined. Therefore, good-bye to the wide-winged condor, to the torrent of falling water, and to the blue of the morning glory; good-bye to the Pacific, and to the Andes. Good-bye to those Islands of the North that are treeless, where in October fall no autumn leaves but where, instead, is only fall of star.

Good-bye to the East; to the sweetness of wild honey eaten together, the honey sucked of orchids; to the cool water of the nut from which they had drunk together under the palm trees—the palm trees always cool, the serene guardians of pleasantness even in the great heats. Only the South held no memories.

Good-bye to that body, the beauty of which had been the feast of her eyes; to the shapeliness of those hands and those feet; to that form which had been attuned to the great heats and the great colds, which had offered endurance to the extreme of hardship. Slowly, like a coral island, the ages had built up that form of a man. Nearly a thousand years of privileged beings lay behind it. Good-bye to the efflorescence of a line that had spent itself in blood, and sacrifice, and wealth.

Good-bye to the communion with his mind, his mind that was stored with love of strange people, stored with poetry. Mind that was free of the barriers of religion, and of class, and of nationality, free of illusions, but without bitterness. His mind and hers, so understanding the one of the other that a few words sufficed; subtler than words the intercourse between them.

Never a flight of birds, never a silver squall of rain, but he called her to come and share the seeing of the precious thing—waves betossed by wind, stags in the forest fighting—"Come, Vi, and see!"

Good-bye to the cloak of love always mantled about her. He had enshrined her high up, almost beyond his need to touch, or his wish to tell. "I should love you just as much if you were in a case of crystal," he had said when she was yet his bride. He had endowed her with dangers; he had shared his solitudes with her, the solitudes of distant islands, the silences of far-away places. That was the wealth of his offering, that was the proof of his love, more binding than embraces. In her he had found his desire for love and peace, and thus he had named her breasts. Good-bye, and good-bye, and, because the feast had been great, the famine was the sharper. But love never faileth, so rise up love, and be greater than grief!

'Oh! I have lost him off the earth and we have not died to-gether as always I thought we should.' Then this certainty en-compassed her: 'I have lost him off the earth but he is in Christ and so am I; there is our common life.'

Then slowly, and throughout time, love showed Violet how she could still spend herself for Talbot. He must be in need of prayers, and in need of the offering of the Sacrifice. If perhaps he did not stand in need, then he would use the healing unguents for some soul in Purgatory. 'He who was generous and giving will be glad to have these gifts in his hand,' she thought. And again: 'I can be his bard, I can tell the tale of his life, interpret him to other men, translate his thoughts so native to himself. Hasten his soul to Heaven, and on earth, among men, strive to make him immortal.' 'Spend yourself thus,' urged love.

And so the days and nights, instead of being as ashes and
as shadows, were like the great wells of oil that,
in some mountains, burn perpetually. The
tongues of flames leaping upward—
to God, for Talbot.

NOTES

★   ★   ★

THE LITTLE BOOK OF ALASKA

1. Talbot Clifton's mother was married a second time (to Sir James Drummond, Bart., of Edwinsford, Llandilo) and Talbot was brought up by his grandmother, Lady Cecily Clifton.

2. At Mrs. Clifton's request for recollections of Talbot Clifton, Mr. M. R. M. Tobin on February the nineteenth, 1931, wrote this letter to Mr. Harry Simpkins.

3. Talbot Clifton knew fear often before he flung himself into adventure; knew it, but disregarded it. He hated to watch horse-races, so filled was he with trepidation for the riders.

4. January 1895 the Canadian Government sent out a force of police; at that time the boundaries between U.S.A. and the Canadian Government were still in dispute.

5. The Lewes River below Lake Laberge.

6. They had passed the mouths of the Hutalinkwa and Big and Little Salmon Rivers without special mention.

7. Tribe of Tinné. The Indians of the Yukon are often called Kutchin.

★ The author's best thanks are due to Professor Coleman, Ph.D. (Toronto), who kindly corrected the proofs and supplied the matter used in notes 4, 5 and 6.

THE BOOK OF THE BARREN LANDS

1. 'Clefts in the ice on the Great Lakes are a serious menace. They are formed by the ice contracting in the severe midwinter when the thermometer falls to − 40 or − 50 degrees Fahrenheit, and they may be several feet wide. Horses with no take-off cannot make much of a jump. The sled sometimes is laid across the crack and dogs can so walk over.' [Dr. Alex. Milne.]

2. 'Talbot was, as you know, quite fearless. I remember we had to cross a big stretch of ice which we knew was very rotten and had continually to sound with a pole to see if it was safe. T. was quite unconcerned. At all events I can't recollect that he looked at all anxious.' [Lines out of a letter from Arthur Clifton.]

3. 'A first attack of snow-blindness is very severe and alarming; not only is one quite blind, but there is considerable pain and complete intolerance of light. I recall my own first experience, my head wrapped in a shawl for two full days at Churchill, then a delightful evening with the Lofthouses with tolerable vision under the subdued light of a single candle, and then out into the soothing darkness of night completely recovered. Mr. Clifton does not exaggerate the feeling of misery one has while the attack lasts. Later attacks are less severe, and one is careful not to expose oneself so carelessly to an attack.' [Dr. Milne.]

4. Their language. . . . When well spoken the Cree language leaves no doubt as to what a phrase may mean; every action is described exactly, is

428

Notes

made as crystal clear as it is in Latin. The Cree has no written language, but the spoken language is conserved with piety and is taught with exactitude; is passed on as an heirloom, and is exalted and publicly acclaimed when given forth in oratory.

5. 'I am sorry we did not hit it off, but, as I said before, I was so young and he was then probably old for his years, and so we were only trekking together for a few months.' [Lines out of a letter from Arthur Clifton.]

6. Dixon found that on some leaf-cells is a pressure of thirty atmospheres and a pressure reaching as much as four hundred and fifty pounds to the square inch.

7. 'The ordered regularity and relatively strict discipline at York Factory made life there perhaps too much like what Mr. Clifton was seeking to get away from. It seemed that he was disappointed not yet to be clear of civilization—becoming the more impatient as delay succeeded delay.' [Dr. A. Milne.]

8. 'I am sorry Mr. Clifton seems to have rather despised my Indians as sailormen. He was unfortunate in his first impression of the Indians being gained at Norway House, where intercourse with white men of the frontier and a new-found independence had demoralized them.

'The navigation along the shores of Hudson's Bay so early in the year is fraught with infinite danger from icefloes, especially in frail open boats, and doubtless Mr. Clifton realized this later on, and came to appreciate the skill of the boatmen and the wisdom of hugging the shore.' [Dr. Milne.]

9. "In spring the polar bears go to the woods to bear their young. Near Fort Churchill they were numerous. I have seen eleven." [Note written by Talbot Clifton in the margin of a book on the arctic.]

10. 'I have only a dim memory of the people you mention; with the exception of the missionary, they must have been Hudson Bay factors who seemed to lead a very monotonous life and rarely saw a white man from year's end to year's end.' [Lines out of a letter from Arthur Clifton.]

11. The Hudson's Bay Company had no established stations yet beyond Churchill, where Eskimos came to trade; but a yearly expedition was made by boats and meeting-places arranged as far north as the vicinity of Chesterfield Inlet.

12. *Fort Churchill.* In 1750 the Fort had been yielded to the French by Hearn without a blow being struck for it, although the Fort had been well armed with cannon.

13. *George Oman.* 'It is but due to the memory of the interpreter, George Oman, to say that he was a valued servant of the Company for a long number of years, faithful and trustworthy. The Eskimos had the same confidence in him, and I have no doubt Atonguela was influenced in attaching himself to Mr. Clifton to a large extent by George's assurances that he could be quite sure of his reward if he did what was required of him. But George's work amongst the Eskimos was to him but the routine duty of day-to-day life. The spirit of adventure was not in him. Mr. Clifton evidently came to realize all this, and to feel that the venture was for him alone, and so let Oman go back.' [Dr. Alex. Milne.]

14. It must be remembered that Talbot Clifton was a martyr to dyspepsia, and makes several references, not all here repeated, to feeling weak because of the fare.

People who only have meat to eat must eat an enormous amount more than those who eat farinaceous food as well. In Hudson Bay one man will eat two geese at a meal.

15. Often he gave them rhubarb pills, which they asked for in large quantities without any discretion, so that for their own good he refused them. His own cough he cured with quinine.

16. The writer believes that Talbot Clifton so named the nameless places; now and again throughout the entire journey and sojourn, certain places are named perhaps according to a Hudson Bay map made, very possibly, by guesswork, and based on Eskimo report.

17. This island was Long. 93°, Lat. 64°, and was named by Talbot Clifton "Nondescript Land".

18. At this time Talbot often had nothing to eat excepting captain biscuits, and he records that "the stopping has come out of my tooth, and I wish it had stopped in. Ha! Ha!" He did not perhaps foresee what terrible agony this would cause him later.

19. The recurring simile in Talbot's mind when complaining of the leisurely ways of the Eskimos was: "It would be as hard to hurry an Eskimo as to hurry a Lytham cab-horse."

20. Length 52½ in. Circumference 5½ in. Tip to tip 15 in. Widest inside 26½ in. Points 17 and 12.

21. 'On the morning after his return to York Factory, he called to me, stretching his arm out from under the bedclothes with his watch for me to look at. I was shocked to see that he was wearing no nightshirt, but he hastened to assure me he had discarded night clothes for all time—it was so much more restful to sleep in the nude!' [Dr. Alex. Milne.]

22. 'Ce qu'il y a encore de frappant dans la complexion de ces barbares, c'est l'extrême chaleur de leur estomac et de leur sang; ils échauffent tellement, par leur haleine ardente, les huttes où ils assemblent en hiver, que les Européens s'y sentent étouffés, comme dans une étuve . . . aussi ne font-ils jamais de feu dans leur habitation . . . et ils ignorent l'usage des cheminées sous le climat le plus froid du globe.' [De Pauw.]

23. Piblokto was probably Illanah's affliction, a form of hysteria that affects the Eskimos and their dogs.

24. *Jubilee Lake.* Talbot Clifton later reckoned it to be some 60 miles long; 80 miles broad, and near to the River Kaaga.

25. The spelling adopted for these words is from memory of their sound as repeated by Talbot Clifton.

26. The head of the musk-ox is at Lytham.

Breadth of palm	7½ in.
Length outside	24½ in.
Tip to tip	19 in.

Notes

27. It is supposed that the name of the musk-ox is derived from a musky taste in the meat, but Talbot Clifton did not mention any such taste.

28. The snow-house is like a diving-bell. Cold air is heavier than hot. Hot air rises, hence the sleeping platforms.

29. The journey took them 45 days.

30. By sail, he referred to the sail he knew would be hoisted on the sleigh, but though the wind would help its progress, imagine the added agony that wind would lend to arctic cold.

31. *Atonguela.* 'When Mr. Clifton on the return journey arrived at York Factory, he told me Atonguela had agreed to accompany him on the strict understanding that he would take him all the way to 'the white man's country.' Of a truth he was a fine-looking man, as Mr. Clifton says, and in character must have been as outstanding, to have harboured so bold an ambition. The travel through the bush country, multitudes of white men and women, railway trains, the roar of traffic in the streets of Winnipeg, hotel life, all seemed to come to him as a matter of course, although my men told me when they would camp in a grove of good timber, he would stand and gaze at a great tree as with a feeling of awe. He to whom a stick of drift-wood was of priceless value would naturally see the fulfilment of his keenest desires, could he but transport these into his country. In the newness and variety of his experiences nothing seemed to daunt him. The work of the unseen creator in the silent forest growth was more to him than all the petty endeavour of man, the bustle and noise of streets, the ever anxious-looking crowds, and his thoughts may have run not far remote from those conse-crated in holy writ—Consider the lilies how they grow, they toil not neither do they spin, yet Solomon in all his glory was not arrayed like one of these.

'When Mr. Clifton parted from Atonguela at Winnipeg, the Company fortunately found near by a Churchill woman, through whom as interpreter everything was arranged for starting Atonguela on his homeward way. At Norway House he met an old Churchill acquaintance in the person of the blacksmith, who regaled him with a fine, fat, frozen lake fish raw—the first square meal really to his liking since many months. When he reached York Factory he still had his Winnipeg purchases securely baled up, and stayed with us until the ship arrived from England. On board ship he seemed at last to feel himself amongst friends to be trusted, and at once the great bale was opened and he set about to deck himself out in his new finery.

'We landed him in due course at Churchill, and I should think Mr. Binney could find more to tell of the after life of one who, considering his environ-ment, was a traveller with but few peers.

'Many years afterwards one little curious incident relating to him I did come across. In Amundsen's book, *The North West Passage* I think it is called, it is told that as they were resting in their winter quarters, on the arctic coast north-west of Chesterfield Inlet, an Eskimo broke in upon them in a too-familiar way, greeting them in English. Amundsen gives his name, and no doubt it was our Atonguela, whose reception would have probably been more cordial had they known he too was a traveller renowned amongst his people.' [Dr. Alex. Milne.]

431

32. 'Mr. Clifton made a very remarkable journey, especially as to that part of it where he made the great venture of trusting himself alone amongst the Eskimos, and then undertaking the long winter journey through the Barren Lands, with Atonguela the Eskimo his sole companion. That he should have come through so much privation, enduring misery unspeakable in the squalor of Eskimo tents and snow huts and the pitiless arctic winter weather and yet returned to us quite cheerful and in perfect health, proves the gallant manhood that was in him and that his fearlessness in taking any hazard had never paled. His fine figure and great stature combined with his contempt of danger doubtless appealed to the Eskimos, who themselves are notoriously careless of life, and his good sense in realizing he had in Atonguela a man deserving of his trust, probably saved him from disaster, trying though it would have been to a man of his independent spirit to submit to guidance. He, born to enjoy all that life could give in the way of luxurious living, wearied perhaps of its narrowness and conventionality, found a much fuller joy in a life of adventure. His intercourse with the Eskimos will have added interest to their lives, and done much to preserve the prestige of the white man amongst them. The vast solitudes of the arctic will have had a soul-inspiring effect on himself, which I feel sure he would never have quite thrown off.

'Mr. Clifton, in my opinion, might very well have entertained the hope of hearing at first hand from the Eskimos details of the fate of the last surviving members of the Franklin Expedition. It was from amongst these people that Dr. Rae got the first definite information which gained for him the Government award. Dr. Rae's interpreter, Ouligberck, died at Chesterfield Inlet, the result of an accident, not a very old man, only a year or two before Mr. Clifton was there, and it was not so many years before then that Schwatka, exploring in the same district, found odds and ends of articles which I think were definitely proved to belong to the Franklin party. *Schwatka's Search* is a book dealing with the subject; it is written by Gilder, who accompanied Schwatka. Gilder was at York Factory some 10 years before Mr. Clifton, intending to go north again, but he was recalled.

'Mr. Clifton, in his notes, speaks of the boon which the Library at York Factory was to him. It is most likely that the books there he was mainly, if not altogether, interested in, were the works of the arctic explorers, Parry, Franklin, Ross, Bach, McClintock, Rae, etc. There were first editions of most of these, presentation copies probably, and one could not have stayed at York Factory without studying the contents and perhaps envying the explorers their fame.' [Dr. Alex. Milne.]

THE BOOK OF BOREAS

1. The names may be inaccurate, but Talbot Clifton thought that such were the flowers.

2. Kamlanie—the shaman ritual.

3. Hysteria and epilepsy abound in Siberia.
Such a state is called navani.
Talbot Clifton brought back a shaman dress, which is at Lytham Hall,

Lancashire; the iron of it weighs thirty pounds. He also brought back a shaman drum.

4. On rising ground a cairn supports the wooden cross erected by Melville, chief engineer on board the U.S.N. *Jeanette*, sent by the United States Government to explore the arctic in 1879. The *Jeanette* was commanded by de Long, and was crushed by ice in January 1880. Eventually, after being hauled over ice, three boats put off to sea. Melville's cutter made Yakutsk; one boat was lost entirely and without trace, whilst two men of de Long's party were found by Melville at Bulkur. Led by them, the bodies of the other eleven of de Long's men were found, and also that of de Long. These twelve men lie beneath the great cross.

5. Another nervous illness, bane of the mature, resembling that one, which, in Malay, is called lâtah.

6. A sect of Flagellants. Their name 'Khlysty' became deformed into 'Khristy'—the Christs.

7. *Ovis Poli*. Quite probably *Ovis Ammon* which, like *Ovis Poli*, is of the Argali, 'Largest and finest of all wild sheep. Many local modifications exist of this widely spread and variable species.' [R. Lydekker.]

8. This word is used in the Diary; it is not a Russian word, but perhaps a word of local derivation from the word 'povar', meaning 'cook'.

9. This bear Talbot Clifton gave to Henry, Duke of Norfolk, and it is at Arundel Castle. The measurements are:

Height - - - - - -	6 ft. 5 in.
Girth - - - - - - -	5 ft. 6 in.
Weight - - - - - -	400 lbs.
Spread of arms - - - - -	7 ft. 4 in.

10. The ram shot about forty miles from the mouth of the Yana River, at the north-west end of the Verkhoyansk Mountains, is set up in the British Museum (Natural History). Mr. Lydekker in *Proc. Zool. Soc.* 1902 said: 'It is, I believe, the first example of its kind ever brought to England.' The Museum gives its measurements as follows:

Length of outside curve - - - - -	33 in.
Circumference - - - - - -	13 in.
Tip to tip - - - - - -	22½ in.
Height at shoulder, about - - - -	37 in.

At Lytham Hall are the heads of a similar male and of a female, but these seem to be those referred to on page 204. The female's head is cloud-colour, passing into white at the forehead and muzzle, and has short hairy ears. The male is remarkable with his brown transverse bar, below the eyes and above the nostrils, that spreads over the cheeks. These were shot on the delta of the Lena.

11. This was a kind of marmot not known before, afterwards named Arctomys Cliftoni, and is in the Natural History Museum. See *Annals and Magazine of Natural History*, Ser. 7, vol. IX, June 1902. Innes Pocock says, 'the total or almost total lack of respiration accompanied by power to survive immersion for a considerable time in water or asphyxiating gases, which prove rapidly fatal to the same animals when normally active.'

12. The paws of the bear looked unpleasantly like human hands. When a Batak, who had been a cannibal, told Talbot Clifton that of all parts of the human body the hand is the most palatable, Talbot's thoughts turned at once to the gelatinous delicacy of the bear's paws.

13. The mammoth remains were without odour until received by the Museum authorities, when, according to the description of their *Proceedings*, 'it made up for lost time'.

14. See *From Paris to New York by Land*, by Harry de Windt, pp. 37, 39, 41.

15. 'Any luggage, sir?' said a porter at Victoria station to a gaunt tall man from the Channel Boat. "Yes, look in the van for things marked Clifton." He looked and found the ram still frozen, the bear as stiff as iron, and the head of the white reindeer.

THE BOOK OF BARUCHIAL

1. Arthur Bourchier.

2. Before having become engaged, Talbot had arrived at Edwinsford with his leg, from ankle to knee, torn by the crude machinery of one of the first motor-cars to travel the roads. Refusing to wait for an anaesthetic Clifton, smoking, watched the doctor putting the many stitches into his leg.

In this same car he afterwards crossed Shap, being, I believe, the first motorist to do so. Just before the birth of their first child, Talbot and Violet arrived at Edwinsford on the chassis of a racing car, Clifton could not wait for the body. Perched beside him, Violet hugged a bandbox—their only luggage. John Green had disappeared; "fallen off" Talbot told Violet. The guests, censorious about this method of motoring, were appeased when they saw Talbot making a wreath of montbretias for his wife's hair.

3. Coming out of church after a wedding, Violet's uncle said : 'Was that Talbot sitting next to you?'

'No, Talbot was just behind me.'

'Thank God for that; I'd never seen Talbot, and I nearly prayed that you would not look behind—for if those two meet now there will be trouble I thought.'

4. Live bucolically, but socially too. They entertained their friends to shoot the coverts; "shooting pheasants over this country is tame" thought Talbot. ('He would not tolerate the escape of a wounded pheasant. I once saw him leave the shooting party and go far across a very wet field in order to put a runner out of its misery. The keepers had strict instructions that they must follow up any birds noticed to have escaped with wounds, and see that they did not linger in misery.'—Lines out of a letter from H. Thorpe.)

When the Clifton Park Racecourse was inaugurated, the Earl of Lonsdale, Sir Peter Walker, and Talbot, the owner of the site, were granted the licence for the Course, which was designed after Hurst Park. A host of racing people was round them.

At Squire's Gate, on Talbot's property, was held in 1909 the second Flying Contest to happen in England. Lord Lonsdale again was interested, and the Grand Duke Michael; Grahame-White, Farman, Lathom and Dietrich flew; Sir Hiram Maxim was warden of the nascent art.

Notes

From across the Atlantic famous golfers came to play on the Lytham-St. Anne's Golf Course. Some years later Talbot and Violet were able, through the influence of one in a high place, to have the designation of 'Royal Golf Club' conferred by charter upon the Course.

In their home at Lytham was also the coming and going of musicians and actors, and other famous men and women.

5. The Law of Property Act, 1922, which enfranchises copyhold lands and converts them into freeholds, only deals with the manorial rights in such enfranchised lands. Manors existing in freehold estates are not affected and the Acts do not in any way interfere with Mr. Clifton's Manors.

At the time of the Norman Conquest, practically the whole of the country was divided up into Manors, the Lords of which granted out from their Manors certain feuds or fees which became ancient freeholds, and though these lands were held of the Manor, they did not remain parcel of it, so that the Manor, as it became recognized, was exclusive of such lands. They are just ordinary freeholds, and may be conveyed from one person to another as the usual freeholds.

There are still three separate Manor Courts (Courts Baron) regularly held in connection with the Clifton Estates, those at Lytham, Westby and Marton.

6. Cecily Lowther. When her brother succeeded as Earl of Lonsdale of Lowther Castle, Carlisle, Mrs. Talbot Clifton (formerly Miss Lowther), became Lady Cicely Clifton.

7. See *Pilgrims to the Isle of Penance*, by Mrs. Talbot Clifton (Violet Clifton), published by Messrs. Long.

8. *Four Days*, by G. Spencer-Pryse, pp. 1 and 2.

9. See *A Diplomatic Diary*, by Hugh Gibson, pp. 235 *et seq.* Talbot Clifton and his wife are referred to as Mr. and Mrs. W.

10. The Mons Star, and the War and Victory, medal were sent to Talbot. Clifton's widow in 1931. He never knew he had obtained this reward. These medals were also conferred on Mrs. Clifton.

11. See *Islands of Queen Wilhelmina*, by Violet Clifton.

12. Gilan long afterwards sent word to Clifton through Conboy, saying that he had long lain on his back and bethought him, son of a sometime police-constable, of his jolly end—how easily he might have been killed unconfessed. He said that if Talbot Clifton ever needed a faithful servant he Gilan was his man.

13. G. K. Chesterton and Augustus John were among the guests of honour. Someone blaming John for some of his pleasures, Clifton said in extenuation: "A man with all the faults of all the gods."

14. Gertrude Bell translated these into English.

15. Jaafar Pasha, afterwards Prime Minister of Iraq.

16. The Sheik, and his brother, and two of their eight wives stayed at Kildalton in Islay. Palms in pots, and wild rabbits pleased them most. The fire lit in their room terrified them. The women allowed Michael to unveil

them; not ashamed to be seen of Talbot or of Michael, they shrank from the look of the Arab brothers-in-law; but they allowed it.

17. Summary of Benefactions made by John Talbot Clifton in the vicinity of Lytham-St. Anne's.

	£.	s.	d.
1. Cash donations for religious, educational and other purposes - - - - - - - -	5,499	0	0
2. Gifts of Sites for religious and educational purposes -	24,025	0	0
3. Gifts of Lands for general public purposes - - -	114,282	0	0
4. Church Endowments - - - - - -	8,400	0	0
	£152,206	0	0

18. This honour paid to him was also a consolation, as the Liberal peer, Lord Shuttleworth, refused to make Talbot Clifton a Deputy Lieutenant. He gave as reason that Clifton had lived too long out of England.

19. Mahomed Noa wrote these accounts of the journey, years later, for Mrs. Clifton.

20. Violet's recent operation had dashed her hopes of such journeying.

21. As amongst the Eskimos, so here, the primitive man deserts the sick man. Likely enough the aversion from—or the fear of—sickness, is instinctive to savages as it is to animals.

22. ". . . the most beautiful of all the stags." *Proaig Forest Stag*. Length 35 in. Girth 5⅛ in. Tip to tip 16¾. Widest inside 27 in. Outside 33 in. Points 6 and 7.

Mr. Reginald Loder made measurements slightly more. Talbot Clifton was apt to minimize.

23. 'I only knew Talbot Clifton during the last two years of his life. In June, 1926, I went to Islay with Dr. O. H. Wild to work at natural history for a few weeks. We drove out to Kildalton one evening, and introduced ourselves to Clifton. He had been on the point of leaving Islay on some fishing excursion, but when he learnt what we were doing he apparently abandoned that plan, and during the next week or two gave a good deal of his time to us.

'Driving back from Kildalton on that evening, Wild remarked to me that it was easy to see that his knowledge of natural history was immense. We had been discussing the Malay Archipelago, where he had travelled. Twice in the next couple of years I spent short winter holidays with Talbot Clifton, and was with him on Islay immediately before he went to Africa for the last time. During part of that last visit he was ill, but never apparently entertained the idea of changing his plan.

'To me he was one of the two or three most entertaining companions that I have ever had. His interest covered an extraordinarily wide field. His house was filled with pictures by Archibald Thorburn for whose work he had an intense admiration. He had collected a library of, I think, six thousand volumes on sport, travel, history, poetry, biography. One section was devoted to books on pirates. He apparently classed this as a branch of sport. When looking at some of these treasures with me, he remarked that the worst point about collecting books was that no one would care a rap about them after we were gone. He was always ready to discuss politics and politicians, but in a very detached way. He loved to talk about his friends. He was enormously interested in his own past life.

'Two of his characteristics impressed me during my stay. One was his strong sense of possession. We were talking about D—, whose house at Port Askaig looks towards Jura. "Never could understand D— sitting down at a writing-table in front of a window overlooking another man's land," he said. The second characteristic was his way of dressing in clothes which, without being odd, were yet peculiar to himself. His homespun shooting clothes were of wools of blended colours; his evening smoking-suits, and particularly a tartan one, were very pleasant to the eye.

'What distinguished him from most other men was, I think, that everything in him was on an exaggerated scale. If he had been toned down in some way he would have been a more or less ordinary man. He helped me to understand what the great adventurers of the past must have been like. He was more ruthless in conversation than any person that I have ever met. At the same time he could listen with the greatest patience to any person who had information to give him. His mind would leap over two or three stages in an argument, so that it often required a moment's thought to see what he meant. He was not of a temper to be patient with fools. He held very strong opinions on most matters, but then he generally had some grounds for doing so. He loved to tease people, to see how they would take it. At times he would play with a person like a cat with a mouse. This was all combined with a tender seriousness lit up by a very whimsical turn of wit. The result was that one was never dull with him. Behind all this there lay the most intense and unresting energy. He had the most restless spirit that I have ever known. Even when he was ill, it never occurred to him to call a halt. If he had any fixed plan for his life, it must have been to keep on travelling as long as he was able to walk. He loved danger and hardship for their own sake. It is the fashion in these days to explain this unusual energy by tracing it to an excess of some physical constituent. He was like a man who was greatly 'overcharged' in some way. Probably, however, the explanation is rather in his intense curiosity about the world, and in his simple determination to see as much of it as he could. Then, from the circumstances of his life, he had never been forced to adjust himself to any groove. He had never been forced, as most people are, to give in to other people's ways and ideas. He rather reminded me of an Elizabethan adventurer carrying on the business into a later and duller generation. He might have been a soldier or an administrator, if circumstances had led him that way. There certainly was no grain of fear or self-distrust in his whole make-up. Probably, on the whole, he fulfilled his destiny with a completeness that is given to few. He explored the world with the same simplicity as a bird migrates, or a bee makes honey, and he kept at it to the end.

'My only regret about him was that he never wrote his travels, and never would have done so if he had lived to be a hundred. He was almost secretive about what he had done. That is a pity, as the record of his travels, written with his curious point of view towards life, would certainly have been of

Notes

absorbing interest. No one but a few friends will ever have any idea of the kind of man that he was.

'My main recollection of him is as we sat at the dinner-table at Kildalton, surrounded by his racing cups and his Thorburn pictures, beside a great open fire, talking about natural history and travel, and laughing occasionally, after a day out in the open when I had massacred one or two of his pheasants and been scolded for it. I do not know any person now living who could give pleasure of just the same kind to a chance friend, and I certainly know no one who showed more generous and disinterested kindness to me.' [The Revd. J. M. McWilliam, author of *The Birds of the Island of Bute*.]

THE LAST JOURNEY

1. In reference to p. 412: More than once during the years of their marriage he had said to her that if he died before she did he hoped she would marry again rather than go into a Convent.

In all the letters written to his widow the same refrain: 'How can he be dead, he so vital, so dominant?' The word 'intrepid' was in most of the letters. The word 'intrepid' and the word 'kind', for Talbot, so impatient of weighty people, so open in his dislikes or scorns, was in action good to the many.

Folk whom he had met walking on the roads wrote to say how never he had passed without offering them the help of the carriage, more lately of his car. An artist wrote: 'for pure fun he had driven perilously near me day after day to make me look up from my easel'; and, as he had not looked up, Talbot had stopped at last, talked to him, taken him back to Rhidoroch, given him a sudden quiverful of hunter's lore, shown him red-deer and golden eagles.

Sailors wrote—to one he had given money which had now been put to a new keel, another owed him his nets.

An Irish peasant wrote: 'Well, I am surprised: he was the last I expected death for.' That said everything, for it seemed against nature that Talbot should be dead whilst the earth was teeming with people who always had been so very little alive. Round such men as he have been woven legends of a continual life; they have been spirited away; they have fallen asleep in a secret cave; but they have not died; they will suddenly return.

From Persia, Allah Khan wrote in his own language: 'whenever I and my wife wanted to be happy we talked of you two.'

And from Bahrein the Lady Ayesha: 'It hurts very much, but since it is Allah's will we will say no more of the matter.'

A poet wrote: 'I never met a man with so great a heart and so noble an outlook—in this age he was unique.' Also this poet wrote as Epitaph to an Explorer:

'He walks Death's well-worn path; but, were he first,
Even where Danger feared to go, he durst.'

And thus to Violet a Highland lady wrote: 'You were always able to share his life and never failed to make everything that he enjoyed more joyous for him.'

Lest the people of Lytham should feel it a slur that Talbot Clifton was not

Notes

buried there in the vault of the Cliftons, his widow wrote a public letter explaining to the Vicar that her husband had asked once to lie in the Green Hill where the deer feed, and over which fly the birds coming in from the north—on the hill overlooking the sea.

Because of that letter, from smoking towns in England two women, wives of working men, wrote saying that in the drab of their lives the very thought of such a resting-place 'seemed to stand out like a gleam'.

'Perhaps houses never will creep up that hill, nor people overrun this Island;' Violet hoped; 'it may be that the miracle of his resurrection, jewel of my hope, may be staged on the still-unspoiled Green Hill.'

A cairn with a cross was raised, a cairn because it is the traveller's help, a landmark. The old forester had almost refused to quarry the stone on Cnoc Maine, because he feared the anger of the fairies. But for love of Talbot he hewed out the granite. The bards of Islay wrote songs in Gaelic about the place.

Later on, came (as it were) messages to Violet: two carpenters in Lytham, each on the same night had had a dream, vivid as a vision. Talbot in their dreams had said that he was in light after much suffering.

As in far countries men had followed Talbot, so now from Lytham a working man with a disease of the heart who, if he walked, was in danger of death, travelled from Lytham and walked up the Green Hill. He came down refreshed. He said to Violet: 'Now I'll die in peace, for I've seen my master's grave, and why should I stay behind when he has gone away.'

To
DOLLIE BORTON
I give the primrose of my thanks. She—the first to help me.

To
F. E. DORAN
the woven homespun of my tribute. He gave, to my work,
his time, and his care.

To
NEVILL COGHILL
the grain, the oil, the wine of thankfulness. Without his teaching, without his sustaining charity—I had faltered.

To
WALLACE WOOD
lilt of wings; and violet, and magnolia of my offering. Secret
sweetness, and a form he showed me.

To
HERBERT READ
the golden August of my gratitude. He, in time, last of the five
to add a glory.